VOICES OF ISLAM

VOICES OF ISLAM

Volume 2

VOICES OF THE SPIRIT

Vincent J. Cornell, General Editor and
Volume Editor

PRAEGER PERSPECTIVES

Westport, Connecticut
London

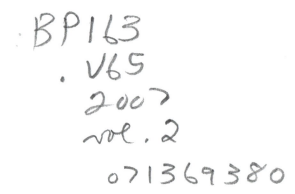

Library of Congress Cataloging-in-Publication Data

Voices of Islam / Vincent J. Cornell, general editor.
  p. cm.
  Includes bibliographical references and index.
  ISBN 0–275–98732–9 (set : alk. paper)—ISBN 0–275–98733–7 (vol 1 : alk. paper)—ISBN 0–275–98734–5 (vol 2 : alk. paper)—ISBN 0–275–98735–3 (vol 3 : alk. paper)—ISBN 0–275–98736–1 (vol 4 : alk. paper)—ISBN 0–275–98737–X (vol 5 : alk. paper) 1. Islam—Appreciation. 2. Islam—Essence, genius, nature. I. Cornell, Vincent J.
  BP163.V65 2007
  297—dc22   2006031060

British Library Cataloguing in Publication Data is available.

Library of Congress Catalog Card Number: 2006031060
ISBN: 0–275–98732–9 (set)
     0–275–98733–7 (vol. 1)
     0–275–98734–5 (vol. 2)
     0–275–98735–3 (vol. 3)
     0–275–98736–1 (vol. 4)
     0–275–98737–X (vol. 5)

First published in 2007

Praeger Publishers, 88 Post Road West, Westport, CT 06881
An imprint of Greenwood Publishing Group, Inc.
www.praeger.com

Printed in the United States of America

The paper used in this book complies with the Permanent Paper Standard issued by the National Information Standards Organization (Z39.48–1984).

10 9 8 7 6 5 4 3 2 1

Contents

Voices of Islam

———————————————— • ————————————————

Vincent J. Cornell

It has long been a truism to say that Islam is the most misunderstood religion in the world. However, the situation expressed by this statement is more than a little ironic because Islam is also one of the most studied religions in the world, after Christianity and Judaism. In the quarter of a century since the 1978–1979 Islamic revolution in Iran, hundreds of books on Islam and the Islamic world have appeared in print, including more than a score of introductions to Islam in various European languages. How is one to understand this paradox? Why is it that most Americans and Europeans are still largely uninformed about Islam after so many books about Islam have been published? Even more, how can people still claim to know so little about Islam when Muslims now live in virtually every medium-sized and major community in America and Europe? A visit to a local library or to a national bookstore chain in any American city will reveal numerous titles on Islam and the Muslim world, ranging from journalistic potboilers to academic studies, translations of the Qur'an, and works advocating a variety of points of view from apologetics to predictions of the apocalypse.

The answer to this question is complex, and it would take a book itself to discuss it adequately. More than 28 years have passed since Edward Said wrote his classic study *Orientalism,* and it has been nearly as long since Said critiqued journalistic depictions of Islam in *Covering Islam: How the Media and the Experts Determine How We See the Rest of the World.* When these books first appeared in print, many thought that the ignorance about the Middle East and the Muslim world in the West would finally be dispelled. However, there is little evidence that the public consciousness of Islam and Muslims has been raised to a significant degree in Western countries. Scholars of Islam in American universities still feel the need to humanize Muslims in the eyes of their students. A basic objective of many introductory courses on Islam is to demonstrate that Muslims are rational human beings and that their beliefs are worthy of respect. As Carl W. Ernst observes in the preface to his recent work, *Following Muhammad: Rethinking Islam in the*

Contemporary World, "It still amazes me that intelligent people can believe that all Muslims are violent or that all Muslim women are oppressed, when they would never dream of uttering slurs stereotyping much smaller groups such as Jews or blacks. The strength of these negative images of Muslims is remarkable, even though they are not based on personal experience or actual study, but they receive daily reinforcement from the news media and popular culture."[1]

Such prejudices and misconceptions have only become worse since the terrorist attacks of September 11, 2001, and the war in Iraq. There still remains a need to portray Muslims in all of their human diversity, whether this diversity is based on culture, historical circumstances, economic class, gender, or religious doctrine. Today, Muslims represent nearly one-fourth of the world's population. Although many Americans are aware that Indonesia is the world's largest Muslim country, most are surprised to learn that half of the Muslims in the world live east of Lahore, Pakistan. In this sense, Islam is as much an "Asian" religion as is Hinduism or Buddhism. The new reality of global Islam strongly contradicts the "Middle Eastern" view of Islam held by most Americans. Politically, the United States has been preoccupied with the Middle East for more than half a century. Religiously, however, American Protestantism has been involved in the Middle East for more than 150 years. Thus, it comes as a shock for Americans to learn that only one-fourth of the world's Muslims live in the Middle East and North Africa and that only one-fifth of Muslims are Arabs. Islam is now as much a worldwide religion as Christianity, with somewhere between 4 and 6 million believers in the United States and approximately 10 million believers in Western Europe. Almost 20 million Muslims live within the borders of the Russian Federation, and nearly a million people of Muslim descent live in the Russian city of St. Petersburg, on the Gulf of Finland.

To think of Islam as monolithic under these circumstances is both wrong and dangerous. The idea that all Muslims are fundamentalists or anti-democratic religious zealots can lead to the fear that dangerous aliens are hiding within Western countries, a fifth column of a civilization that is antithetical to freedom and the liberal way of life. This attitude is often expressed in popular opinion in both the United States and Europe. For example, it can be seen in the "Letters" section of the June 7, 2004, edition of *Time* magazine, where a reader writes: "Now it is time for Muslim clerics to denounce the terrorists or admit that Islam is fighting a war with us—a religious war."[2] For the author of this letter, Muslim "clerics" are not to be trusted, not because they find it hard to believe that pious Muslims would commit outrageous acts of terrorism, but because they secretly hate the West and its values. Clearly, for this reader of *Time,* Islam and the West are at war; however the "West" may be defined and wherever "Islam" or Muslims are to be found.

Prejudice against Muslim minorities still exists in many countries. In Russia, Muslim restaurateurs from the Caucasus Mountains must call themselves "Georgian" to stay in business. In China, being Muslim by ethnicity is acceptable, but being a Muslim by conviction might get one convicted for antistate activities. In the Balkans, Muslims in Serbia, Bulgaria, and Macedonia are called "Turks" and right-wing nationalist parties deny them full ethnic legitimacy as citizens of their countries. In India, over a thousand Muslims were killed in communal riots in Gujarat as recently as 2002. As I write these words, Israel and Hizbollah, the Lebanese Shiite political movement and militia, are engaged in a bloody conflict that has left hundreds of dead and injured on both sides. Although the number of people who have been killed in Lebanon, most of whom are Shiite civilians, is far greater than the number of those killed in Israel, television news reports in the United States do not treat Lebanese and Israeli casualties the same way. While the casualties that are caused by Hizbollah rockets in Israel are depicted as personal tragedies, Lebanese casualties are seldom personalized in this way. The truth is, of course, that all casualties of war are personal tragedies, whether the victims are Lebanese civilians, Israeli civilians, or American soldiers killed or maimed by improvised explosive devices in Iraq. In addition, all civilian deaths in war pose a moral problem, whether they are caused as a consequence of aggression or of retaliation. In many ways, depersonalization can have worse effects than actual hatred. An enemy that is hated must at least be confronted; when innocent victims are reduced to pictures without stories, they are all too easily ignored.

The problem of depersonalization has deeper roots than just individual prejudice. Ironically, the global village created by international news organizations such as CNN, BBC, and Fox News may unintentionally contribute to the problem of devaluing Muslim lives. Depictions of victimhood are often studies in incomprehension: victims speak a language the viewer cannot understand, their shock or rage strips them of their rationality, and their standard of living and mode of dress may appear medieval or even primitive when compared with the dominant cultural forms of modernity. In her classic study, *The Origins of Totalitarianism,* Hannah Arendt pointed out that the ideology of human equality, which is fostered with all good intentions by the international news media, paradoxically contributes to the visibility of difference by confusing equality with sameness. In 99 out of 100 cases, says Arendt, equality "will be mistaken for an innate quality of every individual, who is 'normal' if he is like everybody else and 'abnormal' if he happens to be different. This perversion of equality from a political into a social concept is all the more dangerous when a society leaves but little space for special groups and individuals, for then their differences become all the more conspicuous."[3] According to Arendt, the widespread acceptance of the ideal of social equality after the French Revolution was a major reason why genocide, whether of Jews in Europe, Tutsis in Rwanda, or Muslims in the former Yugoslavia, has become a characteristically modern phenomenon.

The idea of equality as sameness was not as firmly established in the United States, claimed Arendt, because the "equal opportunity" ideology of American liberalism values difference—in the form of imagination, entrepreneurship, and personal initiative—as a token of success.[4] This ideology enabled Jews in America to assert their distinctiveness and eventually to prosper in the twentieth century, and it provides an opportunity for Muslim Americans to assert their distinctiveness and to prosper today. So far, the United States has not engaged in systematic persecution of Muslims and has been relatively free of anti-Muslim prejudice. However, fear and distrust of Muslims among the general public is fostered by images of insurgent attacks and suicide bombings in Iraq, of Al Qaeda atrocities around the globe, and of increasing expressions of anti-Americanism in the Arabic and Islamic media. In addition, some pundits on talk radio, certain fundamentalist religious leaders, and some members of the conservative press and academia fan the flames of prejudice by portraying Islam as inherently intolerant and by portraying Muslims as slaves to tradition and authoritarianism rather than as advocates of reason and freedom of expression. Clearly, there is still a need to demonstrate to the American public that Muslims are rational human beings and that Islam is a religion that is worthy of respect.

Changing public opinion about Islam and Muslims in the United States and Europe will not be easy. The culture critic Guillermo Gomez-Peña has written that as a result of the opening of American borders to non-Europeans in the 1960s, the American myth of the cultural melting pot "has been replaced by a model that is more germane to the times, that of the *menudo chowder*. According to this model, most of the ingredients do melt, but some stubborn chunks are condemned merely to float."[5] At the present time, Muslims constitute the most visible "stubborn chunks" in the *menudo chowder* of American and European pluralism. Muslims are often seen as the chunks of the *menudo chowder* that most stubbornly refuse to "melt in." To the non-Muslim majoritarian citizen of Western countries, Muslims seem to be the most "uncivil" members of civil society. They do not dress like the majority, they do not eat like the majority, they do not drink like the majority, they do not let their women work, they reject the music and cultural values of the majority, and sometimes they even try to opt out of majoritarian legal and economic systems. In Europe, Islam has replaced Catholicism as the religion that left-wing pundits most love to hate. Americans, however, have been more ambivalent about Islam and Muslims. On the one hand, there have been sincere attempts to include Muslims as full partners in civil society. On the other hand, the apparent resistance of some Muslims to "fit in" creates a widespread distrust that has had legal ramifications in several notable cases.

A useful way to conceive of the problem that Muslims face as members of civil society—both within Western countries and in the global civil society that is dominated by the West—is to recognize, following Homi K. Bhabha, the social fact of Muslim *unhomeliness.* To be "unhomed," says Bhabha, is not to be homeless, but rather to escape easy assimilation or accommodation.[6] The problem is not that the "unhomed" possesses no physical home but that there is no "place" to locate the unhomed in the majoritarian consciousness. Simply put, one does not know what to make of the unhomed. Bhabha derives this term from Sigmund Freud's concept of *unheimlich,* "the name for everything that ought to have remained secret and hidden but has come to light."[7] Unhomeliness is a way of expressing social discomfort. When one encounters the unhomed, one feels awkward and uncomfortable because the unhomed person appears truly alien. Indeed, if there is any single experience that virtually all Muslims in Western countries share, it is that Islam makes non-Muslims uncomfortable. In the global civil society dominated by the West, Muslims are unhomed wherever they may live, even in their own countries.

This reality of Muslim experience highlights how contemporary advocates of Muslim identity politics have often made matters worse by accentuating symbolic tokens of difference between so-called Islamic and Western norms. The problem for Islam in today's global civil society is not that it is not seen. On the contrary, Islam and Muslims are arguably all too visible because they are seen as fundamentally different from the accepted norm. Like the black man in the colonial West Indies or in Jim Crow America, the Muslim is, to borrow a phrase from Frantz Fanon, "overdetermined from without."[8] Muslims have been overdetermined by the press, overdetermined by Hollywood, overdetermined by politicians, and overdetermined by culture critics. From the president of the United States to the prime minister of the United Kingdom, and in countless editorials in print and television media, leaders of public opinion ask, "What do Muslims want?" Such a question forces the Muslim into a corner in which the only answer is apologetics or defiance. To again paraphrase Fanon, the overdetermined Muslim is constantly made aware of himself or herself not just in the third person but in *triple person.* As a symbol of the unhomely, the Muslim is made to feel personally responsible for a contradictory variety of "Islamic" moral values, "Islamic" cultural expressions, and "Islamic" religious and political doctrines.[9]

In the face of such outside pressures, what the overdetermined Muslim needs most is not to be seen, but to be heard. There is a critical need for Islam to be expressed to the world not as an image, but as a narrative, and for Muslims to bear their own witness to their own experiences. The vast majority of books on Islam written in European languages, even the best ones, have been written by non-Muslims. This is not necessarily a problem, because an objective and open-minded non-Muslim can often describe Islam for a non-

Muslim audience better than a Muslim apologist. The scholars Said and Ernst, mentioned above, are both from Christian backgrounds. The discipline of Religious Studies from which Ernst writes has been careful to maintain a nonjudgmental attitude toward non-Christian religions. As heirs to the political and philosophical values of European liberalism, scholars of Religious Studies are typically dogmatic about only one thing: they must practice *epoché* (a Greek word meaning "holding back" or restraining one's beliefs) when approaching the worldview of another religion. In the words of the late Canadian scholar of religion Wilfred Cantwell Smith, it is not enough to act like "a fly crawling on the outside of a goldfish bowl," magisterially observing another's religious practices while remaining distant from the subject. Instead, one must be more engaged in her inquiry and, through imagination and the use of *epoché*, try to find out what it feels like to be a goldfish.[10]

Through the practice of *epoché*, the field of Religious Studies has by now produced two generations of accomplished scholars of Islam in the United States and Canada. Smith himself was a fair and sympathetic Christian scholar of Islam, and his field has been more influential than any other in promoting the study of Islam in the West. However, even Smith was aware that only a goldfish truly knows what it means to be a goldfish. The most that a sympathetic non-Muslim specialist in Islamic studies can do is *describe* Islam from the perspective of a sensitive outsider. Because non-Muslims do not share a personal commitment to the Islamic faith, they are not in the best position to convey a sense of what it means to *be* a Muslim on the inside—to live a Muslim life, to share Muslim values and concerns, and to experience Islam spiritually. In the final analysis, only Muslims can fully bear witness to their own traditions from within.

The five-volume set of *Voices of Islam* is an attempt to meet this need. By bringing together the voices of nearly 50 prominent Muslims from around the world, it aims to present an accurate, comprehensive, and accessible account of Islamic doctrines, practices, and worldviews for a general reader at the senior high school and university undergraduate level. The subjects of the volumes—*Voices of Tradition; Voices of the Spirit; Voices of Life: Family, Home, and Society; Voices of Art, Beauty, and Science;* and *Voices of Change*— were selected to provide as wide a depiction as possible of Muslim experiences and ways of knowledge. Taken collectively, the chapters in these volumes provide bridges between formal religion and culture, the present and the past, tradition and change, and spiritual and outward action that can be crossed by readers, whether they are Muslims or non-Muslims, many times and in a variety of ways. What this set does *not* do is present a magisterial, authoritative vision of an "objectively real" Islam that is juxtaposed against a supposedly inauthentic diversity of individual voices. As the Egyptian-American legal scholar and culture critic Khaled Abou El Fadl has pointed out, whenever Islam is the subject of discourse, the authoritative quickly elides into the authoritarian, irrespective of whether the voice of authority is

Muslim or non-Muslim.[11] The editors of *Voices of Islam* seek to avoid the authoritarian by allowing every voice expressed in the five-volume set to be authoritative, both in terms of individual experience and in terms of the commonalities that Muslims share among themselves.

THE EDITORS

The general editor for *Voices of Islam* is Vincent J. Cornell, Asa Griggs Candler Professor of Middle East and Islamic Studies at Emory University in Atlanta, Georgia. When he was solicited by Praeger, an imprint of Greenwood Publishing, to formulate this project, he was director of the King Fahd Center for Middle East and Islamic Studies at the University of Arkansas. Dr. Cornell has been a Sunni Muslim for more than 30 years and is a noted scholar of Islamic thought and history. His most important book, *Realm of the Saint: Power and Authority in Moroccan Sufism* (1998), was described by a prepublication reviewer as "the most significant study of the Sufi tradition in Islam to have appeared in the last two decades." Besides publishing works on Sufism, Dr. Cornell has also written articles on Islamic law, Islamic theology, and moral and political philosophy. For the past five years, he has been a participant in the Archbishop of Canterbury's "Building Bridges" dialogue of Christian and Muslim theologians. In cooperation with the Jerusalem-based Elijah Interfaith Institute, he is presently co-convener of a group of Muslim scholars, of whom some are contributors to *Voices of Islam,* which is working toward a new theology of the religious other in Islam. Besides serving as general editor for *Voices of Islam,* Dr. Cornell is also the volume editor for Volume 1, *Voices of Tradition;* Volume 2, *Voices of the Spirit;* and Volume 4, *Voices of Art, Beauty, and Science.*

The associate editors for *Voices of Islam* are Omid Safi and Virginia Gray Henry-Blakemore. Omid Safi is Associate Professor of Religion at the University of North Carolina at Chapel Hill. Dr. Safi, the grandson of a noted Iranian Ayatollah, was born in the United States but raised in Iran and has been recognized as an important Muslim voice for moderation and diversity. He gained widespread praise for his edited first book, *Progressive Muslims: On Justice, Gender, and Pluralism* (2003), and was interviewed on CNN, National Public Radio, and other major media outlets. He recently published an important study of Sufi-state relations in premodern Iran, *The Politics of Knowledge in Premodern Islam* (2006). Dr. Safi is the volume editor for Volume 5, *Voices of Change,* which contains chapters by many of the authors represented in his earlier work, *Progressive Muslims.*

Virginia Gray Henry-Blakemore has been a practicing Sunni Muslim for almost 40 years. She is director of the interfaith publishing houses Fons Vitae and Quinta Essentia and cofounder and trustee of the Islamic Texts Society of Cambridge, England. Some of the most influential families in Saudi

Arabia, Egypt, and Jordan have supported her publishing projects. She is an accomplished lecturer in art history, world religions, and filmmaking and is a founding member of the Thomas Merton Center Foundation. Henry-Blakemore received her BA at Sarah Lawrence College, studied at the American University in Cairo and Al-Azhar University, earned her MA in Education at the University of Michigan, and served as a research fellow at Cambridge University from 1983 to 1990. She is the volume editor for Volume 3, *Voices of Life: Family, Home, and Society.*

THE AUTHORS

As stated earlier, *Voices of Islam* seeks to meet the need for Muslims to bear witness to their own traditions by bringing together a diverse collection of Muslim voices from different regions and from different scholarly and professional backgrounds. The voices that speak to the readers about Islam in this set come from Asia, Africa, Europe, and North America, and include men and women, academics, community and religious leaders, teachers, activists, and business leaders. Some authors were born Muslims and others embraced Islam at various points in their lives. A variety of doctrinal, legal, and cultural positions are also represented, including modernists, traditionalists, legalists, Sunnis, Shiites, Sufis, and "progressive Muslims." The editors of the set took care to represent as many Muslim points of view as possible, including those that they may disagree with. Although each chapter in the set was designed to provide basic information for the general reader on a particular topic, the authors were encouraged to express their individual voices of opinion and experience whenever possible.

In theoretical terms, *Voices of Islam* treads a fine line between what Paul Veyne has called "specificity" and "singularity." As both an introduction to Islam and as an expression of Islamic diversity, this set combines historical and commentarial approaches, as well as poetic and narrative accounts of individual experiences. Because of the wide range of subjects that are covered, individualized accounts (the "singular") make up much of the narrative of *Voices of Islam,* but the intent of the work is not to express individuality per se. Rather, the goal is to help the reader understand the varieties of Islamic experience (the "specific") more deeply by finding within their specificity a certain kind of generality.[12]

For Veyne, "specificity" is another way of expressing typicality or the ideal type, a sociological concept that has been a useful tool for investigating complex systems of social organization, thought, or belief. However, the problem with typification is that it may lead to oversimplification, and oversimplification is the handmaiden of the stereotype. Typification can lead to oversimplification because the concept of typicality belongs to a structure of general knowledge that obscures the view of the singular and the different. Thus,

presenting the voices of only preselected "typical Muslims" or
"representative Muslims" in a work such as *Voices of Islam* would only aggra-
vate the tendency of many Muslims and non-Muslims to define Islam in a single, essentialized way. When done from without, this can lead to a form of
stereotyping that may exacerbate, rather than alleviate, the tendency to see
Muslims in ways that they do not see themselves. When done from within,
it can lead to a dogmatic fundamentalism (whether liberal or conservative
does not matter) that excludes the voices of difference from "real" Islam
and fosters a totalitarian approach to religion. Such an emphasis on the legitimacy of representation by Muslims themselves would merely reinforce the
ideal of sameness that Arendt decried and enable the overdetermination of
the "typical" Muslim from without. For this reason, *Voices of Islam* seeks to
strike a balance between specificity and singularity. Not only the chapters in
these volumes but also the backgrounds and personal orientations of their
authors express Islam as a lived diversity and as a source of multiple well-
springs of knowledge. Through the use of individual voices, this work seeks
to save the "singular" from the "typical" by employing the "specific."

Dipesh Chakrabarty, a major figure in the field of Subaltern Studies, notes:
"Singularity is a matter of viewing. It comes into being as that which resists
our attempt to see something as a particular instance of a general idea or category."[13] For Chakrabarty, the singular is a necessary antidote to the typical
because it "defies the generalizing impulse of the sociological imagination."[14] Because the tendency to overdetermine and objectify Islam is central
to the continued lack of understanding of Islam by non-Muslims, it is necessary to defy the generalizing impulse by demonstrating that the unity of Islam
is not a unity of sameness, but of diversity. Highlighting the singularity of
individual Islamic practices and doctrines becomes a means of liberating
Islam from the totalizing vision of both religious fundamentalism (Muslim
and non-Muslim alike) and secular essentialism. While Islam in theory may
be a unity, in both thought and practice this "unity" is in reality a galaxy
whose millions of singular stars exist within a universe of multiple perspectives. This is not just a sociological fact, but a theological point as well. For
centuries, Muslim theologians have asserted that the Transcendent Unity of
God is a mystery that defies the normal rules of logic. To human beings,
unity usually implies either singularity or sameness, but with respect to
God, Unity is beyond number or comparison.

In historiographical terms, a work that seeks to describe Islam through the
voices of individual Muslims is an example of "minority history." However,
by allowing the voices of specificity and singularity to enter into a trialogue
that includes each other as well as the reader, *Voices of Islam* is also an example of "subaltern history." For Chakrabarty, subaltern narratives "are mar-
ginalized not because of any conscious intentions but because they
represent moments or points at which the archive that the historian mines
develops a degree of intractability with respect to the aims of professional

history."[15] Subaltern narratives do not only belong to socially subordinate or minority groups, but they also belong to underrepresented groups in Western scholarship, even if these groups comprise a billion people as Muslims do. Subaltern narratives resist typification because the realities that they represent do not correspond to the stereotypical. As such, they need to be studied on their own terms. The history of Islam in thought and practice is the product of constant dialogues between the present and the past, internal and external discourses, culture and ideology, and tradition and change. To describe Islam as anything less would be to reduce it to a limited set of descriptive and conceptual categories that can only rob Islam of its diversity and its historical and intellectual depth. The best way to retain a sense of this diversity and depth is to allow Muslim voices to relate their own narratives of Islam's past and present.

NOTES

1. Carl W. Ernst, *Following Muhammad: Rethinking Islam in the Contemporary World* (Chapel Hill and London: University of North Carolina Press, 2003), xvii.

2. *Time,* June 7, 2004, 10.

3. Hannah Arendt, *The Origins of Totalitarianism,* rev. ed. (San Diego, New York, and London: Harvest Harcourt, 1976), 54.

4. Ibid., 55.

5. Guillermo Gomez-Peña, "The New World (B)order," *Third Text* 21 (Winter 1992–1993): 74, quoted in Homi K. Bhabha, *The Location of Culture* (London and New York: Routledge Classics, 2004), 313.

6. Bhabha, *The Location of Culture,* 13.

7. Ibid., 14–15.

8. Frantz Fanon, *Black Skin, White Masks* (London, U.K.: Pluto, 1986), 116. The original French term for this condition is *surdéterminé.* See idem, *Peau noire masques blancs* (Paris: Éditions du Seuil, 1952), 128.

9. Ibid., 112.

10. Wilfred Cantwell Smith, *The Meaning and End of Religion* (Minneapolis, Minnesota: The University of Minnesota Press, 1991), 7.

11. Khaled Abou El Fadl, *Speaking in God's Name: Islamic Law, Authority, and Women* (Oxford, U.K.: Oneworld Publications, 2001), 9–85.

12. Paul Veyne, *Writing History: Essay on Epistemology,* trans. Mina Moore-Rinvolucri (Middletown, Connecticut: Wesleyan University Press, 1984), 56.

13. Dipesh Chakrabarty, *Provincializing Europe: Postcolonial Thought and Historical Difference* (Princeton and Oxford: Princeton University Press, 2000), 82.

14. Ibid., 83.

15. Ibid., 101.

INTRODUCTION: VOICES OF THE SPIRIT

———————————————— • ————————————————

Vincent J. Cornell

Frithjof Schuon, whose Muslim name was Nur al-Din ‘Isa and who is one of the contributors to this set in Volume 4, *Voices of Art, Beauty, and Science,* ends his book *Spiritual Perspectives and Human Facts* with the following reflection on prayer:

> Man prays and prayer fashions man. The saint has himself become prayer, the meeting-place of earth and Heaven; and thereby he contains the universe and the universe prays with him. He is everywhere where nature prays and he prays with her and in her: in the peaks which touch the void and eternity, in a flower which scatters its scent or in the carefree song of a bird.
> He who lives in prayer has not lived in vain.[1]

I was strongly drawn to Schuon's words from the first time I read them. However, they initially expressed to me a sentiment that was honored more in the breach than in practice. Schuon's view of prayer expresses a spirituality that is rare in today's Western religions. Whether in Judaism, Christianity, or even in much of contemporary Islam, the materialistic tenor of the times has crept into religious observance. The evangelism that pervades Sunday morning television in the United States is often materialistic, and expresses its worldliness both in its association with partisan politics and in its equation of religious virtue with worldly success. In the early 1970s, when I was a student at the University of California, Berkeley, a preacher from Oakland, California, named Reverend Ike preached a gospel of wealth that bore the motto, "You can't lose with the stuff I use." Today's gospel of prosperity in the United States may come in a more appealing package, but its message has changed very little. The equation of virtue with material success in evangelicalism has roots that go far back into the history of American Protestantism. The Catholic and Orthodox traditions of Christianity may be less overtly materialistic than Evangelical Protestantism, but they too have not emerged unscathed from the effects of materialism. In Judaism, to escape the influence of materialism, many believers approach God's commandments through an esoteric tradition such as Hasidism or Kabbalah. When more secularized

Americans seek the type of spirituality expressed in Schuon's statement, they often follow the example of the Trappist monk Thomas Merton and look not to the West but to the East—to the Dalai Lama, a Zen master, or a Hindu sage.

In the present age of late capitalism and high materiality, it often seems enough for the seeker just to find a religious message that gives practical advice on how to attain a sense of balance and harmony in one's life. This is a major reason for the popularity of preachers such as Houston Evangelist Joel Osteen, whose practical and commonsense approach to what might be called the "gospel of wellness" deals with universal principles of faith and works that are as acceptable to a Muslim or a Jew as they are to a Christian. It is also a reason why much of the religious revival in the West is moralistic and legalistic in nature, including the revival of Islam. In a complex world, the Law of God provides the most visible and easily graspable thread that can lead lost souls out of the labyrinth of modern life.

At the end of the fifteenth century CE, 'Ali Salih al-Andalusi (d. ca. 1508), a Sufi from Granada, noted that adherence to religious law is necessary for maintaining both the theological and the ethical boundaries of religion.[2] The law counteracts the weakness or inadequacy of the human being by applying basic principles of spiritual training and discipline. For this reason, many religious reform movements stress the importance of sincerity and ethical virtues and require strict obedience to God's Law. By comparison, spirituality receives less attention. According to Andalusi, religious reformers who see God's Law as the ultimate path to salvation take as their motto the phrase, "We hear and obey." It is sometimes said by such reformers in Islam that the root of *insan,* the Arabic word for "human being," is *nasiya,* "to forget." Because human beings are forgetful, they need to be reminded of God through revelation and redirected toward salvation by the Law (*Shari'a*) that God has mandated.[3]

However, there is another possible root for *insan,* which is *anisa,* "to come close." According to this understanding, human beings are close to God by nature because they are created in God's image. This view of human nature, which is common to the Sufi perspective in Islam, gives greater attention to the transcendental potential of the human spirit than does the legalistic path to religious reform. As outlined by Andalusi, a model of reform based on the Sufi view of human potential starts from the assumption that human beings are fully prepared to fulfill their role as God's representatives on Earth. The development of a greater sense of the sacred thus becomes a matter of spiritual pedagogy and character building, which supplements, rather than replaces, outward conformity to religious law. Because their view of the human being is more optimistic, such theologies of human potential often combine pedagogies of love and nurturance with disciplinary training and concentrate on the inward assimilation of divine commands without rejecting their outward practice. According to Andalusi, whereas the exoteric religious reformer follows the dictate, "We hear and obey," the Sufi reformer responds, "We have witnessed and understand."

This Sufi theology of human potential lies behind Frithjof Schuon's notion of prayer in the selection reproduced above. The person who lives in prayer does not live in vain because she understands that prayer is more than a mere act of obedience. It is above all a means of communication between the worshipper and the Absolute, an act of communion for which every person is predisposed. According to a Holy Tradition (*hadith qudsi*) that can be found in Daniel Abdal-Hayy Moore's chapter on the remembrance of God (*dhikr*), "Allah Almighty says, 'I am whatever My slave thinks of Me and I am with Him when He remembers Me. When he remembers Me in himself, I remember him in Myself. If he mentions Me in an assembly, I mention him in a better assembly. If he comes near to Me by a hand-span, I come near to him by a cubit. If he comes near to Me by a cubit, I come near to him by a league. If he comes to Me walking, I come to him running." Commenting on this tradition, Moore's spiritual teacher, the Moroccan Sufi Muhammad ibn al-Habib, states in his collection of poems: "If the breath of God's remembrance were to fill the west and there were/A sick man in the east, that man would be cured of his affliction." In other words, and especially in today's global Islam, what the Spanish Sufi Ibn 'Arabi (d. 1240 CE) called the "Breath of the All-Merciful" (*nafas al-Rahman*) blows everywhere: when it blows in the east, it can heal the west; when it blows in the west, it can heal the east.

This volume of *Voices of Islam* is dedicated to *Voices of the Spirit* because, outside of Sufism, no aspect of Islamic thought and practice has been more overlooked in recent studies of Islam than spirituality. For most observers in Western countries, Islam embodies three traits that are antithetical to liberal views of religious expression: traditionalism, legalism, and authoritarianism. The spiritual dimension of Islam is seldom mentioned except with respect to Sufis. To a certain extent, this blindness to the spiritual side of Islam is the result of a prejudice that has existed for more than two centuries in the West. According to this view, "real" Islam (somewhat like "real" Judaism) is traditionalistic and legalistic but not deeply spiritual. When Sufi spirituality is brought up, it is usually not as a religious perspective within Islam but rather as an importation of spirituality from the outside, such as from Christian monasticism or from the Indian philosophies of Hinduism or Buddhism. Since Sufi spirituality is not seen as "real" Islam, Sufism is often treated as a separate sect or even as a de facto alternative religion. This is why some New Age practitioners of Sufism in the West feel comfortable calling themselves Sufis but refuse to identify themselves as Muslims.

More than twenty-five years ago, Edward W. Said noted in his book *Orientalism* that the European and American view of the Middle East and the Islamic world is premised on the notion of exteriority, which allows complex cultural phenomena to be simplified into discrete representations of an artificially constructed "essence."[4] The traditions, laws, and politics of Islam are easily visible, exteriorized phenomena. As such, they can be observed and studied by the outsider and turned into symbolic representations of a "real" Islam that has been reduced to its predetermined "essential" characteristics. Spirituality, however, is premised on the notion of interiority. What is on the inside is hard to see, and what is hard to see cannot easily be observed, measured, and subjected to regimes of control and domination. If "real" Islam is exteriorized as a set of rules that determine right behavior and right belief instead of a deeper orientation toward God, it becomes easy to separate the interior aspects of Islam, such as theology and spirituality, out of Islam's supposed essence. Such an Islam would be an Islam with neither a mind (theology) nor a soul (spirituality) and hence would pose no challenge either to Western religions or to secular notions of ultimate truth.

However, the exteriorization of Islam is not just the result of a Western Orientalism that refuses to die out. Part of the blame for this situation also lies with Muslims themselves. Much of Muslim discourse today consists of an anti-Western, "clash of civilizations" type rhetoric that conceives of Islam not as a spiritual approach to the Absolute, but as an ideological system that is opposed to the hegemonic culture of Western modernity. This perspective is embodied in the title of one of the key chapters of the Muslim Brotherhood ideologue Sayyid Qutb's (d. 1966) manifesto *Ma'alim fi al-Tariq* (Signs Along the Road). Chapter 8 of Qutb's work is titled, "The Islamic Concept and Culture" (*al-Tasawwur al-Islami wa al-Thaqafa*). Qutb's *Signs Along the Road* has arguably been the most influential political manifesto since *The Communist Manifesto* of Karl Marx and Friedrich Engels. It has provided inspiration for a vast array of Islamic activists from Morocco to Malaysia, and Usama Bin Laden is perhaps its most loyal reader. The chapter "The Islamic Concept and Culture" was the inspiration for an intellectual movement known as the "Islamization of Knowledge," which is still followed in many parts of the Muslim world.[5] In this chapter, Qutb warns Muslim youths to avoid the Western sciences of sociology, cosmology, and anthropology, saying, "It is not permissible for a Muslim to learn them from anyone other than a God-fearing and pious Muslim, who knows that guidance in these matters comes from God."[6] For Qutb, the touchstone of Islamic piety is less the spiritual awareness of God as it is a means of inoculation against ideological and intellectual viruses from the West.

Lest one dismiss the exteriority of Qutb's view of Islam as the ideology of a political extremist and hence unrepresentative of Islamic reformism in general, one may also bring forward the statement of Farid Esack, a South African Muslim activist and intellectual living in the United States, who champions human rights, social and political pluralism, and intellectual freedom. In his book *Qur'an, Liberation, and Pluralism* he states, "Despite the regular reminders of the inevitable return to God, the spiritualizing of human existence, which regards earthly life as incidental, is unfounded in the qur'anic [*sic*] view of humankind.''[7] One must ask in response to this assertion: If Islam cannot transcend the material world, then why is it called a religion and not just an ideology? The views of Qutb and Esack reflect a common tendency among Muslim reformists to reduce the religion of Islam to a system, to reduce Islamic theology to ideology, and to reduce the cultural diversity of Islam to a monoculture. In this perspective, piety is not denied per se but rather is transformed from an integral part of religion into an instrumental means of social and political liberation.

Although Muslims have long fought for social justice, modern Islamic Liberation Theologies such as those of Qutb and Esack—like the Marxist-oriented Liberation Theology that was popular in Latin America in the 1970s and 1980s—are fundamentally materialistic. This is because they seek a state of political and worldly perfection that is far more un-Qur'anic than the spiritualism that Esack decries. While the Qur'an calls on believers to strive to better their condition, nowhere does it predict the return of an earthly paradise. Quite the opposite: Islamic tradition is unanimous that things will get worse as humanity approaches the End Times. Despite this fact, the quest for a social and political utopia has become a dominant theme in Islamic reformism virtually everywhere in the world. This constitutes a crisis of faith because the purpose of Islam, like that of Christianity, Judaism, and other salvation religions, is to prepare individual souls to meet God. Today, however, politically minded Islamic reformers routinely criticize Muslims who stress piety for being socially irresponsible. For the despairing Muslim pietist, it seems that Islam has not just failed to change the world but that the world has taken over Islam in the name of Islam itself. Has the notion that the believer is his brother's keeper caused Muslims to forget that the traditional legal view of Islamic society was not of a corporate entity but rather of a collection of individuals? Have Muslims forgotten the admonition of the Qur'an that ''Each soul is the hostage of its own deeds'' (Qur'an 74:38) and not of the deeds of the collectivity? The fate of the individual soul in Islam is not dependent on the fate of the community. The righteous person can still expect God's mercy, even if one's entire society lives in sin. And even if the whole world were to embrace Islam, it would not help a single Muslim attain salvation.

Of course, there are millions of ordinary Muslims around the world who are not political activists but are deeply pious in the ways advocated by the Qur'an and Islamic tradition. This set would be remiss if it did not include their voices too. Before modern times, it was possible to express one's piety in Islam in a variety of theological and philosophical perspectives. However, it seems that today, if one wants to find a reformist intellectual who sees piety as foundational for Islam, one must look for a person who has been exposed to Sufism, even if one is not a Sufi oneself. An example of such a reformist intellectual is Enes Karić, Dean of the Faculty of Islamic Studies in Sarajevo, Bosnia-Herzegovina. The intellectual culture of Bosnia includes both Sufis and non-Sufis, but it is resolutely opposed to the imposition of a single dominant interpretation of Islam. In his writings on Islam, Kariç evokes the modernist notion of an *efficient Islam*, "an Islam that would be a viable proposition in the present world, an Islam that would confer strength and respectability on its followers in the world, particularly in this part of Europe."[8] However, unlike other reformist writers, Kariç does not overlook the importance of individual piety and spirituality. If Islam is indeed a "system," Kariç observes, "It is a system of piousness. To be a Muslim transparently means to be a Muslim simply because Islam has revealed the faith through a total, wholesome practice of piousness. This mighty wave of piousness grants to Islam as a faith an ever new freshness: schools of theology may succeed one another, the legal elaboration of the Message may later be renewed, political systems may vanish, but Islam remains as piousness, Islam as commitment to the One and Only God."[9]

This statement reflects the underlying premise of *Voices of the Spirit*. Rather than viewing spirituality as an obstacle to a progressive Islamic social consciousness, the editors of *Voices of Islam* regard spirituality as the necessary ground for all religiously directed action. Not only is spirituality the soul of Islam, but it also constitutes Islam's most valuable contribution to world religions. One must not deny the importance of social justice and political action in the Islamic world, but what is one to do with the heart? If one accepts the Greek metaphor of society as a body, which was adopted by many Muslim political theorists such as the philosopher Farabi (d. 950 CE), then treating outward social ills without giving sufficient importance to the spiritual well-being of the person is as foolish as treating gangrene from outside an infection and ignoring the poison that is already circulating in the bloodstream. Even when viewed instrumentally, a sense of spirituality is undeniably important for curing the diseases of the soul. What are these diseases? Frithjof Schuon's essay once again provides the answer:

> A false life, a false death, a false activity, a false rest. A false life: passion which engenders suffering; a false death: egoism which hardens the heart and separates it from God and his mercy; a false activity: dissipation, which casts the soul into an insatiable vortex and makes it forget God, who is Peace; a false rest or a false passivity: the weakness and laziness which deliver up the soul without resistance to the countless solicitations of the world.[10]

Tragically, as can be seen in recent articles and television reports on the problem of "home-grown" Muslim terrorists in countries such as the United Kingdom and Spain, and among jihadists who have been trained by Al Qaeda or its allies, many of the most sincere and religiously committed Muslim youths have, for want of a heart and a soul in their Islam, condemned themselves to a false life, a false death, a false activity, and a false rest. The April 8, 2002, issue of *Time* magazine carried an essay on suicide terrorism by Eyad Sarraj, a secular and politically moderate Palestinian psychiatrist and founder of the Palestinian Independent Commission for Citizens' Rights. Sarraj asserted that young Palestinians become suicide bombers because of the shame and despair they feel at the Israeli occupation of their country. "Shame is the most painful emotion in the Arab culture," said Sarraj, "producing the feeling that one is unworthy to live. The honorable Arab is the one who refuses to suffer shame and dies in dignity."[11]

If this is indeed the motivation for suicide bombing, then Schuon's words, which were written in the 1960s, have been proved prophetic in ways that no one at that time could have imagined. A feeling of despair that causes a person to seek death is not only the sign of a false life, but it is also a grave sin in Islam, as attested by Qur'an 4:29, "Do not kill yourselves, for God is merciful to you." Killing oneself out of despair means despairing of God's mercy, which no Muslim should ever do. Suicide bombing is a false death because suicide, especially a suicide that inflicts pain and suffering on the innocent, is a selfish act of egoism, which results, as the Qur'an implies, from a hardening of the heart and a spiritual separation from God and His mercy. False activity can be found in the often strident and obsessive concern with activism for its own sake, which goes beyond the necessary struggle for social and political justice, and casts the soul, as Schuon says, "into an insatiable vortex and makes it forget God, who is Peace." Finally, the false rest or passivity that Schuon decries can be found in indoctrinated minds that abandon the will to question—which, after all, is part of the human instinct for self-preservation—and deliver up their souls to the world in a false desire for a death that they wrongly believe will be virtuous, painless, and paradisal.

Ironically, it is the converted Alsatian Muslim Frithjof Schuon, more than the secular Palestinian psychiatrist Sarraj or the born Muslim suicide bomber from Iraq, Chechnya, or the United Kingdom, who is consistent with the teachings of the Qur'an and historical Islamic tradition. Nowhere is this truer than when Schuon provides his antidote for the troubles of our times:

> To this false life is opposed a true death: the death of passion; this is a spiritual death, the cold and crystalline purity of the soul conscious of its immortality. To false death is opposed a true life: the life of the heart turned towards God and open to the warmth of his love. To false activity is opposed a true rest, a true peace: the repose of the soul which is simple and generous and content with God, the soul which turns aside from agitations and curiosity and ambition, to rest in the Divine beauty. To false rest is opposed a true activity: the battle of the spirit against the multiple weaknesses which squander the soul—and this precious life—as in a game or a dream.[12]

Despite the distortions of jihad that are committed by Muslim terrorists and suicide bombers, Muslim pietists and political activists both agree on one point: struggle in the way of God in Islam is an intensely spiritual act. This is why the chapter, "Jihad in Islam," by the Syrian-born Sufi shaykh Muhammad Hisham Kabbani is included in this volume. Islam still retains, in a way that has become rare in the United States since the end of the civil rights movement, the notion that struggling to establish God's justice is a path to salvation. For this reason, it is important to remind the readers, as Shaykh Kabbani does, that jihad against the unbelievers is only one of many forms of what Schuon has termed "the battle of the spirit" in Islam. Following the fourteenth-century Muslim scholar Ibn Qayyim al-Jawziyya, Shaykh Kabbani notes that frequently encountered forms of jihad include those against hypocrisy, Satan, and the self. All of these jihads depend on a deep and profound sense of spirituality. In fact, these above three forms of jihad, if followed carefully by Muslim activists, would serve as an antidote to the distortions of jihad that are now committed in the name of Islam. The irony of political Islam is that it often seeks to win the world at the cost of the soul. As a friend of the Saudi intellectual Muhammad Asad once observed of the Wahhabi insurgents who opposed King Abdul Aziz of Saudi Arabia for entering into treaties with non-Muslims, Muslim political extremists "are like the *jinns*...who know neither joy of life nor fear of death.... They are brave and strong in faith, no one can deny that—but all they dream about is blood and death and Paradise."[13] The ultimate tragedy for many Muslims is that they forget that such a "Paradise" is in fact Paradise lost.

This volume does not contain a complete inventory of spirituality in Islam, as it would take an entire set of volumes to produce. However, the volume was designed to provide a representative sample of spiritual perspectives, both Sufi and non-Sufi and both Sunni and Shiite. The volume begins with a reflection on prayer in Islam that links Islamic spirituality to its origins through the sacred space of the Ka'ba in Mecca and to the wide varieties of prayer that one finds in the universe of Muslim spiritual experiences. The discussion then moves to the concept of remembrance and links the remembrance of God in Islam through the formal prayer (*Salat*) and supererogatory invocation (*dhikr*) to the popular remembrance of the Prophet Muhammad, without whom the historical religion of Islam would not exist. In this section, the reader is taken from a reflection on the Prophet's inner nature, through a spiritual tour (*ziyara*) of Medina, the Prophet's City, and finally to the experience of sitting in the remembrance of the Prophet before his tomb. From the remembrance of the Prophet Muhammad, the reader is next led to the remembrance of the Prophet's descendants in Shiite Islam, through the visitation by women of the tombs of Imams and their descendants in Iran and then via a discussion of 'Ashura, the important Shiite commemoration of the martyrdom of the Prophet's grandson Husayn.

From the theme of remembrance, the narrative next moves to other important spiritual themes in Islam: Shaykh 'Ali Jum'a, the Mufti of Egypt, discusses the heart as a seat of spiritual guidance; the eminent Iranian-born scholar Seyyid Hossein Nasr discusses evil in Islam as an absence of the good rather than as an actively malefic presence; and Virginia Gray Henry-Blakemore discusses the spiritual value of fear in the tradition of the great Spanish Sufi Abu Madyan (d. 1198 CE), who said: "Fear is a whip that urges and restrains; it urges one toward obedience and restrains one from disobedience."[14] Next the reader is introduced to Sufi spirituality, first with a chapter that describes the Catholic monk Thomas Merton's encounter with a Sufi saint, then with a discussion of the Sufi way of love and peace by Nasrollah Pourjavady, the foremost academic specialist on Sufism in Iran. Sufi women's spirituality is explored by Rkia E. Cornell, who discusses the theology of servitude practiced by early Sufi women, and by Leslie Cadavid, who recounts the biography of Fatima al-Yashrutiyya, a twentieth-century woman Sufi master from Palestine. A more counterintuitive approach to spirituality for the Western reader is found in Daniel Abdal-Hayy Moore's poem about his encounter in Mecca with a man who was "attracted to God" (*majdhub*) as a moth is attracted to a flame; such a person may appear mad on the outside but is profoundly in touch with the spirit on the inside. This poetic depiction precedes the important chapter on jihad by Shaykh Muhammad Hisham Kabbani, discussed above, which thoroughly discusses the inner, spiritual dimension of struggle in the way of God in Islam. The volume ends with "Letter to Mankind," another poem by Abdal-Hayy Moore that eloquently summarizes what it means for one to have experienced the spiritual dimension of Islam.

This volume of *Voices of Islam*, like the others, contains the voices of Muslims from several parts of the world, from the Arab countries of Morocco, Egypt, and Syria to Iran. However, its path also detours into the United States and includes the voices of converts to Islam who have spent large portions of their lives in the Muslim world. For the most part, this was not a conscious editorial decision but reflects the topics on which the authors who were solicited for this set wished to write. Looking back on the mix of authors, both those who were born as Muslims and those who embraced Islam by way of personal choice, one cannot help but feel that their choice of topics was more than a mere coincidence, for it reflects in very tangible terms the point made by the Moroccan Sufi Muhammad ibn al-Habib: The Breath of the All-Merciful blows in every corner of the world. If it blows in the east, it heals the west, and if it blows in the west, it heals the east. In the Introduction to Volume 4, *Voices of Art, Beauty, and Science*, I discuss the hybridity of European and American voices of Islam and their importance as an expression of what culture theorist Homi Bhabha calls "contra-modernity." For me, "contra-modernity" is best understood as a secular and postmodern way of saying with Shyakh Ibn al-Habib that the Breath of the Merciful—the spirituality that is so essential to Islam—can blow just as strongly in the west as in the east.

Muslims who have been born into the faith should not dismiss this opinion as just another argument for an Orientalism that still seeks to dominate the Muslim world. For some nationalistic Muslims, those who have embraced Islam from other religions pose a threat to Islam, in that such "Muslims by conviction" may act as a fifth column that promotes the domination of Islam by Western values now imposed from the inside. However, more traditionally minded Muslim scholars often have very different opinions. A little more than twenty years ago, 'Umar al-Rish, former administrator of Islamic endowments in Rabat and religious advisor to King Hassan II of Morocco, told me that in his opinion, the intellectual and spiritual future of Islam would be found in America and Europe, not in the countries that have historically been associated with Islam. Agreeing with the views of the Sufis Ibn 'Arabi and Ibn al-Habib, Sidi 'Umar believed that the effects of colonialism and the stresses of modernization would render those who lived in the so-called Muslim world insensitive to the Breath of the All-Merciful as it blew across their societies. If Islam were not to become a stranger in its own lands, he felt, it needed a re-infusion of spirituality from the countries of the West, lands whose inhabitants were already jaded with materialism and who sought a deeply spiritual perspective in their own lives.

Time will tell whether or not 'Umar al-Rish was correct. However, it is fitting to dedicate not only this volume of *Voices of Islam*, but also the entire set to his vision. This project could never have been successful without a panoply of voices from throughout the Islamic *Umma*, including those parts of the community that can be found in countries whose majorities are non-Muslim. This Introduction began with the words of Frithjof Schuon, an Alsatian Christian convert to Islam who spent most of his career in Lausanne, Switzerland, and Bloomington, Indiana. Its conclusion can be found in the words of the Saudi intellectual Muhammad Asad, who entered Islam as a Jewish reporter named Leopold Weiss for the newspaper *Frankfurter Zeitung*. Reflecting on the changes that occurred in the Islamic world from his first exposure to Islam in the 1920s to the publication of his memoir *The Road to Mecca* in the 1950s, he surmised:

> Never before...have the worlds of Islam and the West come so close to one another as today. This closeness is a struggle, visible and invisible. Under the impact of Western cultural influences, the souls of many Muslim men and women are slowly shriveling. They are letting themselves be led away from their erstwhile belief than an improvement of living standards should be but a means to improving man's spiritual perceptions; they are falling into the same idolatry of 'progress' into which the Western world fell after it reduced religion to a mere melodious tinkling somewhere in the background of happening.... If the Muslims keep their heads cool and accept progress as a means and not an end in itself, they may not only retain their own inner freedom but also, perhaps, pass on to Western man the lost secret of life's sweetness.[15]

NOTES

1. Frithjof Schuon, *Spiritual Perspectives and Human Facts*, trans. P.N. Townsend (1969 Eng ed., repr; Pates Manor, Bedfont, Middlesex: Perennial Books

Limited, 1987), 223. This work was initially published in French under the title, *Perspectives Spirituelles et Faits Humains*.

2. See Abu al-Hasan 'Ali Salih al-Andalusi, *Sharh rahbat al-aman* (Rabat: Bibliothèque al-Hasaniyya (Royal Library), manuscript number 5697, 970/1562-3), 4–20. The only discussion in print of Andalusi's doctrines can be found in Vincent J. Cornell, *Realm of the Saint: Power and Authority in Moroccan Sufism* (Austin, Texas: University of Texas Press, 1998), 213–218.

3. On the notion of the Shari'a, see Mohammad Hashim Kamali, "The *Shari'a*: Law as the Way of God," vol. 1, *Voices of Tradition*.

4. Edward W. Said, *Orientalism* (New York: Vintage Books/Random House, 1994 anniversary edition of 1978 original), 20–21.

5. The most significant theoretical discussion of the Islamization of Knowledge can be found in Syed Muhammad Naquib al-Attas, *Prologomena to the Metaphysics of Islam: An Exposition of the Fundamental Elements of the Worldview of Islam* (Kuala Lumpur, Malaysia: International Institute of Islamic Thought and Civilization, 1995).

6. Sayyid Qutb, *Ma'alim fi al-Tariq* (Beirut: Dar al-Shuruq, 2000), 139; see also the English translation of this work, Seyyid Qutb, *Milestones* (Damascus: Dar al-'Ilm, n.d.), 109–110.

7. Farid Esack, *Qur'an, Liberation, and Pluralism: An Islamic Perspective of Interreligious Solidarity against Oppression* (Oxford, U.K.: One World Books, 1997), 95.

8. Enes Karič, "Islam in Contemporary Bosnia: A Personal Statement," in *Essays (on Behalf) of Bosnia* (Sarajevo: El Kalem, 1999), 96.

9. Enes Karič, "The Universe of the Qur'an," in *Essays,* 168.

10. Schuon, *Spiritual Perspectives,* 222.

11. Eyad Sarraj, "Why We Blow Ourselves Up," *Time*, April 8, 2002.

12. Schuon, *Spiritual Perspectives,* 222.

13. Muhammad Asad, *The Road to Mecca* (Gibraltar: Dar al-Andalus, 1980 revision of 1954 first edition), 237.

14. This quotation is from Abu Madyan's collection of aphorisms, "The Intimacy of the Recluse and the Pastime of the Seeker" (*Uns al-Wahid wa nuzhat al-murid*). See Vincent J. Cornell, *The Way of Abu Madyan: Doctrinal and Poetic Works of Abu Madyan Shu'ayb ibn al-Husayn al-Ansari (c. 509/1115–1116—594/1198)* (Cambridge, U.K.: The Islamic Texts Society, 1996), 122.

15. Asad, *The Road to Mecca*, 347–349.

1

Abraham's Call: The Pilgrimage and the Call to Prayer

Virginia Gray Henry-Blakemore

No longer able to tolerate the community of idol worshippers in whose presence he had grown up, Abraham departed from the Sumerian town of Ur in the Euphrates river valley in about 1750 BCE. He journeyed to Palestine where he settled in Hebron, south of Bethlehem. In Arabic, Hebron is called *al-Khalil,* the City of the Friend of God. It was there that he purchased the cave of Machpeleh, where later he would be buried along with Sarah, Isaac, Rebecca, Leah, Jacob, and possibly Joseph. The Tomb of the Prophets in Hebron, which is revered by both Muslims and Jews, stands over the site of this cave. When Sarah, Abraham's wife, was very old and had still not been blessed with children, she suggested to Abraham—in keeping with tradition —that he marry Hagar, her Egyptian handmaiden, in the hope that there would be a child. Hagar soon bore Ishmael and it was not long before Sarah miraculously gave birth to a son, Isaac. God told Abraham that he would have two sons from whom two nations would be founded, and for this reason, Abraham must take Hagar and Ishmael to dwell in a new land. From the descendants of Sarah's son, Isaac, would come Moses and Jesus. Muhammad would come from the family of Ishmael, thereby making Abraham the father of the Jews, the Christians, and the Muslims.

Abraham took Hagar and Ishmael into an arid valley called Bakka, which was located on one of the great Arabian caravan routes where Mecca stands today. Abraham traveled back and forth between his two small families. On one of these visits, after Ishmael had become a young man, God commanded Abraham to rebuild, on the site of a most ancient place of worship, a sanctuary—a sacred House. This is recorded in the Qur'an: "The First House (of worship) appointed for humanity was at Bakka; a holy place and a guidance for all beings" (Qur'an 3:96).

Precise instructions were given by God as to how to build this structure for worship, called the *Ka'ba,* a word that means "cube" in the Arabic

language. In the Qur'an, God states: "Remember that We made the House
a place of assembly and safety for humanity, so take the station of
Abraham as a place of prayer. And we covenanted with Abraham and
Ishmael that they should sanctify My House for those who circle round it,
or use it as a retreat, or bow, or prostrate themselves [therein in prayer]"
(Qur'an 2:125).

When Abraham and Ishmael were raising the foundations of the House,
Abraham prayed: "O Lord! Receive this from us; Thou, only Thou, art the
All-hearing, the All-knowing. Our Lord, make us submissive unto Thee and
of our seed a nation that will be submissive unto Thee. Show us our ways of
worship, and turn towards us. Lo! Thou, only Thou, art the Relenting, the
Merciful. Our Lord, raise in their midst a Messenger from amongst them
who shall recite unto them Thy revelations, who shall instruct them in the
Scripture and in wisdom, and shall make them grow. Lo! Thou, only Thou,
art the Mighty, the Wise" (Qur'an 2:127–129).

After Abraham and Ishmael had completed the construction of the Ka'ba,
God said to Abraham, "Proclaim unto mankind the pilgrimage. Call them to
come and worship Me here." There stood Abraham, in the midst of a vast
and remote stretch of desert. "How far will my call reach?" he asked. God
replied, "You call and it is upon Me to make it reach." Then Abraham called,
"O mankind, the pilgrimage to the ancient House has been prescribed for
you—so make the pilgrimage."[1]

More than 2,000 years later, in the sixth century CE, Muhammad grew
up in Mecca, and, as his forefather Abraham had done in Ur, he despaired
of the corruption and idolatry that had come to pervade the sacred precincts.
He made meditative retreats in the cave of Hira at the summit of a mountain
outside the city. On one of these retreats, the Archangel Gabriel appeared
to him and recited the first of the revelations of the Qur'an. Later revelations
instituted the *Hajj*, or annual pilgrimage, that is incumbent on every
Muslim—who is able to afford it—to make at least once in his or her lifetime.
The Hajj is one of the Five Pillars of the Islamic faith.

As the pilgrim moves forward from his or her homeland in the direction of
Mecca—from the time he or she walks out of the door of his or her home,
travels in a car, flies in a plane, walks, or rides a donkey—he or she verbally
answers the Call of Abraham, made nearly 4,000 years ago. The pilgrim
repeats certain phrases, referred to as the *Talbiya*, taught by the Prophet
himself:

Labbayka Allahumma labbayk,
Labbayka la sharika lak.
Labbayka.
Inna al-hamda wa an-ni'amata
Laka wa al-Mulka.
La sharika lak.

Ever at Thy service O God! Ever at Thy service!
Ever at Thy service, Thou hast no partner.
Ever at Thy service!
Surely all Praise and Blessings
And Dominion are Thine.
Thou hast no partner.[2]

The word *Labbayka*, translated as "Ever at Thy service," literally means, "I am answering and responding to You (your call)."

Upon arriving in Mecca, the pilgrim circumambulates the Ka'ba[3] and then retires to the valley of Mina. On the Day of Arafat, he or she stands on the Plain of Arafat, amidst millions of pilgrims from all the nations of the world, asking God's forgiveness. That evening, at sunset, the pilgrims move together through mountain passes, preparing for the next rite, which commemorates Abraham's overcoming and rejection of the temptation to forgo sacrificing his son. These pilgrims, all humbly attired in *ihram*—a simple garb not unlike a shroud—experience there in the moonlight something like a preview of the Last Judgment. Men and women of all races are intermingled—indistinguishable as regards worldly rank. All stand together before God, who alone knows what is in their hearts.

Just as the call to pilgrimage and the response of the pilgrim are integral to this rite, so also is the *adhan,* the call to prayer in Islam. The word *adhan,* which means "call," shares the same linguistic root with the words for "ear," "listen," and "permission." When the Prophet Muhammad fled from Mecca and the severe persecutions of his birthplace in 622 CE, he settled in the town of Yathrib (Medina today). There a vision came to one of his companions, 'Abd Allah ibn Zayd, in which the exact words of the call to prayer were given:

Allahu Akbar, Allahu Akbar!
Allahu Akbar, Allahu Akbar!
Ashhadu an la ilaha illa'llah.
Ashhadu an la ilaha illa'llah.
Ashhadu anna Muhammadan Rasul Allah.
Ashhadu anna Muhammadan Rasul Allah.
Haya 'ala as-sala, Haya 'ala as-sala.
Haya 'ala al-falah. Haya 'ala al-falah.
Allahu Akbar, Allahu Akbar!
La ilaha illa'llah.

God is most great. God is most great!
God is most great. God is most great!
I testify that there is no god but God.
I testify that there is no god but God.
I testify that Muhammad is the Messenger of God.

I testify that Muhammad is the Messenger of God.
Come to prayer. Come to prayer.
Come to salvation. Come to salvation.
God is most great. God is most great!
There is no god but God.[4]

At this time, the second mosque, the mosque now known as the
Mosque of the Prophet, was being constructed in Medina. It is interesting to know that Muslims originally prayed in the direction of
Jerusalem.[5] Bilal, an African who had been a slave in Mecca and endured great torture for his conversion to Islam, was chosen by the
Prophet Muhammad to be the first to make the call announcing the
five daily prayers. And so, today, as the sun rises and sets at ever-
changing moments around the globe, the call to prayer could be said to
be continuous—with one slightly overlapping the next as the earth journeys
around the sun.

ACKNOWLEDGMENTS

The author would like to thank Mr. Akram Safadi of Lebanon and
Mr. Adnan Bogary of Saudi Arabia for their invaluable assistance in preparing
this chapter.

NOTES

The verses from the Qur'an were taken from the translation made by Abdullah
Yusuf Ali, Washington D.C., 1946 edition, as well as A.J. Arberry, *The Quran
Interpreted* (Oxford: Oxford University Press, 1964).

This chapter first appeared in *Parabola,* spring 1994, 61–65. It is reproduced
with slight modifications in this volume with the permission of the editors of
Parabola.

1.   The phrase, "Call of Abraham," comes from a statement by the Prophet
Muhammad's cousin, Ibn 'Abbas, and is found in the Qur'an commentary or *Tafsir*
of Tabari: vol. 10, Surat al-Hajj 22:27.

2.   These phrases repeated by the pilgrim in response to Abraham's Call are known
as the *Talbiya*. The *Talbiya* is found in an authentic *hadith* (prophetic saying) reported
by Muslim and others from Jabir ibn 'Abdallah al-Ansari. See *Sahih Muslim,* ed.,
Muhammad Fuad 'Abd al-Baqi (Cairo: Dar Ihya' al-Kutub al-'Ilmiyya 1374/1954–
1955), vol. 2, 886, hadith no. 1218.

3.   Abraham, Sarah, and Isaac are buried in Hebron, below the spot
where a mosque stands today. It is interesting to add that Hagar (*Hajar* in
Arabic) and Ishmael (*Isma'il*) are buried in Mecca at one side of the Ka'ba in
a spot known as *Hijr Isma'il* (The Lap of Ishmael). "Abraham" in Arabic is
Ibrahim.

4. Martin Lings, *Muhammad: His Life Based on the Earliest Sources* (Cambridge: The Islamic Texts Society, 1991), 130–131.

5. Ibid., 137. A short time later, another verse of the Qur'an was revealed (Qur'an 2:144), which changed the direction of prayer toward the "Inviolable Mosque" (*al-Masjid al-Haram*) in Mecca.

2

PRAYER AT THE KAʿBA

—————————————— • ——————————————

Daniel Abdal-Hayy Moore

Oh Lord, the orange cat lying asleep on the
   shoe rack outside the Kaʿba
     looked tranquil, lean from
living wild in Mecca, but still
     cat-like and sweet-faced—
surely some of this peacefulness
     could come to me?

Oh Lord, You raise up giant roof-beams in the
   world and
     hurl great foundations
       as deep as the seas—
I am only your creation of
       flesh and bone,
but surely some of those
    depths and heights
      could be mine?

Oh Allah, I sit here facing Your House on
   earth, beseeching Your Grace,
     seeking Your Face,
       my own not good enough in
         this life,
my own face a combination of
   lusty panther and
     awkward ostrich
    in this life,
    yet I'm grateful for its
      miraculous properties in
       facing the world,

especially the eyes—close them
   and light spreads,
      open them and
         miracles appear—
especially Your stark square of black cloth rising
endlessly up into the night in front of me now
   but Your Face, Lord,
      could I catch a
      glimpse of it at least?

A white owl flies in the night somewhere,
its impassive face and saucer eyes
fleeing through the air.

Is this my face, Lord, or
Your Face

searching everywhere?

NOTE

This poem first appeared in Daniel Abdal-Hayy Moore, *Mecca/Medina Time-Warp*. Reprinted from a Zilzal Press chapbook, by permission from the author.

3

THE IMPORTANCE AND MEANING OF PRAYER IN ISLAM

⎯⎯⎯⎯⎯⎯⎯⎯⎯ • ⎯⎯⎯⎯⎯⎯⎯⎯⎯

Shaykh Muhammad Hisham Kabbani

Prayer is one of the central elements of Islamic practice and worship. Indeed, it is the second of the Five Pillars of Islam and, along with the testimony of faith, the pilgrimage to Mecca, fasting the month of Ramadan, and paying the poor tax, forms the essential framework of religious life for Muslims. More than that, the observance of the ritual prayer forms the framework of each Muslim's day, from the predawn morning prayer to the night prayer that precedes sleep.

Prayer, in the ritual sense, is an obligation of the faith, to be performed five times a day by adult Muslims. According to Islamic law, prayers have a variety of obligations and conditions of observance. However, beyond the level of practice, there are spiritual conditions and aspects of prayer which represent its essence.

WHAT IS PRAYER IN ISLAM?

In the Holy Qur'an, God says:

I created the jinn and humankind only that they might worship Me.

(Qur'an 51:56)

Thus, prayer first and foremost is the response to this Divine directive to worship the Creator. Prayer represents the individual's affirmation of servant-hood before the Lord of Creation and submission to His Omnipotent Will. It also represents a willing acknowledgment of our weakness and neediness by seeking Divine Grace, Mercy, Abundance, and Forgiveness. Prayer, then, is a willful, directed action by the believer, seeking direct, unmediated communication with God, for Muslims believe that every human being is of interest

to the Divine. It also represents a concrete manifestation of the Islamic conception of freewill, in that the decision to pray is one that must be made by
each individual. In this way, prayer is a uniquely "human" form of worship,
for all other creatures submit without question to God's Will and are engaged
in His praise, glorification, and remembrance, as the Holy Qur'an asserts:

> and there is not a thing but hymneth His praise; but ye understand not their
> praise.

> (Qur'an 17:44)

Prayer, by its very nature, is a form of request or entreaty, and thus requires
the full conscious participation of the one praying, with will, intellect, body,
and soul. The one engaged in prayer is in direct connection with the
Creator Who hears everything the supplicant says and responds—though
not necessarily in the affirmative—to each request. This is the concrete
manifestation of God's role as The Hearer, The Aware, and The Responsive,
which represent 3 of the 99 Holy Names and Attributes of God that form the
basis of the Islamic conception of the Divine.[1]

In Islam, there are two forms of prayer. One has ritual, formal requirements and manners, which are essential to its correct observance. This is
called *Salat*. The other form is supplicatory prayer, and in its more general
sense, represents an open-ended conversation with God, which may occur
at any time or place, with few restrictions or requirements. It is called *du'a*.

Supplicatory Prayer

The term *du'a* is derived from the Arabic verb meaning "to supplicate"
or "to call upon." Other similar terms for such prayer are *munaja, nida,*
and *al-daru'a.*

Munaja means "a secret conversation with God," usually with the
intention of seeking delivery and relief. Referring to this form of prayer,
God says in the Holy Qur'an:

> Say: Who delivereth you from the darkness of the land and the sea? Ye call upon
> Him humbly and in secret, (saying): If we are delivered from this (fear) we truly
> will be of the thankful.

> (Qur'an 6:63)

Nida means "to call upon God while withdrawn from people." The Holy
Qur'an relates the story of the Prophet Zachariah who, having no son,
beseeched God in his old age to give him a successor to inherit his prophetic
knowledge and duties:

A mention of the mercy of thy Lord unto His servant Zachariah. When he cried
unto his Lord a cry in secret, Saying: My Lord!...give me from Thy Presence
a successor who shall inherit of me and inherit (also) of the house of Jacob...
(It was said unto him): O Zachariah! Lo! We bring thee tidings of a son
whose name is John; We have given the same name to none before (him).

(Qur'an 19:2–7)

Al-daru'a means "a loud entreaty to God for safety," as mentioned in the
Holy Qur'an:

Before thee We sent (apostles) to many nations, and We afflicted the nations
with suffering and adversity, that they might submissively entreat (Him)!

(Qur'an 6:42)

Ritual Prayer

The Linguistic Root of Prayer: Salat

Ritual prayer in Islam is called *Salat*, a word whose full meaning is best
understood by examining its linguistic roots. One of the origins of *Salat* is
the root word *silat*, which means "connection" or "contact." One of Islam's
most renowned philosophers, Ibn Rushd, said:

It derives from the word "connection" (*silat*) in that it connects the servant with
his Creator, meaning that the prayer brings him near His Mercy and connects
him to His Generosity and His Heavenly Paradise.[2]

This word is also used in the context of close relations (*silat al-rahim*)
whose connections with an individual are due to blood ties and are therefore
imperishable in the eyes of the Divine. In this sense, prayer is seen as the
unseverable bond between the individual and his or her Lord.

Commenting on this, another renowned Qur'anic exegete, Qurtubi said:

The word *Salat* derives from the word *silat*, one of the names of fire as when it is
said, "The wood is burned by fire."[3]

Qurtubi attributed six different meanings to the word *Salat* in his
commentary on the Holy Qur'an:

Prayer is the invocation of God; it is mercy, as when one says, "O God,
bestow prayers on Muhammad"; it is worship, as when God says, "And
their worship at the (holy) House" (Qur'an 8:35); it is a supererogatory
prayer, as when God says, "And enjoin upon thy people worship"
(Qur'an 20:132); and it is God's praise, as when He says, "And had he

not been one of those who glorify (God)…" (Qur'an 37:143); Prayer is also recitation.[4]

RITUAL PRAYER IN DIVINE LAW (*SHARI'A*)

Ritual prayer is bound by detailed obligations and structure. It encompasses both obligatory (*fard*) prayers, which are observed five times daily at specified intervals, and voluntary prayers, which are performed by the worshipper before or after the obligatory prayers as well as at other times.

The Obligatory Nature of Ritual Prayer

The Prophet Muhammad, upon whom be peace and blessings,[5] called prayer "the pillar of religion." No fundamental element of Islam is stressed as much as prayer in the Holy Qur'an. Indeed, God mentions it in over 700 verses of the holy text. Among those that define its role in the religion of Islam are:

Worship at fixed hours hath been enjoined on the believers.

(Qur'an 4:103)

Be guardians of your prayers, and of the midmost prayer.

(Qur'an 2:238)

Enjoin prayer on thy people, and be constant therein. We ask thee not to provide sustenance: We provide it for thee. But the (fruit of) the Hereafter is for righteousness.

(Qur'an 20:132)

Recite that which has been revealed to thee of the Book, and observe Prayer. Surely, Prayer restrains one from indecency and manifest evil, and remembrance of God indeed is the greatest virtue. And God knows what you do.

(Qur'an 29:46)

(They will be) in Gardens (of Delight): they will question each other, and (ask) of the sinners: "What led you into Hell Fire?" They will say: "We were not of those who prayed.

(Qur'an 74:40–43)

The Messenger of God made ritual prayer the second of the Five Pillars of Islam:

Islam is built on five: testifying that there is no god except God and that Muhammad is the Messenger of God, establishing ritual prayer, paying the poor-due, pilgrimage and fasting Ramadan.[6]

Thus, the ritual prayer is an obligation from God on every sane, adult Muslim. The Prophet said:

The first thing about which a person will be questioned on the Day of Judgment is prayer. If it is found to be sound all his other actions will be sound as well. If his prayer is not sound all his remaining actions would be spoiled.[7]

The Prophet also said:

Giving up prayer is tantamount to disbelief and associating partners with God.[8]

He also said:

The one who misses one of the ritual prayers, is as if he has lost all his family and property.[9]

And he said:

Ritual prayer is the best means of struggle in the way of God (*Jihad*).

It is reported that the Prophet's last words were:

Prayer! Prayer! And fear God regarding those whom you are in charge of.[10]

Abu Bakr ibn al-Jaza'iri states:

Among the wisdoms in the implementation of prayer is that it purifies and welcomes the worshipper to converse with God and His Messenger, and, while he or she remains in the material world, brings him or her into proximity with the Divine in the next life and wards off indecency and manifest evil.[11]

God's Messenger Muhammad said:

The simile of the five prayers is like a flowing river of sweet water in front of the door of one of you, in which he plunges five times a day. What dirt will remain on him? They said, "None." He said, "Surely the five prayers eliminate sins just as water eliminates dirt."[12]

God's Messenger also said:

> Five (daily) prayers and from one Friday prayer to the (next) Friday prayer, and from Ramadan to Ramadan, are expiations for the (sins) committed in between (their intervals) provided one shuns the major sins.[13]

One of the primary aims of prayer is to prevent iniquity and vice. The Prophet of God said:

> The one whose prayer does not prevent him from iniquity and vice, gains nothing from God except remoteness.[14]

While the five prayers are an obligation, Muslims are also enjoined to perform other prayers in accordance with the practices of the Prophet Muhammad. These include

- *Witr* (the final prayer to end the day)
- The two festival (*'Id*) prayers
- The Eclipse Prayer (*Salat al-Kushuf*)
- The Prayer for Rain (*Salat al-Istisqa*)

All the above are given in established traditions of the Prophet. Other than these are what are classified as voluntary worship.[15]

In addition, there are a number of supererogatory prayers (*sunan*), which were part of the normative practice of the Prophet Muhammad, and which remain part of the everyday worship of many traditional Muslims.

History of Ritual Prayer

After the Prophet Muhammad was commissioned with prophethood in his 40th year, the first order he was given by God was to pray. It is related that the Archangel Gabriel came to him, and a spring of water gushed out from the rocks in front of them. Gabriel then showed the Prophet how to perform the ablution that is a prerequisite of the ritual prayer in Islam. Gabriel then showed the Prophet how to offer the ritual prayer to God. The Prophet then went home and showed his wife Khadija what the Archangel Gabriel had taught him.

After that, the Messenger of God began to pray two cycles (*raka'at*) of ritual prayer twice a day—once in the morning and once in the evening. From that time forward, the Prophet never went through a day without praying. In the ninth year of the Prophet's mission, he was taken by the Archangel Gabriel on a miraculous journey by night to Jerusalem and, from there, ascended to the heavens and the Divine Presence. During this tremendous journey, God commanded the Prophet and his followers to observe the ritual prayer 50 times a day. Returning from the Divine Presence, the Prophet Muhammad met the Prophet Moses who said, "Seek a reduction, for your people cannot bear it." The Prophet did so and it was granted. After many such dialogues, the command was reduced to observe five prayers, which would be the equivalent of the original command to observe 50. For this reason, Muslims feel a great debt to the Prophet Moses for this intercession on their behalf.

Requirements of Ritual Prayer

In Divine Law (*Shari'a*), there are a number of requirements for valid ritual prayer:

- Purification
- Time
- Direction
- Covering
- Fundaments of prayer

In addition to these essentials, there are a number of normative practices of the Prophet, which are strongly recommended as part of the ritual prayer, known as *sunna:*

- Congregation/Imamate
- Humility before the Divine (*khushu'*)
- Place
- Attire

Prayer Is According to the Prophetic Pattern

The practice of the Prophet is essential to understand the Holy Qur'an. God said:

Establish prayers (*Salat*) and pay the poor-due (*Zakat*).

(Qur'an 2:43)

From this, it is clear that both prayer and the poor-due are obligations. However, to find the necessary details to complete the prayer, that is, the manner and timing of the prayer and upon whom it is obligatory, and so on, we must turn to the practice of Prophet Muhammad. Islamic doctrine states that for every single event in his lifetime God revealed to the Prophet's heart what to say and what to do. The Qur'an and the Prophetic Narrations (*ahadith*) both derive from revelation and are thus inseparable sources for understanding and implementing Islam's divine guidance.[16]

The Prophet said, "Pray as you see me pray."[17] What is meant here is to follow the method of observing prayer, both in its form and in its inward composure and states.

The Prophet used to practice the ritual prayer constantly, outside the obligatory times. In doing so he was observing God's recommendation:

> Nay, seek (God's) help with patient perseverance and prayer: It is indeed hard, except to those who bring a lowly spirit.

> (Qur'an 2:45)

According to the scholars of Divine Law, recommended acts are divided into three categories: those acts whose demand is confirmed, known as the "confirmed normative practice of the Prophet" (*sunan al-mu'akkada*). According to Ahmad ibn Naqib al-Masri, "Someone who neglects such an act...deserves censure and blame."[18] Second are those acts that are rewardable in Divine Law, but the one who neglects them deserves no blame. These are called the extra *sunan* (*sunna nafila*). The third category is the superlatively recommended, "meaning those acts considered part of an individual's perfections."[19] These are called the desirable acts (*mustahab*) or decorum (*adab*).

Purification

A precondition of ritual prayer in Islam is that the worshipper be in a ritually pure state and perform his or her prayer in a ritually pure location.

There are two levels of ritual impurity, each with its own remedy:

(1) *Major impurity:* This occurs as a result of menstruation, childbirth, and sexual intercourse or emission. Its remedy is ritual bathing, as prescribed in the Holy Qur'an:

> O ye who believe! Approach not prayers with a mind befogged, until ye can understand all that ye say,- nor in a state of ceremonial impurity (Except when travelling on the road), until after washing your whole body.

> (Qur'an 4:43)

(2) *Minor impurity:* This occurs due to answering the call of nature, bleeding, vomiting, or sleeping. Its remedy is ritual ablution. This, too, is mentioned in the Holy Qur'an:

> O you who believe! When you get ready for ritual prayer [salat], wash your faces, and your hands up to the elbows, and lightly rub your heads and (wash) your feet up to the ankles.
>
> (Qur'an 5:6)

The Holy Prophet said:

> Ablution is the key to prayer as prayer is the key to Paradise.[20]

The various schools of Islamic jurisprudence differ slightly in the precise details of ritual ablution and bathing. Emphasized in all, however, is the need to use pure water, free from all contamination, for pure water contains the secret of life and of revivifying what is dead. God says in the Holy Qur'an:

> We made from water every living thing.
>
> (Qur'an 21:30)

And:

> In the rain which God Sends down from the skies, and the life which He gives therewith to an earth that is dead. . . .
>
> (Qur'an 2:164)

If water is unavailable, extremely scarce or its use would harm the worshipper, it is permitted to perform substitute ablution using dry earth. The Holy Qur'an says:

> And if ye are sick or on a journey, or one of you cometh from the closet, or ye have had [sexual] contact with women, and ye find not water, then go to clean, high ground and rub your faces and your hands with some of it. God would not place a burden on you, but He would purify you and would perfect His grace upon you, that ye may give thanks.
>
> (Qur'an 5:6)

Besides cleansing the body, the worshipper must also take care to ensure that his or her clothes are free from impurities that would nullify the prayer. Traditionally, shoes are removed before the prayer because of their tendency to retain impurities.

THE SPIRITUAL SIGNIFICANCE OF PURIFICATION

Ibn Rushd states that the word for ablution, *wudu'*, derives from the word
for light in Arabic, *daw*, signifying the resultant spiritual light that accrues
to the one who performs it.[21]
The Messenger of God said:

> On the Day of Resurrection, my Community will be called "those with the
> radiant appendages" because of the traces of ablution. Therefore, whoever can
> increase the area of his radiance should do so.[22]

Abu Hurayra related:

> I heard my intimate friend (the Messenger of God) saying, "The radiance of the
> believer reaches the areas that the water of ablution reaches."[23]

Ablution signifies spiritual purity, which the Prophet was granted when
the angels washed his heart, both in his youth and again, later, when
angels washed it with the water of the holy well of Zam Zam on the Night
of Ascension.

To gain the full benefit of ablution, the worshipper must perform it with
the realization of its inner aspects, washing away the burdens and darkness
of worldly life that distract him or her from Divine service. By removing both
the physical and the mental filth that accumulate through the day, one ignites
and seals the latent spiritual energy of one's being by means of the special
attributes of water. The extremities washed during ablution are the primary
means of interacting with the worldly life, and these must be cleansed of the
taint left by that contact.

Ablution begins with washing the hands, signifying that the first level of
spiritual energy is in the hands. Human hands contain a Divine secret, for
they are a reflection of the Divine Attribute of Power, which God has
bestowed in a limited degree on humankind. They provide the means for
the outward manifestations of humankind's will to change its circumstances.
Thus, hands are a source of change, control, and healing. No other creature
has been endowed with so great an ability to manipulate its surroundings,
and the hands are the main physical instrument of that ability.

The hand can act as a receiver of positive energy. The circle of the body, so
clearly illustrated by Leonardo da Vinci's famous drawing *Ecce Homo*, is
reflected on a smaller scale in the circle of the hand. Energy can be drawn in
through the hands and channeled throughout the body. When one rubs the
hands together during ablution, one activates a spiritual code that God has
given us within our hands: the power of the 99 Beautiful Names and Attributes that God has inscribed on every person's palms.[24] The friction between
the two hands creates energy in the form of heat and rubbing them together
under water locks in that energy, preventing it from escaping. The water

keeps the energy that is generated by rubbing the hands together within the body, where it can be released later.

During the process of ablution the hands are used to convey the water to each other limb and organ, thereby functioning as a dispenser of that divine energy. As the limbs and organs are washed in ablution, each undergoes similar spiritual alterations based on the water, the hands and their energy, and the various movements and recitations that are part of the ablution. For the believer to benefit from the water, it must be pure and clean, otherwise its secret blessings do not reach the body.

On an esoteric level, ablution becomes a metaphor for purifying the heart. Water is always clean in its essence, so the degree of spiritual reception is dependent on keeping the water free from external impurities. If we expand the spiritual metaphor, the water symbolizes the remembrance of God. That remembrance is pure, in and of itself, but can be tainted by the darkness of negativity which derives from wrong intent, wrong will, and wrong action.

The most powerful energy we carry as human beings is our spiritual energy. Second to that is the physical energy of creativity, which manifests during the act of procreation. In the course of physically expressing this creative energy God has placed within us, we enter into a state similar to the spiritual state of annihilation, but not related to the Divine Presence; on the contrary, it is related to the lower self. When this occurs, it is essential to wash the body completely, with the intention to restore the spiritual state of purity lost during the act.

Purification of the heart blocks the influence of Satan on the believer. For this reason, the Prophet is reported to have said:

Ablution is the weapon of the believer.[25]

Ablution protects the believer from four enemies of the soul: the lower self or ego (*nafs*), worldly desire (*hubb al-dunya*), lust (*hawa*), and Satan. However, only through the remembrance of God can the believer maintain this defense throughout the day. When the heart begins to beat with God's Holy Name, "Allah," Satan is prevented from entering, and the gossips and insinuations of the lower self are gradually reduced until they are no more than a whisper.

At an even higher level of understanding, ablution signifies the state of dissolving the self in the Divine Presence. According to the Sufi master Jili:

...the requirement of using water signifies that purity is not achieved except by the emergence [in the worshipper] of the manifestations of the Divine Attributes, which is the water of life, for water is the secret of life. Dry ablution (*tayammum*) as a substitute [for ablution with water] is the station of purity by necessity, and is thus a symbol of purifying one's self by opposing one's lower-self, combating the tyrannical selfish ego and spiritual exercises. However, even after someone is purified, there is still a chance for [the ego] to exist.[26]

This is what the Prophet alluded to when he supplicated, "O my Lord give my self its piety and its purity, for You are the best one to purify it."[27] His saying "Give my self its piety," is an indication of [the need for] combating the lower-self by means of spiritual exercises. His saying "…and its purity, for You are the best one to purify it," is an indication of the heart's attraction to the Divine, for this [attraction] is far more effective than purifying by means of action and opposing the lower-self.[28]

Prayer Times

The five times of obligatory ritual prayer are

- *Fajr:* From dawn to sunrise;
- *Zuhr:* From noon until mid-afternoon;
- *Asr:* From mid-afternoon to sunset;
- *Maghrib:* From sunset to early evening;
- *Isha':* From early evening to the middle of the night.

These times coincide with the significant temporal changes that are part of each day's cycle on earth as this planet moves through its various stations in relation to the Sun. The Sun, which is the focal point of the solar system, thus becomes a guiding light for the worshiper, indicating the beginning and ending of each prayer's interval. In this way, Muslims are reminded of the story of Abraham, as mentioned in the Holy Qur'an.

In his yearning and seeking for God, Abraham holds a metaphorical debate within himself. His first inclination is to bow before a bright star that shines forth at night, taking it as his Lord. However, when that star sets, his intellect rejects it, seeking something greater as Lord. Seeing the Moon, he determines it to be his Lord until it too sets and he seeks something greater still. Seeing the Sun rise, he supposes it must be his Lord, but despite its blazing glory, it too sets. Finally, Abraham concludes that none of these heavenly bodies—and by inference, no created thing—could be his Lord, and thus sets himself firmly on worship of the Unseen Lord:

> …when [the sun] set he exclaimed: O my people! Lo! I am free from all that ye associate (with Him). Lo! I have turned my face toward Him Who created the heavens and the earth, as one by nature upright, and I am not of the idolaters.
>
> (Qur'an 6:75–79)

Muslims consider the day to begin at sunset, with the evening (*Maghrib*) prayer. This holds tremendous significance on an esoteric, or spiritual, level. The masters of the science of Islamic spirituality, Sufism, see the cycles of prayer as symbolic of the cycles of creation itself. The sunset prayer represents the station of leaving existence. The night prayer, which follows it, represents the station of darkness and death, annihilation, and nonexistence.

In some Islamic traditions, funeral prayers for those who have passed away during the preceding day are read immediately after the sunset prayer, indicating this time's correlation with death and the afterlife.

The Holy Qur'an says:

> It is God that takes the souls (of men) at death; and those that die not (He takes) during their sleep: Those on whom He has passed the decree of death, He keeps back (from returning to life), but the rest He sends (to their bodies) for a term appointed.

> (Qur'an 39:42)

Awakening to pray just before dawn represents the return to life, the descent through the darkness of the womb to emerge into the light. Metaphorically, the worshipper moves from the station of nonexistence and annihilation back to the station of existence and rebirth. A new day has come, and with it the worshipper is reborn.

The apex of existence is marked by the noon prayer, which begins just as the Sun reaches the peak of brightness. At the zenith, two kingdoms are present and the prayer joins them: the kingdom of heaven and the kingdom of earth.

The afternoon prayer takes place at a time that signifies the approach of the end, autumn, and the last era of worldly life. According to Islamic tradition, the Prophet Muhammad and the community of believers he raised appear at the end of humanity's spiritual history, just prior to the Day of Judgment. The coming of the afternoon prayer thus represents the approach of Judgment Day and the Divine Reckoning that it brings. With the setting of the sun, life comes to an end. The worshipper returns to God, taking with him an account of his deeds. With the darkness comes annihilation in the oceans of God's Endless Mercy. It is for this reason that Islam places a strong emphasis on the afternoon prayer.

Thus, each day is a full life cycle, from creation out of nonexistence to Judgment Day and annihilation. Each day has its birth, life, and death. In similar fashion the prayer times reflect the five major stages of life: infancy, childhood, youth, maturity, and old age.

Direction

The worshipper faces the Ka'ba, the holy shrine of Islam, as determined to the best of his or her ability by simple means. This directional focus is called the *qibla*.

The Ka'ba is the House of God, located in the holy city of Mecca in Arabia. It is the goal of the pilgrimage, which is the fifth pillar of Islam. In Islamic teachings, the Ka'ba is said to mark the location where the Divine House in the Seventh Heaven, beyond which stands the Supreme Throne, which angels constantly circle in praise and worship of God, descended to Earth after the first man and woman, Adam and Eve, were cast out of Paradise for their mistake. In the time of Noah's flood, this heavenly sanctuary was taken up to heaven again. Millennia later, Abraham and Ishmael built the Ka'ba in the same location, where it stands today, the first house of worship dedicated to God. By facing this location in prayer, each Muslim aims and hopes to reach that holy location at some point in his or her life.

Initially, in the early days of Prophet Muhammad's mission, the believers faced Jerusalem when they prayed, out of respect for the Temple there. This direction represented respect for the previous Divine dispensations brought by Moses and Jesus and the Israelite prophets. Later, Divine legislation altered the direction of prayer to face the Holy House in Mecca:

> We see thee (O Muhammad) turning of thy face for guidance to the heavens: now shall We turn thee to a prayer-direction that shall please thee. Turn then thy face in the direction of the Sacred Mosque [Ka'ba]: Wherever ye are, turn your faces in that direction.

> (Qur'an 2:144)

Thus, wherever Muslims live, their prayers have a common focus: the Ka'ba.

Because of the presence of this blessed shrine, the area surrounding the Ka'ba is holy. These environs are called the *Haram,* literally "prohibited," meaning a place where sins are prohibited. The Ka'ba itself is located within the "Prohibited Mosque," *al-Masjid al-Haram.*[29] The name Prohibited Mosque was given because no one may act on bad desires there. While it is called a mosque, God made it more than that. In reality, it is a place where sins are utterly rejected, not only in their outward forms but also in their inner realities. There, even negative thoughts and intentions are considered blameworthy. Only pure, positive desires, and good thoughts are accepted. Indeed, within the confines of that holy sanctuary, no hunting is allowed; even the cutting of trees and vegetation is proscribed.

God said in the Holy Qur'an:

> Glory to (God) Who did take His servant for a Journey by night from the Sacred Mosque to the farthest Mosque, whose precincts We did bless, in order that We might show him some of Our Signs: for He is the One Who Heareth and Seeth (all things).

> (Qur'an 17:1)

This verse describes the important journey that the Prophet Muhammad made between the Prohibited Mosque in Mecca and the Temple in Jerusalem (referred to as the "Farthest Mosque," *al-Masjid al-Aqsa*[30]), a journey that in one moment bridged three divinely revealed religions.

SPIRITUAL SIGNIFICANCE OF THE KA'BA

One of the distinctive characteristics of Islamic ritual prayer is that the worshipper is obliged to keep his vision, both external and internal, concentrated upon the *qibla*. The focus of every worshipper is, and must be, a holy place. People whose understanding is purely external believe facing the Ka'ba is of intrinsic value.

Those with a mystic understanding know that the Ka'ba represents the spiritual pole of this world, around which all creation turns. Looking at photographs of the Ka'ba taken from above, we see the worshippers moving around it in perfectly arranged concentric circles. This assembly gathers in imitation of the heavenly kingdom, for all these circles have one center regardless of their distance from it. At the spiritual level, that center is the Divine Presence. While each worshipper faces the Ka'ba's walls of stone and mortar, these are not the focus. If we remove the four walls, what do we find? Each person facing someone else. In this is a deep and subtle secret that we leave for the reader to ponder.

When the spiritual seeker realizes his or her station on the circle of the People of the *Qibla*, he enters what is known as the Circle of Unconditional Lovers (*da'irat al-muhibbin*). That is the circle of Muslims at the first level in the way of God: the level of love. Such love is not related to any desire, but is a purely Platonic, spiritual love between the believer and his or her Lord. God is the center of the circle, and the believers are each a point on its circumference. Each has his or her own connection to the center. That means each has his or her own direction, *qibla*, toward the Divine Presence. As this connection becomes apparent to the believer, that radius becomes like a tunnel into which the seeker begins to step from the circumference of the circle. Upon making his first steps into that tunnel, he begins to discover countless negative characteristics within himself. As he discovers one characteristic after another, he begins to eliminate them, progressing down the tunnel to become a "seeker in the circle of lovers on the spiritual journey," progressing ever nearer to the *qibla* at the center. In the metaphysics of Ibn 'Arabi, the renowned mystic scholar speaks of a spiritual hierarchy in which the emanations from the Divine are received by a single human receptor who is the leader of all these circles of lovers and through him spreads to the rest of humanity, each according to his or her degree or station. This individual represents the Prophet in his or her time as the perfect servant of God. Thus, under one spiritual leader, all are moving constantly closer to the Divine Presence.

In the Sufi understanding, which delves deeply into the mystic knowledge and symbolism of Islam's outward forms, it is said that the Prohibited

Mosque represents the heart of the believer. Thus, the inner direction of prayer is toward the sanctified heart. What is the sanctified heart? At the first level of spirituality, the sanctified heart is the heart that is purified of all wrong thoughts, negativity, and dark intent. This level is called the Level of the Secret (*sirr*). Once that secret is opened within the sanctified heart, the seeker moves to the heart of the heart, known as Secret of the Secret (*sirr al-sirr*). This is the level of purification from any attachment to worldly desires. Beyond these levels of the heart are "the Hidden" (*khafa*) and "the Innermost" (*akhfa*) levels, representing further stations of purity, in which the heart becomes ever more removed from attachments, turning away from all that is worldly to focus instead on the spiritual realm of the Hereafter. At the highest level, the heart turns away from even that and begins to focus solely on the Divine Presence.

These are levels of achievement. On the spiritual dimension, the believer's focus is to reach a perfected level of character, to learn from it and to be enlightened from it. In order to progress beyond our state of ignorance we must strive to learn and educate ourselves. This can only be accomplished by keeping the company of enlightened individuals who have successfully traversed the Path of God, to God, and who are granted the ability to guide others. God says:

> O ye who believe! Fear God and be with those who are true (in word and deed).

> (Qur'an 9:119)

God is aware of every heart. The Holy Qur'an states:

> Those who struggle for Us, We will guide them in the right ways, the ways that are suitable to them.

> (Qur'an 29:69)

The polished heart of the sincere and true believer (*sadiq*) is a receptacle for God's Heavenly Lights and Divine Blessings. Such a person is like the sun. When the sun rises, the whole world shines from that source of energy and light, the light of mystical gnosis that makes all things visible. For that reason, the Prophet said, "The heart of the [true] believer is the House of the Lord."

Covering

The Islamic schools of jurisprudence concur that it is essential (*wajib*) for both men and women to cover those parts of their bodies during prayer which should ordinarily be kept covered before strangers. For men, this includes what is between the navel and the knee. For women, it is the entire body, except the face and hands.

As we have said, the purity of what covers the body is essential for the prayer to be acceptable. In one of the first revelations to the Prophet Muhammad, God says:

> And thy Lord do thou magnify! And thy garments keep free from stain! And all abomination shun!
>
> (Qur'an 74:3–5)

The body is not the only thing that must be covered in prayer. During *Salat,* the worshipper is commanded to look only at the location where he or she will prostrate, not to the left or right. In this way, one covers one's gaze and directs oneself to the Vision of God, for the Prophet said:

> The perfection of religion (*al-Ihsan*) is to worship God as if you are seeing Him and if you do not see Him, know that He sees you.[31]

Thus, the gaze of the believer must be veiled at the time of worship from everything other than God. This derives from a spiritual understanding of the Verse of the Veil in the Holy Qur'an, in which God says:

> Say to the believing men that they should lower their gaze and guard their modesty: that will make for greater purity for them: And God is well acquainted with all that they do. And say to the believing women that they should lower their gaze and guard their modesty; that they should not display their beauty and ornaments except what (must ordinarily) appear thereof; that they should draw their veils over their bosoms and not display their beauty....
>
> (Qur'an 24:30–31)

The emphasis in these verses is on lowering the gaze, meaning to guard the eyes from looking at what is forbidden or impure. In the outer sense, this means to refrain from looking with lustful desire at other than one's spouse, for the Prophet said, "The two eyes are two adulterers."[32]

In this regard, a renowned contemporary Sufi saint, and my teacher and guide on the spiritual path, Shaykh Muhammad Nazim Adil al-Haqqani, relates the story of a judge (*qadi*), called by a woman to annul her husband's marriage to a second wife. The judge asked the plaintiff, whose face was hidden by a face veil (*burqa*), "Why are you asking me to prevent something permitted in Islamic Divine Law?" The first wife replied, "Your honor, were I to remove my face-veil you would wonder how someone married to so stunning a beauty could seek another woman's companionship!" Upon hearing this the judge swooned. When he came to, his associates asked him what had happened. He replied, "On hearing this woman's reply, I had an epiphany. How is it that our hearts turn to all manner of worldly interests, when God Himself is asking us to be with Him alone?"

The next verse says:

> they should not display their beauty and ornaments except what (must ordinarily) appear thereof; that they should draw their veils over their bosoms and not display their beauty. . . .

> (Qur'an 24:31)

calling on women to veil their beauty from other than the men in their immediate family, to protect them from men who are all too easily overpowered by desire, and to protect men from their own weaknesses.

Esoteric commentators state that "women" here symbolizes attachments to the worldly life. The spiritual meaning of this prohibition then is that, when coming before the Lord of Creation, the seeker must veil himself or herself from all distractions of the worldly life and focus on the One to Whom prayer is directed.

At an even higher level of spiritual understanding, the word "women" refers to the Divine Attributes of Beauty. Thus, the worshipper is advised to call to mind the Divine Attributes of Majesty, and not become lost in the Attributes of Beauty, which may lead the seeker to lose his or her balance in approaching the Divine Presence.

In the Holy Qur'an, God also said:

> O Children of Adam! wear your beautiful apparel at every time and place of prayer (*masjid*).

> (Qur'an 7:31)

Here, believers are called upon by God to wear their best and most attractive garments when going to pray. The call to manifest "beautiful apparel" at the "place of prayer" can be interpreted as well to be an instruction to adorn the mosques and beautify them, keeping in mind that:

> The places of worship (*masajid*) are for God (alone).

> (Qur'an 72:18)

The three major holy mosques of Islam—al-Masjid al-Haram in Mecca, the Prophet's Mosque in Medina, and al-Masjid al-Aqsa in Jerusalem—are all highly ornamented with gilding, decorative calligraphy, mosaic tiles, inlaid wood, brilliant lamps, and other decorations. All other mosques are connected to these for, as we have said, when worshippers stand to pray in any mosque, they must face the Ka'ba, God's Holy House.

> God said, "Neither My heavens contain Me nor My earth. But the heart of My Believing Servant contains Me."[33]

The heart, too, then is a mosque, and for this reason it also must be decorated. The ornamentation of the heart involves removing everything that distracts one from the worship of God and replacing these impurities with love of the Divine, as we have seen earlier. Anything that brings impurity to the heart extinguishes the light that God has placed there. This is a form of tyranny, for the Arabic word for tyranny (*zulm*) also means darkness. Thus, any darkness which veils the heart from God's Holy Light is a form of oppression. This darkness cannot be removed except through repentance and seeking the intercessory prayers of the Prophet. This is why the aforementioned verses about modesty are followed closely by:

> God is the Light of the heavens and the earth. The parable of His Light is as if there were a niche and within it a lamp: the lamp enclosed in glass: the glass as it were a brilliant star: Lit from a blessed tree, an olive, neither of the east nor of the west, whose oil is well-nigh luminous, though fire scarce touched it: Light upon Light! God doth guide whom He will to His Light: God doth set forth parables for men: and God doth know all things.

> (Qur'an 24:35)

"God is the Light" does not mean that God is light, rather The Light is His while God's Essence is unknown. The created cannot know The Creator except by means of His Beautiful Names and Attributes, His Descriptions. God's saying "He is the Light of the heavens and earth" means that whatever is found in the heavens and earth contains that light.[34] Since we are from earth, that light is within each of us, for God, being the Just, bestows on all with Divine Fairness. Shaykh Ibrahim Hakki, a renowned Ottoman scholar of the Qur'an, said:

> Without a doubt the complete potential for perfection is found within every human being, because God the Most High has placed His own Divine Secrets within the essence of man, in order to manifest from the Unseen His Beautiful Names and Attributes.[35]

Therefore, as the Prophet said, "Human beings are born of a natural disposition,"[36] meaning each human being carries that light of primordial faith and predisposition to submission before God.

Therefore in the Prophet Muhammad, being the epitome of humankind and its highest standard bearer, is found the perfect manifestation of the human embodiment of Divine Grace and the corporeal manifestation of Divine Attributes. It is due to the Prophet's utter submission, in the state of perfect servanthood, that made him the perfect receptacle for Divine Appearances. That is, the Muhammadan Reality (*al-haqiqa al-Muhammadiyya*) reflects the heart of the Divine Essence, since the Prophet's heart moves without restriction in the orbit of the 99 Divine Names and Attributes. He has been blessed by being adorned with the 99 Names inside of which is a glowing pearl which has yet to appear. Thus, many commentators assert that the "Light of the heavens and earth" referred to in the above verse is the Light of Muhammad, whom God created from His own Divine Light, and it is this light which shines in the hearts of believers, for the Light of the Prophet is the source of the light of all believers.

APPEARANCE

God says in the Holy Qur'an:

O Children of Adam! wear your beautiful apparel at every time and place of prayer. . . .
Say (O Muhammad): "Who has forbidden the adoration with clothes given by God, which He has produced for His devotees?"

(Qur'an 7:31–32)

Nafi' related:

'Umar entered upon me one day as I was praying in a single garment and he said, "Don't you have two garments in your possession?" I said, "Yes." He said, "In your opinion, if I sent you to one of the people of Medina on an errand, would you go in a single garment?" I said, "No." He said, "Then is God worthier of our self-beautification or people?"

An adjunct to proper covering is proper physical appearance. The most direct method for establishing one's identity as a traveler upon the path of self-purification is to adopt the correct outward appearance, abandoning the dress of the worldly life and putting on instead the apparel of the Hereafter. This is an outward indication of rejecting servitude to the material world (*'abd al-dunya*) and asserting one's true identity as a servant of the Divine (*'abd Allah*).

The dress most conducive to spirituality is the garb of the Prophet Muhammad, the traditional clothing worn by all the Prophets and

Messengers of God. For men, this includes wearing the turban, the cloak (*jubba*), and a ring, and using perfume and a tooth-stick (*miswak*). For women, it involves wearing loose clothing, covering the hair, arms, and legs, with white clothing being the most preferable. Such is the honored dress of the ascetics and lovers of God and His Prophet, those who reject the illusion of the material world and will settle for nothing less than the perfection and truth of reality.

Fundaments of Prayer

The first and foremost fundamental part of the ritual prayer is intention (*niyya*).

As in all Islamic worship, the worshipper intends the prayer as a fulfillment of God's order done purely for God's sake. The Prophet Muhammad established this as a paramount rule of worship when he said, "Verily all deeds are based on their intention."[37]

The prayer is initiated by the consecratory magnification of God (*takbir*), followed by multiple cycles, each of which follows the same series of postures and recitations: first standing, then bowing, brief standing, prostrating, a brief sitting, a second prostration, and in the even cycles, sitting after the second prostration. Each of these positions also involves specific recitations. While standing, the first chapter (*Surat al-Fatiha*) and other portions of the Holy Qur'an are recited, either silently or aloud, depending upon the time of prayer. In bowing, the brief standing, prostration, and the brief sitting, God is glorified and praised in short formulas. While sitting, the testimony of faith (*tashahhud*) is recited, along with greetings to and prayers for the Prophet Muhammad, the Prophet Abraham, and their families. In addition, there are a variety of supplemental invocations and recitations that are traditionally part of the practice of most worshippers. The basic essentials of ritual prayer number about 15, depending on the school of jurisprudence followed.[38]

Each obligatory prayer has a prescribed number of cycles to be observed (see the following table).

Prayer	Number of cycles
Maghrib (sunset)	3
Isha' (night)	4
Fajr (dawn)	2
Zuhr (noon)	4
Asr (afternoon)	4

The Positions of Prayer

The movements of the prayer identify the one praying with all other forms of creation, for the prayer's postures are designed to remind the worshipper of mortality and the traversal through the different stages of life. They also resemble the rising and setting of the celestial bodies, as well as the rotation of the planets upon their axes and the orbits of the moons, planets, and suns. These are signs which demonstrate the hierarchical nature of creation and its submission to Divine regulation at every level, for as the Holy Qur'an states:

> Among His Signs are the night and the day, and the sun and the moon. Adore not the sun and the moon, but adore God, Who created them, if it is Him ye wish to serve.

> (Qur'an 41:37)

God further draws our attention to their submissive nature, saying:

> Hast thou not seen that before God prostrate whosoever is in the heavens and whosoever is on the earth, and the sun, and the moon, and the stars, and the hills, and the trees, and the beasts, and many of mankind...?

> (Qur'an 22:18)

The postures of prayer, then, are symbolic of humanity's relationship to the Divine, moving as they do from standing in assertion of existence and strength, to the bowing of humility and servitude, to prostration in the face of God's overwhelming Magnificence and Power and the corresponding realization of one's utter nonexistence. From this station of utter abasement, the worshipper returns to the intermediate position, between annihilation and independence, to sit between the hands of the Prophet Muhammad, greeting the one who is the intermediary between the Divinity and His creation. The Prophet stands at the station of Perfect Servanthood and is the ultimate exemplar of the condition of servanthood to God. Unlike all other creations, the Prophet Muhammad was divested of all selfhood, dissolved in the Presence of God.

> Whithersoever ye turn, there is the presence of God. For God is all-Pervading, all-Knowing.

> (Qur'an 2:115)

THE PEAK OF PRAYER IS PROSTRATION

The Prophet said, "Nothing brings the servant of God nearer to the Divine Presence than through his secret prostration (*al-khafi*)." The Prophet also said, "Any believer who prostrates himself, will be raised one degree by God." As for what that degree consists of, know that it is not something small, for each heaven might consist of one degree.

For these reasons, many among the pious observe extra voluntary prostrations to God after completing their obligatory prayers. Whenever they encounter a difficulty, whether spiritual or worldly, they seek refuge in their Lord through prostration to Him.

One must cut down self-pride and make the inner self prostrate, for one who truly submits to his or her Lord can no longer submit to his or her self. Once that state is reached, prayer is purely for God. That is why the Prophet said, "What I fear most for my Community is hidden polytheism."[39] He feared for his community not the outward polytheism of idol worship, for he was informed by God that his community was protected from that forever,[40] but the secret polytheism, which is to do something for the sake of showing off.

A man came and asked the Prophet, "O Prophet of God, pray for me to be under your intercession on Judgment Day and grant me to be in your company in Paradise." The Prophet replied, "I will do so, but assist me in that." The man asked, "How so?" The Prophet said, "By frequent prostration [before God]."

The Prophet related that, on the Day of Judgment, as the believers emerge from their graves, angels will come to them to brush the dust from their foreheads. However, despite the best efforts of the angels, some of that dust will remain. Both the resurrected believers and their angelic helpers will be surprised that this dust cannot be removed. Then a voice will call out, "Leave that dust and do not try to remove it, for that is the dust of their prayer-niches, thus will it be known in Paradise that they are My [devout] servants."

This Prophetic Tradition indicates the spiritual value of the prostration of the believers, making as it does even the dust touched by their foreheads hallowed. The power of prayer has a similar effect on the place of prayer itself, as exemplified in the story of the Virgin Mary, as mentioned in the Holy Qur'an:

> Whenever Zachariah went into the prayer-niche where she was, he found that she had food. He said: O Mary! Whence cometh unto thee this (food)? She answered: It is from God. God giveth without stint to whom He will.

(Qur'an 3:37)

It was there, in the Virgin Mary's hallowed sanctuary, where she used to find her daily provision in the form of fruits out of season, that the Prophet Zachariah went to prostrate himself before God and beseech Him for a child, and it was there that God granted his request.

The places where a Muslim prostrates will bear witness to his or her devotion on the Day of Judgment. It is for this reason that one often sees Muslims changing the location of their prayers, praying the obligatory cycles in one spot and then moving to another area to observe the voluntary cycles (*sunan*).

Ibn 'Abbas, a cousin of the Prophet and the greatest early exegete of the Qur'an, said, "When God commanded Adam to descend to Earth, as soon as he arrived, he went into prostration, asking God's forgiveness for the sin he had made. God sent the archangel Gabriel to him after forty years had passed, and Gabriel found Adam still in prostration." He had not raised his head for 40 years in sincere and heartfelt repentance before God.

The Holy Qur'an tells us that, after God created Adam, He ordered the angels to prostrate before the first man.

When We said to the angels, "prostrate yourselves to Adam," they prostrated themselves, but not Iblis [Satan]: he refused.

(Qur'an 20:116)

Imam Qurtubi, one of the great commentators on the Holy Qur'an, writes in his exegesis that one of the four Archangels, Rafael, had the entire Qur'an written on his forehead. God had given Rafael knowledge of the Holy Qur'an and wrote all of it between his eyes, and he is the angel who inscribed the destinies of all things in the Preserved Tablets before they were created.[41] Rafael's name in Arabic, which differs from his Syriac name Israfil, is 'Abd al-Rahman, Servant of The Merciful. This theme of mercy pervades Islamic thought, for it was through God's Mercy that the Holy Qur'an was sent down to the Prophet, about whom The Merciful said:

We sent thee not but as a Mercy for all creatures.

(Qur'an 21:107)

When God ordered the angels to make prostration to Adam, Rafael was the first to obey, making prostration and placing his forehead, containing the entire Qur'an, on the earth, out of respect and honor for Adam, for he perceived the whole of Qur'an written on Adam's forehead.[42] Other commentators say the angels fell prostrate before Adam for they perceived the Light of the Prophet Muhammad shining from his form. There is in reality no discrepancy here, for God said in the Holy Qur'an:

Yasin. By the Qur'an, full of Wisdom.

(Qur'an 36:1–2)

The Prophet Muhammad said that Yasin, the 36th chapter of the Holy Qur'an as well as one of his own blessed names, is the heart of the Holy Qur'an, the very Qur'an that the Prophet was carrying in his breast. Thus, the light that shone forth from Adam was the Light of the Prophet within him, who in turn was blazing with God's Holy Word.

The Inner Meanings of the Different Positions of Prayer

Shah Waliullah al-Dihlawi said:

Know that one is sometimes transported, quick as lightning, to the Holy Precincts (of the Divine Presence), and finds oneself attached, with the greatest possible adherence, to the Threshold of God. There descend on this person the Divine transfigurations (*tajalli*) which dominate his soul. He sees and feels things which the human tongue is incapable of describing. Once this state of light passes away, he returns to his previous condition, and finds himself tormented by the loss of such an ecstasy. Thereupon he tries to rejoin that which has escaped him, and adopts the condition of this lowly world which would be nearest to a state of absorption in the knowledge of the Creator. This is a posture of respect, of devotion, and of an almost direct conversation with God, which posture is accompanied by appropriate acts and words.... Worship consists essentially of three elements: (1) humility of heart (spirit) consequent on a feeling of the Presence of the Majesty and Grandeur of God, (2) recognition of this superiority (of God) and humbleness (of man) by means of appropriate words, and (3) adoption by the organs of the body of postures of necessary reverence...

Still greater respect is displayed by laying down the face, which reflects in the highest degree one's ego and self-consciousness, so low that it touches the ground in front of the object of reverence.[43]

Jili says:

The secrets and inner-meanings of prayer are uncountable so what is mentioned here is limited for the sake of brevity. Prayer is a symbol of the uniqueness of the Divine Reality (*al-Haqq*), and the [position of] standing in it is a symbol of the establishment of the uniqueness of mankind in possessing something from the Divine Names and Attributes, for as the Prophet said, "Verily God created Adam in His Image."[44]

Then the standing towards the Qibla is an indication of the universal direction in the quest of the Divine Reality. The intention therein is an indication of the connection of the heart in this direction. The opening magnification of God's Greatness (*takbir*) is an indication that the Divine Proximity is larger and more expansive than what may manifest to him because nothing can limit its perspective. Even so, it is vaster still than every perspective or vision that manifests to the servant for it is without end.

The recitation of the Opening Chapter, *al-Fatiha,* is an indication of the existence of His Perfection in man because man is the opening of creation, for God initiated creation by him when He brought from nothingness the first creation.

What Jili is referring to here is the Light of Muhammad, known also as the First Mind, the Universal Man, and the Microcosm of the Macrocosm.[45] He continues:

> Then there is bowing, which is an indication of acknowledging the nonexistence of all creation under the existence of divine emanations and power. Then standing in the prayer is an indication of the station of subsistence (*al-baqa*). Therefore, one says in his prayer, "God hears the one who praises Him,"...an indication of subsistence in that he is the Vicegerent of the Divine Reality. In this way, God relates about Himself by Himself by relating on hearing its truth through the praising of His creation. The prostration is an expression of pulverization of the traits of humanness and their extermination before the unending manifestation of the sanctifying essence. The sitting between the two prostrations is an indication of obtaining the realities of the Divine Names and Attributes. This is because the sitting is firmly positioned in a place as indicated by the verse where God says: "The Merciful was established on the Throne" (Qur'an 20:5).
>
> The second prostration is the indication of the station of servanthood and it is the returning from the Divine Reality to creation. The salutations [upon the Prophet] are an indication of the attainability of human perfection, for they are an expression of praising God, His Messenger and His righteous servants. This is the station of perfection, for the saint is not complete except by his attainment of the Divine realities, by his accord with the Messenger and accord with all of the servants of God.

The two sections of the testimony of faith are *La ilaha illa'llah*, "there is no diety except the one God," and *Muhammadun rasulullah*, "and Muhammad is the Messenger of God." Scholars say that *La ilaha illa'llah* represents the Creator and *Muhammadun rasulullah* symbolizes the entirety of creation. The prayer is considered a dual communication: one is between the worshipper and God, the second is between the worshipper and God's perfect servant, the Prophet Muhammad, the archetype of all the Prophets and Messengers. Thus, one part of the prayer is a communication with the Divine, by means of God's Holy Words revealed in the Qur'an and through bowing and prostration, reciting God's glorification, magnification, and praise. The other part is the salutation on the Prophet, in which the worshipper addresses the Prophet personally and directly, as leader of the worshippers and the believers, followed by invoking the Lord's blessings on him and on his family.

These realities in fact reflect the doctrine of the Prophet's having attained the zenith of servanthood (*'ubudiyya*) to God, and thus the entirety of prayer in itself is built around his person. For the Words of God recited are the words revealed to the Prophet and the remainder of the prayer acknowledges his leadership and spiritual primacy in both this life and the next. Thus, scholars assert that even the positions of the prayer are an indication of the Muhammadan Station, for the physical positions reflect the shapes of the letters of the Prophet's heavenly name, Ahmad, where the first letter *Alif* is represented by the standing position, *Ha* by the bowing stance, *Mim* in the prostration, and *Dal* in sitting for salutation.

Prayer in Daily Life

One may pray individually or communally, in the home, outside, at the mosque, or in virtually any clean place. However, observing the prayers at the mosque and in congregation is strongly encouraged. In addition to the regular daily prayers, there is a special Friday noon prayer, called *Jumu'a.* It, too, is obligatory, and must be performed in a mosque, in congregation. It is accompanied by a sermon (*khutba*) and replaces the normal noon prayer.

Since ritual prayers are performed throughout the waking cycle of the day, they influence the rhythm of the entire day in many Muslim nations. Although it is preferable to worship together in a mosque, a Muslim may pray almost anywhere, such as in fields, offices, factories, and universities. Visitors to the Muslim world, where the call to prayer, the *adhan,* is made publicly from every mosque at the onset of each prayer time, are often struck by the centrality of prayer in daily life.

Traditionally, the call to prayer is the first thing a newborn baby hears after birth, as the father or a person of piety recites the prayer call in the infant's right ear and the call to start the prayer (*iqama*) in the left.

Mosques

God says in the Holy Qur'an:

Say: My Lord hath commanded justice; and that ye set your whole selves (to Him) at every time and mosque, and call upon Him, making your devotion sincere as in His sight: such as He created you in the beginning, so shall ye return.

(Qur'an 7:29)

When performed in congregation, prayer provides a strong sense of community, equality, and brotherhood. All Muslims are welcome in every mosque, regardless of their race, class, or nationality. There is no minimum number of congregants required to hold communal prayers. Traditionally, mosques were the centers of their communities, where believers gathered five times daily or, at a minimum, once a week. There, the poor found food and assistance; the homeless, shelter; the student of religion, learning. Because of the centrality of prayer in Muslim religious life, mosques are often the dominant structures in Muslim villages, towns, and cities. Traditionally, great attention was paid to making these houses of worship more than just halls for prayer. Governments, individuals, and communities invested huge sums to make their mosque the visual focus of its neighborhood. In particular, the great mosques, in which the Friday obligatory congregational prayer was held, often became magnificent examples of architecture and art.

The faithful take off their shoes before entering the house of worship out of respect for its sanctity and in keeping with the commandment to the Prophet Moses, when he entered the hallowed ground around the burning bush:

> When he came to the Fire, a voice uttered: O Moses! I am thy Lord, therefore put off thy shoes, for thou art in the sacred valley of Tuwa.

> (Qur'an 20:11–12)

THE SINCERE PRAYER

Ibn 'Ata Allah, a renowned Egyptian Sufi scholar of the fourteenth century CE, wrote:[46]

> The ritual prayer is the focal point of heavenly discourse, the source of purity by which the avenues of secrets expand and the gleams of lights radiate. So, if you want to know yourself, it is all by the prayer how you would weigh it. If it causes you to desist from worldly influence, then you know you are one who is given happiness. Other than that, you should be aware of what your feet have dragged along to your prayer, and then you will know that you have not obtained the secrets of prayer. Have you ever seen a lover that does not desire whom he loves?
>
> This is what you take from the prayer of discourse with God: when you say, "You alone do we worship, and from You alone do we seek assistance" (Qur'an 1:4)—and from the discourse with the Messenger, when you say in your prayers, "Peace be upon you, O Prophet, and the Mercy of God and His Blessing." You say this in every prayer, whereupon you are cleansed of your sins, only to return to them yet again after receiving the blessings with which the Lord has favored you, which is meeting with your Lord, the highest of blessings.
>
> If one wishes to know his reality and to see his state with his Lord, let him look at his prayer. Either it will produce humility and tranquility or heedlessness and hastiness. So, if your prayer is not of the first type, then seek to throw dirt on your head out of neglect and sorrow.[47] The one who sits with a perfume maker is given the fragrance of his perfume. The prayer, therefore, is the association with God, so when you attend it and you do not obtain from it anything, it indicates a sickness that resides in you, which is either pride or the absence of proper manners. God says:

"I shall turn away from My revelations those who magnify themselves wrong-fully in the earth" (Qur'an 7:146).

It is not desired that one rushes from the mosque after his prayer. Rather, he should remember God after it and seek His forgiveness from his shortcomings in doing so. For perhaps his prayer is not in a state for it to be accepted. But if you were to seek God's forgiveness, thereafter it will be accepted.[48]

Ibn 'Ata Allah's warning not leave the mosque too quickly after perform-ing the ritual prayer also has an esoteric meaning. The mosque, in the sym-bolism of Sufism, signifies the heart, while prayers signify the connection between the worshipper and the Divine Presence. Thus, Ibn 'Ata Allah here calls on the faithful to maintain the connection with the Divine Source in the heart and not be too quick to push it aside to return to worldly concerns. This means one should strive to keep the connection with the Divine Presence that has been built up through remembrance and prayer, and not fall into heedlessness.

After the Messenger of God used to pray, he would seek God's forgiveness three times. This was related by Thawban, who said:

When he finished from prayer, he would seek God's forgiveness three times and say, "O God, you are the peace and from you is peace. Blessed are you, O Owner of Greatness and Honor."

Ibn 'Ata Allah also wrote:

The simile of one who had performed his prayer without tranquility and humility of heart or presence of contemplation is like the one who presents to the king one hundred empty boxes. Thereafter, he deserves the admonishment of the king because of his lack of intelligence and thought, which the king will utter about him whenever he is mentioned. But the one who prays with tranquility and presence of heart is like the one who presented the king with boxes of precious jewels, for surely the king will delight in that and will return the favor on him and he will always mention to others about the gifts he had received from him. This is because the one who gives has purity of heart, perfection of thought and high aspiration.[49]

I say to you, O servant of God, when you enter prayer you are conversing with your Lord and speaking with the Messenger of God in the Witnessing, because you are saying, "Peace be upon you, O Prophet, and God's mercy and blessings." It is not said, "O you," or, "O so and so," in the language of the Arabs, except to someone who is present in the assembly. So, in your prayers, you should summon his greatness in your mind.[50]

If you wish to know how you will traverse the Bridge on the Day of Judgment, then look at your state in proceeding to prayer in going to the mosque...for in this world, the prayer is the bridge of uprightness that is not seen by the eyes, but by the enlightened hearts and clear vision. God says: "This is my straight way, therefore follow it" (Qur'an 6:153).

So, the one for whom the path is enlightened follows thereon, but the one for whom his path is darkened does not see where he is stepping and is not able to travel the way; therefore, he will remain in his place standing and bewildered. Abu Hurayra related that the Messenger of God said: "The poor of the Muslims will enter Paradise before the rich by half a day, and each day is five hundred years."[51]

This is because they were foremost in the world in worship and constant in the Friday prayer and the congregation.

VOLUNTARY WORSHIP

In addition to the fixed, obligatory ritual prayers (*fara'id al-Salat*), Muslims consider supererogatory prayers of great importance. Great emphasis is placed on observing the prayers that the Prophet, upon whom be peace and blessings, used to observe in addition to the five prescribed prayers.

In addition to the obligatory prayers, the Prophet observed certain sets of supererogatory ritual prayers just before and after them. These confirmed *sunan* are well documented.[52] In addition to these, the Prophet would add additional prayer cycles known as *nawafil*. Each of the schools of Islamic jurisprudence classifies these cycles slightly differently, but all agree on the merit of performing these supplemental acts of devotion. Finally, the Prophet would pray additional ritual prayers independently of the obligatory ones. These include

- Prayer just after sunrise (*ishraq*)
- From 4 to 12 cycles in the forenoon (*duha*)
- Six cycles after the evening prayer (*awabin*)
- The night vigil (*tahajjud* or *qiyam al-layl*).

When asked why he used to pray so much, to the point that his feet were swollen, the Prophet replied, "Should I not be a thankful servant of God?"[53] In saying this, the Prophet expressed the essence of supererogatory worship, to show gratitude to the Lord and thus to draw nearer to the Divine Presence. The Prophet related regarding the words[54] recited in every prayer from the Opening chapter of the Holy Qur'an, "Praise is to Allah, the Lord of the universe," that God responds by saying, "My servant has praised Me."[55]

The Night Vigil

One of the most important supererogatory prayers is the Night Vigil (*Qiyam al-Layl*). The ideal time for voluntary prayer, and indeed for spiritual endeavors in general, is at night—preferably after midnight. This is the time when the world is asleep, but the lovers and seekers of God (*al-ʿibad*) are awake and traveling toward reality and their divine destinations. It is under the veil of the night that the plane of consciousness is clear from the chaos of worldly affairs, for it is a time when the mind and heart operate most effectively.

Prayer before midnight, whether supplicatory or ritual, is very slow; after midnight, it is very fast.

In one of the first revelations, God ordered His Messenger:

> Stand (to prayer) by night, but not all night, half of it or a little less. Or a little more; and recite the Qur'an in slow, measured rhythmic tones.

> (Qur'an 73:2–4)

And the Messenger of God said:

> Two cycles of prayer in the late hours of the night are more valuable than all the riches of this world. But for fear of overburdening my followers, I would have made these obligatory.

Salman, a renowned Companion of the Prophet, in describing the observance of the night vigil said:

> The man who considers the darkness of night and people's unmindfulness a boon, and stands up and says the prayer till the morning, he is a man for whom there is all gain and no loss...adopt those medium-type of supererogatory prayers (*nawafil*) which you may put up with perpetually.[56]

The Prophet's wife 'A'isha related:

> I used to stand with God's Messenger throughout the night. He would recite *Surat al-Baqara, Surat Al ʿImran* and *Surat al-Nisa* [i.e., the four longest chapters of the Qur'an].[57]

It is related that the third caliph, 'Uthman ibn 'Affan, would recite the entire Qur'an in one prayer during the night.[58]

A renowned contemporary Sufi saint, and my teacher and guide on the spiritual path, Shaykh Muhammad Nazim Adil al-Haqqani, says:

> The last third of the night is the best of times to pray at night because God the Most High is looking therein at His servant. Our master 'Abd-Allah al-Daghestani, may God always elevate his stations, used to invite me to his association during the last third of the night because it is the time of heavenly manifestation. He would say that, in this time, there is no veil between God and His servant. So, each of you should awake in the third

part of the night to pray and be present in the hour of heavenly manifestations. Oh God, make us among those who stand in prayer at night, seeking the vision of Your Face.

There is no possibility to receive sainthood without the night vigil. The night vigil is ordained for the Prophet, also for the Friends of God it is considered obligatory and, as related to the community, it is a strong practice (*sunna*). Without a doubt, the servant will not receive the station of sainthood if he is not connected to God. And a token of the one who is connected with the Lord Almighty is the night vigil. This is the greatest means of sainthood, by which God adorns His servant with the secret of sainthood during the last third of the night. Therefore, be awake at this time of the night, whether engaged in your prayer or in something else, so that nothing will obstruct you from being present in this time for which you will obtain this special mercy.[59]

The renowned Egyptian Sufi Ibn 'Ata Allah as-Sakandari said:

Two cycles of ritual prayer before God during the night is better than thousands of cycles of prayer during the day, for the Messenger of God says:

"Keep to observing the night prayer for it is the devotion of the righteous before you, it brings you closer to God, it wipes away offenses, replaces sins and wards off illness from the body."[60]

Without a doubt you do not pray two cycles in the night except that you will find its rewards on your scales on the Day of Requital. Is a servant purchased for any reason other than to serve? Do you see a servant who is purchased merely to eat and sleep, who does not perform his duties? You are nothing more than a servant that God has brought into existence for His worship. He created you for His obedience; your purchase is for His service:

"Lo! God hath bought from the believers their lives and their wealth because for them is Paradise" (Qur'an 9:111).

We conclude this section with the words of Shaykh Abd Allah al-Fa'iz al-Daghestani, may God preserve his sanctity, who said about the night vigil:

Even if a servant rises in the time of heavenly manifestations and he is a non-Muslim in faith, and he does something in that hour, because of that he too would obtain the level of belief before passing from this life. He will be guided and safe because he was awake during the hours of heavenly manifestations, and he would consequently receive that special mercy. It is not possible for anyone who receives even a drop from that mercy, to remain wretched or to remain in unbelief. He is safe even if a tyrant; in time he will turn back to God, and if he is a sinner, he will repent. There is no ambiguity that this mercy will change his state.

THE PERFECTION OF PRAYER

In reality, prayer is a state of heedfulness that must be kept constantly and perpetually throughout the day. Those committed to this path seek to maintain a state of mindfulness in each breath, not forgetting their Lord for even a single moment.

The perfection of prayer means to be aware of God's Presence, "as if you see Him," and to demonstrate one's devotion and servitude to Him. God said:

> I created the jinn and humankind only that they might worship Me. No Sustenance do I require of them, nor do I require that they should feed Me.

> (Qur'an 51:56)

God initially commanded the Prophet Muhammad's followers to observe 50 prayers a day, but with His mercy this obligation was reduced to 5. In the Divine Balance, the 5 prayers are thus considered as 50. Calculating the time required to observe 50 prayers, it would require all of a worshipper's waking hours, including one's time to eat and make ablution. Thus, those who observe the five prayers perfectly, with complete submission to God and complete presence before God, will be in fulfillment of the above verse. For those, God will provide sustenance without their needing to work, for they are fulfilling the Divine Directive properly.

The Summit of Worship

Ritual prayer is known as the "summit of worship," for it contains the essential aspects of all five pillars of Islamic worship: the testimony of faith, prayer, charity, fasting, and pilgrimage.

The first pillar, the testimony of faith (*al-Shahada*) is observed in each ritual prayer, when one bears witness to the Oneness of God and the Prophethood of Muhammad during the sitting phase.

Charity (*Zakat*), the third pillar consists of giving 2½% of one's wealth to the needy for the sake of God. Ritual prayer encompasses this pillar in the sense that the most important thing that one possesses is the body and spirit. In ritual prayer one give one's whole person and time to God.

The fourth pillar, fasting (*Sawm*) is accomplished immediately on entering the prayer, for one must withhold oneself from all worldly actions, including eating, drinking, relations with others, and, even more stringent than the ritual fast, one may not converse except with the Lord.

The last pillar of Islam, the pilgrimage (*Hajj*) is encompassed when the worshipper directs himself or herself to the Ka'ba, the focal point of the pilgrimage.

Prayer is Ascension to the Divine

The Prophet said:

Ritual prayer is the ascension (*mi'raj*) of the believer.

The Prophet therefore had, according to Islam's esoteric scholars, not just one, but 24,000 ascensions during his life.

When the worshipper begins a sincere prayer, saying "God is Greatest," the ascension begins. If one is truly observant of the rights and duties of the prayers with their perfection, this will be apparent, for as soon as you enter the prayer inspiration of Divine knowledge will begin to enter your heart along with increased yearning for the Divine Presence. If these secrets are not coming to you, it signifies that your prayers are not ascending to the Divine Presence and that you are falling into Satan's traps.

Sayyid Haydar Amuli writes:

His [the Prophet's] words, "I have been given coolness of the eye in prayer," refer to nothing else but the contemplation of the Beloved by the eye of the lover, who draws near in the stillness of the prayer.... On seeing the Beloved, the eye too becomes stilled and it ceases to look at anything other than Him in all things.[61]

Thus, the worshipper attains the state, related in the Holy Tradition:

...My servant shall continue to draw nearer to Me by performing the supererogatory acts of virtue until I love him; when I love him, I become his ears with which he hears, his eyes with which he sees, his hands with which he grasps, and his feet with which he walks; if he were to ask of Me, I will grant his request, if he were to seek refuge in Me, I will protect him.[62]

As to the Messenger's state during prayer, his wife 'A'isha reported:

He would weep continuously until his lap became wet. He would be sitting and keep weeping until his auspicious beard became drenched. Then he would weep so much the ground became wet.[63]

Abu Bakr al-Siddiq, the first caliph after the Prophet, would stand in prayer as if he were a pillar. Commenting on this, one of the early transmitters of traditions, Mujahid, said, "this is the fearfulness (*khushu'*) in prayer."

The Prophet said, "Pray as you see me pray."[64] He did not say, "Pray as you have heard I prayed," nor "Pray as I taught my Companions." This hints at something very profound. The vision of the Prophet is something that is true, and has been witnessed by countless Friends of God. Thus, the Prophet's saying, "Whoever saw me in a vision, in truth saw me,"[65] to the Sufi commentators carries the meaning, "Whoever saw me in a vision will see me in reality." For Sufis, the first level of witnessing (*mushahada*) is to sense the Prophet present before them. The final stage of witnessing, which is "to worship God as if you see Him,"[66] was achieved by the Prophet during the Ascension when he was brought to the station of Nearness (*qurb*), "two bow's lengths or nearer" (Qur'an 53:9) to the Divine Presence. The Sufis affirm that true prayer brings the worshipper to the state of witnessing God and His Prophet, thereby attaining true unity with the Beloved. For this reason, prayer is compared to the union of marriage, *wisal*. Indeed, they explain the two salutations of peace, made to end the prayer, as a return from extinction, to greet the world as a new person.

It is said of the Prophet's fourth successor, his cousin 'Ali ibn Abi Talib, that when he prayed, he was utterly oblivious to his surroundings. Once he was injured by an enemy arrow, which penetrated his foot. It could not be removed without causing immense pain. He said, "I will pray, at which time remove it." They did as he directed. Upon completing the prayer he asked his companions, "When are you going to remove the arrow?" 'Ali ibn Abi Talib used to say, "Even if the Veil were lifted, it would not increase my certainty," referring to his state of witnessing the Divine Presence.[67]

We conclude with a story, related about the great Sufi master Shaykh Abu al-Hasan al-Shadhili.

> The scholars of Alexandria came to him to test him and he read what was in their hearts before they spoke and said, "O pious scholars, have you ever prayed?"
>
> They said, "Far be it from any of us to leave prayer."
>
> He then recited the verse:
>
> "Lo! man was created anxious, Fretful when evil befalleth him, And, when good befalleth him, grudging, except those who (really) prays" (Qur'an 70:19–22).
>
> "So," he asked, "do any of you pray like this?" They were silent. Then the shaykh said to them, "Then, none of you has ever prayed!"
>
> The real prayer is performed purely for the pleasure of God, conversing with Him in variations of delight, humbleness and awe which is void of hypocrisy and repute. No doubt it brings about the remembrance of God and the heart inherits awe of Him.[68]

CONCLUSION

Prayer as Divine Service

While the ritual prayer we have just examined in detail is one of the Five Pillars of Islam, in reality all of Islam is essentially a form of prayer. For the meaning of prayer is worship, and the essence of all worship is to seek God. Seeking the Face of God is the goal of Islam, and the means are the Divinely prescribed forms of action as well as voluntary forms of bringing the worshipper closer to the Divine Presence.

God says:

And to Him prostrate all that is in the heavens and on earth; willingly or by compulsion.

(Qur'an 13:15)

And to God prostrate all that is in the heavens and the earth.

(Qur'an 16:49)

And there is not one thing except that it glorifies with God with His praise.

(Qur'an 17:44)

These verses indicate that all of creation, regardless of form or substance, are in fact in a state of prayer, for prostration and glorification are the essence of prayer. They cannot be other than that—even those who disobey, in their disobedience—are in fact submitting to the ultimate Holy Will of God and the Destiny prescribed for them.

However, the key to the Lord's Bounty is to seek Him and submit willingly with one's entire being. To become a Muslim means to say, "O God! I admit that You are the Creator and I am your slave." This is the first level of submission, slavery, but it is not servanthood. Servanthood is higher.

True servanthood of God means to become obedient. The servant has no will of his or her own but is subject to the will of the master at all times. Islam does not ask human beings to serve a cruel and whimsical master, but rather the Creator of all things, Who is the Aware, the Subtle, in His all-encompassing knowledge of both the needs and the desires of His servants.

One who attains this level of submission in Islam becomes *'abd,* servant to the Lord. In Islam this is considered the highest achievement—the state of servanthood, known as *'ubudiyya.* For that reason the Prophet said, "The names dearest to God are Abdullah (servant of God) and 'Abdur-Rahman (servant of the Most Merciful)."[69]

God says:

Glory to (God) Who did take His Servant for a Journey by night from the Sacred Mosque to the farthest Mosque, whose precincts We did bless, in order that We might show him some of Our Signs.

(Qur'an 17:1)

God specified the Prophet Muhammad in this verse with the title "servant," *'abd,* and again, relating to Prophet Muhammad's ascension to the Divine Presence, when He says:

So did (God) convey the inspiration to His Servant- (conveyed) what He (meant) to convey.

(Qur'an 53:10)

...For truly did he see, of the Signs of his Lord, the Greatest!

(Qur'an 53:18)

Of the station the Prophet Muhammad attained in that rapture, Imam Nawawi, one of the great scholars of Islam, says, "Most of the scholars say that the Prophet saw his Lord with the eyes of his head."

The unique greatness of God's Messenger, Muhammad, is that he saw the Lord of Creation, thus making him the perfected monotheist (*muwahhid*). The Prophet Muhammad's grasp of Divine Unity, *tawhid,* was perfected by ascension to the Divine Presence. Everyone else's understanding of Divine Unity falls short of the Messenger's. Despite this, the Prophet maintained absolute humility, never seeing himself as important, but rather as a servant, honored by the Master of masters.

It is related that when the Prophet reached the highest levels and most distinguished stations God revealed to him, "With what shall I honor you?" The Prophet said, "By relating me to You through servanthood (*'ubudiyya*)."[70]

Thus, true prayer is nothing less than Ascension to the Station of true Servanthood, which is the Station of Submission. In that station, Divine Unity becomes manifest, and there, the servant reaches the state where he hears what no ears have heard, sees what no eyes have seen, and tastes the reality of Divine Oneness. In this state of witnessing, the servant perceives only the Lord. He sees all existence through His Existence and the realization that all proceeds from the One. This is known as the Station of Annihilation, in which the servant no longer sees himself or herself, no longer sees anything, but only sees, feels and is immersed in the Presence of the Lord without any partner and with no likeness.

NOTES

1. The Hearer—*al-Sami'*, The Aware—*al-'Alim,* Responsive to those who call on Him—*al-Mujib.*

2. Ibn Rushd (Averroes), *al-Muqaddima,* the chapter of Prayer (Beirut: Dar al-Kutub al-'Ilmiyya, 1994), 50.

3. See *Fiqh al-Lugha,* from al-Thaʿlabi. Also in Qurtubi's commentary on the Qurʾan and others.

4. Cited from Qurtubi's commentary by Ibn Rushd (Averroes), *al-Muqaddima.*

5. The traditional reverential phrase used whenever the Prophet's name or titles are mentioned.

6. Bukhari, Muslim, and others.

7. Tabarani.

8. Muslim.

9. Bukhari. The specific prayer mentioned is the afternoon prayer (*Salat al-ʿAsr*).

10. Mawlana Muhammad Yusuf Khandalvi, *Hayat al-Sahaba* (New Delhi, India: Idara Ishaʿat-e-Diniyat Ltd, 1992), 101.

11. Abu Bakr ibn al-Jazaʾiri, *Minhaj al-Muslim,* chapter on Prayer, 1st ed. (Mecca, Saudi Arabia: Dar al-Fikr, 1995), 184.

12. Muslim from Jabir and others from Abu Hurayra.

13. Muslim, Tirmidhi.

14. Tabarani reported it from Anas in his *Kabir.* In another report it reads "... then his prayers are not prayers."

15. Al-Jazaʾiri, *Minhaj al-Muslim,* 184–185.

16. The Prophet said:

Verily this Qurʾan is difficult and felt as a burden to anyone that hates it, but it is made easy to anyone that follows it. Verily my sayings are difficult and felt as a burden to anyone that hates them, but they are made easy to anyone that follows them. Whoever hears my saying and preserves it, putting it into practice, shall come forth together with the Qurʾan on the Day of Resurrection. Whoever dismisses my sayings dismisses the Qurʾan, and whoever dismisses the Qurʾan has lost this world and the next.

Narrated from al-Hakam ibn ʿUmayr al-Thumali by Khatib in *al-Jamiʿ li Akhlaq al-Rawi* (1983 ed. 2:189), Qurtubi in his *Tafsir* (18:17), Abu Nuʿaym, Abu al-Shaykh, and Daylami.

17. Bukhari.

18. A. Al-Masri, *The Reliance of the Traveller,* trans. N. Keller (Dubai, United Arab Emirates: Modern Printing Press, 1991), 34.

19. Ibid., 35.

20. Ahmad ibn Hanbal.

21. Ibn Rushd, *al-Muqaddima.*

22. Bukhari and Muslim from Abu Hurayra.

23. Muslim from Abu Hurayra.

24. On the right palm one sees the Arabic numerals 1 and 8, signifying 18, and on the left 8 and 1, signifying 81. The sum of these is 99.

25. Often cited, but not traced to a known hadith from the Prophet.

26. Without annihilation, that is, to see himself as existent before the Ultimate Divine Reality, which at the highest understanding of spirituality, is associating one's self as partner with God.

27.   Muslim, Ahmad ibn Hanbal in his *Musnad,* and others from Zayd ibn Arqam.

28.   Jili, *al-Insan al-Kamil* (the Perfect Human), Chapter "Secrets of Religion and Worship," section "The Spiritual Symbolism of Prayer," 260–261.

29.   Also translated as the "Sacred Mosque."

30.   Abdullah Yusuf Ali's commentary on this verse summarizes traditional commentaries: "The Farthest Mosque," he writes, "must refer to the site of the Temple of Solomon in Jerusalem on the hill of Moriah." Muslims purposely built a mosque on this hill, according to tradition on the verified site of earlier sanctuaries. It was a strong concern of the early Muslims to restore the site to its earlier function as a place of supplication venerated by all the prophets, including Abraham, David, and Solomon. Tradition relates that when the Caliph 'Umar visited Jerusalem after its conquest, he searched for David's sanctuary or prayer niche (*mihrab Dawud*), which is mentioned in the Qur'an (38:21), the same site on which David's son Solomon later erected the Temple. Satisfied that he had located it, the Caliph 'Umar ordered a prayer niche (*musalla*) to be established there which evolved into a mosque complex later known as the *al-Haram al-Sharif,* according to Prophetic tradition the third most venerated location in Islam.

31.   Bukhari and Muslim.

32.   Bukhari.

33.   Ghazali mentioned this in his *Revival of the Religious Sciences.* It is similar to an Israelite tradition related by Ahmad ibn Hanbal in *Kitab al-Zuhd* from Wahb bin Munabbih.

34.   Ka'b al-Ahbar makes the entire verse refer to Muhammad, it is a metaphor of the Light of Muhammad. The Messenger of Allah is the niche, the lamp is prophethood, the glass is his heart, the blessed tree is the revelation and the angels who bought it, the oils are the proofs and evidence which contain the revelation.

35.   Ibrahim Hakki Erzurumi, *Marifetname* (Cairo: Bulaq [Printing House], 1835).

36.   Bukhari.

37.   Bukhari and Muslim.

38.   The basic essentials of the ritual prayer are:

1. Standing in an upright posture (*qiyam*).

2. The opening affirmation of God's Supreme Greatness (*takbirat al-ihram*).

3. Recitation of the Opening chapter of the Qur'an (*Surat al-Fatiha*).

4. Bowing (*ruku'*).

5. Calm composure (*tuma'nina*) in the bowing posture.

6. Straightening up from the bowing posture.

7. Calm composure in the erect posture resumed after bowing.

8. Prostration (*sujud*).

9. Calm composure in the posture of prostration.

10. Sitting between the two acts of prostration.

11. Calm composure in the sitting posture.

12. The final testimony (*tashahhud*).

13. Adopting the sitting posture in order to pronounce the final testimony.

14. The invocation of blessing on the Prophet (*al-Salat al-Ibrahimiyya*).

15. The salutation (*taslim*).

39. Al-Hakim in *al-Mustadrak* (authentic). In a similar vein, the Prophet is reported to have said, "Association with God (*shirk*) is stealthier in this community than creeping ants."

40. The Prophet said, "I do not fear that you will become polytheists after me, but I fear that, because of worldly interests, you will fight each other, and thus be destroyed like the peoples of old." Bukhari and Muslim.

41. Hajjah Amina Adil, *Lore of Light* (Columbo, Sri Lanka: Arafat Publishing House, 1989), p. xiii.

42. Ibid., 9.

43. Shah Waliullah al-Dihlawi, *Hujjatullah al-Baligha,* vol. 1, Secrets of Worship.

44. Muslim, Ahmad ibn Hanbal.

45. What is meant here is that Muhammad is the overall, universal opening of creation due to the fact everything was created from his light.

46. Ibn 'Ata Allah as-Sakandari, *al-Tuhfa fi al-Tasawwuf,* from the Chapter on Prayer, arranged and compiled by Dr. 'Ali Hasan al-'Aridh, The Library of the Superior Achievement, al-Fajalah Egypt, pages 94–98.

47. It is related that Ibn 'Abbas said, "If you had performed your prayers and you didn't find in your heart humility, when you read the Qur'an and you don't find a meaning in it and when you remember God by yourself and your tears don't flow, then throw dirt on your head and cry about your loss. Then ask God to provide for you another heart."

48. What Ibn 'Ata Allah means here is that after the prayer, one remembers God by magnification, praise, and glorification following the obligation prayers. It is related from Abu Hurayra in *Sahih Muslim*:

> The one who remembers God at the end of every prayer 33 times (by glorification [*tasbih*], praise [*tahmid*] and magnification [*takbir*]) and ends it with, "There is no god except God, He has no partners. To Him belongs the Kingdom and all praise and He has power over all things," his sins will be forgiven even if they were as numerous as the foam of the ocean.

49. Suyuti recorded in his *Jami'* that Abu Hurayra said: "When any of you are in prayer, he is conversing with his Lord."

50. To have the image of the Prophet in prayer is the highest summoning, even outside the prayer. Suyuti reported from Ibn 'Abbas that he had a dream in which he saw the Messenger. Thereafter he went to the house of the Prophet's wife 'A'isha, the Mother of Believers, in which he was shown a mirror. But he did not see himself, he saw the image of the Messenger. Khalid al-Baghdadi added it in his *Treatises in Obtaining Connection*, reporting from al-Hafi in Suyuti's, *Tanwir*. It is noted that this stage is reached after one has obtained constant connection with his spiritual guide (*murshid*) through meditation (*muraqaba*) which guides

him into the presence of the Messenger. Thus, meditation is an evolution after one has passed the higher stations of *dhikr;* by tongue, by heart, then by the combination of both.

51. Tirmidhi related this and it is sound.

52. These are two cycles before the dawn prayer, two or four before the noon prayer and two after, either none or two cycles before the afternoon prayer, two after the sunset prayer and two after the night prayer.

53. Bukhari and Muslim.

54. Part of the Opening chapter of the Qur'an (*Surat al-Fatiha*) whose recitation in prayer is obligatory.

55. Muslim, Malik, Tirmidhi, Abu Dawud, an-Nasa'i, and Ibn Maja.

56. Yusuf Khandalvi, *Hayat as-Sahaba,* 101.

57. Ibid., 105.

58. Abu Nu'aym al-Isfahani, *Hilyat al-Awliya wa tabaqat al-asfiya* (The Beauty of the Righteous and Ranks of the Elite), trans. M. Akili (Philadelphia, Pennsylvania: Pearl Press, 1988), 56.

59. Mawlana Shaykh Muhammad Nazim Adil al-Haqqani, *al-Irshad ash-Sharif,* private manuscript.

60. Ibn Asakir reported it from Abu al-Darda' and Ibn al-Sina from Jabir. Daylami recorded something similar from Ibn 'Umar with the notable addition, "...it extinguishes the anger of God and wards off the heat of hellfire from his family on the Day of Judgment." Ahmad recorded it in his *Musnad,* and Tabarani in his *Kabir,* from Ibn Anas, "You should pray the night prayer, even if it's only one cycle." Al-Hafi in Suyuti graded it as sound.

61. Sayyid Haydar Amuli, *Inner Secrets of the Path* (London: Element Books, 1983), 233.

62. Bukhari.

63. Yusuf Khandalvi, *Hayat as-Sahaba,* 101.

64. Bukhari.

65. Musnad of Ahmad ibn Hanbal.

66. Part of the long "Gabriel Hadith" in which the Prophet describes the three levels of religion: submission, faith and perfection of character. The latter he described as "to worship God as if you see Him, and if you do not see Him, know that He sees you." Narrated by Bukhari and Muslim.

67. Haydar Amuli, *Inner Secrets of the Path.*

68. Ibn 'Ata Allah as-Sakandari, *at-Tuhfa fi at-Tasawwuf,* from the chapter of Prayer, pages 94–98.

69. Abu Dawud.

70. Related by Abu Qasim Sulayman al-Ansari.

4

VIGIL

Barry C. McDonald

Men dream the shadow play of history;
We live and die, together and alone.
The here below is not our final home;
All men are born to face eternity.

Why am I on the earth? And should I fear?
Sit quietly, invoke the Name of God.
Stay vigilant, although the night draws near,
Repeat again the liberating Word.

5

DHIKR, A DOOR THAT WHEN KNOCKED, OPENS: AN ESSAY ON THE REMEMBRANCE OF GOD

Daniel Abdal-Hayy Moore

In the Name of Allah, the Merciful, the Most Merciful

I begin with praise of the One Who has given us His Name to call Him by: Allah, Creator of every creation conceivable and inconceivable, our breaths and heartbeats, our origins and destinies, He Who has no origin other than Himself nor destiny other than Himself, in Whose formless form we have been fashioned in order to be reflections back to Him of His Grace in His creation, He Who is both Origin and Destination of our praise and gratitude, upon Whom we rely when all supports have been removed and we are left facing life and death with none but Him, and upon Whose Mercy we throw ourselves when the world is dark, relying on His endless Light alone.

And praise be to His prophets, from His first reflected light, Adam, to the last of the prophets, His beloved Seal of Prophethood, Muhammad, son of Abdullah, peace of Allah's praises be upon him eternally, he both Praiser and Praiseworthy in one, door from Eternity into time and the Next World into this world, living example of God's qualities and translator of His will and continuous blessing upon us, dispenser of the macrocosm into the microcosm, straightener of prayer rows and releaser of sorrows, the Prophet and Messenger Muhammad, from whose heart line come the saints, scholars, and teachers of purity and deepest devotion living among every people on earth and in every age on earth until the end of time, those who teach remembrance of God and who have it on their tongues and in their beings both asleep and awake, in good times and bad, and whose generosity is God's generosity, and whose wisdom in all moments is His wisdom from whose milk we may freely ladle divine knowledge and illumination suited to every circumstance in our lives perfect for this life and the hereafter.

And to my own shaykh, Sidi Muhammad ibn al-Habib ibn al-Siddiq al-Amghari al-Idrisi al-Hasani, may God be pleased with him and grant him light in the grave, whose *zawiya* in Meknès, Morocco (al-Maghrib, *The West*), contains his light that radiates out into this world of forgetfulness to awaken it to its original remembrance of God with every person's breath and heartbeat, knowingly or unknowingly. As he says in his *Diwan:*

> If the breath of His *dhikr* were to fill the west and there were
> A sick man in the east, that man would be cured of his affliction.

This echoes in mirror image the words of the Sultan of the Lovers, the Egyptian mystic poet Ibn al-Farid (d. 1235 CE), from *al-Khamriyya, The Wine Ode,* that being the wine of God intoxication:

> Could the breaths of its bouquet spread out in the East,
> One stuffed-up in the west would smell again.

And may Allah bless and expand all present shaykhs and guides, and my present *shaykha* (female spiritual master) Baji Tayyiba Khanum, in her deepest light and loving compassion, spreading the way of the *dhikr* of Allah to the West to open the passages of our hearts again to love of Allah and His Prophet Muhammad in at least some small measure of the vast dimension in which they should be loved.

Though I grew up in Oakland, California, in a nonreligious family, I was always drawn to music and words and a particular sacred aspect of the joining of the two, but perhaps not any more than any other child with a newly minted mind open to new experiences. Sacred music, Bach, Stravinsky, and generally classical and modern serious music attracted me more than the then-current pop music, but so did jazz, which in its spontaneity has always seemed to have a touch of the sacred and philosophical in it. California in the 1950s was also influenced by everything Japanese, in spite of being on the coast most vulnerable to possible attacks from Japan during the war, so that we had high-class framed Japanese prints on the wall and generous decorative elements of bamboo and *ikbana* flower motifs.

It seemed natural, then, in my twenties, already writing poetry and avidly reading spiritual texts from all the traditions, especially Zen Buddhism and the early Hindu sutras, to sit in the *zendo* of Sensei Shrunyu Suzuki in San Francisco, in the Japanese Buddhist Temple on Bush Street, and to recite the short Prajña Paramita Sutra in phonetic Japanese, that ends, *Ji ho san shi i shi hu shi son bu sa mo ko sa mo ko ho ja ho ro mi* ("Ten directions, past, present, and future, all Buddhas, the world-honored one, Bodhisattva. Great Bodhisattva, Great Prajña Paramita!"). After an hour or more of silent meditation in Zen, cross-legged, attempting (but only rarely succeeding) to let thoughts drift by without attachment, such chanting in the large, empty hall with its polished wooden floors and simple Buddhist altar with bowl-shaped bells and gladiolas spraying out of tall vases went deeply into the heart and cleared one's consciousness of its daily cobwebs.

But we were nothing if not eclectic in those heady days of 1960s in California, and we chanted Hindu chants during Hatha Yoga practice, the Sanskrit version of the Prajña Paramita Sutra ending, *Gate, gate, paragate, parasamgate, bodhi, swaha!* ("Gone, Gone, Gone Beyond Goneness, Gone to the Other Side, into Bodhi consciousness, *Swaha!*"), Tibetan chants of *Om mani padme Hum!* ("O Jewel in the Heart of the Lotus, *Hum!*"), and any other invocations we thought might be efficacious in transforming our consciousness, wafting on streams of the various smokes traveling through our rooms, brightening a sense of worlds beyond our senses and the mysterious workings of the cosmos shivering its lights through our walls and ceilings, in the leafy woods in our exploratory retreats, or alone in our incense-rich rooms in the dark of night.

Invocation: the repetition of phrases meant to call up spiritual reality, or halt our normal minds, to descend into our hearts to metamorphose our daily lives into awakened attention and delight. *Transformation* is the key element in all invocation, to change our central focus from individual consciousness to the greater "cosmic" consciousness, or, as in the case of the Sufi practices I later encountered, which have a very pure metaphysic, to be annihilated from our effective ego-self and allow God, Who Alone exists, to be experientially realized in His singular existence.

From the moment we first find we can make audible and effective sounds, we might become focused and energized in our being by repeating certain words or phrases over and over again, such as the ubiquitous *dada* and *mama,* our first real invocation to those flawed but beloved, mortal gods, to increase our sense of an intimate universe with all its vastness somehow encompassed within our hearts. And when we later discovered the existence of the no-less mortal but far less-flawed saints of the religious paths, who have repeated mantras or chanted sutras or intoned simple phrases up to and past their shattering and transforming point of enlightenment, this for us in those dropout days was enough to increase our thirst and determination to engage in the practice of what I later would be able to call: *Dhikr of Allah.*

The era of the 1960s, however, was remarkable for the amount of new material that was suddenly flushing into our culture, music from India listened to with full and devotional attention, Tibetan monastery music, the rumbling chant of monks along with their sad artifacts that were then being sold very inexpensively at various import stores in San Francisco and elsewhere, no doubt from refugees willing to part with them for any amount of money more useful to them for much-needed food and clothing. I had a theater company in Berkeley in the 1960s that based its sacred theatrics imaginatively on Tibetan rituals I was reading at the time and that seemed fitting for our crazed consciousness experiments within the overall background environment of the Vietnam War. We had Tibetan longhorns and conch shells and gongs and bells in our orchestra to authenticate our serious intentions, and a sense of radical spirituality based on Zen but ritualized into a drama of good versus evil to try to exorcise the specter of war from our collective consciousness. We listened to newly available UNESCO records of real monks from the Himalayas, with their deep-throated chanting also capable of intoning two sounded notes at the same time, punctuated by the clanging of cymbals and bells, and the deep bellowing drone of the long horns, with drums and the high-pitched melodies of double reed trumpets. It was a real cacophony of spiritual sound, recalling something indescribably ancient in which we bathed our senses for a time. We tried to include all of this in our theatrical performances, recollecting our cosmic source through action, poetic chanting, and stylized choreography at night by torchlight to an avid audience waiting for a spiritual experience; all of us, performers and audience, attuned to the transformative possibilities for our souls and totally expectant of a positive outcome for all of the energies we poured unstintingly into the proceedings.

At the end of this period however, and after the disbanding of the troupe at the tail end of the 1960s, I met a Muslim Sufi who introduced a few of us to Islam and the stories of the Prophet Muhammad, peace be upon him, and his Companions, the revelation of the Qur'an, and the existence of a living, enlightened Sufi shaykh of instruction of well over a hundred years of age residing in Meknès, Morocco. I accepted the invitation to become a Muslim and simultaneously entered the Sufi Path at his hand with full confidence that this was a furthering and refining of everything I had superficially experienced so far, for it presented an immediate spiritual world of Light that I should not, in all consciousness, resist entering. By so doing, I was also accepting the invocatory formulas of Sufism (a long initiatory litany of invocations given by the shaykh, known as a *wird*), which signified a serious break with earlier practices and a total immersion in new prayers, both formal and informal, with their attendant courtesies and obligations that needed to be learned. This level of commitment and immersion was something new to me and beyond what I had experienced so far, even as an itinerant Zen practitioner. What was required was to take the new Light seriously, since it promised (and continues to promise) the total transformation of our lives to lives closer to human perfection.

To taste the community of the Sufis directly, of course, we were invited by the shaykh to a giant *moussem* (celebration) gathering in Meknès, Morocco, to meet him and his many disciples arriving on donkeys or by train or airplane from the deserts, the mountains, and even other countries to worship and acknowledge the divinity of Allah and praise with our deepest hearts His Messenger, Muhammad, peace and blessings be upon him, in days that were to be filled with invocation and worship almost nonstop. This took place in the shaykh's *zawiya* or center, a smallish nondescript building with a mosque in it, near the Jama'a Zaytuna mosque that was used by the general, not necessarily Sufi population. Here would be a time of intense *dhikr* of God, singing, ritual dancing, and repetitions of God's Divine Name (His Greatest Name, *Allah,* and His 99 Names as well), throughout a protracted period of time.

In Islam, *dhikr* is an Arabic word that has a cluster of meanings. From the Hans Wehr Arabic dictionary we see that it means: *recollection, remembrance, reminiscence, commemoration, naming, mentioning, invocation of God, mention of the Lord's Name, and (in Sufism), incessant repetition of certain words or formulas in praise of God, often accompanied by music and dancing.*[1] But the *dhikr* of God encompasses so many things, all of which are a way of remembrance. When we sat with the Sufis of Meknès and elsewhere we found that they recited the Qur'an in the *Warsh* style of recitation, in unison, in an elongated and rhythmically emphasized monotone that seemed to us like a rushing ocean with no discernable shores; the Qur'an came alive as its oral recitation was always meant to be, alive on the tongues of the believers. Its words and nontuneful melodies sank deep into our blood, filled the room, recited from memory by hundreds of men (separate from the woman in this case in the *zawiya* complex), with Russian Volga depth and seriousness and a free and sweeping sonic scope particular to the Maghribi (Moroccan) Muslims, and not just the Sufis. This incredibly wide-sweeping and over-whelmingly vast musical manner of recitation is what Moroccan children have been traditionally taught in their schools from childhood, so that some-one who is a *hafiz* of the Qur'an—one who knows it in its entirety by heart—was not (and hopefully today still is not) that much of a rarity in North Africa.

Here was true *dhikr Allah:* a gathering of folks for Allah's sake, reciting the words transmitted by the Prophet Muhammad in the Qur'an every day of their lives, in unison, thus filling the mosques to their very rafters with the divinely revealed Word of God. In the Sufi *zawiya,* after the Qur'an recitation, they would sing songs from the *Diwan* (poetry collection) of our shaykh, many of them composed by the shaykh himself—songs of illumina-tive instruction—as well as many from other respected shaykhs of the Sufi Path. With mint tea served in little glasses in our midst, and the shadows of the *zawiya* with its high windows to cool the outside heat, and sandalwood incense permeating the atmosphere, somehow the essence of the remem-brance of God was sounded in us as if from a garden in Paradise, its reverber-ations deeply extending through the passageways of our lives forevermore.

When we first arrived, we were greeted at the main *zawiya* in Meknès (the shaykh was suffering from a cold at the time, so we were not able to greet him until a few days later), and then after sunset we were trooped to a small ramshackle mosque at the poorest edge of town (the Prophet Muhammad said in an established hadith tradition: "Look for me among the poor"), where a gathering of Sufis was already in full swing. This was such a heart-opening experience that I can still enter into it in my imagination 35 years later. We entered a packed mosque over a muddy ditch, whose minaret was just a few boards hammered together as a kind of tower one could not climb up into, and found men in *jallabas* shoulder to shoulder, singing the *Diwan* and invoking Allah and His Prophet with incredible beauty and joy. The house was truly rocking! This little mosque (only when I saw it empty did I see how really small it was) seemed like the fields of heaven, and when we had sung for about an hour or two and got up to stand in the dance that is known among Moroccans as the *hadra* (the Presence) or the *raqs* (the Dance), it seemed as if the ceiling was a flashing bright blue sky of a very exalted heaven rather than the low wooden ceiling of a ramshackle mosque under the cloudy black sky of the Moroccan night. This was indeed high-octane *dhikr* of the finest kind!

This was also direct remembrance of the heart and limbs, perhaps the active result of scholars' ink but in full-bodied practice, not restrained in an atmosphere of dry scholarship. The atmosphere here was of passionately engaged participation, of all the theological reasons and back stories of Islamic recollection now made manifest and directly palpable. Here were rough mountain men in coarse woolen robes alongside elegant imams and scholars from Fez with their pressed gabardines and desert Sufis with long, narrow fingers clasping the hands of pale-skinned Americans and Europeans new to the experience. These knowledgeable veterans of the Sufi Path embraced us all with a sweetness and openness rarely encountered in our own countries of origin, a sweetness transcending languages and life experiences, a Londoner clasping the hand of a desert goat herder, a university graduate holding onto an "illiterate" imam's hand who was the living protector (*hafiz*) of the Qur'an by virtue of knowing it all by heart, word for word and perfectly pronounced (bringing into question, of course, as to which of the two was "illiterate" or which of the two was "educated").

This was a place of pure joy, of true ecstasy, of inner recognition of spiritual realities clothed always (according to the way of the Shadhiliyya Tariqa) in an outward sobriety, which meant that the "dance" was performed within strict limits, avoiding extreme expressions of joy (usually associated with Persian or Turkish Sufis, especially in the miniature paintings of their gatherings), such as the tearing of garments, swooning, or wildly entering into psychic states, all forbidden and controlled in our circles, thereby leading to deeper understandings than those gained by the drunken momentary fireworks of thrilled tasting, which usually vanishes into thin air when morning comes.

The dance itself is strong and ecstatic, the motions of the body, including bowing forward, while taking deep breaths on the words *Hayy* (The Living One), then leaning back on the Divine Name, *Allah*. This is the first phase. Then at a signal of the leader, who takes his place in the center of the circle, the second phase begins with standing in one place while still more deeply breathing the repeated single name of The Living One (*Hayy, Hayy, Hayy*), breaking slightly at the knees and stiffening straight again, as if boldly shaken up and down by the overwhelming force of an inspired state. During this time one concentrates on the *dhikr* of the heart, letting the body loose within its physical limits, but focused on the Divine Name, even imaginatively writing it in Arabic on our hearts and writing it again and again with each breath. Then, at the very end of the *hadra,* the energy turns to a throaty whisper, until finally the words *Muhammadun Rasulullah* (Muhammad the Messenger of God) are intoned to signal the finish of the *hadra* and everyone sits down on the floor where they stood.

It is said by the Sufis that at the beginning of the *hadra,* we do the *dhikr,* but in the second part Allah Himself does it and we are spiritually taken over—we are no more, we have been annihilated in Allah. Afterward, in the calm that follows such a vibrant storm, someone recites the Qur'an in the most gorgeously melodic way, which is like cool water from a mountain spring poured over us to flow throughout our limbs and consciousness. A person of some wisdom and experience (everyone usually knows who this is in any gathering) then gives a teaching, again not a scholarly discourse, but one that seems to have come on the wind, from the heart of the speaker as well as from all those present, filled with the wisdom of the Prophet Muhammad, peace be upon him, and his almost palpable presence among us, and all the teachers over the centuries that have proceeded from him. After that everything is calm and peacefulness; we relax and talk among ourselves, and on this first night in that ramshackle mosque on the edge of town, tables were suddenly brought into this vast but cramped space and a wonderful meal was served, somehow, between all those tightly packed men grazing now with open hearts in the fields of heaven.

This form of standing *dhikr,* the *hadra,* is not performed by every Sufi *tariqa* (the Path or Order, the transmitted line of teaching through various shaykhs with its particular practices and obligations) in exactly the same way, and in some cases, is dispensed with or even frowned upon. The most famous "dance" of the Sufis, of course, is that of the whirling dervishes of Mevlana Jalaluddin Rumi of Konya, Turkey, where men in wide white skirts and tall felt hats turn to a slow and solemn but rhythmic music and singing, including musical instruments, particularly the wailing and poignant *ney* flute and dry taps of drums. Other standing *adhkar* (the plural of *dhikr*) may vary in form and intensity, such as the lines of Egyptian Sufis with whom I have stood, who bowed and repeated the divine phrases but did not follow quite the same phrases as I was used to from the Moroccan experiences. Some of the *turuq* (the plural of *tariqa*), notably the Naqshbandi, prefer silent *dhikr,* without outward performance, although I have heard recently that due to the depth of today's corruption some Naqshbandi shaykhs are instructing their disciples to intone outwardly as well. The varieties of *dhikr* may be endless; one evening we were with a shaykh from Bosnia who led us in the many different forms of standing and dancing *adhkar* from all the *turuq* in his homeland with which he was acquainted, some in spiral lines leading into the center and then out again. And then there are Sufi groups, particularly in the West, that have seemingly eschewed the basic practices of Islam but do various "dances of peace," which are somewhat deracinated and improvised but artful, to bring people to a place of inner tranquility.

What I learned in those first few years as a Muslim and ever after in my life, coming as I did from my California experiences with various practices of remembrance, including the very ancient Hindu and Buddhist ones, was that the Prophet Muhammad, the final revealer of God's Way to mankind, brought the specific science of *dhikr* to us and taught his Companions and family and all who met him directly to remember God in every circumstance and with every breath. All of the specific formulas of *dhikr* are based on the key to entering into Islamic knowledge, *La ilaha illa Allah, Muhammadun Rasulullah* ("There is no god but God [Allah], and Muhammad is the Messenger of God"). This simple statement is recited on the tongues of Muslims all over the world, day and night, incessantly, because it miraculously contains all one needs to know to live a life of compassionate meaning from birth to death.

The Prophet was given the direct word of God in the Qur'an through the Messenger (there is always a Messenger behind every Messenger) Gabriel, *Jibril* in Arabic, who received the revelation from Allah and transmitted it through various experiences to Muhammad, peace be upon him. Every word of the Qur'an has a resonance that cannot be fathomed—even the most mundane-seeming practicalities—especially when discerned and explained by Gnostic teachers who have been bathed in the Qur'an in the deepest sense of the word. The Qur'an itself is a major *dhikr* of Allah, from which all other *adhkar* have been derived. Thus, the recitation of the Qur'an puts us in direct contact with God's Light, and with the very heart and tongue of the Prophet, peace be upon him, from whom we received it, word for word and unchanged, to this day. Each time we open the Qur'an and recite its Arabic with pure intention we find ourselves in sacred territory.

Scholars, of course, from the Companions of the Prophet onward, have expounded on the meanings of the Qur'an and lead us to God through every phrase. The libraries of Islam are packed with diligently and lovingly hand-written copies of books, or their valuable and precious originals, which pour over every phrase of the Qur'an to find its most elemental and useful meaning to our lives. Books have been written on the grammar of the Qur'an as well, not from a pedantic point of view, but because it is a sacred grammar, and knowledge of it brings one into an awed remembrance or invocation of the grammar's source, that being God Himself, Who has speech as one of His key attributes, as we clearly find manifest throughout the ages of mankind and within every culture on our terrestrial globe.

Books have even been written on the simple dot below the letter *ba'* that begins *Bismillah* in Arabic, which means, "In the name of Allah." Treatises on a single dot! Such a treatise is also a *dhikr,* not simply a dry scholarly analysis, but an excitement and regeneration of the heart through profound recollection, which leads to a vision of the universe and how it has proceeded from God's command: "Be!"

So the river of the Qur'an, with all of its illuminative examples and directives, is our major source of remembrance (*dhikr*). And the practices of prayer five times or more a day and in the deepness of night are forms of very intimate remembrance (*dhikr*), as are the Five Pillars of Islam, the testament of God's Oneness (*al-Shahada*), the Prophet Muhammad's Messengership, the formal prayer, the tax on our wealth, fasting Ramadan once a year, and traveling to Mecca to perform the Hajj once in our lifetimes. All of these are incomparable forms of remembrance (*dhikr*) of our Creator and Lord, without whom the entire fabric of the world and us within it would atomize into dust-mote fragments afloat in nothingness.

I made the Hajj pilgrimage in 1972, along with the first six members of our embryonic Sufi community in London. The Hajj is called "the arduous journey." But when you are in Mecca for the Hajj, a state of *dhikr* descends upon you, and it is all a swimming exercise in the great ocean of remembrance from then on. The word *sabaha* in Arabic not only means "to swim" but also "to praise and glorify." The Muslim string of 99 beads for reciting each of God's 99 Divine Names is known as *subha* or *tasbih*, from the same root word, meaning "to swim." Surrounded by millions of Muslims from every part of the world, all there for the one focus—God, and His worship, and His Prophet Muhammad, peace be upon him—with every action and every intention ostensibly for this end, you cannot help but drown in the sweet and salty seas of *dhikr*. But the most astonishing *dhikr*, the most miraculous vision of remembrance, is the Ka'ba itself, the House of Allah, the cubed building draped in black embroidered cloth, which looms up from its surrounding marble courtyard fully material and made of stones and yet fully spiritual and seemingly insubstantial: holy. A rude building with a door in it, a black stone at one corner set in a silver collar that the pilgrims kiss as they circumambulate, and another square stone at the Yemeni Corner, which has been rubbed smooth by the pilgrims' loving and perfumed hands as they pass.

The *dhikr* of the vision of the Ka'ba alone is a monumental proclamation of God's praises. Here people circle seven times, then come to stand and face the harsh wall of their reality and bathe in the Compassionate Grace of Allah that permeates the very air of the Meccan mosque. This anchor in the heart never leaves anyone who has visited Mecca, even if they stray afterward. It is the center of the world for us, and the center of our prayer to which we turn each day. Its depth seems to go straight through the earth's core and straight up to the Throne of God. No one is unmoved at the Ka'ba, it seems, and when I returned to Mecca 24 years later, at the very sight of the outer mosque from the street through the buildings as our bus got closer, I burst into tears. And again at the first sight of the Ka'ba itself through the arches of the mosque entrance, there in its courtyard, serene, waiting for the believers to pay respect to Allah there, openly and with submission, raw heart-burst, naked before it in our being, pierced through and through by its majesty and Light, tears involuntarily come to greet its pure and seemingly undimensional monumentality.

It is said that everyone who goes on the Hajj becomes a Sufi. And if that means that one is overwhelmed with love for Allah, then it is true. We met people at the beginning of the Hajj who were transformed entirely at the end. Their faces stern and puritanical seeming at the beginning were softer and filled with happiness at the end of the Hajj. This is the result of *dhikr,* true *dhikr,* where the heart is made softer and pliant and open to God's whispers from His unseen domains. The Qur'an recitation in the prayer and the act of going down into prostration, the true position of remembrance for all of God's creatures, all of these things are the crowning glory of *dhikr* of God.

A spiritual master, a shaykh of Allah, is also a Ka'ba, a center around which believers pivot in their worship, not of him or her as a person, but of Allah's light made manifest and beamed to the disciples through the shaykh.

Our shaykh in Meknès, Morocco (May Allah protect his secret), Shaykh Muhammad ibn al-Habib, was over a hundred years old when I met him. He barely moved. His voice was indescribably sweet, but honed by the raspiness of age. His face was like the moon. His words were simple, and he wept easily with an inner rationale. But sitting even for a moment in his presence was in itself an automatic *dhikr* of Allah. I did not see an old man. The old man, the young man, the mortal man, was so refined, so essentialized, that he was almost gone. It seemed that he looked at us from the Next World, from Allah's direct Presence. You felt you were in the presence of a heart being constantly filled with direct inspirations from the Absolute. You do not see many people like him in this life. It is the only way that we have for understanding the Prophet of Allah, Muhammad, peace and blessings be upon him, and likewise a true understanding of all the prophets before him, who by their Messengership and their prophethood, looked at humankind from Allah's Presence, not our own earthly reality alone, with their hearts filled to the extent of the divinely lit universe. Each one of them was a *dhikr* of God. The details came later, the revelations in words, the parables, the teachings, and the commandments. God had captured them heart and soul, and sent them back to capture us with remembrance of Him as well.

Our connection to the Prophet through remembering God is that part of our own consciousness which is the human birthright, the consciousness that knows God foremost and hindmost, from first to last. Each of our souls has a portion of prophethood—in dreams, in inspirations, and in our sense of justice or duty—though (praise be to God) we have not been burdened with the Prophet's task in its incalculable measure. It is our chance for illumination. It is our cardiac highway to the center. It is simply our direct way to the living Presence of Allah.

　　The staunch materialists remember God through negation. The scientists who insist that no God made the universe remember him by denying Him. If the materialist says that man created God out of his own insecurities, it is simply a projection of his own consciousness, perhaps a remembrance not of a Divine Reality but of the mythically proportioned Mother and Father when as a baby he saw only their care and compassion; he too is by default in a kind of negative state of divine remembrance. But is this inspiration only mechanical? Was the need for such an invention simply psychological, the panicky reaction to a separation neurosis? The reasoning for such a conclusion is sliver thin. For where the human need to invent things ends and Divine inspiration begins is a fuzzy boundary indeed. It is where worlds overlap, where dimensions of "our" consciousness and "Divine" consciousness shade into each other, and where the intricacy of disentangling one from the other is one of confusion, and ultimately of belief. Either you believe one explanation or you believe the other. And belief is very difficult to analyze, unless the fierceness of your position puts you so firmly in one camp or the other that you will not be budged by any persuasions. This is where the history of revelation takes place, on this playing (or more often battle) field, between the "refuseniks" and the believers. And why one person is of one or the other "camp" is itself a mystery. Nature and nurture are both confounded by this dilemma. Why someone with all the material gifts that life can provide is a refusenik and totally enshrouded in disbelief, while someone with absolutely nothing is a believer seeing the riches of God's illumination in every breath, is a mystery that no amount of psychological analysis can possibly explain. For every conclusion will only appeal to those of one persuasion or another.

　　Ultimately, the litmus test is in which of the two, the refusenik or the believer, is the more content. Which of the two is still filled with light and praise no matter what devastations have taken place in his or her life? Which of the two ultimately is happier in his or her universe? Which universe is an endless bounty of riches: the universe of the one who remembers God or the universe of the one who does not? The person who sees God's actions in everything that befalls him or her, or the person who does not? The person who throws all faith over when a tribulation comes to her, or the person who is increased in faith, even when home and family and livelihood are swept out to sea, as in the recent Tsunami in the Indian Ocean that wrecked the shoreline communities yet left many praying more than before and, although in trauma, affirming God's Mercy? One might say that such people were mad. But whom else but God can they turn to? If their fishing boat has been transported to the roof of their house, whose power put it there? In the midst of a terrible flu this winter when I felt like dying, I had a little insight into this state. In the midst of terrible suffering (far beyond what I was experiencing) one calls out to God. Even atheists have been known to do this. The Qur'an and the Bible both say that when people are at sea and a storm comes up that threatens their boat, they cry out to God to save them, but when they reach shore and safety they forget all about Him, and go on living their oblivious ways.

But God in the Qur'an says, "When you forget, remember." Perhaps it is that simple. It is only a matter of remembering God, but those who remember Him best are those who are purified by their remembrance, who seek Him by their actions and thoughts, who turn away from forgetfulness, and who polish the clapper of their remembrance in the bell of their hearts to make a purer sound.

Because God remembers everyone of His creation, no one is left out. Not a soul on this earth is absent from His consciousness of us. Otherwise, we would not have been born into whatever circumstances we find ourselves. Each of us who takes a breath remembers Allah. *Al-Hayy*, the Living One, breath, the sound of breathing, that thing we do last before we die, that thing that starts us once we are out of the womb, breath, upon which our words sail like boats into profanity or divinity. And how much better to speak well-shot words whose target is God than to spend our lives in the styes of pigs. Perhaps it is this simple. How much more harmonious somehow to have the Name of God on our tongues and in the moisture of our mouths than profanities and rages. And how soothingly the naming in this way cools our rages, although some use the Name of God to kill and destroy, betraying His Reality in deepest insincerity while telling themselves that they are His righteous servants.

The difference between a true person of *dhikr* and a fake one is evident, sooner or later. No wanton destruction in His Name enters history as a boon. But somehow a person of true *dhikr* of Allah who may even sit still in the shade of an arch or in the deepest recesses of *khalwa* (retreat) outlasts every historic tragedy that may befall mankind at the hands of natural disasters (God's Majesty) or at the hands of humankind itself. In Kastamonu, Turkey, in the mosque *tekke* and tomb of Shaykh Saban-i-Veli, there are little wooden closet rooms in which his disciples retreated to practice a protracted regimen of *dhikr* of Allah. The little dark rooms are empty. The practitioners are in the graveyard outside. A bit of inquiry would probably reveal more about them, their names, or some of their spiritual legacy. But even so, in the stillness of the mosque, facing these little rooms of *dhikr*, one is struck by the sheer power of their simplicity and their function. Not battlefields, which now are empty glades, hillsides, valleys, with no trace of bloodshed, only the memories of war historians, but these little dark prisons for the willing liberation of souls and hearts. A peace falls over the entire place, as if in the hush one might experience the men and women who might be behind the little doors entering the world of reality by means of their *dhikr*. And in any case, while we are alive, before we enter the already purchased grave (by the sheer destiny of our deaths), how better to pass our days than to practice the remembrance of our Creator? And when called upon to act in the world, how better to grease the castors of our actions than with His divine *dhikr?*

We are all the same, with bodies and internal organs, men and women, our consciousnesses and mental processes, not that different really from one to another, although one might be a genius and solve the Unified Theory and another might die in jail a convicted felon. But the act of remembrance of God, in whatever Path, through whatever means, even the Buddhists turning their prayer wheels, I believe, on high Himalayan peaks, these folk are in another world, parallel to this one, moving in and out of it or staying permanently within it, according to their spiritual stature.

Everyone who breathes in this atmosphere is of another order of human being, and an assurance, as long as there is one of them among us, that the world will not be wasted and its people ruined entirely. There is a *hadith* of this, of an angel about to destroy a town, but finding one person devoted to God; so God says to the angel to hold his hand from destroying it.

We need to be these people, these pivots.

One day, I came from the modern city on the opposite hill in Meknès, Morocco, after tending to some bank business—since all the banks are in the modern city across from the old walled city, in which the *zawiya* of my shaykh was situated—and was heading back to the *zawiya* to do the noon prayer and join in the *dhikr* the disciples do after the prayer, usually including a short *hadra.* As I approached the hill that crests just before you can look down into the little valley and see the alleyway in the distance that leads to the great wooden doors of the *zawiya,* I noticed a group of men sitting in a circle under a tree playing cards. They were concentrating very hard on their cards, grunting as card players do, slapping cards down in front of them, and just over their heads, in the distance, I could see the alleyway that would lead to a similar circle, but of men remembering their Lord with deep conviction and concentration, their hearts filled with devotion. This world and the next world were so vividly manifest! No judgment was implied—these card players could be saints, and the disciples in the *zawiya* rogues at heart, but the image has remained with me to this day of the different intentions and actions available in this world within the Clement Gaze of God.

Dhikr is a door that when knocked, opens. And when it becomes second nature and as much a part of our physical beings as breathing is, then it is a door that knocks *us* open. Allah *subhana wa ta'ala* (may He be glorified and exalted) says that when we do *dhikr* of Him, he does *dhikr* of us.

What a mystery, but *not* a mystery! Why have we been created in a manifest universe if not by Him Who created us to become vehicles to reflect Him back to Himself? He *subhana wa ta'ala* says in a *Hadith Qudsi* (non-Qur'anic divine saying), "I created the creation in order to be known." We are not one with Allah, but we are not separate from Him either. "The whole universe cannot contain Me, but the heart of the believer can contain Me," He says in another *Hadith Qudsi.* What separates us from Him is His utter transcendence of this entire known and unknown cosmos. However, He has sent word of Himself, or else how could I be writing this, a human born of a human into a material world, but whose spirit is really from God's world and has never been detached from it? One call and the wires tremble, the phone rings, He answers the call. And it is His Voice that answers. Our *dhikr* of Him, over and over, as the illusory celluloid of motion flashes frame by frame to give us an image of movement, aging, experience, ego-identity, and change. "He is always on a major task." It is not static, but He is not changed by change nor made static by stasis. How do I know this? Men and women much wiser than I am have alluded to this in every verbal and grammatical way they know. They are also flesh and blood, and heat and energy, and they have also engaged in *dhikr* of Allah and remembered when they forgot.

Dhikr of Allah is the only reliable shore against this world's ocean too vast to feel comfort in, too deep not to be drowned in, too shoreless and ungraspable, with every material flotsam of wood a mere splinter in majestic space. *Dhikr* of Allah gives us instead the splendid shore of the Next World, God's imperishable domain, and heaven's unfathomable dimension within our human compass. For the human compass itself is seen to pass away and only the living remembrance of Allah remains.

Dhikr connects heart and head; otherwise, the heart would be just a mechanical clock, ticking away, sooner or later to run down and leave us bereft. *Dhikr* puts a door in the heart that opens both ways, a crystal cabinet in which we can see Allah's Mercy, a small human-sized dimension in which a vast and greater-than-human dimension fits with ease—the cosmos in a ventricle, in a heartbeat, in the repetition of the Divine Names to tell, within us with our physical star-stuff, the beads of the farthest constellations.

Dhikr is wealth beyond materiality. It connects us to the ineffable, though in itself it is articulated, whether silently or aloud. Where before there was nothing, now there is something—a word, a Name for God, a phrase—and it unfreezes us, like the tiny forest frog that freezes entirely to the point of seeming dead in the fall to endure the winter, but begins spontaneously and miraculously thawing *from its heart outward* when spring arrives.

Dhikr is a rope to the shore of the next world, as much as it is a rope to this world that will not break. Paradoxically, it is also the happy drowning of itself in God's ocean.

God gave us *dhikr* of Himself. It is His gift, direct. It is even He Himself. Not "His only begotten son," to be sacrificed on untold numbers of bloody altars to leave us confounded by a triangular mystery. The *dhikr* of God in Islam is both direct and indirect. It is incorporeal, though it gives us bodies to withstand annihilation. It is annihilation in the greater dimension of God. So it is both drowning and saving.

"Do dhikr of Allah until people say you are mad," said the Prophet, may peace be upon him. Salvador Dali said, "The only difference between me and a madman is that I'm not mad." The *majdhub,* the Sufi who is "attracted" to God, is drawn magnetically, and it is beyond his power to resist either the Beauty or the Majesty of Allah. He is lost within that magnetic field. He is out of his own control. Left to God's devices in even simple things like taking a step to the right or to the left, or going up one street or another, he has become a human *dhikr* of Allah; thus one can indeed say he is mad. A shaykh of *ma'rifa* (highest recognition, highest direct knowledge of Allah) is needed to bring him out of the state of mad attraction, which is a danger to himself and anyone who comes within his radius, for another might become infected with his divine madness, and be thrown raw and nakedly unprepared into a state of direct gnosis. The way of Shaykh Abu al-Hasan al-Shadhili (d. 1258 CE), the founder of our *tariqa,* was to be outwardly sober and inwardly drunk—to experience the inner ecstasy, but to continue acting in the world with cool aplomb and responsibility.

Truly, without *dhikr* of Allah, we are lost. If our Creator created us, and did not set us down without His guidance, did not cut us loose and set us adrift, and did not disdain us and turn His back on us, but instead kept the lifeline that is our hearts always open, and pumps into it the blood of His direct Presence—if this is so, then when we remember Him we are plugged in, our rope is pulled taut to the shore, and by following it even takes us to the depths.

A great shaykh of our Path, Shaykh Ibn 'Ata'illah of Alexandria in Egypt (d. 1309 CE), said about *dhikr:* "*Dhikr* is a fire which does not stay or remain. So if it enters a house saying: 'Me and nothing other than me'—which is from the meaning of *la ilaha illa Allah*—and if there is firewood in the house, it burns it up and it becomes fire. If there is darkness in the house, it becomes light, its Light. If there is light in the house, it becomes Light upon Light."[2]

There is no lovelier thing on earth than the *dhikr* of Allah. Take me to the gardens of the Alhambra, the heights of Macchu Pichu, the Atlas mountains, or the valleys of Afghanistan carpeted with wildflowers, all of these pale in comparison before the remembrance of God. For the breeze that blows through those wildflowers is His breeze, the shining glitter atop the Atlas of snows and bright lights is His Light, the ruins of Macchu Pichu are the faint traces of His wisdom, and the gardens of the Alhambra with their fountains and esplanades and sound of rushing water are a fuzzy reflection of the Garden of Paradise in His domain, where the sound is of *dhikr* of Allah, where the air is of *dhikr* of Allah, where the fountains run with the remembrance of Him through unabated repetition of His Divine Names.

Take me to the most exalted being on earth, man or woman, filled with the greatest wisdom, a true saint, and he or she is simply an embodied *dhikr* of Allah, a remembrance made flesh, whose every gesture (and I have seen this up close) is a reminder and an awakening in the tranquil certainty of His glory.

From the biography and study by the late Martin Lings of Shaykh Ahmad al-ʿAlawi of Mostaganem, Algeria, concerning his shaykh's mystical instruction and technique of invoking the Greatest Name of Allah:

> But the course which he most often followed, and which I also followed after him, was to enjoin upon the disciple the invocation of the single Name with distinct visualization of its letters until they were written in his imagination. Then he would tell him to spread them out and enlarge them until they filled all of the horizon. The *dhikr* would continue in this form until the letters became like light. Then the Shaikh would show the way out of this standpoint—it is impossible to express in words how he did so—and by means of this indication the Spirit of the disciple would quickly reach beyond the created universe provided that he had sufficient preparation and aptitude—otherwise there would be need for purification and other spiritual training. At the above-mentioned indication the disciple would find himself able to distinguish between the Absolute and the relative, and he would see the universe as a ball or a lamp suspended in a beginningless, endless void. Then it would grow dimmer in his sight as he persevered in the invocation to the accompaniment of meditation, until it seemed no longer a definite object but a mere trace. Then it would become not even a trace, until at length the disciple was submerged in the World of the Absolute and his certainty was strengthened by Its Pure Light. In all this the Shaikh would watch over him and ask him about his states and strengthen him in the *dhikr* degree by degree until he finally reached a point of being conscious of what he perceived through his own power. The Shaikh would not be satisfied until this point was reached, and he used to quote the words of God which refer to: *"One whom his Lord hath made certain, and whose certainty He hath then followed up with direct evidence."*[3]

Abu Hurayra reported that the Messenger of Allah said, "Allah Almighty says, 'I am in My slave's opinion of Me and I am with Him when He remembers Me. When he remembers Me in himself, I mention him in Myself. If he mentions Me in an assembly, I mention him in a better assembly than them.' If he comes near to Me by a hand-span, I come near to him by a cubit. If he comes near to Me by a cubit, I come near to him by a fathom. When he comes to Me walking, I come to him running." (*Sahih al-Bukhari* and *Sahih Muslim;* the *Musnad* of Ahmad ibn Hanbal has at the end of it, "Qatada said, 'Allah is quicker to forgive.'")

Abu Saʿid al-Khudri reported that the Messenger of Allah said, "Do a lot of remembrance of Allah until they say, 'He is mad.'" (*Musnad* of Ibn Hanbal)

Abu Hurayra reported that the Messenger of Allah said, "Allah Almighty has angels who travel the highways and by-ways seeking out the people of *dhikr*. When they find people remembering Allah, the Mighty and Majestic, they call out to one another, 'Come to what you hunger for!' Then they enfold them with their wings stretching up to the lowest heaven. Their Lord—who knows them best—asks them, 'What are My slaves saying?'

They say, 'They are glorifying You, proclaiming Your greatness, praising You and magnifying You.' He says, 'Have they seen Me?' They say, 'No, by Allah, they have not seen You.' He says, 'How would it be if they were to see Me?' They say, 'If they were to see You, they would worship You even more intensely and magnify You even more intensely and glorify You even more intensely.' He says, 'What are they asking Me for?' They say, 'They are asking You for the Garden.' He says, 'Have they seen it?' They say, 'No, by Allah, they have not seen it.'" He says, 'How would it be if they were to see it?' They say, 'If they were to see it, they would yearn for it even more strongly and seek it even more assiduously and would have an even greater desire for it.' He says, 'What are they seeking refuge from?' They say, 'They are seeking refuge from the Fire.' He says, 'Have they seen it?' He says, 'How would it be if they were to see it?' They say, 'If they were to see it, they would flee from it even harder and have an even greater fear of it.' He says, 'I testify to you that I have forgiven them.' One of angels says, 'Among them is so-and-so who is not one of them. He came to get something he needed.' He says, 'They are sitting and the one sitting with them will not be wretched.'" (*Sahih al-Bukhari*)

'Amr said, "I heard the Messenger of Allah say, 'I know some words which, if a person says them truly from his heart and dies after that, he will be unlawful to the Fire: "There is no god but Allah."'" (*Sunan al-Tirmidhi*)

Umm Hani said, "The Messenger of Allah passed by me one day and I said, 'Messenger of Allah, I am old and weak, so command me something I can do sitting.' He said, 'Say "Glory be to Allah" a hundred times: it is equal to a hundred slaves of the descendants of Isma'il you set free. Say "Praise be to Allah" a hundred times: it is equal to a hundred horses saddled and bridled and ridden in the Way of Allah. Say "Allah is most great" a hundred times: it is equal to a hundred camels garlanded and facing the direction of Mecca (*al-qibla*). Say, "There is no god but Allah" a hundred times. (I think he said) this fills up what is between heaven and earth. On that day no one will have a better action presented than that which will be presented for you, unless he brings the like of what you bring.'" (*Musnad* of Ibn Hanbal)

NOTES

1. *Arabic-English Dictionary, The Hans Wehr Dictionary of Modern Written Arabic,* ed. J.M. Cowan (New York: Spoken Language Services, Inc., 1976), 310.

2. Quoted in 'Abd al-Qadir Sufi, *The Way of Muhammad* (London and San Francisco: The Diwan Press, 1975), 105.

3. Martin Lings, *A Sufi Saint of the Twentieth Century: Shaikh Ahmad al-'Alawi* (Berkeley and Los Angeles: University of California Press, 1973), 54–55.

6

There Was No One Like Him

Daniel Abdal-Hayy Moore

To say there was no one like him
   is to say
there was no one like him!

God knows best about this
   but we say
"There was no one like him."

The best way to get even a tiny glimpse of who he was
is to recall some person with extraordinary qualities
who passed by in a moment
or stayed for a season, whose
   sweet nobility awed you, or whose
spontaneous depth of knowledge,
   taken out from some
     deepsea nets whose
strings you couldn't see
       nor whose source fathom,
light after light,
load of richness,
   dredged from the deeps...

Or someone you loved whose every gesture was
   meaning, whose
    still center was a
camp of tents, in each tent a
   prince whose otherworldly
    beauty swept you away.

A snowbound romance
between two summers
whose heat melted it away
leaving only a positive memory and no
    sculptor's regret
not to have "caught it in stone," or to have
        kept it forever frozen.

Someone whose strength seemed to be
summoned from an ancient animal kingdom
against a violence of nature that flooded from nowhere,

or someone whose sudden sweetness surprised you
and made you want it to last your whole lifetime
    past the closing door down the hallway,
but who went on to a similar succession
        of such personal sweetnesses.

Or the Buddha, sitting crosswise to everything.

Or the linkage of radiances connecting its dots
    through the globe
in discrete places, in out-of-the-way
        locations—
a generosity that saved someone from drowning
or a word that turned a life all the way around—

this, these, one after the other,
commonly continuous, all of them and more,

forming a whole man in this world where everyone is a
    partial enigma jigsaw,

forming a clear focus in a
    dangerous fog,
a light standing up
    in a subway of shadows.

In a world gone galvinized tin,
    a sensitive liquid.

He was like no one.

The peaks of all possible humanness
   folded into one.

He had time for everything and everyone.

Nothing that exists kept him from
   anything else in existence.

He himself was an empty mirror, but
   the frame was the cosmos
     aflame in the dot

that sits below the letter *ba* in *Bismillah*
   —*in the Name of Allah*—
and bathes everything in light.

This is no fiction.

His Companions
   like lenses
on the same occasion
   caught sight of him the same
and recorded identical conversation
     as multiple observers,
so that a movie of him exists, walking
alone among them,
a world not gone in a burst
   once gone,
but alive forever on the transmitted
   heart screen of emptiness.

Gentle humility shook the earth's foundations
since true knowledge funneled in discs of exploding
    light through it.

Tattered poverty sent proud kings flying
since it endures after golden thrones have turned
   impossibly to dust.

Face down in the dust
the tyrant is wild-eyed.
He fears for his neck
as God's rose-thorn digs in.

But the Prophet's face down in the dust
pushed its light through the stars,
spread out in an array
that will never go away.

There was no one like him.

NOTE

This poem was first published in *Maulood*. It is reprinted here from a Zilzal Press chapbook by permission of the author.

7

A SPIRITUAL TOUR OF THE PROPHET'S CITY (MEDINA)

Daoud Stephen Casewit

It is Ramadan. I have just spent four days at the center of Islam's ritual universe. The glow of Mecca dims into the desert darkness as our car glides northwards. My next destination: the oasis sanctuary of Medina. I have accomplished the reverential visit, or *ziyara,* to the Prophet's City before, but never in such a distinguished company. Mustafa, my guide, is a leading expert on the sacred history and geography of his native Medina. Having met me in Mecca with a car and driver, he is to be my companion for the next three days.

"My brother," he says, "I am sure you know why this freeway is called Emigration Road."

Like any good teacher, Mustafa is testing me. For a Western convert, I am considered well read in the vast Arabic literature on the hallowed township.[1] However, keen to benefit from his erudition, my reply is brief. "Because the Prophet was forced to take flight from Mecca to Medina."

"Indeed," he affirms, "for thirteen years God's Messenger strove to sow the seeds of Islam in the hostile, pagan soil of Mecca. As his small group of followers grew, the persecution they faced intensified. Meanwhile, in Yathrib, as Medina was then called, the nascent faith had been embraced by an influential number of its citizens, who offered protection and refuge to the Muslims of Mecca. In the early fall of 622 CE the Prophet undertook the *hijra* ('emigration' or 'flight') to Medina, joining the *émigrés* who had preceded him.[2] In the shelter of this oasis, the vulnerable seedling of God's Final Revelation was able to take firm root, growing into a strong, unified community of believers composed of indigenous allies (*ansar*) and emigrants."

"Wasn't the emigration to Medina a religious obligation at one time?" I ask.

"Yes. In the early years, Medina was like an island of monotheistic faith and moral rectitude in a sea of polytheistic ignorance and depravity. The sacrificial act of severing ties to kin and homeland for God and His Prophet was the ultimate touchstone of sincere belief. Thus, Medina is known as The Abode of Emigration (*Dar al-Hijra*) and The Abode of Faith (*Dar al-Iman*). However, following the conquest of Mecca in 630 CE and the submission of Arabia's tribes, the *hijra* to Medina lost its imperative nature. Indeed, given the city's inability to support endless waves of new inhabitants, emigration was actually discouraged. Henceforth, increased emphasis was placed on its profound connotations of personal effort in the Way of God and living in conformity with the practice of the Prophet Muhammad."[3]

Meditating on Mustafa's words, it occurs to me that the timeless implications of the emigration might still have a bearing on my present journey. "But isn't it true, my brother, that the Messenger of God permitted some new converts to make a vow of a limited-term emigration to Medina?"

"There are some recorded examples of this. Such provisional residence in Medina enabled new Muslims to deepen their knowledge and practice of Islam. It also allowed them to imbibe the sanctity and wisdom of the Prophet and to be inspired by the example of his luminary companions."

Summoning my courage, I suggest, "Could the *ziyara* to Medina be considered a temporary emigration?"

"I have never quite looked at it in that way," Mustafa admits. After a few moments, he remarks, "Perhaps one could think of your question in light of the famous *hadith* (saying) of the Prophet:

> Verily actions will be judged by God according to the intentions behind them, and verily a man will have a reward for what he intends. So whoever's emigration is for the sake of God and His Messenger, his emigration will be counted for the sake of God and His Messenger; and whoever's emigration was for the sake of some worldly gain or for a woman he wishes to marry, then his emigration will be counted for the sake of that for which he emigrated."[4]

Gratified by his response, I take further inspiration from a verse in the Qur'an, which speaks of believers "fleeing unto God and His Prophet" (Qur'an 4:100). For me, the past days spent in Mecca have been a means of seeking refuge in God. I pray that He will accept my sojourn in Medina as a mode of emigration to His Prophet.

A few minutes later, Mustafa speaks again, "Tonight we should complete this 420 kilometer trip in less than four hours. Not so long ago it used to take up to two weeks by caravan. For centuries, countless generations of pilgrims braved the hardships and perils of this overland trek to Medina. In our age, millions of Muslims travel to the sanctuary every year. Since the *ziyara* is not, legally speaking, an obligatory component of the Greater or Lesser Pilgrimage, what is it that continues to motivate the believers to visit the Prophet's City?"

Suspecting that his question is only rhetorical, I nevertheless respond, "Love of the Prophet."

"No doubt," he nods. "As the Messenger of God once said, 'Not one of you truly believes unless I am more beloved to him than his father and son and all of humanity.'[5] This devoted affection naturally manifests itself in an ardent desire to visit the Prophet's tomb in Medina. The word *ziyara* itself implies the visitation of a grave. However the basis of this motivation in Islamic law is controversial. Some scholars have argued that the only admissible intention for traveling to Medina is to pray in the Prophet's Mosque, after which it is highly recommended to offer salutations at his grave. Among the Prophet's reported sayings that support this reasoning is one which states that there are only three mosques which justify a long journey to worship in them: that of Mecca, his own mosque in Medina, and the al-Aqsa Mosque in Jerusalem."[6]

Muslim theologians and jurists have written tomes about the contentious question of what constitutes a legitimate intention for traveling to the City of the Prophet. Ultimately, their opinions are based on divergent emphases on the transcendent and immanent aspects of God. The Muslim Testimony of Faith (*al-Shahada*) embraces both by declaring the truth of God's absolute oneness as well as the status of the Prophet Muhammad as His Messenger.

"Yet it is extraordinary," Mustafa continues, "that Medina shelters the only burial place of God's many prophets that can be unmistakably identified. The fact that the Messenger is interred in its hallowed soil is viewed by some as the most peerless of the city's distinguishing virtues.[7] A couple of traditions of the Prophet indicate that each of us is made of the specific earth in which our bodies will eventually be buried.[8] Thus, the Prophet, the Best of God's Creation, is of the same substance as the blessed dust of Medina. Some have argued that this unique distinction renders Medina superior to any other spot on earth, including Mecca. Not all scholars accept this conclusion, but none would contest that the city is unrivaled in the number of Prophetic references to the special spiritual blessing (*baraka*) it embodies, especially localizations of Paradisiacal grace."

After a few minutes, Mustafa resumes. "As with Mecca, Medina's status as a holy sanctuary carries with it a number of legal restrictions. My brother, do you know what any of these are?"

I venture a partial reply. "I believe that it is not permitted to hunt game within its precincts."

Glancing at me approvingly, Mustafa cites several other prohibitions, including bearing arms with hostile intent, damaging its trees, and transporting rocks or soil outside of its boundaries. He then falls silent and I drift off to sleep.

I am awakened an hour later as we pull into a brightly lit truck stop. It is 2:30 AM in the morning; time to take our final meal. Soon we are eating and sipping tea in a simple coffee house. Our joint repast allows me to study my companions more closely. Mustafa's serene face shows few signs of age, but his wispy grey beard suggests he is in his sixties. His dignified comportment bespeaks an upbringing in which piety and propriety were the unquestioned norm. Our driver, Ahmed, is Pakistani. With his handsome smile and jet-black hair, he looks to be about 35. In pidgin dialectical Arabic, he tells me he has been working as a Medina-based chauffeur for 10 years. After our meal, we offer the predawn prayer with other clientele in an adjoining room where a rudimentary, hand-painted arch on the southern wall indicates the direction of Mecca.

After driving for about 45 minutes, a distinctively Saudi road-sign flashes past. Like those on the outskirts of Mecca, it bars non-Muslims from pro-ceeding toward the sacred territory, instructing them to take the next exit to a detour road. We come to a checkpoint, where our identification papers are checked. Soon we are moving again in a roughly northeasterly direction and I eagerly scan the landscape for a glimpse of our destination. To our right a jagged mountain is etched against the eastern sky, which grows brighter by the minute. As we pass beyond the rocky curtain, the morning sun is just breaching the horizon. Spread out beneath it is the legendary, forbidden City of the Prophet, *Madinat al-Nabi*.

Halting at the side of the road, we emerge to take in the full panorama. In the heart of the sprawling patchwork of white and green, I can make out the minarets of the Prophet's Mosque. The sight fills me with inexpressible joy. I exclaim, "May God shower His blessings and benedictions upon His Envoy Muhammad!" Mustafa then draws my attention to several prominent land-marks. Gesturing to center left, he points out a solitary massif at Medina's northern flank. "That is Mount Uhud," he explains, "which lies just within the sanctuary's boundary in that direction." Then, pointing to our right, he says, "The southern limit of the sacred territory extends to the base of that other peak, which is called Jabal 'Ayr. Some Prophetic traditions depict these two mountains as antipodes. While Jabal Uhud is a blessed mountain of Paradise that loves us and is loved by us, Jabal 'Ayr is described as a cursed mountain of Hell that detests us and is detested by us."[9]

Mustafa looks at me, as if to gauge my reaction. "This may sound irrational in our age, but we must remember that the Prophet's perception embraced the spiritual dimensions of both time and space. In Medina, he gave voice to numerous supernatural observations, especially those related to divine *bar-aka*, which is so abundant here." He then points out the course of a dry streambed to our left. "An example of this is Wadi al-'Aqiq. When the Prophet prayed there he felt an exceptional celestial presence and referred to it as *al-Wadi al-Mubarak* (the Blessed Valley).[10] The large mosque you see nearby is where the people of Medina don the pilgrim's garb and make the vows of pilgrimage to Mecca."

Motioning toward a dark expanse east of Wadi al-'Aqiq, Mustafa observes, "That lava tract, called Harrat al-Wabra, marks the western perimeter of the sanctuary. Harrat Waqim, a larger plain of volcanic rock, defines its limit to the east. The two lava tracts merge to the south of the oasis of Medina. Because the sharp, rough surface of this basalt terrain is almost impossible for loaded camels or mounted warhorses to traverse, it provided Medina with a natural defensive barrier on three sides. For this reason, armies or caravans coming from Mecca or the coast usually followed the sandy bottom of Wadi al-'Aqiq northward to a point just southwest of Mount Uhud, from where they could advance southward across a saline plain towards the city. The armies of the Quraysh twice attempted to attack Medina by means of this route."[11]

"Wouldn't the city have been protected by its fortified walls?" I ask, now doing a bit of testing myself. I am aware that the common image of Medina as a walled stronghold has virtually nothing to do with the actual layout of the city in the Prophet's time.

"No," Mustafa replies. "The first city walls weren't constructed until more than two-and-a-half centuries after the Prophet's death. During his lifetime, the Prophet's mosque and the residential quarter around it constituted the nucleus of the oasis, but most of the inhabitants lived in widely dispersed farming settlements according to tribal affiliation, including several indigenous Jewish clans. Each settlement had one or more fortified communal keeps to which residents retired in times of conflict."

Mustafa then points toward the suburb of Quba, whose celebrated mosque gleams white among date palm gardens. "Because of its relative elevation, the southern area of Medina is often referred to as *al-'Aliya* (the Heights).[12] The northern zone, including the district around the Prophet's Mosque, is called *al-Safila* (the Lowlands). The south-to-north inclination determines the flow of rare surface water and also that of underground channels, which feed the wells of the oasis. When there is a heavy rain, several rivulets drain off the surrounding lava plains, eventually merging into a major torrent bed that traverses the entire length of Medina. Called Wadi Buthan, this gulley was described by the Prophet as lying upon one of the channels of Paradise."[13]

With that final reminder of the heavenly nature of Medina, we continue driving eastward toward the city. "The Prophet and Abu Bakr (d. 634 CE), his faithful friend and disciple," Mustafa says, "descended near here after their miraculous escape from Mecca. Their arrival was the cause of great rejoicing among the Muslims. They stayed in Quba for a number of days, and the Prophet participated in the construction of its mosque."

We exit right and turn northward in the shadow of the magnificent prayer hall of the mosque of Quba. "When the Prophet departed Quba in search of a more permanent place of local residence," Mustafa continues, "each settlement he passed through beseeched him to reside with them. But the Messenger of God told them that his undirected she-camel was under God's Command. The Prophet only stopped when it was time for the noon prayer. It was Friday, and on that occasion he led the first public congregational prayer and sermon." Mustafa points out a mosque to our right, built at the historic spot, and continues, "Then he again let his camel wander until it finally kneeled at the location where he was to build his mosque and adjoining dwellings." Looking ahead, still some distance away, I behold the green dome of the Prophet's Mosque.

The *ziyara* to Medina is governed by traditional protocol and, obviously, I must begin with the Prophet's Mosque. But first I stop at my hotel, where I perform ritual ablutions and change into clean robes. Half an hour later, Mustafa and I set out on foot across the vast, marble-decked esplanade surrounding the sanctuary. For well over a millennium, the mosque was nestled in dense residential quarters behind fortified walls, but beginning in the late 1970s, these were gradually razed. By the late 1980s bulldozers had demolished the last vestiges of the old city to allow for the mosque's unprecedented expansion and the radical reconfiguration of its environs. It saddens me to think of all the historic sites that were permanently erased, but, given the unprecedented numbers of pilgrims that now converge on Medina, the Saudi authorities probably had few options.

As a Saudi citizen, Mustafa evinces an understandable pride in the most recent expansion of the Prophet's Mosque, which he often simply refers to as *al-Haram,* the Sanctuary. The floor space of the gargantuan prayer hall is five times greater than the older structure, making it the second largest mosque in the world after Mecca. When the roof and the paved surface around it are used, up to a million Muslims can pray together here simultaneously. The nine-year project was personally inaugurated in 1984 by the late King Fahd, whose honorific title, "Custodian of the Two Holy Sanctuaries," is indicative of the immense prestige attached to the Kingdom's guardianship of Mecca and Medina.

At the southwestern entrance of Bab al-Salam, the Portal of Salutation and Peace, we place our footwear in cubbyholes at the door. Pausing, Mustafa reminds me of the Qur'anic verse urging the believers not to raise their voices above that of the Prophet (Qur'an 73:2–4). He then whispers, "According to a hadith, Prophets continue to be conscious in their graves, so let us speak only in hushed voices inside."[14] As we enter, we utter the time-honored formula, "Peace be upon you, Oh Prophet of God, and God's Mercy and Blessings! Oh God, forgive me my sins and open for me the doors of Your Mercy!"

Before us is a long passage through a section of the mosque dating back to the Ottoman reconstruction of 1860. To our left is a low brass work partition, beyond which lies the main prayer hall. To our right, facing Mecca is the lavishly ornamented southern wall. It is adorned with three superimposed calligraphic bands of Qur'anic verse. Below these runs a row of square frames, inscribed with names and titles of the Prophet, including Beloved of God, Mercy unto the Worlds, and Key of Paradise. These alternate with circular medallions, which read, "May God bless him and grant him peace." With every forward stride, my longing to greet the Prophet swells more intensely in my breast. Suddenly, Mustafa takes my arm and directs me through an opening in the low barrier on our left. "Let us now perform the two cycles of prayer in ritual greeting of the mosque," he instructs me. Just as the Muslim affirmation of God's unity precedes the attestation of Muhammad's function as His Messenger, our first devotional act, even here, should be worship of the One, the Transcendent Divine Being.

As we advance eastward, the color of the lush carpets beneath our bare feet changes from red to white, signaling that we are now within the sanctum of the *Rawda* (Garden). According to numerous traditions, this area of the mosque, extending from the Prophet's house, where he died and was interred, to his *minbar* (pulpit), is one of the gardens of Paradise.[15] A few paces ahead of us is an ornate, free-standing marble prayer niche, erected at the spot where the Prophet would lead his followers in worship. Before we worship, Mustafa reminds me of the tradition stating that a prayer in this mosque is superior to a thousand prayers observed elsewhere, with the exception of the Great Mosque at Mecca.[16] At that point we offer individual prayers. In the final kneeling position, the air around me seems to pulsate with an inexplicably benevolent presence, as if gently stirred by the beating of angels' wings. I conclude my devotions with the customary salutations of peace. "*As-Salamu 'alaykum*," I utter, turning to my right and then again to my left, where my gaze falls upon the Noble Burial Chamber of God's Most Honored Envoy.

It is there that Mustafa now escorts me. We move forward through the *Rawda* and, passing beyond the partition, turn left into a crowded vestibule between the tomb enclosure and the southern wall. A Qur'anic verse on a nearby ornamental plaque commands: "Verily God and His Angels shower blessings upon the Prophet. Oh you who believe, call down blessings upon him and greet him with salutations of peace (Qur'an 73:56)." At this point, Mustafa performs the most important service of a *ziyara* guide by leading me in the recitation of the time-honored salutations and prayers that are made at the tomb of the Prophet Muhammad. It is an inspirational moment of pure verticality, for we are literally joining God and His angels in blessing the Prophet:

> Peace be unto you, oh magnanimous noble leader and prodigious Messenger, gentle and compassionate. May the Mercy of God and His Blessings be upon you! Peace be unto you, oh Prophet of God! Peace be unto you, oh purest of God's Creation! Peace be unto you, oh beloved of God! I testify that there is no god but Allah, alone and without associate, and that you are His devoted servant and His Envoy. I testify that you have delivered the Message and completed your mission, and that you have given good counsel to the community of believers and striven in the path of God. May God then shower you with permanent blessings until the Day of Judgment. Our Lord, grant us the Good in this lower world and the Good in the Hereafter and preserve us from the punishment of Hellfire. Oh God, grant him every favor and the supreme merit,

and grant him the loftiest status and resurrect him to the praiseworthy station, which You have promised him. Verily You are not one to break Your promise.[17]

Despite the throngs of people surrounding the Prophet's tomb, the feeling that one gets in the vicinity of God's Messenger is one of extreme intimacy and affection. In this spot, one stands in front of the Prophet, who lies on his right side facing Mecca. The Messenger reportedly said that when someone greets him in his grave, God returns his spirit to him so that he may hear and personally return the greeting.[18] The ardor of the subdued voices all around reminds me of a well-known hadith, which relates how a Bedouin once entered the mosque and asked the Messenger of God when the Final Hour would come. The Prophet responded, "Woe unto you! What have you done to prepare yourself for it?" Admitting that he had not accomplished much, the man stressed his love for God and His Messenger. At this the Prophet reassured him, saying "Verily you will be included [in heaven] among those you have loved." At this, the other Muslims present asked if the Prophet's promise also applied to them. When the Prophet replied affirmatively, their happiness was boundless.[19]

Besides a feeling of intimacy and affection, the atmosphere around the Prophet's tomb is also charged with profound deference and humility. In the presence of the Prophet, who will be the principal intercessor for his followers on Judgment Day, I am painfully aware of my own failings and unworthiness. During the Messenger's lifetime, the Qur'an urged believers to come to him after having committed transgressions in order that he might entreat God's forgiveness for them (Qur'an 94:63). Thus, for me and for many other visitors, this blessed encounter with the Messenger of God is also an opportunity to address fervent pleas to the Prophet to mediate on our behalf with God. In the view of the Wahhabi scholars of Saudi Arabia, this traditional practice is viewed as unacceptable and even bordering on idolatry. Stern guards are posted here to make sure that we do not raise our hands in supplication toward the tomb, or attempt to touch or kiss the enclosure around it.

Mustafa then ushers me a couple of steps further eastward, where we recite greetings and benedictions at the tomb of the Prophet's close friend Abu Bakr al-Siddiq, whose epithet means "The True Believer." After the Messenger's death, Abu Bakr held the office of Commander of the Faithful (*Amir al-Mu'minin*, the official title of the Caliph of the Islamic state) for two years before his own death. The hallowed chamber where Abu Bakr is buried was part of the dwelling belonging to his daughter 'A'isha (d. 678 CE), the Prophet's favorite wife. Two or three paces further, we pay our respects at the tomb of 'Umar ibn al-Khattab (d. 644 CE), the second of the Rightly Guided Caliphs, whose strength of character and integrity were legendary. His 10-year rule was cut short by an assassin's knife while leading the prayer only a few meters away in this mosque.

Having performed the most essential rites of *ziyara,* I am led around the enclosure of the tomb chamber back toward the main prayer hall. As we walk, Mustafa whispers, "Both the original mosque and the adjoining houses of the Prophet's wives were built of the most rustic materials. The walls were of unfired mud brick. Date tree trunks served as columns and were split for beams to support a roof made of layered palm branches and covered with earth. Over its long history, the mosque has been enlarged and renovated many times by successive rulers. Twice it was destroyed by fire, and it had to be entirely rebuilt. But with each reconstruction, the position of the original columns, along with the location of the Prophet's places of prayer and pulpit, were carefully preserved. And with each expansion the names and relative locations of historic doorways were also maintained."

Within the precincts of the *Rawda,* Mustafa points out several historic columns clad in white marble. Among them is The Pillar of Delegations, at whose base the Prophet sat when receiving representatives of Arabian tribes who came to swear their allegiance to him following the conquest of Mecca. Another is The Casting of Lots Pillar, before which the Prophet showed a marked preference for offering voluntary, individual prayers. Concerning the name of this column, the Prophet once said that if people realized the special grace that is to be found in worshipping at that spot, they would cast lots for the privilege.[20] In this most prized place of devotion, I wait my turn to offer a supererogatory prayer.

We then approach the intricately carved and gilded white marble pulpit (*minbar*). Dating from the late sixteenth century, its arched doorway gives way to a tall set of railed steps leading to dais housed in an ornamental pillared turret. The Prophet's original *minbar,* destroyed in the great fire of 1256 CE, was a kind of raised wooden armchair mounted on two steps. In many traditions, it is depicted as standing astride the Prophet's water basin (*hawd*) in Paradise, from which he will dispense to the blessed a drink that will forever banish all thirst.[21] Mustafa recounts the wondrous story of the pulpit's first use. "For several years the Messenger of God delivered the Friday sermon standing on this spot, occasionally supporting himself on the trunk of a date palm erected there for that purpose. When his fatigue became more apparent, he agreed to have a pulpit constructed for him. When he first ascended it, the assembled congregation was astonished to hear the palm trunk begin to moan like a she camel yearning for her offspring. It continued to moan until the Messenger came down from the pulpit and embraced it."[22]

Moving northward through the colonnaded hall, we enter a wide court-yard. Here the sun's light and heat are refracted through six enormous, but elegant, fabric umbrellas, installed during the latest expansion project. "The original Mosque of the Prophet also had a courtyard," Mustafa explains. "Besides being an extension of the prayer space, it was used for other communal purposes. To its rear was a small shaded area, which served as a shelter for indigent male immigrants and occasional groups of visitors.

As a result of living here in such close proximity to the Prophet, a number of these companions became leading scholars."

The shaded court suddenly echoes with the amplified, melodious call for the midday prayer. The space around us quickly fills up with men attired in a diverse range of traditional dress. The screened-off women's section to our distant left is no doubt witness to a similar scene. When the second, final call to prayer sounds, we coalesce into long, orderly lines for worship. Afterward, as we exit, Mustafa proposes that I return to my hotel for a brief siesta. Suddenly feeling light-headed in the glaring midday sun, I happily submit to his suggestion.

Later, after the mid-afternoon prayer, I meet Mustafa at the southeast corner of the *Haram*. A brief stroll eastward across the geometrically patterned plaza brings us to the gates of Islam's most hallowed cemetery, *Baqi' al-Gharqad,* said to shelter the remains of more than 10,000 of the Prophet's venerable companions. "The Prophet" Mustafa tells me, "made a regular habit of visiting this graveyard late in the night and he would say, 'Peace be upon you, house of the believing folk. Coming upon you is that which you were promised, soon at a time decreed. And verily, God willing, we will be joining you. O God! Forgive the people of Baqi' al-Gharqad!'"[23]

Inside the cemetery, I am struck by the austerity of the vast expanse. Less than a hundred years ago, the tombs of its most illustrious personages were adorned with domed mausoleums and ornate headstones. In 1925, after conquering Medina, the forces of the Saudi King 'Abd al-'Aziz obliterated all of these funerary structures. Like their Wahhabi predecessors, who had flattened the graveyard in 1805, these puritan warriors ascribed to the reformist doctrines of the theologian Muhammad ibn 'Abd al-Wahhab (d. 1792), from whose name the term "Wahhabi" derives. While this demolition of tombs was and continues to be decried as a shameless desecration by many Muslims worldwide, the perpetrators saw it as an enforcement of a legal prohibition against the building of raised structures on Muslim tombs. From their uncompromisingly literalist perspective, they were simply doing their righteous duty in eradicating inadmissible innovations and objects of reverence that detracted from the worship of the One, utterly Transcendent God. Though I am sympathetic with the pious intentions of those who had erected the beautiful burial monuments that once stood here, I am forced to admit that the barren, bone-littered terrain now before me does serve to emphasize one of the principal reasons the Prophet encouraged Muslims to visit graveyards: the remembrance of death.

Beginning with the members of the Prophet's family, we recite salutations and prayers at each major gravesite. First, I am led to the graves of eight of the Prophet's wives, referred to collectively as "Mothers of the Believers." Then we visit the resting place of three of the Messenger's daughters, Ruqayya, Zaynab, and Umm Kulthum. Next we move to an area, once covered by a large cupola, where several of his most eminent kinfolk are interred. These include his revered daughter Fatima (d. 632 CE). Her marriage to the Prophet's cousin 'Ali (d. 661 CE) produced al-Hasan (d. 669 CE) and al-Husayn (d. 680 CE), from whose loins issued the entire lineage of the Prophet's descendents. Al-Hasan's blessed body lies nearby. The same spot shelters a paternal uncle of the Prophet, al-'Abbas (d. 653 CE), whose progeny founded the 'Abbasid Dynasty in 750 CE. Here, too, is the revered tomb of Imam Ja'far al-Sadiq (d. 765 CE), a great-great-grandson of the Prophet through al-Husayn, and a central figure for both Imami and Ismaili Shiites. Further on, Mustafa guides me to the burial spot of Imam Malik ibn Anas (d. 798 CE), founder of one of the four great schools of Sunni jurisprudence. At a surprising distance from the graves of his contemporaries, is the tomb of the third Rightly Guided Caliph, 'Uthman ibn 'Affan. In 656 CE, he was murdered by rebels, who prevented his interment next to the Prophet or even in the main cemetery. Instead, he was buried in a small garden, which was incorporated into the enlarged graveyard by his clansmen after they had established the Umayyad Caliphate.

Retracing our steps to the entrance, we turn and offer final general benedictions and salutations to the folk of *al-Baqi'*. "According to a hadith," Mustafa tells me, "those buried here will be the first to be resurrected after the Prophet on the Day of Judgment.[24] God's Messenger also encouraged all those who have the possibility of dying in Medina to do so, promising to intercede for them."[25]

The declining sun shines in our faces as we head back to the *Haram*. To the north, Mount Uhud glows in hues of pink and purple. The polished deck ahead of us has been transformed into a ritual picnic space. Countless rows of people are seated at long sheets of plastic laid out with provisions to break the fast of Ramadan. The benefactors at each makeshift table implore passersby to join them for the sunset supper. Mustafa exchanges familiar greetings with many of his fellow townsmen, but politely moves on. Inside the mosque, the same scene repeats itself. After much effort we reach a spot in the crowded *Rawda*, where Mustafa's brother has saved two places for us at his breakfast spread. Greeting him warmly and offering salutations to those around us, we take our seats on the carpeted floor. Hailing from diverse corners of the Islamic World, most of our table companions speak no common language. However, they are unified by the common bond of faith and by the generosity of our host, who in the spirit of the Helpers (*al-Ansar*), the people of Medina who provided shelter and support for the Prophet and his Companions, provides for us in the hope of otherworldly recompense. Together we wait patiently for the *muezzin* to signal sunset and permission to still the thirst and hunger each of us feels. It is a moment to be cherished, for beyond this holy place and this holy time, the community of the faithful is, alas, often more of an ideal than a reality.

"*Allahu akbar*, God is Most Great," sounds the call to prayer. Parched lips murmur the traditional formula of consecration, and fingers reach for dates

laid out before us. This is followed by a sip of water, which Mustafa reminds
me is brought from the blessed well of Zam Zam in Mecca. A cup of
unsweetened Arabian coffee is then pressed into my hand. Made from
unroasted beans and flavored with cardamom, it is light green in color.
Bread and more water, coffee and dates are passed around. The dignified
atmosphere reflects the ritual nature of this fleeting feast. "*Allahu akbar,*"
the second call rings out. Almost instantaneously, utensils and uneaten food
are packed away, plastic sheeting is rolled up and lines for prayer are formed.
I find myself standing between an Indonesian and a Nigerian and together we
worship the Sustainer of Creation.

When the prayer is finished, Mustafa goes home to take a more substantial
meal with his family, and I to dine at my hotel. An hour later, I return and
find a place in an arcade at the rear of the foremost courtyard for the evening
prayer. With the giant umbrellas now retracted, I have a splendid view of a
classic image of the Prophet's Mosque: the Green Dome superimposed upon
the main southeast minaret. The majestic cupola above the Prophet's burial
chamber was rebuilt by an Ottoman Caliph in 1817. The finely contoured
tower to its left was erected in the late fifteenth century at the command of
a great Sultan of Mamluke Egypt.

Following the prayer service, I remain with nearly all those around me
to participate in the prolonged cycles of communal, supererogatory prayer
particular to Ramadan. Each night of the holy month, in mosques throughout the world, successive sections of the entire Qur'an are recited during
these devotions. It is especially rewarding to take part in this observance in
Medina, where the greater part of the Muslim scripture was revealed. It is said
that Medina alone was "conquered by the Qur'an," while other realms
were conquered by the sword. For the next hour, I immerse myself in the
powerful, cleansing stream of God's words, punctuated by the self-effacing
movements of prayer with my fellow Muslims.

I sleep briefly but well that night and rise at 2:30 AM to take a light meal,
before heading to the Prophet's Mosque. After the predawn prayer, I rendez-
vous with Mustafa at one of the rear doors. Our stroll to the car takes us
through a complex of hotels and shopping areas. In shops that never seem
to close, merchants are doing a brisk business in pilgrim goods, including
Qur'ans in a variety of sizes and styles, prayer manuals, prayer carpets and
prayer beads, and Medina dates. The economies of both Mecca and Medina
continue to depend heavily upon their spiritual tourists, who are expected
to return home with gifts and souvenirs. Both sanctuary cities have become
massive commercial clearinghouses for everything from jewelry and perfume
to electronic goods and textiles.

The sky has begun to visibly brighten as we set off northwards to visit the
Graves of the Martyrs at Uhud. As we drive, Mustafa provides background
commentary: "In 625 CE, a Quraysh army of 3,000 warriors, keen to avenge
their bitter defeat at the Battle of Badr the previous year, had advanced from

Mecca and was encamped just southwest of Mount Uhud. After consulting his companions, the Prophet decided to confront the enemy near their camp. So in the dead of night, the Muslim force of about 800 men marched out in the same direction we are moving now."

Halting before a spacious cove at the foot of Mount Uhud, we proceed on foot to the barred gate of the graveyard. Seventy Muslim heroes were killed during this battle, the most celebrated being the Prophet's uncle Hamza, who was known as "The Lion of God" for his great courage and martial skill. "The Prophet used to visit these graves regularly and pray for the martyrs," Mustafa says. He then recites a Qur'anic verse, "And do not imagine that those killed in the path of God are dead, nay they are alive and are receiving provisions with their Lord" (Qur'an 3:169). After offering salutations and benedictions for the martyrs of Uhud, we climb a low hill called The Archers' Mount just south of the graveyard. Above us looms the granite mass of Mount Uhud. Behind us runs the westward course of the dry streambed of Wadi Qana.

Looking down upon the ancient battlefield, Mustafa recounts its principal phases:[26] "The Prophet assigned this strategic spot to about fifty archers, with orders to remain here at all costs to protect the rear and southern flank of his main force from the superior Quraysh cavalry. The main Muslim army was positioned in the center, there, with their backs to the slope of Uhud and facing the enemy's infantry, who stood in formation over there to the left. Despite being outnumbered more than three to one, the holy warriors soon gained the upper hand. Pursued by the prematurely triumphant Muslim soldiers, the Meccans fled in disarray toward their encampment. Seeing this and ignoring the pleas of their commander, the majority of the archers stationed here then abandoned their posts to join in pursuit of the enemy. It was then that the tide of battle turned, as the adversary's horsemen were able to come around the south of this hillock and attack the believers from behind. In the ensuing confusion, the Prophet was injured and was even rumored to have been killed. Many Muslims were slain, while others fled to Medina. A stalwart group gathered around the Messenger and, defending him with selfless courage and tenacity, gradually retreated up that gorge to the safety of higher ground. When the enemy finally retreated, the Prophet descended from Mount Uhud to find that the bodies of the fallen Muslims had been mutilated vindictively. He then ordered graves to be dug here, and led the funeral prayer for all of them."

Spellbound by Mustafa's narrative, I linger on the hilltop meditating on the supreme importance God gives to the intentions behind our acts. In particular, I think of the illuminating tales of two men slain that day. One of them, a native of Medina, had resisted all attempts to convert him to Islam until the eve of the battle, when his heart was suddenly penetrated by faith. Taking up his arms, he had made his way alone to Uhud, where he fought until he was mortally wounded. Recognized by his fellow tribesmen, he told them of his conversion and died in their arms. He is known as the Muslim who entered Paradise without ever having made a single prostration to God.[27] Another man who fought with tremendous bravery and ferocity was also found breathing his last. Those around him comforted him with tidings of a martyr's reward, upon which he insisted that his sole motivation had been to bring honor to his tribe. Then, when his pain became unbearable, he took an arrow from his quiver and killed himself. The Prophet later declared him one of the people in Hellfire, as taking one's own life is forbidden in the strongest terms in Islam.[28]

Mustafa has already begun to pick his way back down the hill and I follow him solemnly. A growing number of visitors now throng the gate of the hallowed cemetery. Above them a large sign in several languages sternly warns against engaging in any prohibited devotional acts. It is curious how this dogmatic zeal to uphold God's transcendence can lead to an indifference—almost an aversion—to the *baraka*, the spiritual blessing, of sacred sites. Alas, I cannot help but notice how the strict guardians of the faith in Arabia, who sanctioned the destruction of the mausoleum over Hamza's grave, have allowed much of this sanctified battlefield to become clustered with ugly cinderblock dwellings and strewn with trash.

As we begin driving back toward Medina, Mustafa points northwest toward the confluence of Medina's three main riverbeds. "There are a couple of traditions about the Last Days, which prophesy that the *Dajjal* (a sort of Islamic Anti-Christ) will establish his camp on the plain there, which lies just outside the boundary of Medina's sanctuary. While many of the city's inhabitants will join him, he will be prevented from entering the sacred territory by armed angels."[29]

After crossing the western lava tract, we soon reach the Mosque of Quba. Reconstructed in the early 1980s, its monumental walls are crenellated and each of its four corners is marked by a commanding minaret. "After the *Haram,* this is the most important mosque in Medina," Mustafa notes. "According to many traditions, those who perform their ritual ablutions and come here with the sole intention of praying will have the reward of performing the lesser pilgrimage (the *'Umra* pilgrimage) to Mecca.[30] The Prophet reportedly came here to pray on a weekly basis." We enter the eastern door of the mosque and pass through a lovely arcaded courtyard before turning left to pray beneath the lofty domes of the main prayer hall.

Mustafa then rises and exchanges friendly greetings with an elderly caretaker. After he introduces me, the three of us walk to the rear of the mosque. At the northwest corner Mustafa's compatriot unlocks a small door. "We are going to the top of the minaret," Mustafa tells me. The narrow stairwell winds around and around. An occasional window and the view from an intermediary gallery reveal our increasing altitude. Finally, we reach the topmost balcony, where we are rewarded by a breathtaking panorama of the entire oasis.

"*Al-hamdu li-Llah,*" Mustafa exclaims. "Praise be to God, you have now visited the four most universally recommended visiting-places (*mazarat*) of Medina. However, as you know, Medina comprises many other places of reverential visitation linked to the life of God's Messenger. While not all scholars encourage visiting these secondary sites, to my mind they constitute precious landmarks in the sacred history of the Prophet's city. From very early times they have been a traditional part of the complete itinerary of *ziyara.*"

Looking northward toward the city center, Mustafa continues. "In the time of the Prophet, Muslims from throughout the oasis of Medina would congregate at the *Haram* for the weekly Friday prayers. However, for the regular daily prayers, inhabitants normally worshipped in smaller tribal mosques, like this one, closer to their dwellings and gardens. God's Messenger prayed in most of these communal mosques. He is also reported to have worshipped in many open-air locations in Medina, especially in the course of military campaigns. In the early eighth century CE, an Umayyad Caliph ordered that commemorative stone mosques be built at all the places where the Prophet's blessed forehead touched the ground in prostration. Historical sources mention more than fifty such shrines, of which the location and identity of only about twenty are known today. God willing, we shall be visiting some of the most important ones."

Then pointing down to the west of our dizzying perch, Mustafa tells me, "Buried beneath the street down there is the Well of Aris, from whose water the Messenger is said to have drunk and purified himself. Its more famous name is Well of the Ring, in reference to an incident in the life of 'Uthman ibn 'Affan. As third caliph, he had inherited the Prophet's silver seal ring from the Caliph 'Umar, who had it from the Caliph Abu Bakr. One day, while he was sitting at the rim of this well, the treasured band slipped from his hand and fell into the well. Though the well was dug for three days in search of it, the ring was never found.[31] Until only recently it was a prominent landmark to which pilgrims flocked to drink its blessed water."

It is almost noon as we head to the Mosque of the Friday Prayer, which we had passed on the first day. After performing the ritual salutation of the mosque, we wait to observe the midday prayer in congregation. Leaning against a column, I watch as fellow Muslims of every conceivable ethnic and racial description stream in. My own blue-eyed and fair-haired presence turns not a single head. Both Mecca and Medina offer a welcome respite from the well-intentioned questions and attention I would inevitably attract in most any other Islamic country. Soon the call to prayer brings all people to their feet and we follow the Imam in worship.

I emerge weary and thirsty from the air-conditioned mosque. Outside, the October sun hammers down on the softened asphalt. Noticing the beads of sweat forming on my brow, Mustafa relates a hadith in which the Prophet promises to be a witness or an intercessor for those who patiently bear the rigors of Medina's climate.[32] I am gratified but am glad when Mustafa proposes that I now return to my hotel to rest.

After an hour's nap, I proceed to the *Haram* alone for the mid-afternoon prayer. Throughout the older prayer hall are groups of men seated around teachers giving lessons in various branches of religious science. The Messenger of God once said that whoever enters his mosque to learn or teach good things is like the holy warrior on the path of God.[33] Since its foundation more than 14 centuries ago, the Prophet's Mosque has been a vibrant center of religious education. Nearly all of the great early scholars of Islam spent periods in Medina, a preeminent halting place for those who traveled in search of knowledge. The function of the mosque in this respect is highlighted in an exquisite anecdote describing how the famed Hadith narrator Abu Hurayra once wandered into Medina's bustling marketplace and expressed his surprise that so many people were there when the inheritance of the Prophet was being distributed in his mosque. The crowds rushed to the *Haram* but soon returned in disappointment to Abu Hurayra. He asked them what they witnessed there, they said they had only seen people teaching and learning religious knowledge and remembering God. "*That* is the inheritance of the Prophet," he reminded them.[34]

When the call to prayer sounds, the study circles dissolve into lines and we prostrate to the All-Knowing One. I then meet Mustafa at the western entrance of Bab al-Rahma, the Gate of Mercy. "The name of this door," he explains, "can be traced back to an incident during the Prophet's life. A period of drought had afflicted the region and while the Prophet was sitting on the pulpit to deliver the weekly sermon, a man came in through this entrance and implored the Prophet to pray for relief. As they watched through this door, the sky began to fill with welcome dark clouds. The rains came and lasted a week. The next Friday, the man came in and begged the Prophet to preserve them from the ceaseless downpour. The Messenger prayed that the rain fall around Medina instead of upon it and this, too, was answered."[35] I recall that rain and mercy are often linked in the Qur'an. In other verses, the image of heavenly precipitation giving life to a desiccated landscape is a common allegory for the resurrection of the dead.

We head southwest across the plaza toward a comparatively small-domed mosque rebuilt in the Ottoman era. "This is Masjid al-Musalla (Mosque of the Outdoor Feast Day Prayers)," says Mustafa. "In this area, the Messenger of God would assemble his followers for open-air services to celebrate the Feast of the Sacrifice (*'Id al-Adha*) and the holy day marking the end of Ramadan (*'Id al-Fitr*). Its more popular name of Masjid al-Ghamama (Mosque of the Cloud) is probably related to the Prophet's having performed communal rain-seeking prayers here."

Further on, we come to a handsome basalt mosque built in late Ottoman times to serve the terminal of the Hijaz Railway, which lies across the street. As we make our way to the derelict train station, Mustafa explains,

"The rail-line linking Damascus to Medina was inaugurated in 1908, but was used for only eight years. During the First World War, it became a favored target of the Arab Revolt against Turkish control. In this they had the active encouragement of Lawrence of Arabia, the British agent charged with opening a southern front against Germany's oriental ally, the Ottoman Empire. The destroyed railway to Medina was never repaired." Mustafa allows me to briefly explore the vast walled yard behind the train station. In a half-collapsed maintenance hangar, I see a couple of century-old German locomotives and the sad remains of some damaged railcars.

Mustafa then directs me toward the real objective of our visit, a tiny triple-domed mosque near the southeastern corner of the terminal enclosure. "This is al-Suqya Mosque," he states. Here the Prophet assembled and reviewed his troops in the spring of 624 CE before marching on to the victorious Battle of Badr, about a hundred and fifty kilometers to the west. On another occasion, the Prophet prayed here and made a famous supplication in which he sanctified the city of Medina:

> O God! Verily Abraham, Your intimate friend, Your devoted servant and Your Prophet, invoked your blessings upon the people of Mecca. I am Muhammad, Your devoted servant, Your Prophet and Your Messenger, and I invoke Your favor for the people of Medina, asking you for that which Abraham asked for the people of Mecca. We entreat You to bless them in the measures of their sustenance and in the fruit of their earth. O God, cause us to love Medina, just as You instilled in us love for Mecca.... O God, I have declared what lies between its two lava tracts to be an inviolable sanctuary just as You established the sanctuary of Mecca through the declaration of Abraham.[36]

Standing before the mosque's closed doors, we recite a brief prayer before returning to the Prophet's Mosque to break the fast. When we finally reach the *Rawda,* only a few minutes remain before sunset. Mustafa places a handful of small, dark, wrinkled dates in front of me. "These are *'Ajwa* dates," he whispers, "The most prized of Medina's nearly one hundred varieties. God's Messenger declared them to be of the fruit of Paradise."[37] When the call for the sunset prayer sounds, I utter the formula of consecration and put one of them in my mouth. Its delicious, licorice-like taste is utterly unique. Soon the brief repast concludes and we rise with the congregation to worship.

Later that night, I am invited to Mustafa's home for dinner. His residence is a modest villa in a residential area not far from Quba. Joining us are two of his grown sons, his brother, and three erudite male friends. No women are visible, as one would expect in a conservative Saudi household. Surrounded by gilded Louis XIV sofas and chairs, we sit on the carpeted living room floor like Bedouins and dine on a memorable feast of whole roast lamb served on a bed of rice. Much of the animated conversation revolves around the deterioration of Medina's cultural and historical heritage.

The next morning, after a light meal, I make my way to Bab al-Rahma. A thick crowd of worshippers waits before the still bolted door. The scene has something apocalyptic about it. In the depths of the night, like mendicant souls at the threshold of Heaven, we are gathered at the mighty gilded gate of Mercy, eagerly anticipating our admittance into the celestial light within. Ten minutes later, the floodgates open and we stream into the mosque, filling every available space.

Following the prayer, I meet Mustafa and we walk north across the still cool marble to our sedan. I am eager to make the most of my third and final day in the Prophet's City. We drive west and turn north beyond the craggy silhouette of Mount Sila'. Then, penetrating deep into the western lava tract, we reach the imposing, white Mosque of *al-Qiblatayn,* the Two Prayer Orientations. Mustafa explains, "In 624 CE, about sixteen months after the emigration, the Prophet received Divine instructions to change the ritual direction of prayer from Jerusalem to Mecca. According to some reports, this occurred while the Prophet was leading a clan of the Helpers in noonday worship at their mosque here. In the middle of the prayer, the command to face the Ka'ba was revealed. So the Prophet changed his position, as did the congregation, with the men and women switching places. Then, facing south instead of north, they completed the rest of the prayer."[38]

We make our way up the steps and into a magnificent prayer hall. As we must wait until the sun rises before performing the devotional greeting to the mosque, I sit and meditate on the significance of this place of worship. While all of Medina's first mosques had to be reoriented, it is fitting that there should be a monument commemorating this important event. When the Prophet was still in Mecca, the Ka'ba was host to a myriad of idols, and the direction of Muslim prayer toward Jerusalem reflected Islam's affinity with the monotheistic faith preached by previous prophets. Later, however, in Medina, the majority of the native Jews proved hostile to the new religion and challenged the Prophet's status and authority. The Qur'an affirms that the Ka'ba was originally erected by Abraham, who was neither a Jew nor a Christian (Qur'an 2:127; 3:68). Thus, God's decree that His Holy House at Mecca should henceforth be the focal point of Muslim devotion served to highlight the primordial nature of Islam. The change of *qibla,* the direction of prayer, differentiated the Muslims in a critical way from the indigenous Jewish tribes of Medina, who continued to pray toward Jerusalem. Once the sun clears the horizon, we perform our individual devotions in the direction of Mecca and then return to our vehicle.

We drive to the southeast past Quba Mosque and turn right. We stop beside an uninspiring cinderblock wall encircling what appears to be a nondescript field scattered with basalt rocks and withered weeds. "The Prophet led the prayers at this spot for several days during the siege of an indigenous Jewish tribe. The commemorative mosque built here was known as Masjid al-Fadikh (The Date Wine Mosque). According to some sources, the prohibition against consuming alcohol was revealed during the siege.[39] Other reports say that a group of companions were drinking fermented date juice (*fadikh*) here when they received news of the prohibition of alcohol, at which point they poured the contents of their wine skins onto the ground.[40] Thus, the unusual name of this shrine embodies the exemplary obedience of the first Muslims."

Looking into the enclosure again, I discern a pattern of stones arranged upon the ground to mark the demolished shrine's *qibla* wall. Further to the left, I now see that the other rocks are simple tomb markers. The Saudi religious authorities most probably sanctioned the razing of the mosque that originally stood here, based on the prohibition of worshipping at or near graves. "Older sources describe Masjid al-Fadikh as located near the banks of a streambed." Pointing eastward to a concrete canal, Mustafa adds, "The principal headwaters of Wadi Buthan flow there." Then, shaking his head with discernable sadness, he remarks, "Today this historical site is largely unknown, and most people now confuse it with another mosque site further east. Praise be to the One who alters things, but Himself does not change!"

Mustafa now leads me toward a dense grove of date palms to the west. "The face of Medina has changed radically in recent years," he says, "but in gardens such as these one can still get a taste of what it must have been like in the Prophet's day." The narrow road is closed in on both sides by high stone walls of evident antiquity. At a breach in one of the walls, we enter a timeless pastoral world. Filtered by the canopy of palm fronds, sunlight dapples plots of herbs and clover. Here and there are clearings planted with grape vines, pomegranate, and also fruit-bearing lote trees, which figure prominently in descriptions of the celestial realms. Eventually, we come to an archaic masonry complex comprising a wide-mouthed well, and an adjoining reservoir overlooked by a small, arcaded veranda, to which we now ascend. Gazing over the idyllic scene, I am reminded of Qur'anic depictions of Paradise as "gardens beneath which rivers flow." Mustafa excuses himself to chat with a local farmer, leaving me in the coolness of the portico to remember the Supreme Gardener for a blessed half an hour. When he returns, we stroll back to the car in silence.

Our route traverses the agricultural area of southeastern Medina, many of whose inhabitants belong to an indigenous Shiite population. This Imami community has a long history of antagonism and rivalry with the majority Sunni population, who refer to them as *al-Nakhawila*, Workers of the Date Palms. We soon reach the district's main boulevard named after 'Ali, the Prophet's valorous cousin and son-in-law. The city also has modern thoroughfares named in honor of Abu Bakr, 'Umar, and 'Uthman, who are likewise revered by Sunnis as pillars among the early Companions of the Prophet and as his four righteous successors. However, most Shiites view 'Ali as having been the sole rightful claimant to the title of Commander of the Faithful and, because they historically denied the legitimacy of his predecessors, they are labeled "rejectionists" by many Sunnis. After 'Ali was assassinated in 661 CE, claims to supreme leadership shifted to his two sons by the Prophet's daughter Fatima and later to their progeny. Over the succeeding centuries, Medina was often a hotbed of Shiite revolt against the Umayyad and Abbasid dynasties. For hundreds of years, autonomous princes of the lineage of al-Hasan or al-Husayn ruled Mecca and Medina.

A short while later, we come to the eastern perimeter of the Baqi' Graveyard. Eventually, our car stops next to a modest new mosque, surmounted by a single squat minaret. "This is Masjid al-Ijaba (Mosque of the Response), site of the prayer hall of an *Ansari* clan (a clan of Helpers, who welcomed the Prophet Muhammad and his followers to Medina). Its name derives from a personal supplication the Prophet once made after praying here. A hadith relates the Messenger's plea: 'I asked my Lord for three favors, and he granted me two of them, and withheld the third. I asked my Lord not to wipe out my community of followers by famine, and this He granted. I asked Him not to obliterate my community by flood, and this He granted. Finally, I asked Him not to incite them to make war against each other, and this He denied me.'"[41]

It is time for the midday prayer, so we enter. As we wait for the *muezzin*'s second call, I contemplate the hadith cited by Mustafa. By the grace of God, the Prophet had been able to put an end to decades of rancor and armed conflict between Medina's indigenous Arab clans. Forging an alliance of faith between the Helpers and a diverse group of emigrants, the Messenger had brought nearly the whole of the Arabian Peninsula into the fold of Islam by the time of his death in 632 CE. However, without his harmonizing presence and God-given authority, the unity of his theocratic state rapidly showed signs of serious fissures. Much of Abu Bakr's brief rule as first caliph was taken up with repressing bloody secessionist rebellions. Although the dominions of Islam expanded tremendously during the Caliphates of 'Umar and 'Uthman, both were murdered. So was 'Ali, whose five-year reign witnessed almost continual civil strife, in which some of the Prophet's most eminent companions found themselves on opposing sides. Even the sanctuary of Medina was not immune from this internecine bloodshed. In 683 CE, in the nearby eastern lava tract, a local group of pious rebels was slaughtered by the army of the Umayyad Caliph, whose Syrian troops plundered the Prophet's City for three days. By the end of the first Islamic century, political, tribal, ethnic, and theological rifts had given rise to a multitude of endlessly warring factions. How truly and sadly prophetic was the Messenger's exchange with his Lord at this spot!

The noon prayer briefly unifies the focus and movements of the assembled worshippers, and then each one exits the mosque to go in diverse directions. We continue along the inner ring road, which now curves westward. Just before Mount Sila' we turn north and descend toward Uhud. A short while later, we turn right and halt at the bottom of a steep hillock. As we hike up the sloping road, Mustafa explains that the mosque we are about to visit is linked to the Battle of the Trench. "In the spring of 627 CE, the Meccans again marched against Medina with an allied force of ten thousand warriors, determined to destroy Islam once and for all. The Prophet had received advance warning of the impending attack, and sought counsel on how best to meet the threat. In the end he adopted the innovative proposal of Salman the Persian, to protect Medina's most vulnerable flank by digging a defensive trench between the two lava tracts to the north of Jabal Sila'."

At the top of the prominence, wedged between nondescript houses, we come to the tiny mosque of Masjid al-Raya, Mosque of the Battle Banner. It marks the spot where the Prophet's campaign tent was erected to enable him to supervise the digging of the trench and its subsequent defense. Passing through a modest courtyard, we enter the diminutive prayer chamber, covered by a single low dome. Here, in what feels like a masonry tent, we offer prayers. As we emerge to return to the car, I ask, "Isn't this near the place where the miracle of the rock occurred?"

"Yes, my brother," Mustafa says. "Just to the north of this hill a group of diggers encountered a large rock, which they were unable to break or dislodge. When the Prophet was asked for guidance, he descended to the ditch and shattered the stone himself by striking it three times with a pick. At each blow a great bolt of light shot forth, one to the east, one to the north and one to the south. He later said this was an omen that the Muslims would one day conquer Iraq, Syria and Yemen.[42] Though the hypocrites mocked the Messenger for making this prophecy at a time when the Muslims were being threatened by an overwhelmingly superior enemy at their doorstep, it later proved true."

Mustafa continues his commentary as we drive around the north of Jabal Sila': "The five-kilometer-long ditch had barely been completed when the enemy forces arrived and established their camps to the north. After more than twenty days of relentless siege, the morale, stamina, and even the faith of the thinly stretched lines of defenders began to falter. The desperate condition of the Muslims at this time is described in the Qur'an: 'When you were being assailed from above and from below, and when your vision failed you, and your hearts were in your throats and you began to think strange thoughts about God, then were the believers put to a trial and shaken to their roots'" (Qur'an 73:10–11).

Just then we pull into a broad paved bay on the northwestern flank of Mount Sila', another site associated with the Battle of the Trench known as the Seven Mosques. Pointing to a whitewashed shrine erected on a rocky spur of the mountain to our left, Mustafa tells me, "That is The Mosque of Victory, marking the spot where the Prophet implored God for three consecutive days to come to the aid of the Muslims with this supplication: 'O God! Revealer of the Covenant Scripture, Swift of Reckoning! O God! Vanquish the enemy confederates! O God! Put them to flight and cause them to tremble!"[43] On the third day, his petition was granted, and he announced that victory was at hand. God then sent troops of angels and a raging gale to wreak havoc upon the camps of the Quraysh and their allies. Terrified and thrown into utter confusion, the assailants soon raised the siege and departed."

By means of a steep set of stone steps, we ascend the outcropping to the mosque. Entering a small walled court, we find the vaulted prayer vestibule tightly packed with pilgrims. While we wait for our turn to pray there, Mustafa reveals a secret: "It is recorded that the Prophet's entreaty was granted on a Wednesday, between the midday prayers and the afternoon prayers. Ever since then, sincere supplications made at this spot and at this time have been known to be answered by God." Today, I realize, *is* Wednesday, and *now* is the propitious hour. When we finally manage to secure the necessary space inside, my devotions are charged with exceptional fervor.

Mustafa suggests that we forgo visiting the other mosques, named in honor of several eminent Companions of the Prophet, in order to reach another more important mosque for the mid-afternoon prayer. We backtrack around Jabal Sila', and eventually find ourselves on the airport road, where I am sadly reminded of my imminent departure.

We are dropped off near the Mosque of Abu Dharr, named after a Bedouin tribesman famed for his great asceticism. But the shrine has a more ancient name, Masjid al-Sajda, Mosque of the Prostration, whose story Mustafa relates: "It is reported that the Prophet once walked from his mosque to an enclosed garden here. Unbeknownst to him, one of the Meccan emigrants had followed him and watched as he made his ritual ablution and prayed at this spot. The Messenger remained in the position of the final prostration for such a long time that his unseen companion feared that God might have taken his soul. Eventually, the Messenger assumed the final kneeling position and completed his devotions. It was then that he noticed he was not alone. His escort told him of the concern he had felt at his protracted prostration, so the Prophet informed him: 'Verily Gabriel, upon whom be Peace, came to me and communicated to me God's glad tidings that whoever blesses me, I will bless, and whoever greets you with a benediction, I will greet. And so I prostrated to God the Mighty, the Majestic.'"[44] We then go in and perform the prayer in honor of the mosque and subsequently join the congregation for mid-afternoon worship. Both rituals include reverential greetings and blessings on the Prophet. I am deeply moved to recall the Divine reciprocity inherent in this act, which constitutes such an important facet of Islamic piety.

Outside, Mustafa recommends that I now return to my hotel to pack my luggage, promising to fetch me for my final sunset meal at the Prophet's Mosque. Not having rested that afternoon, I am dazed with fatigue, but the spiritual nourishment of the day's tour has dissipated every thought of the thirst and hunger. Later, I stroll across the great plaza one last time with Mustafa. In the celestial precincts, we break the fast with heavenly dates washed down with water from a sacred well. Then we perform the communal prayer toward the *qibla* wall upon which the Messenger saw a vision of the delights of Paradise and the torments of Hell. I end my devotions with a voluntary prayer, remaining in thankful prostration for a prolonged period. Mustafa then escorts me to the Gate of Mercy, where I turn in the direction of the Noble Chamber and offer a closing salutation to the Prophet. Leading with my left foot, I exit while uttering the traditional prayer, "O God! Verily I ask of You Your abundant grace."

Mustafa walks beside me in the direction of the car. Taking my hand, he says, "You know the story of how the Prophet, not long after his emigration to Medina (*hijra*), instituted ties of brotherhood between individual émigrés and the Helpers." "Of course," I reply. "Well, though your emigration has been brief, I regard you as my permanent brother in love for our Prophet and his city."

Deeply moved by his words, I tell him, "You have given me a great gift in the past three days, and I feel I have nothing to give to you in return."

"You are wrong," he interjects, "for your interest in the sacred history and geography of my city has given me hope that Medina's remaining visitation sites will be preserved and remembered for what they embody of the life and times of our blessed Prophet."

At the car, we embrace and exchange final farewells. The journey to the airport takes us across the eastern lava tract beyond Mount Uhud. When we reach the terminal, I thank our driver Ahmed for his faithful service and patience. Inside the departure hall, I check in for my southbound flight to Jeddah, from where I expect to make the long westward trip home. As a departing blessing, I am assigned a window seat.

Once we are airborne, I am offered a dazzling vista of *al-Madina al-Munawwara*, the Luminous City. The most brilliant glow emanates from the *Haram* in the middle of the city. Overflowing into the plaza on three sides, I can vaguely discern the massed rows of the faithful engaged in the night vigil prayers. The scene makes me think of the Prophet's vow: "By Him in Whose hand is my soul, things will revert to how they began; surely all true faith will return to Medina, just as it began from there, until all true faith will be in Medina."[45] It is impossible to escape feelings of profound regret at leaving the Abode of Faith. At the same time, I am filled with immense gratitude. For my sojourn in the Prophet's City has permitted me to partake of the eternal significance of the *Hijra* Emigration, which is, in essence, an inspired movement away from darkness toward the light.

NOTES

(Ed.) following a note signifies that the note was added by the general editor of this set.

1. For a scholarly but dated review of Arabic sources on Medina, see Jean Sauvaget, *La Mosquée Omeyyade de Médine: Etude sur les Origines Architecturales de la Mosquée et de la Basilique* (Paris: Vanoest, 1947).

2. Dates are provided in Common Era format for general readership. The year 622 CE corresponds to year one of the Muslim Hijra dating system based on a lunar calendar.

3. See Daoud Casewit, "Al-Hijrah Between History and Metaphor: An Analysis of Quranic and Hadith Sources," *The Muslim World* 88, no. 2 (April 1998): 105–128.

4. Muslim Ibn al-Hajjaj, *Sahih Muslim* (Beirut: Dar al-Kutub al-'Ilmiya, 2001), 760, no. 1907; Muhammad Ibn Isma'il al-Bukhari, *Sahih al-Bukhari* (Beirut: al-Maktaba al-'Asriya, 2002), 15, no. 1.

5. Bukhari, *Sahih*, 20, no. 15; Muslim, *Sahih*, 41, no. 44.

6. Bukhari, *Sahih*, 207, no. 1189; Muslim, *Sahih*, 517, no. 1397.

7. See Daoud Casewit, "Fada'il al-Madinah: The Unique Distinctions of the Prophet's City," *The Islamic Quarterly*, 35, no. 1 (1991): 5–22.

8. 'Abd al-Razzaq Ibn Humam al-Sana'ani, *Musnaf*, ed., 'Abd al-Rahman al-'Azami, vol. 3 (Beirut: al-Maktab al-Islami, 1970), 515, no. 6531.

9. 'Umar al-Numayri al-Basri Ibn Shabbah, *Kitab Ta'rikh al-Madina al-Munawwara*, ed., 'Ali Muhammad Dandal and Yasir Sa'd al-Din Bayyan, vol. 1 (Beirut: Dar al-Kutub al-'Ilmiyya, 1996), 83; Sulayman Ibn Ahmad al-Tabarani, *al-Mu'jam al-Awsat*, ed., Mahmud al-Tahhan, vol. 2 (Riyadh: Maktaba al-Ma'arif, 1985), 104.

10. Bukhari, *Sahih*, 267–268, no. 1534, no. 1535.

11. The tribe of Quraysh, to which the Prophet Muhammad belonged, controlled Mecca in the seventh century CE. During the time of the Prophet's mission, most of the powerful members of this tribe opposed Islam. The leaders of Quraysh commanded the armies that attempted to attack Medina and destroy the nascent Muslim community. (Ed.)

12. For an in-depth study of the historical geography of *al-'Aliya* see Michael Lecker, *Muslims, Jews and Pagans: Studies in Early Islamic Medina* (Leiden and New York: E.J. Brill, 1995).

13. Ibn Shabbah, *Ta'rikh*, 167.

14. Muhammad Ibn 'Abdallah al-Nisaburi al-Hakim, *al-Mustadrak 'ala al-Sahihayn*, vol. 5 (Aleppo and Beirut: Dar al-Fikr, 1978), 560.

15. Bukhari, *Sahih*, 208, no. 1196; Muslim, *Sahih*, 515, no. 1390.

16. Bukhari, *Sahih*, 207, no. 1190; Muslim, *Sahih*, 516, no. 1394.

17. Author's translation of the Arabic text from Ahmed Kamal, *The Sacred Journey* (London: George Allen & Unwin, 1961), 102.

18. Abu Dawud Sulayman ibn al-Ash'ath al-Sijistani, *Sunan*, vol. 2 (Cairo: Dar al-Hadith, 1988), 224.

19. Bukhari, *Sahih*, 647, no. 3688; Muslim, *Sahih*, 1017, no. 163.

20. Tabarani, *al-Awsat*, vol. 1, 475–476.

21. Bukhari, *Sahih*, 208, no. 1196; Muslim, *Sahih*, 515, no. 1391.

22. Bukhari, *Sahih*, 358, no. 2095; and 630–631, no. 3584; Muhammad Ibn Yazid Ibn Maja, *Sunan*, ed., Muhammad Fu'ad 'Abd al-Baqi (Cairo: 'Isa al-Halabi, no date), no. 1417.

23. Muslim, *Sahih*, 348, no. 974.

24. Tabarani, *al-Mu'jam al-Kabir*, vol. 2 (Baghdad: Dar al-'Arabiyya, 1978–1983), 305, no. 13190; Hakim, *al-Mustadrak*, vol. 2, 465–466.

25. Muhammad Ibn 'Isa al-Tirmidhi, *Sunan*, vol. 5 (Madina: Maktaba al-Salafiya, 1967), 377, no. 4009; Ibn Maja, *Sunan*, no. 3112.

26. For a fuller account of the battle of Uhud, see Muhammad Hamidullah, *The Battlefields of the Prophet Muhammad* (New Delhi: Kitab Bhavan, 1992).

27. Muhammad ibn 'Umar al-Waqidi, *Kitab al-Maghazi*, ed., Marsden Jones, vol. 1 (London: 'Alam al-Kutub, 1966), 262; 'Abd al-Malik Ibn Hisham, *al-Sira al-Nabawiya*, ed., Taha 'Abd al-Ra'uf Sa'd, vol. 3 (Beirut: Dar al-Jil, 1987), 35.

28. Ibn Hisham, *al-Sira*, 34.

29. Muslim, *Sahih*, 1129, no. 2943.

30. Ibn Maja, *Sunan*, no. 1412; Ibn Shabbah, *Ta'rikh*, 41–42.

31. Bukhari, *Sahih*, 1065, no. 5866; Muslim, *Sahih*, 832, no. 54, 55; Muhammad Ibn Sa'd, *al-Tabaqat al-Kubra*, vol. 1 (Beirut: Dar Beirut, 1985), 476.

32. Muslim, *Sahih*, 512, no. 1377; Malik Ibn Anas, *al-Muwatta'*, vol. 2 (Beirut: Dar Ihya' al-'Ulum, 1988), 885.

33. Ibn Maja, *Sunan*, no. 227; Hakim, *al-Mustadrak*, vol. 1, 91.

34. 'Abd Allah ibn Muhammad Ibn Farhun, *Ta'rikh al-Madina al-Munawwara*, ed., Husayn Muhammad 'Ali Shukri (Beirut: Dar al-Arqam, 2001), 29–30.

35. Bukhari, *Sahih*, 179, no. 1013; Muslim, *Sahih*, 320, no. 8.

36. Ahmad Ibn Hanbal, *Musnad*, vol. 5 (Beirut: Dar Sadir and Maktab al-Islami, 1954), 309.

37. Tirmidhi, *Sunan*, vol. 4, 401, no. 2068; Ibn Maja, *Sunan*, no. 3453, 3455.

38. Ibn Sa'd, *al-Tabaqat*, vol. 1, 241–243.

39. Ibn Hisham, *al-Sira*, 109.

40. Ibn Shabbah, *Ta'rikh*, 65, 69.

41. Muslim, *Sahih*, 1107, no. 2890; Ibn Shabbah, *Ta'rikh*, 68.

42. Ibn Sa'd, *al-Tabaqat*, vol. 4, 83–84; Waqidi, *al-Maghazi*, vol. 2, 449–550.

43. Bukhari, *Sahih*, 720, no. 4116; Ibn Shabbah, *Ta'rikh*, 58–50.

44. Ibn Hanbal, *Musnad*, vol. 3, 130, and 129; Hakim, *al-Mustadrak*, vol. 1, 222.

45. Hakim, *al-Mustadrak*, vol. 4, 454; Ahmad b. al-Husayn al-Bayhaqi, *Dala'il al-Nubuwwa wa ma'rifa ahwal Sahib al-Shari'a*, ed., 'Abd al-Mu'ti Amin Qal'aji, vol. 6 (Beirut: Dar al-Kutub al-'Ilmiya, 1985), 330–331.

8

SPARROW ON THE PROPHET'S TOMB

Daniel Abdal-Hayy Moore

1

O sparrow perched on a corner of the
    Prophet's tomb
cheeping above thousands of bowed heads murmuring,
whose glassy chirps hit high notes of
    purity under the eaves in this
      Mosque of God's Messenger
that resides in two territories of space—
    this world seen, the next world
      unseen—

in this shadow existence of his signal presence among us
    visitors from even farther away than
      China pass by to greet him,
and in your little feathered body is the swooping freedom to
    come and go all day to visit him
speeding from a tall beam
    across choruses of hearts
gratefully weeping or tranquil with an ecstatic
      inner moon rise

just to be here.

2

Sparrow, what is your name? Is it *"Constant Devotion?"*
Is it *"I Want To Be Near?"* *"Praiseworthy Friend?"*
Is your name *"Generations To Come?"*
You fluff your breast and preen your wing
where men cannot go, you dart into the
dark of the tomb for deeper conversation.

We would all go with you if we could,
squeeze our tiny feathery bodies through the
    gold grille work, past the
        guards in their pea green uniforms,
to sit on a corner of the Prophet's tomb in the
    dark to hear him
return the salutations of
such outpouring awed adorations of men and women,
        each one
passing by that undying presence, trying to
sneak a peak through the golden porthole,
hearts boiling with overwhelming emotions.

You land and sing.
You cock your head.
You watch us from your high perch with a
    cool eye.

3

Sparrow, you are more than a sparrow.
You are a continent of sparrows.
You are The Minister of Internal Affairs of all
    sparrows.
You are the song that laces the margins of the deep message,
    the message of God's Magnificence, the
Thunder of Tremendous Shock, Earthquake and
        heaven crash of the
Stark Glare of God's Might.

You trill and fly,
your song like a tiny tune from paradise,
    delicate celesta of celestial light.

The mosque in Medina expands
    all the way to the
        ends of the earth.

Forget about walls, where
marble pillars mark
the mosque's original dimensions,
the Prophet's precincts now
encompass our houses and the
    invisible courtyards of our
        love, interconnected by
sparrow-song, perched on a
    Turkish cornice,
singing to Timbuktu,

Medina song bird
    heard around the
        world!

NOTE

This poem first appeared in Daniel Abdal-Hayy Moore, *Mecca/Medina Time-Warp*. Reprinted from a Zilzal Press chapbook, by permission from the author.

9

In the Realm of Mercy: A Visit to a Shiite Shrine

Karima Diane Alavi

It is my last Friday—the Muslim day of communal prayer—in Iran. After a 26-year absence from the country, my first return is coming to a close. I gaze out the window that overlooks the city of Shiraz and I am filled with memories of my time here as an exchange student. Raw emotions make their way to the surface, as I wonder if I will ever make it back again. I feel a strong need to leave my fellow tourists behind and head to a sacred site—one of the city's many shrines—where I can be alone with my thoughts; alone in a crowd of fellow believers. I do not try to understand this need. I just recall the words of my grandmother: "Listen to the voice within you. It's the voice of wisdom." Although I dress in traditional Islamic clothing, I know that my blue eyes and light skin reveal my Western origin. With a touch of trepidation about how Iranians might react to a foreigner in their shrine, I force my hands to open the drawer that holds my veil.

I leave the hotel wrapped in a black shroud that enables me to fade into the world of the sacred, as if I had surrounded myself in eternal prayer that keeps the touch of the profane away from my skin, my face, and my heart. I cannot help but chuckle at the Western feminists who will never know the delicious anonymity one gains under a veil. As they speak of rescuing me from the "oppression" of becoming a drop in a sea of black fabric, I luxuriate in the freedom from trying to be someone special, someone different, a person who seeks everyone else's admiration and approval. I turn away from this world and focus on God.

The shrine rises like a glistening mountain of gold and blue. The ceramic tiles of the minaret call me to a higher place and my spirit—which is so fragile on this day—rises to the sunny sky above me while clouds drift by as if they have all the time in the world. "They do," I tell myself, and lower my head, humbled by their beauty. My heart beats to an ancient rhythm as I take my first steps through the shadow of the minaret that lays prostrate across the central courtyard and points toward the door of the inner shrine.

I follow the other women and enter the door only to encounter a man who is quietly telling the men to continue straight, while the women are directed to walk through a black curtain to the right. Stooping forward, I make my way through the layers of fabric that separate the men's area from the women's, and all is dark. For a short moment, I have the sensation of traveling through a womb, wrapped in warmth and heading toward an exit that will lead me to unknown territory. I gasp when I emerge, enshrouded in shimmering lights that seem to come from another world. My eyes are immediately drawn to the ceiling: a domed structure completely covered in mirrors with delicate chandeliers swaying in a slight breeze. Light is everywhere.

Women engulf me in a sea of prayers and tears. They sweep me along their river of movement toward the tomb. Though I want to stop and look, I cannot fight the flow. I surrender and touch the wall to my left to steady myself as the crowd pushes toward their ultimate goal—the final resting place of Sayyed Amir Ahmad, brother of one of the twelve Shi'a Imams, saintly men who are direct descendants of the Prophet Muhammad.

The tomb is enclosed in walls of gold and silver that are decorated with Qur'anic verses and arabesque filigree. In the center, several arched openings become windows to the world of the afterlife, where the grave sits in silent repose. Each window is filled with a metal lattice that women cling to in devotion while they pray for their loved ones who are suffering from illness, sorrow, or the inability to conceive that greatest gift of all, a child. Their hands hang on to the grid and their bodies shake with sobs, filling the room with an intense longing for God's mercy to be shown to those for whom their hearts ache.

I am suddenly overwhelmed with thoughts of my brother's daughter, who had just been in a car accident, and had held on to her best friend whose life quietly flowed away and drifted to a place unknown. Tears stream down my face and I find solace in holding on to the bars of the shrine and feeling the hands of the other women pat mine gently before moving on. I think of the Iraqis who are burying their children in between bombing raids that drop from the sky as if heaven and hell have been reversed, making death come down like rain. An overwhelming weight comes upon me and I have to sit before I succumb to its power and fall to the ground.

Making my way to one of the marbled walls of the shrine, I slump to the floor and cover my face in the safety of the veil. All else drifts away and I beseech God to help my niece and all the other people who have suffered the final gaze of the ones they love. I have no concept of how long I remained there, wrapped in my own world, when a soft touch on the shoulder brings me back to the room that glistens with rays of light bouncing off the ceiling and showering us with its grace.

"*Khanoom*, Ma'am."

I look up to see the rugged, sun-dried face of a village woman who had obviously spent much of her life toiling in a field.

"*Khanoom*, Ma'am. Who are you crying for?" she asks.

"*Dohktareh baradar-eh man*. The daughter of my brother."

"What happened?"

"Her friend died, and she was hurt," is all I can say before crying again. The woman stands up and walks to the wall that separates the men from the women. It is just a couple of feet taller than the top of our heads, and she must have heard her husband's voice on the other side of the wall. "Hossein," she calls.

"Yes?"

"Tell all the men to pray for the foreigner's niece."

I hear the sound of a man telling everyone to pray for my brother's child. The voices of at least a hundred men hum with prayer. On our side of the wall, the other women look at me, raise their palms in the air and pray. It is then that I realize that I am the only person who came to this shrine alone; everyone else is with family and friends. They sit in tightly knit groups and comfort each other—sometimes laughing, sometimes crying—and I sense an enormous loss for not being part of a group of women this day. Yet I am surrounded by their loving prayers, and I feel threads of destiny weaving us together in an endless tapestry of mothers, daughters, and sisters who have shared this blessing of life since the dawn of time. My loneliness drifts away like embers in the night.

Those seated along the wall inch toward me until I am embraced between the shoulders of two women I would share this moment with, but never get to know. They have powerful shoulders that speak of strength—of lifting rocks and sowing fields before the setting sun allows them to surrender to the day's exhaustion.

I find comfort in our shared silence as we wrap chadors over our faces and peer out at the crowd that moves past us like moments in eternal time. Because I am seated on the floor, what I see first is the women's feet. As they move along, their veils open up just enough to reveal their life stories to me. There are ancient feet with bony lumps bulging from the side; feet that have walked so many miles of life that they seem weary and ready for eternal rest. There are delicate city feet with golden bracelets resting peacefully on the ankle. One woman hobbles along with a wrinkled clubfoot covered in the brown-black skin of southern Iran where Arab tribes have lived since migrating there centuries ago.

Shimmering fabrics in red and green swish past me as Qashqai tribal women take time from their mountain migrations to seek the blessings of the venerated man whose body rests a few feet to my left. The gold threads that are woven into their skirts flash rays of light across space and time as the women seem to float along the marble floor. I am in awe of their ability to maintain traditions in the onslaught of our televised McWorld. Enormous silver bracelets jingle around their wrists as they move to the back of the shrine to perform their prayers.

The women next to me slowly drift into a gentle slumber and I rise to say goodbye to this mystical place before heading back to the outside world. I wander in silence and take in the sights for the last time. Prayers are engraved in marble slabs along the walls that women touch as they recite the Qur'an. Ceramic tiles in brilliant blue and white reflect the flood of light that pours down from the mirrored ceiling, filling the room with a blaze of white. I watch two little girls in blue jeans and pink sweatshirts dancing in front of a floor fan as their grandmother looks on affectionately. There are grown women lying with their heads on their mother's laps. Their heavy eyelids rise and fall in an effort to take in all the sights and sounds before it is time to depart. I understand their need to make the experience last.

Meandering slowly toward the door, I recall one of my favorite verses of the Qur'an, the verse about light:

> God is the Light of the heavens and the earth.
> The parable of His Light is as if there was a niche,
> And within it a lamp: the lamp enclosed in glass
> The glass, as it were, a brilliant star lit from a blessed tree
> An olive, neither of the East nor of the West
> Whose oil is well nigh luminous, though fire scarce touched it
> Light upon light! God doth set forth parables for people
> And God doth know all things.

(Qur'an 24:35)

I take one last look at the women who surround the tomb and bend down to reenter the black cloth that leads to the outdoor courtyard of the shrine. Suddenly, a clap of thunder shatters the air and shouts of "Alhamdu Lillah!" (God be praised!) echo through the crowd like a wave of joy. I step into that enchanted mixture of sunshine and rain that has puzzled me since I was a child. Wrapping my chador around me, I run across the glistening pavement to the columned portico on the other side of the courtyard. The delicately carved wooden pillars have eagerly absorbed the rain and are already filling the air with the musky scent of their ancient lives.

I turn around and feel a joy like I have never encountered before. It seems to rise on wings from the horizon of my soul and embrace the sunlight, the raindrops, and the whimsical scene before me, where people are laughing and covering each other with jackets, chadors, and oversized purses. I see the touch of God's plan for our salvation and it is Love.

It is time to leave, and yet I have no remorse. A content serenity embraces me as I lift my hand and quietly call for a taxi. A young Mullah jumps out from the passenger's seat to open the back door for me, hesitating momentarily when he notices my foreign features. Smiling sheepishly, he waits till I am seated and then jumps back into the car. In typical Iranian fashion, we will share a taxi through this wonderful city and then never see each other again.

I smile behind my veil and watch the taxi driver and the Mullah trying to make sense of me without staring; the rearview mirror seems to hold a new fascination for them. They give each other puzzled looks and then we joyfully splash through puddles of God's mercy as we pull away from the shrine, listening to the comforting rhythm of the rain on the roof of our car.

10

THE PASSION OF 'ASHURA IN SHIITE ISLAM

•

Kamran Scot Aghaie

Shortly after American and coalition troops removed Saddam Hussein from power in Iraq in 1983, people around the world witnessed an amazing phenomenon. In the days leading up to the Shiite commemoration of 'Ashura, hundreds of thousands, possibly millions, of people poured onto the Iraqi streets and began passionately beating their chests and heads with their hands and chains, while chanting religious elegies, prayers, and slogans. A few even used blades to draw blood as the world watched in confusion, shock, and disbelief. This massive outpouring of religious sentiment was due in part to decades of frustration at the restrictions that were placed by the Sunni but largely secular Baathist regime of Hussein on Shiite public religious practices in Iraq. Being able to commemorate 'Ashura freely was an important event for the Shiites of Iraq. But what was the world to make of the apparently violent and self-abusive rituals of 'Ashura? Many Sunni and non-Muslim observers thought that the participants must be crazy. Many thought that they must be extremist religious zealots. However, those who were familiar with Shi'ism and its distinctive rituals realized, despite the shocking impression these rituals left in the minds of many people around the world, that by and large the participants were ordinary Shiites involved in traditional expressions of piety and spirituality. In order to properly understand these rituals it is first necessary to understand the historical development of the symbols and rituals associated with the day of 'Ashura, which is at the core of the beliefs of Shiite Muslims.

'Ashura is the 10th day of the month of Muharram, which is the first month of the Islamic calendar. The day of 'Ashura is important to Muslims for two main reasons. First, the Prophet Muhammad identified the 10th of Muharram as a holy day of fasting.[1] Second, it was the day on which the tragic massacre of Karbala took place in 680 CE, in which the Prophet's grandson Husayn was killed along with most of his close family members. The symbols and rituals of 'Ashura have evolved over time and have meant different things to different people. However, at the core of the symbolism of 'Ashura is the moral dichotomy between worldly injustice and corruption on the one hand, and God-centered justice, piety, sacrifice, and perseverance on the other. Also, Shiite Muslims consider the remembrance of the tragic events of 'Ashura to be an important way of worshiping God in a spiritual or mystical way. The emotional reactions of believers to the tragedy of 'Ashura are thought to build a closer relationship between the individual Shiite Muslim and the martyred Imam Husayn, who serves as an intermediary between God and the average believer. It is said that if a believer sheds even one tear for the tragedy of 'Ashura, he or she is guaranteed admission to Paradise.

Politically, the symbolism of 'Ashura has been important in many rebellions and reform movements throughout Muslim history, such as in the overthrow of the Umayyad caliphs by the Abbasid caliphs in 749–750 CE. More recently, in Iran, the symbolism of 'Ashura was a central part of the antimonarchy discourse of the Islamic Revolution of 1979, and in Lebanon the symbolism of 'Ashura played an important role in promoting Shiite communal identity and in mobilizing Shiites against the Israeli occupation of southern Lebanon. Central to the political dynamic of 'Ashura has been its association with the tragic massacre of Husayn and his followers at Karbala. As a commemoration of Karbala, 'Ashura serves as a vindication of the Shiite cause and also provides the foundation for a diverse array of beliefs and rituals, such as mourning rituals, funeral-style commemorative processions, verbal and performed reenactments of the events at Karbala, self-mortification rituals, and of course, politically oriented rallies and speeches. However, the commemoration of 'Ashura has not always been associated exclusively with sectarianism or even with Shi'ism. Many non-Shiite Muslims, especially those oriented toward popular Islam, also commemorate 'Ashura. For example, in Sunni countries like Egypt and Morocco, Muslims commemorate 'Ashura in ways that are distinct from Shiite practices. In the twentieth century, Sunni involvement in the commemoration of Karbala has gone through a relative decline, whereas among Shiites it has continued to evolve and change as it did in previous centuries.

This being said, the sectarian aspect of 'Ashura is critically important to understanding the significance of this commemoration. Islam, like other world religions, has always been characterized by a great deal of internal diversity. One of the most important examples of diversity in Islam is the Sunni–Shiite divide. Today, Sunnis make up approximately 85 to 90 percent of the Muslims in the world, while Shiites constitute approximately 10 to 15 percent. While Shiites live all over the Muslim world, approximately half of them live in Iran. The other major concentrations of Shiites are in Iraq, Lebanon, Yemen, Bahrain, Azerbaijan, eastern Saudi Arabia, Turkey, Afghanistan, and various parts of South Asia. In many of these countries, Shiites are either a minority or a majority who have little or no influence in the government. Today, the only explicit Shiite government is the Islamic

Republic of Iran, which was established through revolutionary upheaval in 1978–1979. At the moment, Iraq seems to be heading toward a Shiite-dominated state, but if the country remains unified its constitution precludes an explicit Shiite government. A small 'Alawi (also called Nusayri) Shiite minority dominates the Syrian government, but the Syrian Baath regime, as was case of Baathist Iraq under Hussein, is explicitly secular in nature. The same is true for Yemen, where Zaydi Shiites are present in considerable numbers.

Shi'ism has numerous internal divisions, such as the Ismailis, Zaydis, 'Alawis, and of course, the Ithna' 'Asharis or Twelvers. The roots of the divisions among different strains of Shi'ism can be found in the historical development of Shi'ism in the centuries after the Prophet Muhammad's death. The distinctions between these different branches of Shi'ism are based on different legal systems, ritual practices, and theological doctrines. More specifically, these different Shiite groups have historically disagreed among themselves regarding the identity, nature, and sequence of the Shiite Imams. The office of the Imam, called the *Imamate*, is a distinctive feature of all branches of Shi'ism. It is both the primary difference between Sunnis and Shiites, and the basis of internal disputes among Shiites, which led to the diversity of Shiite groups. Because they are the largest single Shiite group and because their celebrations of 'Ashura are the most prominent, this chapter will focus on the Ithna' 'Ashari, or Twelver, branch of Shi'ism. Also called Imami Shiites, the name of this sect derives from the belief that there were 12 Shiite Imams, the last of whom has existed in a supernatural or metaphysical state of occultation since 874 CE.

The sectarian division between the Sunnis and the Shiites took several centuries to fully develop. Upon the death of the Prophet Muhammad in 632 CE, there was a crisis of succession. The main challenge facing the young Muslim community was who should succeed the Prophet and in what capacity. It was also unclear whether the Prophet had selected a successor. The imperial caliphate is the system of government that eventually evolved out of this crisis. According to this system, the Islamic state was ruled by a caliph, who commanded both temporal and religious authority, but did not possess any of the supernatural or metaphysical qualities of the Prophet, such as infallibility, supernatural knowledge, or the ability to receive revelation. While some Muslims supported the ruling caliphs, others believed that the Prophet's son-in-law and cousin 'Ali ibn Abu Talib should have succeeded the Prophet upon his death. Later, they believed that 'Ali's descendants should be his successors, beginning with his sons Hasan (d. 669 CE) and Husayn (d. 680 CE). These Muslims are typically referred to as *'Alids* because of their support for 'Ali and his descendants.

These Muslims believed that the Prophet selected 'Ali as his successor on more than one occasion before his death. For example, they believed that the Prophet gave a speech shortly before his death at a place called Ghadir

Khum. According to one account, "[The Prophet] took 'Ali by the hand and said to the people: 'Do you not acknowledge that I have a greater claim on the believers than they have on themselves?' And they replied: 'Yes!' Then he took 'Ali's hand and said: 'Of whomsoever I am Lord [*Mawla*], then 'Ali is also his Lord. O God! Be thou the supporter of whomever supports 'Ali and the enemy of whomever opposes him.'"[2]

Over the centuries support for 'Ali and his descendants slowly evolved into a theory of leadership called the Imamate. The Imamate differed from the Sunni caliphate in that the Imam had to be a descendant of the Prophet Muhammad and was usually considered to have supernatural qualities and abilities, such as infallibility and supernatural religious knowledge. The Imam also had to be appointed by either the Prophet or the previous Imam in an unbroken chain of succession leading back to the Prophet. According to this view, the Prophet endorsed the Imamate before his death in 632 CE.[3] Sunnis and Shiites have passionately disagreed about both the authenticity and the correct interpretation of these accounts. The crisis of succession after the Prophet's death, followed by a series of political events that unfolded during the first few centuries of Islamic history, turned what was originally a political dispute into a religious or sectarian division.[4]

In response to this crisis of succession, Sunnis developed the doctrine that the caliphs, especially the so-called Rightly-Guided Caliphs—Abu Bakr (d. 634 CE), 'Umar (d. 644 CE), 'Uthman (d. 656 CE), and 'Ali (d. 661 CE)— were all legitimate successors to the Prophet Muhammad. The caliphs, who were selected as a result of a political process, were generally considered as both religious and temporal leaders, but were not given the same degree of religious authority as Shiites attributed to the Imams. Shiites considered all of the caliphs except 'Ali to be usurpers of the rightful authority that should have been vested exclusively in the Imams. During the early centuries of Islam, Sunnis tended to be the rulers of the Islamic state, while Shiites were in the opposition. This partly explains the tendency of early Sunnis to preserve the status quo, versus the Shiites who tended to be more critical of rulers and who spoke in more radically utopian terms. While Shiite states eventually developed, particularly in the tenth and eleventh centuries CE, the long-term political influence of Shi'ism was often at its greatest when it took the form of opposition movements that challenged the legitimacy of the ruling Sunni caliphs.

This fundamental disagreement was compounded by later political divisions, which encouraged further divergence in political and legal systems, ritual practices, and theological doctrines. Despite their differing views, relations between Sunnis and Shiites have varied dramatically throughout history, ranging from open conflict or hostility, to relative tolerance and coexistence.

The terms *Shi'a* and *Shiite* derive from the Arabic phrase *Shi'at 'Ali*, "Partisans of 'Ali." The term *Sunni* derives from the phrase *Ahl al-Sunna wa al-Jama'a,* which means, "Followers of the [Prophetic] Tradition and the [Majority] Consensus." As these terms imply, the Shiites support the Prophet Muhammad's progeny as his successors, beginning with 'Ali. Thus, the concept of Sunni orthodoxy developed largely in response to Shiite ideological and political challenges. While the disputes and schisms may have begun with the crisis of succession, they evolved in accordance with later political and theological trends. For example, regional, ethnic, or tribal loyalties frequently sparked political rebellions. Sectarian rhetoric often accompanied such rebellions. Proto-Shiite arguments were often the most effective way to challenge the legitimacy of the ruling caliphs. The Shiite Imams, who were descendants of the Prophet and who had varying degrees of popular support among the masses, were considered rivals of the Sunni caliphs, who actually ruled the Islamic empire.

When 'Ali assumed the position of caliph in 656 CE after the assassination of 'Uthman, the Prophet's widow 'A'isha, with a group from among the Companions of the Prophet, took up arms and challenged 'Ali's authority at the Battle of the Camel, which was so named because the fighting took place around the camel on which 'A'isha rode. In some sources 'A'isha is reported to have stated, "By Allah! 'Uthman has been killed unjustly, and I will seek revenge for his blood!"[5] No sooner had 'Ali put down this rebellion, when he was faced with another military challenge from the powerful governor of Syria, Mu'awiya. Mu'awiya was a cousin of 'Uthman, and he similarly demanded that the murderers of 'Uthman be brought to justice, something that 'Ali was either unable or unwilling to do. This military challenge resulted in a stalemate, and eventually an arbitrated settlement. The unsatisfactory outcome of this conflict turned a small group of zealous supporters against 'Ali. These rebels, who were referred to as *Khawarij* ("secessionists"), condemned 'Ali for failing to decisively crush Mu'awiya's rebellion. Although 'Ali defeated the Khawarij, one of their adherents assassinated him in 661 CE. Ironically, this set the stage for Mu'awiya to assume the office of caliph, thus ending the period of the Rightly-Guided Caliphs and establishing the Umayyad Caliphate, which lasted for nearly a century.

The Umayyad period of Islamic history is critically important for understanding the schism that developed between the Sunnis and the Shiites. During this period, 'Ali's descendants, especially his sons Hasan and Husayn, were increasingly perceived by opposition groups as the ideal rivals of the Umayyad caliphs because of their piety and their relationship to the Prophet. For this reason, Mu'awiya and his successors were particularly hostile toward these supporters of 'Ali and his sons. It was routine for the Umayyads to condemn or persecute the family of 'Ali, and they were even cursed from the pulpit. It is in this environment of tension, distrust, and conflict, along with the crisis resulting from the death of Mu'awiya and the accession to the throne of his unpopular son Yazid I (d. 683 CE), that the battle of Karbala took place in 680 CE.

The battle of Karbala was the ultimate climax of this dizzying series of conflicts, battles, and debates. In many ways it is the most important symbolic event for Shiites since the Prophet Muhammad's mission, because it is the ultimate and ideal example of the Sunni–Shiite conflict. It serves as a religious model for behavior among Shiites, who are expected to struggle against injustice in the path of God, even if they face oppression, persecution, or death. It is no surprise, therefore, that the vast majority of Shiite rituals are derived from events that are believed to have taken place in or around the battle of Karbala.

Like many other famous historical events, the tale of Karbala has been told and retold over the centuries without a single authoritative version emerging to completely supplant all others. The most commonly accepted narratives of the battle of Karbala begin with an account of the discontent of the Muslims of southern Iraq under the rule of the second Umayyad caliph, Yazid. Yazid is typically portrayed as politically oppressive and morally corrupt. The Prophet Muhammad's grandson Husayn, who was living in Medina, received several letters from the caliph's subjects asking him to travel to Iraq in order to lead them in an uprising against Yazid. After sending scouts to assess the situation, Husayn and a number of his close relatives left Medina and began the trip to Iraq.

When they reached Karbala, Husayn's caravan was surrounded by an overwhelmingly large army sent by Yazid. A standoff ensued, because Husayn refused to give an oath of allegiance to the caliph. After 10 days of waiting, negotiating, and occasionally fighting, a final battle took place in which Husayn, all of his adult male relatives and supporters, and some of the women and children were killed in a brutal fashion. The surviving women and children, along with Husayn's adult son 'Ali Zayn al-'Abidin (d. 712–713 CE), who was too ill to take part in the fighting, were taken captive and transported, along with the heads of the martyrs, to Yazid's court in Damascus.

Along the way from Karbala to Damascus, the members of the Prophet's family who were taken prisoner were exhibited in chains in the public markets of the cities through which they passed. Because of this humiliation, Husayn's surviving relatives, especially his sister Zaynab and his son 'Ali, condemned Yazid for his cruelty toward the descendants of the Prophet Muhammad. The role played by women, such as Zaynab, in the events of Karbala and their aftermath is an important focus in Shiite recreations of the Karbala tragedy. Their ordeal of captivity is understood by Shiites to be a terrible injustice and humiliation, especially considering that the prisoners were direct descendants or relatives of the Prophet Muhammad. This captivity also provided an opportunity for Husayn's sister Zaynab to assume a political role by publicly challenging the Umayyad Caliph Yazid. For example, in the following Shiite account, Zaynab rebukes Yazid, saying:

You are not a human being. You are not human. You are an oppressor who inherited bloodthirsty oppression from your father! Even though my heart is wounded and wearied, and my tears are flowing [because of the massacre of Karbala], surely very soon the day of God's punishment will come and everyone will be subjected to God's justice. This is sufficient for us.... If fate has brought me here to face you this was not something that I wished to happen. But now that it is so, I count you as small and I reproach you![6]

The entire Muslim community was deeply traumatized by the massacre of Karbala, both because Muslims were killing other Muslims and because the ruling caliph had ordered his troops to massacre the pious descendants of the Prophet. The events of Karbala were also related to earlier traumatic events, like the Battle of the Camel between 'Ali and 'A'isha, and the Battle of Siffin between 'Ali and Mu'awiya, in which pious and respected Muslims fought on both sides. This negative feeling was compounded by the fact that for many Muslims Husayn and Yazid represented two opposite ends of a religious spectrum. Yazid was widely condemned as impious, tyrannical, and immoral, whereas Husayn was generally seen as being not unlike his grandfather Muhammad or his father 'Ali in his piety, character, and conduct.

Following Karbala, groups in opposition to the Umayyads routinely used the memory of this battle as a rallying cry. Some of these movements were explicitly Shiite, while others were simply hostile toward the Umayyads and looked favorably upon the family of the Prophet. In fact, the Abbasids, who overthrew the Umayyads in 750 CE and established a new Sunni caliphate, made extensive use of the memory of Karbala to gain popular support during their rebellion. However, once they came to power, they ruled over their empire as a Sunni dynasty for the next five centuries.

Mourning for Husayn and the martyrs of Karbala began almost immediately after the massacre, starting with the laments of Husayn's surviving relatives and supporters. As part of the long-term trend toward the development of mourning rituals based on commemoration of Karbala, popular elegies of the martyrs were composed during the remainder of the Umayyad period and the first two centuries of Abbasid rule (ca. 750–930 CE). The following is a short excerpt from one of these elegies:

Now listen to the story of the martyrdom and how [the Umayyads] deprived Hussein of water, and when he was fighting on the plain of Kerbela how they behaved meanly and unjustly. They cut off the head of a descendant of the Prophet in that fiery land! But the Imam lives, his foot in the stirrup and mounted upon his horse! He will not be killed!...The angels in heaven bewailed their deaths and have wept so copiously that water flowed from the leaves of the trees and plants. Thus, you too must weep for a while; for after this tragedy of Taff, laughter is unlawful.[7]

The earliest reliable account of the public mourning rituals that Shiites now call *Muharram* processions concerns an event that took place in 963 CE during the reign of Mu'izz al-Dawla, the Buyid Sultan of southern Iran and Iraq. The Buyids were military commanders from the Caspian Sea region of Iran that ruled in the name of the Sunni Abbasid caliphs. The Buyids, who were Shiites themselves, promoted Shiite rituals, including the celebration of the Prophet Muhammad's designation of 'Ali at Ghadir Khum, in order to promote their legitimacy and to strengthen the sense of Shiite identity in and around Baghdad. The famous fourteenth-century Sunni historian Ibn Kathir states, "On the tenth of Muharram of this year [963 CE], Mu'izz al-Dawla ibn Buwayh, may God disgrace him, ordered that the markets be closed, that the women should wear coarse woolen hair cloth, and that they should go into the markets with their faces unveiled and their hair disheveled, beating their faces and wailing over Husayn ibn 'Ali ibn Abi Talib." He goes on, somewhat apologetically to say, "The people of the Sunna could not prevent this spectacle because of the large number of the Shiites and their increasing power, and because the Sultan was on their side."[8] One of the interesting aspects of this account is that it demonstrates that women have been involved in Shiite rituals from the very beginning and that their role was significant enough to be singled out for comment.

Shiite rituals continued to evolve somewhat unsystematically over the centuries in isolated communities, and under the patronage of regional Shiite notables or rulers. Then, in the sixteenth century, the Safavid dynasty established a Shiite state centered on the Iranian plateau and worked systematically to enhance their religious legitimacy by promoting explicitly Shiite rituals. This turned out to be a watershed event for Ithna' 'Ashari Sh'ism and the rituals associated with it. Unlike their Sunni neighbors the Ottomans, the Uzbeks, and the Mughals, the Safavids declared Ithna' 'Ashari Shi'ism to be the official religion of the dynasty and set out to promote an orthodox Shiite culture, society, and political order. It was in this environment in 1501–1502 CE that the popular religious orator Husayn Va'iz Kashifi composed his seminal work, *Rawzat al-shuhada'* (The Garden of the Martyrs).[9] Kashifi's book represents a new trend in Shiite memorial literature, which involves a synthesis of historical accounts, elegiac poems, theological tracts, and hagiographies in a chain of short narratives that together formed a much larger narrative of Karbala. This book also articulated a complex set of canonized doctrines, which stressed the courage, piety, and sacrifice of Husayn and his followers at Karbala.

The new *Rawza* genre of pious narratives was read aloud at religious gatherings, which progressively evolved into mourning rituals called *Rawza Khani,* which roughly means, "Reading the *Rawza*" (that is, reading the book, *Rawzat al-shuhada'*). Today, the *Rawza Khani* is a ritual in which a sermon is given based on *Rawzat al-shuhada'* or some similar text, with a great deal of improvisation on the part of a specially trained orator.

The objective of the oration is to move the audience to tears through the recitation of the tragic details of the battle of Karbala.[10] This type of mourning ritual is viewed by Shiite Muslims as a means of achieving salvation by developing empathy and sympathy for the martyrs. This belief is illustrated by the often-repeated quotation, "Anyone who cries for Husayn or causes someone to cry for Husayn shall go directly to Paradise."[11]

By the time of the Qajar Dynasty in Iran (ca. 1796–1925), the Rawza Khani had evolved into a much more elaborate ritual called *Shabih Khani* or *Ta'ziyeh Khani*. The *ta'ziya* ("lamentation"), an elaborate theatrical performance of the Karbala story based on the same narratives used in the Rawza Khani, involves a large cast of professional and amateur actors, a director, a staging area, costumes, and props. The Qajar rulers of Iran were great sponsors of these rituals, and social and religious status among the elites were based partly on their ability to sponsor such rituals on a large scale. These rituals, which were also sponsored by a variety of social groups organized around guilds, neighborhoods, tribes, or ethnic groups, also reinforced a variety of social identities. The Iranian Ta'ziyeh ritual reached its greatest level of popularity during the late Qajar period. It entered a relative decline under the Pahlavi Dynasty (1925–1979) and became much less common in the large cities of Iran during the 1930s and the 1940s. However, the Ta'ziyeh continues to exist on a smaller scale in Iran in the traditional quarters of cities and in rural areas.[12]

In the past two centuries, the policies and agendas of the various regimes ruling Iran have influenced manifestations of 'Ashura. However, these symbols and rituals have proven to be substantially independent of the control of the state. The state's ability to make use of the Karbala paradigm has been a very important factor in its ability to maintain its legitimacy and at least some degree of connection or integration with the broader society. The state's failure to adequately incorporate these symbols and rituals into its program and ideology, as was the case with the Pahlavi regime, contributed in part to the state's crisis of legitimacy. This allowed opposition groups to make very effective use of the symbols and rituals of 'Ashura in overthrowing the regime. The government of the present Islamic Republic of Iran has made very effective use of these symbols and rituals to articulate the state's ideology and policies. This has made it difficult for anyone critical of the Islamic regime to use 'Ashura symbols and rituals to critique or oppose the state. However, this state versus opposition dynamic is only part of the modern story of 'Ashura.

'Ashura symbols and rituals remain very important in modern Iranian society, culture, and politics. Although they have exercised an important influence upon the fortunes of the state, the state itself has usually not been the most important factor in the evolution of Karbala symbols and rituals. Rather than a "trickle down" effect, according to which the state's policies determined the nature of these diverse forms of religious expression, the relationship between the state and the society was complex, inconsistent, and above all, a "two-way street." In other words, religious symbols and rituals were produced through a complex process of interaction between the Iranian state and the Iranian society. Much of the evolution of religious expression in Iran was the product of factors that had little or nothing to do with the state. Karbala symbols and rituals have been one of the primary means of expressing social and political ideals on a broad societal level. In some cases, this took the form of direct opposition to the state. In other cases, the rituals that commemorated Karbala served as a means for maintaining social bonds, ideals, and identities that were independent of the agendas and policies of the state. Changing economic and demographic forces transformed preexisting and newly emerging political relationships. Other important factors included changes in ethics, aesthetics, class dynamics, social institutions, groupings, and identities. Discourses on contemporary social and political crises have also found expression in 'Ashura symbols and rituals.

Over the centuries, Shi'ism spread from Iraq and Iran into parts of South Asia. According to popular belief in South Asia, Shiite rituals were first introduced at the end of the fourteenth century by the conqueror Timur Leng (Tamerlane, d. 1405 CE), who is said to have converted to Shi'ism prior to his invasion of the Indian Subcontinent.[13] As Juan Cole has argued, Shi'ism spread along with the migration of Iranian elites (that is, notables, scholars, poets, artisans, and merchants) from the Iranian plateau and Iraq into South Asia. One important side effect of this influx of Iranians was the establishment of an elite culture that was largely derived from Persian elite culture. In some cases, this elite culture was Shiite, which led to the spread of Shi'ism in parts of South Asia. In the sixteenth and seventeenth centuries, Shiite states were established in Southern India. For example, the Nizam Shahi dynasty (r. 1508–1553 CE) ruled in Ahmednagar, the Qutb Shahi dynasty (r. 1512–1687 CE) ruled in Hyderabad, and the 'Adil Shahi dynasty ruled in the Deccan kingdom of Bijapur. These dynasties were able, in varying degrees, to encourage Shiite practices, until the Mughal Dynasty suppressed them from the sixteenth century onward.[14]

While the fifteenth and early sixteenth centuries CE were characterized by Shiite rule in certain provinces of South Asia, one should be careful not to overstate the importance of these political trends. In many ways, the spread of Persian elite culture was a more influential factor in the spread of Shi'ism in South Asia. This is particularly important to note for northern Indian areas like Kashmir and Awadh, where large Shiite minorities lived, mostly under Sunni rule. This elite culture survived well into the modern period and was quite influential in certain areas, where Shiite elites (including some women) promoted Shiite beliefs and ritual practices, depending on the degree of tolerance of the Sunni rulers. For example, elegies were recited both in private and in public, public processions were sometimes organized, and the Karbala Narrative was recalled in the form of sermons and domestic rituals in the homes of Shiite elites. In addition, replicas of the tomb of Husayn were built for use in these various rituals and remain a central feature of South Asian Muharram rituals to this day.[15]

Similar trends can be seen among the Arab Shiite communities that were located outside of Safavid control. In Iraq and Lebanon, major Shiite communities flourished under the rule of the Ottoman Empire, which fluctuated between tolerance and persecution. In fact, during the eighteenth century, when political decentralization, economic chaos, and Afghan invasions weakened the religious establishment in the Iranian plateau, the Shiite shrine cities of southern Iraq, in particular Najaf and Karbala, flourished relatively independently of state influence. The important influence of Iraqi Shiite scholarship continued into the nineteenth century as well. During the period of decline of Iran's religious establishment, many of the greatest Shiite scholars either were from Iraq or chose to study and work there. In this environment, Shiite beliefs, practices, and rituals continued to develop and evolve, as they had in previous centuries.

While 'Ashura rituals were more prevalent in areas where Shiites were concentrated, such as Lebanon, Iran, southern Iraq, Hyderabad, and Awadh, some Sunnis (especially those oriented more toward popular culture and Sufism) also commemorated Karbala in observances that were based on Shiite models. In some areas, such as South Asia, Sunnis have often been enthusiastic participants in Shiite rituals. In the modern era, the rituals of Sunnis and Shiites have become more distinct from each other. However, throughout much of Islamic history the differences between Sunnis and Shiites based on ideological constructs were often less prevalent. This was particularly true of popular practices, which could often be at variance with the views of the ulama.[16]

In summary, the rituals of 'Ashura that are dominant in the world of Shiite Islam have been of three basic types. The first type of ritual is the sermon gathering, in which pious elegies are recited, usually including a combination of chants, elegies, story telling, and sermons. In these rituals, believers mourn the tragedy of 'Ashura and learn ethical or spiritual lessons from the story. They also hope, through their mourning and commemoration, to become closer to the Imams and thereby to be drawn closer to God. The second type of ritual, which involves various forms of reenactment of the battle of Karbala, is a natural extension of the first and can include other actions, such as building or destroying various ritual objects, like a model of Husayn's tomb. The third type of ritual involves public physical mourning rituals, which typically involve self-mortification, often by slapping the chest and head or by hitting oneself with chains. In rare cases, blades are used to inflict more serious pain. Regional variations on such rituals can often be extremely diverse. The object is to inflict pain on oneself, without causing serious injury, because it is believed that pain allows the ritual participants to empathize with the martyrs by experiencing a small fraction of the pain they experienced at Karbala. The willingness of the ritual participants to offer their bodies up for self-inflicted pain is also symbolic of their willingness to be martyred for Husayn. Self-inflicted punishment is also seen as an act of penance for the sins of the Muslim community, who abandoned Husayn and his followers to their tragic fate on the days leading up to 'Ashura.

In addition to the more spiritual or doctrinal functions of the rituals of 'Ashura, these rituals have also served a wide variety of other social and political functions. They have served to strengthen communal identities, especially in relation to Sunni Muslims, but also among ethnic, tribal, neighborhood, and other societal groups. They have helped to cement bonds between patrons and clients, especially in the premodern era. They have been used by modern political movements, including rulers, nationalists, reformists, rebels, and revolutionaries. They have served a wide variety of social functions, such as promoting and preserving social networks and enhancing the social status of individuals and groups, including governments and opposition groups. Many have even argued that 'Ashura rituals serve a variety of psychological or emotional functions for individuals. In short, the rituals of 'Ashura have served, and continue to serve, a dynamic function in Shiite societies. It is therefore reasonable to assume that they will continue to serve important spiritual, ethical, political, and social functions in the foreseeable future.

NOTES

Portions of this chapter are based on material from my two recently published books: *The Martyrs of Karbala: Shi'i Symbols and Rituals in Modern Iran* (Seattle, Washington: University of Washington Press, 2004) and *The Women of Karbala: The Gender Dynamics of Ritual Performances and Symbolic Discourses of Modern Shi'i Islam* (Austin, Texas: University of Texas Press, 2005). Other material may be found in a forthcoming encyclopedia article, "Ashura" in *Encyclopedia of Islam Third Edition,* edited by Rudi Matthee and published by E.J. Brill in Leiden, The Netherlands. Please consult these publications for more detailed discussions of 'Ashura.

1. Early Muslim sources state that when the Prophet Muhammad and his followers emigrated from Mecca to Medina in 622 CE he instructed Muslims to fast on the 10th day of the month of Muharram, the first month of the Islamic calendar. Within the next couple of years, after the month of Ramadan (the ninth month) was prescribed for Muslims as an obligatory period of fasting, the Muharram fast was transformed into an optional fast. There are numerous traditions that describe the events surrounding the adoption of 'Ashura as a holy day. All of these accounts agree that Muslims practiced the fast shortly after the emigration (*hijra*) to Medina and that they abandoned it upon the adoption of the fasting month of Ramadan. However, they disagree on the precise origins of the practice. Some say that Muhammad saw the Jews fasting on the 10th day of the first month of their calendar in commemoration of how God had saved the Israelites from the Egyptians. Other accounts stress the pre-Islamic Arab origins of the holy day, explaining that Muhammad's tribe of

Quraysh, and indeed Muhammad himself, used to fast on the day of 'Ashura in the so-called "Period of Ignorance" (*Jahiliyya*) before the revelation of the Qur'an. Modern scholars have tended to favor the theory of the Jewish origins of the 'Ashura fast, but there is no consensus on the issue. Given the scant historical sources that we have for this early period, scholars must rely on the interpretation of the Hadith and the few other sources that have survived. This is greatly complicated by the fact that the Hadith and other sources, such as the biographical texts about Muhammad (*Sira*), were not written down until one or two centuries after the events they describe. Therefore, it is difficult to resolve this debate definitively.

2. This hadith was reported by the famous Sunni traditionist Ahmad ibn Hanbal (d. 855 CE) in his collection, *al-Musnad*. Moojan Momen, *An Introduction to Shi'i Islam* (New Haven, Connecticut: Yale University Press, 1985), 14.

3. Ibid., 17.

4. For a detailed discussion of the crisis of succession to the Prophet Muhammad, see Wilferd Madelung, *The Succession to Muhammad: A Study of the Early Caliphate* (Cambridge: Cambridge University Press, 1997).

5. Muhammad ibn Jarir al-Tabari, *The History of al-Tabari: Volume 16, The Community Divided,* trans. Adrian Brockett (Albany, New York: State University of New York Press, 1997), 52.

6. Muhammad Muhammadi Eshtehardi, *Hazrat Zaynab, payam risan-i shahidan-i Karbala* (Tehran: Nashr-i Mutahhar, 1997), 26–28.

7. This elegy was written by Sahib Ibn 'Abbad, a prominent poet from the Buyid era (ca. 945–1055 CE). It comes from the collection by Abu Bakr al-Khwarazmi called *Maqtal al-Husayn* (The Killing of Husayn). See Mayel Baktash, "Ta'ziyeh and its Philosophy," in *Ta'ziyeh: Ritual and Drama in Iran,* ed. Peter J. Chelkowski (New York: New York University Press and Soroush Press, 1979), 97.

8. Ibn Kathir, *al-Bidaya wa al-nihaya* (Cairo: Matba'a al-Sa'ada, 1939). The translated passage is adapted from Michel M. Mazzaoui, "Shi'ism and Ashura in South Lebanon," in *Ta'ziyeh,* 231.

9. For a modern edition of this work, see Mulla Husayn Va'iz Kashifi, *Rawzat al-shuhada'* (Tehran: Chapkhanah-i Khavar, 1962).

10. The orators at *Rawza Khanis* are usually men, although sometimes, female orators give sermons in private *Rawza Khanis* attended exclusively by women.

11. Jean Calmard, "Le Patronage des Ta'ziyeh: Elements pour une Etude globale," in *Ta'ziyeh,* 122.

12. For detailed discussions of the *Ta'ziyeh* traditions of Iran, please refer to the following books. In English, Peter J. Chelkowski, *Ta'ziyeh* and Samuel Peterson, ed., *Ta'ziyeh: Ritual and Popular Beliefs in Iran* (Hartford, Connecticut: Trinity College, 1988). In Persian, Sadiq Humayuni, *Ta'ziyeh dar Iran* (Shiraz: Intisharat-i Navid, 1989); Inayatallah Shahidi and 'Ali Bulukbashi, *Pazhuhishi dar ta'ziyah va ta'ziyah khani az aghaz ta payan-i dowrah-i Qajar dar Tihran* (Tehran: Daftar-i Pazhuhish-ha-i Farhangi, Iran UNESCO Commission, 2001); Jaber Anasari, ed., *Shabih khani, kuhan ulgu-i nimayishha-i Irani* (Tehran: Chapkhanah-i Ramin, 1992); Muhammad Ibrahim Ayati, *Barrisi-i tarikh-i Ashura,* 9th ed. (Tehran: Nashr-i Sadduq, 1996); and Laleh Taqiyan, *Ta'ziyah va ti'atr dar Iran* (Tehran: Nashr-e Markaz, 1995).

13. Vernon James Schubel, *Religious Performance in Contemporary Islam: Shi'i Devotional Rituals in South Asia* (Columbia, South Carolina: University of South Carolina Press, 1993) 110.

14. Juan R.I. Cole, *The Roots of North Indian Shi'ism in Iran and Iraq: Religion and State in Awadh, 1722–1859* (Berkeley and Los Angeles: University of California Press, 1988), 22–27; see also, A.N. al-Naqvi, *A Historical Review of the Institution of Azadari for Imam Husain* (Karachi, Pakistan: Peer Mahomed Ebrahim Trust, 1974).

15. See Cole, *Roots of North Indian Shi'ism,* 22–35; Frank J. Korom, *Hosay Trinidad: Muharram Performances in an Indo-Caribbean Diaspora* (Philadelphia, Pennsylvania: University of Pennsylvania Press, 2003); al-Naqvi, *Institution of Azadari.*

16. For Shi'i rituals outside Iran please refer to the following studies: Schubel, *Religious Performance;* Augustus Richard Norton, *Shi'ism and the Ashura Ritual in Lebanon* (New York: Al-Saqi Books, 2003); Cole, *Roots of North Indian Shi'ism;* Yitzhak Nakash, *The Shi'is of Iraq* (Princeton, New Jersey: Princeton University Press, 1994); David Pinault, *The Horse of Karbala: Muslim Devotional Life in India* (New York: Palgrave, 2001); David Pinault, *The Shi'ites, Ritual, and Popular Piety in a Muslim Community* (New York: St. Martin's Press, 1992); Frederic Maatouk, *La representation de la mort de l'imam Hussein a Nabatieh* (Beirut: Université libanaise, Institut des sciences sociales, Centre de recherches, 1974); and Waddah Shararah, *Transformations d'une manifestation religieuse dans un village du Liban-Sud (Asura)* (Beirut: al-Jami'a al-Lubnaniyya, Ma'had al-'Ulum al-Ijtima'iyya, 1968).

11

The Hidden and the Most Hidden: The Heart as a Source of Spiritual Guidance

—————————————— • ——————————————

Shaykh ʿAli Jumʿa

Every Friday thousands of Muslims in Cairo hear the call to prayer and make their way to Sultan Hasan, a fourteenth-century mosque located in the heart of the old city, to pray and listen to the *khutba* (the Friday talk) of Shaykh ʿAli Jumʿa. As one enters the courtyard of the mosque, framed by four enormous vaulted halls, one is struck by the simplicity, beauty, and scale of the structure. It arouses the feeling of man and his Creator.

Shaykh ʿAli climbs the stairs to the *minbar,* faces the congregation, and begins his talk. He invokes the Name of Allah with such intensity that men weep, for it has been said that when you hear the Name of Allah you should weep, and if you do not weep, you should weep because you do not. After the prayer almost the entire congregation remains to hear the lesson that Shaykh ʿAli presents. As he speaks, his soft eyes penetrate, his voice rings with strength and quivers with emotion. He is the embodiment of intelligence and light.

It was after a Friday prayer on a hot Cairo evening that we spoke of the heart. This is the first time Shaykh ʿAli's words have been translated into English.

Shaykh ʿAli Jumʿa is now the *Mufti* (chief jurisconsult) of Egypt. At the time of this interview he was professor of Islamic jurisprudence at Al-Azhar University in Cairo, Egypt.

—Shems Friedlander

SHEMS FRIEDLANDER (SF): What is the heart? Where is it located? Is it the pump that physicians call a heart which remains with man between birth and death? Is it physical or metaphysical?

Shaykh ʿAli Jumʿa (SAJ): There are words, expressions in the Arabic language that speak about this level: the heart (*al-qalb*), the sensitive heart (*al-fuʾad*), the essence (*al-lubb*), and the intellect (*al-ʿaql*). The word *al-qalb* also refers to the physical entity, the pump that pumps blood, the cessation of which separates life and death. But as to this other heart—meaning the inside of a thing, its truth, its central core, and its essence—there are five levels that Sufis speak about regarding this matter. They have spoken of the heart, the spirit, the secret, the hidden, and the most hidden. These five levels are like circles within circles, each circle higher and narrower than the one before. Meaning that if there are 1000 human beings at the level of the heart, at the level of the spirit there are eight hundred, at the level of the secret six hundred, the hidden two hundred, at the level of the most hidden one hundred—and what is beyond this fewer than one hundred. These levels form a pyramidal shape. The heart is a level among the levels, and not a piece of flesh. But there is a relation of sorts between the heart as a piece of flesh and the heart as a level. This relation is not perceived or sensed. It is not possible to touch, see, or experience it through the five senses. And yet, we feel the level of the heart near the breast, below it, and to the left. We feel it in a place lower than or under the part of the body that is the physical heart.

SF: How does one enter this heart?

SAJ: The way leading to the heart is remembrance, repetition of the Names of Allah (*dhikr*) and contemplation (*fikr*). Just as a human being feels that thinking takes place in the head (*Shaykh ʿAli places his hand on his head*) and does not feel that his hand is thinking, so he feels near the heart the unveiling of the secrets and lights in the five realms. There are five realms which the human being experiences. The world of *al-mulk*, this is the visible world experienced by the five senses; the world of *al-malakut*, this comprises the creatures and creation that man cannot see and cannot arrive at through his five senses, like the angels, *jinn*, hell, and heaven. Together, *al-mulk* and *al-malakut* are the world, which is what is other than Allah. Beyond this are three worlds at the divine level; the world of beauty, the world of majesty, and that of completeness. They are also referred to as "what is above the throne" and is what is meant by His saying "*Al-Rahman ala'l-arsh istawa.*" What is above the throne is Allah in His Beauty, Completeness, and Splendor. What is beneath the throne is what is referred to as the carpet. There is a throne and there is a carpet. The aforementioned five levels—the heart, the spirit, the secret, the hidden, and the most hidden—are levels among the levels of lights and secrets in the world of *mulk* and *malakut*, the world beneath the throne, and through which man ascends to the positions of the throne. Above the throne there are five other levels—heart, spirit, secret, hidden, and most hidden—resembling these five, reflected like a mirror, five facing this way and five that way (*Shaykh ʿAli demonstrates with his open palms, one palm toward the listener, one palm toward himself*). Beyond this are three other worlds which are totally obscure, meaning that we absolutely cannot comprehend them, whether with our thought, our minds, our practice of *dhikr*, or our sensory perception. For Allah in His Glory is beyond comprehension.

SF: And so what is the heart?

SAJ: The heart is a level among the levels of piety on the way to Allah, the lights and secrets of which are manifested in a part of the body, the form of which is a pump that pumps blood in the body. In this area, not in the part of the body itself but around it, man feels something of the revelation of secrets, disclosures, and lights.

SF: Where is the heart?

SAJ: It is in man. It is a level among levels of the spirit, meaning a circle of the circles of the spirit. Above it is also the sprit; it is a level in which the spirit finds and comprehends itself. And then there is what is secret. At this level man understands that he is nothing and that Allah is the foundation of all things. In this stage man might lose his way and believe himself to be Allah, and believe himself to be nothing because Allah has totally taken him over and therefore is him. After this he ascends to the hidden and knows that he is one thing and Allah is another. That he is mortal and Allah is permanent and that there is a difference between the creature and the Creator. Then he is elevated beyond this and knows that he is a manifestation among the manifestations of the Beneficent, and that the attributes of Allah are all reflected in him through ability, will, and knowledge. This is the station of the most hidden. The first of all these endless levels is the heart, the instrument of contemplation (*fikr*) and *dhikr* (remembrance by repetition). Allah is eternal, but I perish. I have a beginning and He has no beginning. I need Him but He does not need me, and so a feeling comes from my heart. This is the station of the hidden.

SF: Does the heart have thoughts? Does it have emotions, feelings? Is the spirit, as the philosopher and mystic al-Ghazali (d. 1111 CE) says, a subtle body originating in the cavity of the physical heart, which spreads through the body via the arteries, just as a light from a lantern fills a room?

SAJ: The hidden which we have talked about is a level of the levels that reside in the heart. This heart is a container, a vessel, and these levels of which the first is also called the heart are another thing. Then

there is the spirit, the secret, the hidden, and the most hidden—all
reside in the heart as a vessel. For the spiritual world has a connection
to the physical world, but in reality this material which includes heart,
spirit, secret, hidden, and most hidden is composed of gradations of
the spirit. It is not the pump, but its locus is the pump, just as water is
contained in a glass. The pump is the locus of the spiritual of which
al-Ghazali speaks. So the question is: Does this spiritual entity which
is inside the pump have emotions, feelings? Yes, it has emotions.
These emotions have been the subject of Sufi thinking and are seen as
ten levels. These emotions include a feeling called repentance, which
is when man feels the need to turn away from what is not Allah, as if
his preoccupation with the universe is a sin on his part from which he
wants to turn away, an ugly feeling. There are ten stations and a
section called states. A station is an unchangeable emotion, and the
states are passing emotions that come and go. Man ascends from one
station to the next and does not return to a lower station. If a man does
return to a lower station, it is a major catastrophe, like returning from
faith to unbelief. The states come and go. The Sufis have given them
names such as depressed, happy, union, and separation. The reply then
to this question is: The spiritual heart does have emotions and these
emotions are of two kinds, unmovable and passing.

SF: What closes the heart?

SAJ: According to the Sufis the heart has two doors: a door to
creation, and a door to Truth, therefore to Allah. There is also what is
earned and what is given. By his nature man's heart is open to creation.
He needs food, drink, clothing, a dwelling place, a companion,
company, and he needs to live in the world according to its laws. This
is the door of creation. It is in the nature of man that this door be open.
When *dhikr* is achieved, it opens the other door, the door of Truth, and
this happens in three stages. In the first, the door of Truth is closed. In
the second, it opens, but the door of creation closes from the intensity
of *dhikr,* as if *dhikr* is a wind closing the door of creation and opening
the door of Truth. In the third, the door of creation also opens, and
the heart has two open doors. The fourth case is when both doors are
closed and this is what is called madness. This is someone who is neither
into worship nor into the world—that is, he knows nothing at all. He
has exited from the circle of responsibility. As to the first
case—wherein the door of creation is opened, blocking the door to
Truth—that is from lack of *dhikr* and from man's nature. So what
opens and what closes? This is the answer. The door of creation opens
naturally, and the door of Truth is opened by *dhikr* and *fikr.* The door
of Truth opens little by little until it is wide open. An important issue

to bring up here is that of what is earned and what is given. We can open the door through *dhikr,* but the door can also be opened by Allah without *dhikr.* The Sufis speak of a person who is a seeker and another who is sought. There is one who is on the way and one who is attracted. All these terms lead to the same meaning, namely that there is something man can do that leads to his heart being opened, and there is also a gift from Allah that opens the heart and has nothing to do with the person's effort. The Prophet used to say: "*Allahumma,* let there be in my heart light, and in my hearing light, and in my seeing light, in my hands light, to my right light, to my left light, and let me be light."

SF: Moses threw the staff and it became a snake. He was commanded to pick up the snake. He did and it again became a staff. Then he was told to place his hand on his heart. When he removed it the Name of Allah was written in light on the palm of his hand. Can metaphysical light be transformed into light perceived by the senses?

SAJ: All spiritual things can be transformed into things of a sensory nature. On the Day of Judgment death comes in the form of a ram. Death here is a concept but it becomes materialized. There are two kinds of secrets and two kinds of lights. We spoke of the realm of *al-mulk* and the realm of *al-malakut,* circles of the creation. In each there are secrets and lights. The secrets of *al-mulk* are of the senses. Meaning the benefits of medicinal plants and the laws of building and engineering, of mathematics, and of hydrology—all these are secrets that man discovers every day in the realm of *al-mulk.* There are also sensory lights: electricity, the sun, moon, stars, lasers, and so on. There are also lights and secrets of *al-malakut*—lights and secrets that are nonsensory. But anything from the realm of *al-malakut* can enter the realm of *mulk,* can be transformed into something perceived by the senses. Creation is composed of two sections: *al-mulk,* which is perceived by the five senses, and *al-malakut.* That realm which may be sensed by the five senses is what we are in now. In *al-malakut* it is the spirit ascending the circles which is the perceiver and not the senses.

SF: There is a saying of the Prophet Muhammad: "All things have a polish. The polish of the heart is the Remembrance of God." What rusts the heart?

SAJ: In the Qur'an there are descriptions of what ails the heart. There is the layer of scum on stagnant water, the cover, the locks, veils, pride, and so on, many qualities. These qualities can be removed through faith, others by repetition of the Names of Allah, and others by contemplation. The Sufis link this to the seven levels of the self (*al-nafs*):

domineering, censorious, inspiring, tranquil, contented, pleasing, and pure. They have linked these to the Beautiful Names of Allah and to the gradations of man's attempt to remove rust or scum. Seven Names used are as follows: *la illah illa Allah, Allah, Hu, Al-Hayy, Al-Qayyum, Al-Haqq,* and *Al-Qahhar.* There is some disagreement about this as some Sufis choose *Al-Aziz, Al-Wahid, Al-Wadud, Al-Wahab, Al-Basit,* and *Al-Muhaymin.* There are various formulas given by a sheikh as to the manner and frequency of the repetition of the Names. The invocation of the Names of Allah satisfies the heart and opens the door of Truth.

NOTE

This chapter first appeared in *Parabola,* 26:4, winter 2001, 24–29. It is reproduced in this volume with the permission of the editors of *Parabola.* It has been updated to reflect Shaykh 'Ali Jum'a's appointment as Mufti of Egypt.

12

EVIL AS THE ABSENCE OF THE GOOD

———————————— • ————————————

Seyyed Hossein Nasr

Currently University Professor of Islamic Studies at George Washington University, Dr. Seyyed Hossein Nasr is one of the foremost scholars and writers on Islam and Sufism in the world today. Gray Henry (Virginia Gray Henry-Blakemore) directs Fons Vitae, which publishes books on world spirituality and works with the Thomas Merton Foundation in Louisville, Kentucky.

GRAY HENRY (GH): First is the question of defining evil. Is there absolute evil, and is there relative evil?

SEYYED HOSSEIN NASR (SHN): From the metaphysical point of view, the world itself is a revelation. Revelation is not only the sacred book or an avatar or a divine descent. The universe itself is the primal revelation of God. But it is also a veiling. Only the supreme Good, which is absolute, can be absolutely good. All that is not in that supreme Reality must participate in and partake of the separation from that supreme Good. That's why Christ said, "Only my father in heaven is good." Even Christ said that he was not "the Good;" only his father in heaven was so. Now, this separation from the Good is necessary because we exist. To exist is to be separated from the supreme Reality, to be in the domain of relativity. Separation is the origin of all that we call evil. In *The Divine Comedy*, Dante Alighieri says that Hell is separation from God. God is real; we are relatively real. To the extent that we are relatively real, we are separated from the Divine Reality by a hiatus which itself is the origin of what appears to us to be evil. To the extent that we are real, we reflect the good. That is also why the good has an ontological basis; evil does not.

GH: This is the important point.

SHN: Exactly. Evil is like shadow; the good is like the sun, like light. Now, when you sit under the shade of a tree, you say, "I feel cool."

You think that the shade and the sun ten feet away are equal existentially. Both exist. If you go in the sun, you're hot; if you're under the shade, you're cool. But actually the shade is the absence of the sun. It doesn't have the same ontological status. In the same way, evil is real as much as we, who are relative beings, are real, but it is not real as far as "The Real" is concerned. That is, in God there is no evil. Then why, you might ask, did God bother to create the world? There is the Hindu doctrine of *lila*—the world is divine play. The Islamic response, I think, is most to the point when it asserts that God wanted to be known and therefore created the world so that he would be known. God is infinite. Infinity implies all possibilities, including the possibility of the negation of itself. God is also good. It's in the nature of good to give of itself, as Saint Augustine said, like the light, like the sun. The sun cannot but give of itself. When you understand these two supreme attributes of God, you understand that the possibility of divine self-negation must become realized. And that is the world.

GH: A lot of people say evil is a real force. Does it have its own life?

SHN: That's a very important issue. As you descend down the plane of reality, the veils of darkness increase until you reach the world in which we are, in which the veil is very thick. As the history of the world flows, gradually there's a movement away from the Source, from the Principle. That is, God is not only the center and the above, He's also the beginning and the origin. He's the alpha. In the original creation there were higher levels of reality, closer to the sun. Light dominated completely over darkness. That's the Golden Age, the *Kritayuga* in Hinduism, and so forth. But as the history of the cosmos and our history unfold, the darkness becomes more and more accentuated. This flow, however, is interrupted by revelation and by divine descents throughout human history, each a foundation of a great religion: Christ, Muhammad the Prophet of Islam, the Buddha, Moses on Mt. Sinai, Zoroaster, Lao Tse, and Confucius. There's an intense glow which defines the beginning of each religion, but then the cycle of degeneration begins again.

GH: Now, at the end of the twentieth century, we have the drying up of traditional forms of life.

SHN: Actually, the twentieth century has seen more horrendous forms of evil than any period of human history.

GH: It would appear so.

SHN: There are many people who criticize Traditionalists by saying, "Oh, you idealize the old world. There were also wars in ancient times," and things like that. Of course we do not deny it. But there is a great degree of difference between historical events and events today. And as the cosmic cycle unfolds, and as truths are forgotten, then for a while evil is not even recognized as such. People refuse to recognize it, and it becomes all-invading. This raises an important point of the question you asked a moment ago: Is evil a force? Now, from the *metaphysical* point of view, only God is real. *Evil has no ultimate reality.* Since we live on the level of *relativity,* in our ordinary consciousness this world is relatively real. *Evil is also relatively real.* All religions speak of the battle of good and evil. It would be a great mistake to say, "Well, there is no evil in or around me." In fact, evil is as real as the ego.

GH: Which is separative.

SHN: Yes. We assert the separative ego while denying evil—one of the great strategies of the modern world.

GH: That's a contradiction.

SHN: Absolute contradiction. People don't talk about the devil any more in polite society. Not fashionable. But the devil is the personification of the separative tendency on the human plane. To deny the devil is to deny God. Charles Baudelaire says that in *The Flowers of Evil.* A pasteurized world in which there is no evil and no devil is itself the worst kind of daydreaming and something demonic in the ultimate sense. We must understand that destiny has put us in a moment of cosmic history in which there is a predominance of evil, and we are here to be, in fact, testament and witness to the good. In older days there were so many ways of controlling evil, through religious rites, spiritual disciplines and teachers, through the presence of the sacred…today it's so difficult. And that is the secret of why, in the traditional sources, there are sometimes indications that people prayed for those who would live at the end of the world.

GH: Then the ego is where the force of evil takes place in the human world. And can there be evil without intention?

SHN: In the animal or the plant world—

GH: When there are hurricanes that kill people and so forth.

SHN: That is not completely evil, because a hurricane also cleans up the air and so forth and reestablishes balance. What is metaphysically "evil" is the gradual flow of the cosmos away from its original perfection when it was much more transparent to the archetypal realities. Nature, precisely because it does not have a will to act, is always innocent. Therefore there is no moral evil in nature. Pollution, the greenhouse effect, and the destruction of the coral reefs and the ecology of the oceans: it is we who are destroying nature. Is this only evil if we will it? Morally, yes. The reason we are doing this, and not, let's say, elephants or crocodiles, is precisely because God has given us free will. In the divine plan of things, it is the crown of creation that will finally destroy creation, bring the *Kaliyuga* to an end. Which is what we're doing.

GH: Many people ask, If God is really good, how can he create sinners and then send them to Hell?—a question of predestination and free will.

SHN: Yes, this is important. If everything is determined by God, and we have no free will, then we cannot commit evil. Everything we do is God's will. However, the other side is the question of free will. There can be no moral responsibility without free will. Evil can only be committed if you are free to commit evil. That is why, for example, if you have a fever, that is not an act of evil committed on your part. If you deliberately take a drug which is bad for your body, then you have committed an evil act. But if you eat an apple with something bad for you inside it without knowing it—if you do it without intention—then it's not evil. So evil is always related to intention. As to whether God created sinners deliberately to commit sins and go to Hell, that is not true at all, because those sinners had free will. They were not chosen just to be sinners and sent to hell—that would be a monstrous view of God. Every person has the free will to choose. That is why, for example, in both Islam and Christianity, children or insane people are absolved from committing evil. So the question of intention, free will, and responsibility are part and parcel of reality. You might well say, however, we're put in this world where there's so much evil. Somebody has to commit this evil. So that means most of us have to commit evil. Isn't that unfair? Here I will quote you the famous saying of Christ: "Trouble must needs come, but woe unto him who bringeth it about." Tragedy will come, but woe unto you if you cause its coming. That does not take away our responsibility before God. Each individual, by virtue of the fact that he or she is given the freedom to act, has a moral responsibility. Nobody's forced to become a sinner. We always have the freedom to come out of that state. If you have committed sin, it's always possible, as long as you're human, to eradicate evil by virtue of being human. It's a remarkable gift which God has given us. We can always ask God's pardon, God's mercy.

GH: I have a question about the terms "evil" and "bad." Sometimes things happen and we call them "bad" in our lives—an illness or something. They can be transformed spiritually by us into the good. But can something that seems "evil" be transformed? What is the relationship between "evil" and "bad"?

SHN: Oftentimes events befall us which cause us to suffer. Those are opportunities for the soul to grow. We are in this world, as the Koran says, to be tested. "Evil," however, that which is morally evil, is not only bad in the sense that it's bad for us, but it has no redemptive quality to it unless you recognize it as evil, and perform the *tawba* (turning), and the purging aspect which that brings about. An evil that can befall us can be good for us only in that sense.

GH: *Metanoia.*

SHN: That's right—an occasion for *tawba*, for repentance, for purging something from us by recognizing it as evil. It can also be a challenge for transformation, which is quite something else.

GH: Sometimes people say when a child is born deformed or falls ill, it's a sign of evil. How can we understand that?

SHN: Because of the separation between the material world and the intelligible world, you can never have the perfection of the spiritual world in this one. If you draw a pattern of a hexagon, the perfect hexagon exists only in the intelligible, the mathematical world. Every hexagon that you make is imperfect. It's remarkable how the good predominates over evil. But the imperfection has to be there. We expect everything to be good, everything to be perfect. We want everything without giving anything. We don't want to submit ourselves to God. We do not want to accept our destiny. We always want to assert ourselves as individual egos. And then we expect everything to be perfect. And when it isn't, we—who did not start with truly believing that God is reality and whatever good He has given us we must be thankful for—then begin to criticize God and religion: Oh, if this is a good God, why am I having troubles? But traditional people realized there were imperfections in this world. They took it as a part of terrestrial life and never expected perfection here below. Now, the fact that we are so dissatisfied is proof of our divine origin. Why is it that we expect perfection? That comes from the imprint of the divinity upon us.

GH: Does evil exist cross-culturally? Do, for example, the Buddhists see evil the same way that Muslims do?

SHN: The spiritual and metaphysical significance of evil is universal. It has to do with the ego, with the walls that we draw around it, with the importance of breaking that wall, and with giving of ourselves. However, the forms in which acts take place in which good and evil are defined are bound by the traditions in which human beings live. Then there are formal differences which the various revelations impose as far as what actions are performed. For example, for a Muslim it is considered to be *haram* (forbidden), an evil act, to drink alcoholic beverages or to eat pork. A Jew who follows the *halakhah* will also not eat pork. Whereas for a Christian this is not the case. One might say, "Well, isn't this making evil relative?" But that's to misunderstand the fact that each religion sacralizes the pattern of life according to its own principles.

GH: Is the way we personally overcome evil in ourselves the purification of the ego?

SHN: Yes, but that cannot just be done personally, because who is the person doing the purifying if the ego itself is not purified? That is why you need tradition and objective revelation from the source of All Good. It's important to mention that there is a reality to the human state before what Christianity calls the fallen state of Original Sin. That is what we call in Islam the *fitra* or primordial nature, which was molded in the good and with the good. And that always remains.
We have separated ourselves from our primordial nature. The outer human has forgotten the inner. But always, deep in ourselves, we have the sense of goodness and know what is evil in the deepest moral sense. But we have to delve deeply into ourselves, which many of us do not do. That is why revelation is indispensable.

GH: Every moment, we say, "I should do that, I shouldn't do that." There must be a final accountability because we are in fact continually taking account of ourselves.

SHN: Of course. That tendency, that impulse is still within us. But it's stronger in some people and weaker in others. Unless a society has the objective framework of morality, it cannot survive on this impulse alone.

GH: In the Qur'an, God punishes the mighty who do evil. Why do monstrous heads of state, for example, go seemingly unpunished today?

SHN: That's a question that people often pose, not only about the mighty, but about people who have committed evil and who seem to be living a fairly comfortable life. And some people who've done much good suffer a great deal. The answer, of course, is that we have developed a truncated vision of both divine reality and our own reality, because we associate all of life with only this life. We associate divine justice with our own assessment of it. An evil person may seem to be living a very comfortable life, but he will be punished in the larger curve of life. One has to understand, especially in the case of human beings, that we have a very long journey from our origination in God to our return to the Divine. Our earthly life is only a small part of this circle. To judge things only by the little bit of this trajectory that we are able to observe is false. What appears outwardly as good is not necessarily so inwardly. There are people who seem to have a very comfortable life and live in beautiful surroundings, but who live in hell within themselves.

GH: Can evil, in the end, be overcome? In terms of our own self, that is?

SHN: Evil can *always* be overcome within ourselves. We live in this world in order to do that. We are not in this world to eradicate evil in the whole of the world. This is one of the false ideas that many people have. Outside of us, we must do as much as we can. But our main responsibility is, first of all, to our soul, to God—to cleanse ourselves. One of the great errors of modern society is that by the inversion of all values, people want to eradicate evil in the world without having purified themselves. And so this impulse within the soul for perfection and goodness skips over that which is most difficult—the correcting of ourselves. It is much easier to feed the hungry in India than to fast oneself.

GH: Does evil have an inherent attraction to some people? What would there be in a human being that would attract it to evil?

SHN: Although we were created in the perfect mold, we are also cast into this world and given the possibility of being the lowest of the low. There is within the world a tendency toward what Islam calls forgetfulness of Divine reality; Christianity calls it Original Sin. Although God created us in goodness, we have fallen from that state. There is in fact a tendency in the soul toward falling down. It's what the Hindus call the *tamasic* tendency. Water flows downward. If you let a stone go, it falls down. It takes effort to push something up. God has put us in this world in such a way that He has given us the will, but because He loves us and love needs effort, He wants us to use this effort to move upward.

GH: Is there a difference between evil in thought and evil in deed?

SHN: Yes. We cannot perform an evil deed without having the thought that goes with it. That is the intention. God judges our deeds according to our intentions. Let's say we walk in the street and suddenly step on an animal and hurt it. Or if we're driving, hit a tree, and a bird falls down and dies—we have not premeditated this performance of an evil deed. That is not evil. It's unfortunate, and we have to ask God's pardon that we were the instrument for such a thing, but it is not an evil deed in the theological and moral sense of the term. Every deed is preceded by thought. An evil thought is more dangerous than an evil deed, because it is the source of evil deeds. Society can only judge by the deeds, but evil thoughts are punished by God.

GH: What if one just pops into your head?

SHN: That's temptation. Evil thoughts are evil thoughts when they become *our* thoughts, when we hold them.

GH: One last question. What is a simple thought an average person can hold onto when dealing with questions concerning evil?

SHN: The simplest thought is that God, being good, has created a world in which there is a remarkable predominance of the good over evil, of the beautiful over the ugly, and that no matter what situation we encounter in life, we always have access to the good and the beautiful. It's for us to take advantage of being human and to make this choice of the good over that which is evil, which is ultimately both ugly and a negation.

NOTE

This chapter first appeared in *Parabola* 24:4, winter 1999, 59–66. It is reproduced with slight modifications in this volume with the permission of the editors of *Parabola*.

13

THE BLESSED STATE OF FEAR: REFLECTIONS FROM ISLAM AND CHRISTIANITY

—————————————— • ——————————————

Virginia Gray Henry-Blakemore

There is only one Real Fear: that we do not fully avail ourselves of the opportunity afforded by the human state and that at the moment of death we are not content with the state or degree of spiritual integrity we have realized. Once we are separated from our bodies, our vehicles of "doing" and change, we are left with who we *are*. Even knowing this, we go along abusing the human state.

In the various spiritual traditions, fear and its related attitudes of contrition and repentance can be seen as the blessed impetus and key for the commencement of the spiritual life. Fear incites the soul to move forward. In Islamic mysticism, the movement of the soul toward its true nature is described in three stages: the first is called *makhafa* or Fear of God; the second is called *mahabba,* which refers to the Love of God; and the third stage is *ma'rifa,* which means Gnosis or Knowledge of God. According to Martin Lings, each of these stages has two aspects: "The domain of fear-action is that of 'must not' and 'must'; love has likewise, in addition to its dynamic intensity, the static aspect of contemplative bliss; and spiritual knowledge is both objective and subjective being ultimately concerned with the Absolute as Transcendent Truth and Immanent Selfhood.... Fear of the Lord is the beginning of wisdom, and it is to fear that the first two stations are related. They are thus concerned with danger, and they are two because danger confronts man with two possibilities, flight or attack, that is, abstention and accomplishment. The aforementioned six stations of wisdom might be called dimensions of holiness."[1]

According to Lings, these same three principles of Fear, Love, and Knowledge are apparent in Islamic art and in Qur'anic illumination. The majority of calligraphers were Sufis who had a great fear of intruding on the perfection of the Qur'an with their art. In Islamic art, the geometric aspect of design corresponds with the principles of Rigor and Fear. The arabesque or endlessly entwining plant tendrils represent Love.

Finally, the calligraphy of the Revealed Word corresponds to the domain of Knowledge.

Frithjof Schuon has explained, "Every spiritual path must start with a 'conversion,' an apparently negative turning round of the will, an indirect movement towards God in the form of an inner separation from the false plenitude of the world. This withdrawal corresponds to the station of renunciation or detachment, of sobriety, of fear of God: what has to be overcome is desire, passional attachment, and idolatry of ephemeral things."[2]

The Sufi use of prayer beads or "rosary" (Ar. *tasbih*) can be compared to the Catholic rite of Holy Communion. Both begin with the attitudes of fear and repentance—an emptying of oneself from one's Self. When reciting prayers on the *tasbih,* a Muslim repeats 99 times, "God forgive me." This is said with the intention of *tawba*—Repentance or "turning"—that is, of sincerely desiring to change. The Catholic, before approaching the altar to receive the sacrament, prays, "Lord have mercy upon me, Christ have mercy upon me."[3] Both Muslims and Catholic Christians thus participate in an emptying—a death of all that is unholy or low in themselves. This is the stage that might be referred to as the "death" that St. John of the Cross described when he said, "Die before you die." However, after death comes resurrection, and in the third stage comes eternal life. After the act of emptying comes reformation; according to Meister Eckhart, this leads ultimately to Union with the Godhead: "When I preach, I usually speak of disinterest and say that a man should be *empty* of self and all things; and secondly, that he should be *reconstructed* in the simple Good that God is; and thirdly, that he should consider the great aristocracy which God has set up in the soul, such that by means of it man may wonderfully *attain to God*; and fourthly, of *the purity of the divine nature.*"

In the second stage of prayer with the *tasbih* the Muslim asks for God's blessing and praise upon the Prophet Muhammad with the idea that he himself may return to his own pure and primordial nature, the *fitra,* the condition of the True Man. The Christian, as he kneels before the altar now empty, waits to receive the bread and wine, whether understood symbolically or literally to be the presence of the Word of God. When the Host is taken within his own emptiness he thereby regains his Christ-like nature. He has been *re*-formed for that moment in the Self, which he hopes he will have realized for the time of his resurrection.

The third stage of spiritual movement initiated by fear is that of union or return to the Divine Source of all Being—the froth subsiding into the sea from which it has been manifested. One hopes that if purity of soul has not been realized, if one has not awakened to one's true state of being, God will bestow His Grace and Mercy for the intention of sincere effort in God's direction.

The Muslim in the final stage of prayer with the *tasbih* repeats 99 times, "There is no god but God" (*la ilaha illa Allah*), thereby attesting to the absence of anything but God. Neither the vessel full of itself nor the empty vessel filled with True Man survives; both have returned to the One. A painting by Raphael found at the Vatican provides a similar image for the Christian. In this painting it is as if we are before an altar upon which stands a chalice, and above the chalice appears the dove of the Holy Spirit. At the top of the painting is a depiction of God in the company of heavenly personages including Mary, Jesus, John the Baptist, the Apostles, and angels. What we may understand from this scene is that after the worshipper has received the sacrament and kneels purified before the altar, his or her soul rises up through the medium of the Holy Spirit and back to God. This is a very powerful rite to experience. Also, it reminds the believer on a weekly or more frequent basis of the method of salvation and outcome that one desires for one's human life. By performing these rites, one practices death, resurrection, and eternal life, hoping that during the human state one purifies one's being and in the end will return directly to the Maker.

So just as fear is the blessed beginning, we must never forget its positive nature. Spiritual attainment has frequently been described in the terminology of the alchemical tradition whereby man's leaden, dull nature is returned to its golden original state. When any substance or entity (even a relationship) undergoes dissolution, it must eventually be recrystallized in a new form. In other words, the new entity has the possibility of being reconstituted in a higher and nobler state. What this means for any of us is that when we experience fear, when things seem to be coming apart, we should instead be joyful and grateful for the possibility of moving upward from our present plateau where we perhaps are too comfortably established.

According to Titus Burckhardt, "Lead represents the chaotic, 'heavy,' and sick condition of metal or of the inward man, while gold—'congealed light' and 'earthly sun'—expresses the perfection of both metallic and human existence." He goes on to explain that the *re*-formation of the soul cannot take place until it is "freed from all the rigidities and inner contradictions (so that it may) become that plastic substance on which the Sprit or Intellect, coming from on high, can imprint a new 'form'—a form which does not limit or bind, but on the contrary delivers, because it comes from the Divine Essence.... The soul cannot be transmuted without the cooperation of Spirit, and the Spirit illumines the soul only to the extent of its passive preparedness and in accordance with its manners."[4]

Thus, as the purpose of the human state of being is the sanctification of one's soul, and as one would desire to achieve this before death, I would like to conclude with an extraordinary description of the Saint who no longer fears—although this was the blessed state by which his spiritual life commenced: "The Saint hath no fear, because fear is the expectation either of some future calamity or of the eventual loss of some object of desire; whereas the Saint is the 'son of his time' (resides in the Eternal Present/Presence); he has no future from which he should fear anything and, as he hath no fear so he hath no hope since hope is the expectation either of gaining an object of desire or of being relieved from a misfortune, and this belongs to the future; not does he grieve because grief arises from the rigor of time, and how should he feel grief who dwells in the Radiance of Satisfaction and the Garden of Concord."[5]

NOTES

This chapter first appeared in *Parabola,* fall 1998, 54–57. It is reproduced with slight modifications in this volume with the permission of the editors of *Parabola.*

1. Martin Lings, *Symbol & Archetype: A Study of the Meaning of Existence* (Cambridge: Quinta Essentia, 1991), 114–115.

2. Frithjof Schuon, *Stations of Wisdom* (Bloomington, Indiana: Perennial Books, 1980), 147.

3. "Where reverence is, there too is fear." See Plato, *Euthypho,* 12b.

4. Titus Burkhardt, *Alchemy, Science of the Cosmos, Science of the Soul* (Louisville, Kentucky: Fons Vitae, 1997), 24, 97, 111.

5. A statement attributed to the great Sufi Abu al-Qasim al-Junayd of Baghdad (d. 910 CE).

14

THOMAS MERTON AND A SUFI SAINT

•

Virginia Gray Henry-Blakemore

One of the volumes to be found in Merton's personal library is titled *A Moslem Saint of the Twentieth Century* by Martin Lings.[1] It is heavily underlined throughout. Often in the margins, Merton marked material with several bold vertical lines or with asterisks next to the text. As these highlighted passages must represent what Merton felt best elucidated Islamic mysticism, or were ideas he may have agreed with or found to be useful for his own spiritual growth or understanding, a small selection of these are presented here in order to illustrate some of the concepts and ideas to which Merton was attracted. At the same time, it is hoped that this selection will further inform the reader about the nature and depth of Sufism.

Martin Lings, formerly Keeper of Oriental Manuscripts in the British Museum and the British Library, and author of many important works on Islam and Sufism, opens this wonderful volume with a chapter "Seen from Outside," which presents the impressions of Dr. Marcel Carret, who tended the Algerian saint Ahmad al-'Alawi (1869–1934) in his final years. Dr. Carret's initial impression of Shaikh al-'Alawi is as follows:

> The first thing that struck me was his likeness to the usual representation of Christ. His clothes, so nearly if not exactly the same as those which Jesus must have worn, the fine lawn head-cloth which framed his face, his whole attitude—everything conspired to reinforce the likeness. It occurred to me that such must have been the appearance of Christ when he received his disciples at the time when he was staying with Martha and Mary.

Dr. Carret later recalled:

> Fairly often while I was talking quietly with the Shaikh, the Name Allah had come to us from some remote corner of the *záwiyah,* uttered on one long drawn out vibrant note:
> "A...l...la...h!"

It was like a cry of despair, a distraught supplication, and it came from some solitary cell-bound disciple, bent on meditation. The cry was usually repeated several times, and then all was silence once more.

"Out of the depths have I cried unto Thee, O Lord."

"From the end of the earth will I cry unto Thee, when my heart is overwhelmed; lead me to the rock that is higher than I."

These verses from the Psalms came to my mind. The supplication was really just the same, the supreme cry to God of a soul in distress.

I was not wrong, for later, when I asked the Shaikh what was the meaning of the cry which we had just heard, he answered:

"It is a disciple asking God to help him in his meditation."

"May I ask what is the purpose of his meditation?"

"To achieve self-realization in God."

"Do all the disciples succeed in doing this?"

"No, it is seldom that anyone does. It is only possible for a very few."

"Then what happens to those who do not? Are they not desperate?"

"No: they always rise high enough to have at least inward Peace."

Inward Peace. That was the point he came back to most often, and there lay, no doubt, the reason for his great influence. For what man does not aspire, in some way or other, to inward Peace?

In the chapter "The Reality of Sufism," found in "Part One: The Path and the Order," Merton marked lines to do with spiritual aspiration. For the most part, the passages he noted (indented below) are the exact words of the saint himself. Often Shaikh al-'Alawi cites passages from the Qur'an, hadith—or sayings of the Prophet Muhammad—and from the writings of many of Islam's great saints and mystics of previous centuries. Dr. Lings, for the most part "allows the Sufis...to speak for themselves in a series of texts mainly translated from the Arabic."

The aspiration "to let one's Spirit (that is, as here meant, one's centre of consciousness) rise above oneself" presupposes at the very least some remote awareness of the existence of the Heart, which is the point where the human self ends and the Transcendent Self begins. If the clouds in the night of the soul are so thick as to prevent the moon of the Heart from showing the slightest sign of its presence, there can be no such aspiration. (40)

In a hadith (saying of the Prophet), God states:

"My slave ceaseth not to draw nigh unto Me with devotions of his free will until I love him; and when I love him, I am the Hearing wherewith he heareth, and the Sight wherewith he seeth, and the Hand wherewith he smiteth, and the Foot wherewith on he walketh." (Bukhari) (37)

The Qur'an insists without respite on remembrance of God, *dhikr Allah,* and this insistence holds the place in Islam that is held in Christianity by the first of Christ's two commandments. It is the Quranic use of the cognitive term "remembrance" rather than "love" which has, perhaps more than anything else, imposed on Islamic mysticism its special characteristics. (45)

Many passages which interested Merton seemed to validate the aims and nature of monastic life. The first of many such passages marked by Merton are lines from the early eighth-century saint Hasan al-Basri:

"He that knoweth God loveth Him, and he that knoweth the world abstaineth from it," and the saying of another early Sufi: "Intimacy (*uns*) with God is finer and sweeter than longing." (46)

From "The Spiritual Master," there is more on what would have appealed to a monk who made a hermitage in the forest, as did Merton, in the following paragraphs, which Merton marked, some written by Dr. Lings and some directly quoting Shaikh al-'Alawi.

One of his motives for taking this step [for adding his own name 'Alawî to distinguish his particular branch of the Darqâwî tarîqah] was that he felt the need to introduce, as part of his method, the practice of *khalwah,* that is, spiritual retreat in the solitude of an isolated cell or small hermitage. There was nothing very drastic in this, for if remembrance of God be the positive or heavenly aspect of all mysticism, its negative or earthly aspect is retreat or drawing away from other than God. The Tradition "Be in this world as a stranger, or as a passer-by" has already been quoted, and one of the most powerful aids to achieving this permanent inward spiritual retreat is bodily withdrawal which, in some form or another, perpetual or temporary, is a feature of almost all contemplative orders. In some Sufic brotherhoods—the Khalwatî Tarîqah, for example—it was tradition to make retreat in a special hermitage. But in the Shâdhilî Tarîqah and its branches, the spiritual retreat had usually taken the form of withdrawal to the solitudes of nature, after the pattern of the Prophet's retreats in the cave on Mount Hira, and though inevitably the *khalwah* must have been used on some occasion, to introduce it as a regular methodic practice was something of an innovation for the descendants of Abû 'l-Hasan ash-Shâdhilî. However, the Shaikh no doubt found this form of retreat more practicable than any other in view of the conditions in which most of his disciples lived. We have already seen that he himself had suffered for want of a definite place where he could be alone, and that it was part of his method to supervise at times very closely the invocation of his disciples, which presupposed that the disciple in question would be within easy reach of him.
'Abd al-Karîm Jossot quotes the Shaikh as having said to him:
"The *khalwah* is a cell in which I put a novice after he has sworn to me not to leave it for forty days if need be. In this oratory he must do nothing but repeat ceaselessly, day and night, the Divine Name (Allah), drawing out at each invocation the syllable *âh* until he has no more breath left...."
"During the *khalwah* he fasts strictly by day, only breaking his fast between sunset and dawn.... Some *fuqarâ*[2] obtain the sudden illumination after a few

minutes, some only after several days, and some only after several weeks. I know one *faqîr* who waited eight months. Each morning he would say to me: 'My heart is still too hard,' and would continue his *khalwah*. In the end his efforts were rewarded." (84–85)

It interested Merton that the spiritual retreat demanded by the Shaikh al-'Alawi for his disciples was very difficult for most to endure:

> But what might have been intolerable in other circumstances was made relatively easy because the Shaikh knew how to provoke "a state of spiritual concentration." None the less, some of the *fuqarâ* would come out of the *khalwah* almost in a state of collapse, dazed in both body and soul, hut the Shaikh was indifferent to this provided that some degree of direct knowledge had been achieved. (105)

Other ideas which would also have been of relevance to a monk are:

> Let him examine himself: if what his heart hides is more precious than what his tongue tells of, then he is *one whom his Lord hath made certain* (Qur'an XI, 17), but if not, then he has missed far more than he has gained.... The Prophet said: "Knowledge of the inward is one of the Secrets of God. It is wisdom from the treasury of His Wisdom which He casteth into the heart of whomsoe'er He will of His slaves" and "Knowledge is of two kinds, knowledge in the Heart which is the knowledge that availeth, and knowledge upon the tongue which is God's evidence against His slave." This shows that secret knowledge is different from the knowledge that is bandied about. (89–90)
>
> The Prophet said, "The earth shall never be found lacking in forty men whose Hearts are as the Heart of the Friend [Abraham] of the All-Merciful."...and where else is this body of men to be found save amongst the Rememberers, who are marked out for having devoted their lives to God?
>
> "From men *whose sides shrink away front beds.*" (Qur'an XXXII, 16)
>
> "To *men whom neither bartering nor selling diverteth from the remembrance of God.*" (Qur'an XXIV, 36)

In addition to the Sufi practice of using the rosary, reciting the litanies, and remembering God (*dhikr*) through the invocation of His Holy Name, occasionally members of some orders participate in certain movements which have been called a "sacred dance." Merton highlighted the following:

> None the less, the subjection of the body to a rhythmic motion is never, for the Sufis, any more than an auxiliary; its purpose is simply to facilitate *dhikr* in the fullest sense of remembrance, that is, the concentration of all the faculties of the soul upon the Divine Truth represented by the Supreme Name or some other formula which is uttered aloud or silently by the dancers. It was explained to me by one of the Shaikh's disciples that just as a sacred number such as three, seven or nine, for example, acts as a bridge between multiplicity and Unity, so rhythm is a bridge between agitation and Repose, motion and Motionlessness,

fluctuation and Immutability. Fluctuation, like multiplicity, cannot be transcended in this world of perpetual motion but only in the Peace of Divine Unity; and to partake of this Peace in some degree is in fact that very concentration which the *dhikr* aims at....

If the grace of ecstasy is beyond you, it is not beyond you to believe that others may enjoy it.... None the less I do not say that dancing and manifestations of ecstasy are among the essentials of Sufism. But they are outward signs which come from submersion in remembrance. Let him who doubts try for himself, for hearsay is not the same as direct experience. (95)

God commended the people of the Book [Jews and Christians] for their rapture, mentioning one of its aspects with the highest praise: *When they hear what hath been revealed unto the Prophet, thou seest their eyes overflow with tears from their recognition of the Truth.* (Qur'an V, 83) (93)

The Prophet said: "The solitary ones take precedence, they who are utterly addicted to the remembrance of God." (94)

Thus when the Prophet was asked what spiritual strivers would receive the greatest reward, he replied: "Those who remembered God most." Then when questioned as to what fasters would be most rewarded he said: "Those who remembered God most," and when the prayer and the almsgiving and the pilgrimage and charitable donations were mentioned, he said of each: "The richest in remembrance of God is the richest in reward." (97)

When Dr. Lings explains that the "litany comes as it were from midway between the Heart and the head," Merton boldly marks a following sentence, "Beyond litany is invocation in the sense of the word *dhikr*. This is a cry from the Heart, or from near to the Heart." (111)

A few pages ahead, Merton noted that another form of the invocation is found in groaning: "The Prophet said, 'Let him groan, for groaning is one of the Names of God in which the sick man may find relief.'" (113)

The first chapter in "Part Two: The Doctrine" is titled "Oneness of Being." In the fulfillment of the Gnostics' ascent, "They see directly face to face that there is naught in existence save only God and that *everything perisheth but His face,* not simply that it perisheth at any given time but that it hath never not perished.... Each thing hath two faces, a face of its own, and a face of its Lord; in respect of its own face it is nothingness, and in respect of the Face of God it is Being. Thus there is nothing in existence save only God and His face, for *everything perisheth but His Face,* always and forever." (123)

What a spiritual novice must unlearn struck Merton:

One of the first things that a novice has to do in the 'Alawî Tarîqah—and the same must be true of other paths of mysticism—is to unlearn much of the agility of "profane intelligence" which an al-'Alawî *faqîr* once likened, for my benefit, to the "antics of a monkey that is chained to its post," and to acquire an agility of a different order, comparable to that of a bird which continually changes the level of its flight. The Qur'an and secondarily the Traditions of the Prophet are the great prototypes in Islam of this versatility. (124)

Regarding the three levels of recitation said upon the rosary, Dr. Lings explains:

> What might be called the normal level of psychic perception, is concerned with the ego as such. This is the phase of purification. From the second standpoint this fragmentary ego has ceased to exist, for it has been absorbed into the person of the Prophet who represents a hierarchy of different plenitudes of which the lowest is integral human perfection and the highest is Universal Man (*al-Insân al-Kâmil*), who personifies the whole created universe and who thus anticipates, as it were, the Infinite, of which he is the highest symbol. The disciple aims at concentrating on perfection at one of these levels. From the third point of view the Prophet himself has ceased to exist, for this formula is concerned with nothing but the Divine Oneness. (125)

After Dr. Lings explains that "The soul is not merely immortal but Eternal, not in its psychism but in virtue of the Divine Spark that is in it," Merton boldly marked one line from a poem by Shaikh al-'Alawi:

> Thou seest not who thou art, for thou art, yet art not "thou." (127)

Merton then highlights the words quoted of al-Ghazali (d. 1111 CE):

> There is no he but He, for "he" expresseth that unto which reference is made, and there can be no reference at all save only unto Him, for whenever thou makest a reference, that reference is unto Him even though thou knewest it not through thine ignorance of the Truth of Truths.... Thus "there is no god but God" is the generality's proclamation of Unity, and "there is no he but He" is that of the elect, for the former is more general, whereas the latter is more elect, more all-embracing, truer, more exact, and more operative in bringing him who useth it into the Presence of Unalloyed Singleness and Pure Oneness. (127–128)
>
> I have never looked at a single thing without God being nearer to me than it. (Abû 'Ubaidah, d. 639 CE) (128)

In concluding "Oneness of Being," Lings mentions that "the highest saints are referred to as the *Near*," and that what the Qur'an means by "nearness" is defined by the words:

> *We are nearer to him than his jugular vein and God cometh in between a man and his own heart.* (Qur'an VIII, 24) (129)

Thomas Merton marked many paragraphs as important in "The Three Worlds." The chapter begins with the words of the Moroccan Shaikh ad-Darqâwî:

I was in a state of remembrance and my eyes were lowered and I heard a voice say: *He is the first and the Last and the Outwardly Manifest and the Inwardly Hidden.* I remained silent, and the voice repeated it a second time, and then a third, whereupon I said: "As to *the First,* I understand, and as to *the Last,* I understand, and as to *the Inwardly Hidden,* I understand, but as to *the Outwardly Manifest,* I see nothing but created things." Then the voice said: "If there were any outwardly manifest other than Himself I should have told thee." In that moment I realized the whole hierarchy of Absolute Being. (131)

So realize, my brother, thine own attributes and look with the eye of the Heart at the beginning of thine existence when it came forth from nothingness; for when thou hast truly realized thine attributes, He will increase thee with His. (137)

One of thine attributes is pure nothingness, which belongeth unto thee and unto the world in its entirety. If thou acknowledge thy nothingness, He will increase thee with His Being....

Extinction also is one of thine attributes. Thou art already extinct, my brother, before thou art extinguished and naught before thou art annihilated. Thou art an illusion and a nothingness in a nothingness. When hadst thou Existence that thou mightest be extinguished? Thou art *as a mirage in the desert that the thirsty man taketh to be water until he cometh unto it and findeth it to be nothing, and where he thought it to be, there findeth he God.* Even so, if thou wert to examine thyself, thou wouldst find God instead of finding thyself, and there would be naught left of thee but a name without a form. Being in itself is God's, not thine if thou shouldest come to realize the truth of the matter, and to understand what is God's through stripping thyself of all that is not thine, then wouldest thou find thyself to be as the core of an onion. If thou wouldst peel it, thou would peelest off the first skin, and then the second, and then the third, and so on, until there is nothing left of the onion. Even so is the slave with regard to the Being of the Truth.

It is said that Râbi'ah al-'Adawiyyah met one of the Gnostics and asked him of his state, and he replied: "I have trod the path of obedience and have not sinned since God created me," whereupon she said: "Alas, my son, thine existence is a sin wherewith no other sin may be compared." (137)

The text then refers to what must necessarily be attributed to God as follows: "Being, Beginninglessness, Endlessness, Absolute Independence, Incomparability, Oneness of Essence, of Quality and of Action, Power, Will, Knowledge, Life, Hearing, Speech, Sight." Merton was interested in the comments of Shaikh al-'Alawi:

Here he explaineth what belongeth unto God. See therefore, O Slave, what belongeth unto thee, for if thou shouldst qualify thyself with any of these qualities, thou wilt be contending with thy Lord. (131)

Such a statement reminds a seeker of his own essential emptiness, which were he to realize, he would gain the Divine Presence, for which he yearns.

One can imagine why Merton would have been drawn to the passages above which encourage the spiritual aspirant to recall his own "nothingness," for

> then He will be thy Hearing and thy Sight, and when He is thy Hearing and thy Sight, then wilt thou hear only Him and see only Him, for thou wilt be seeing Him with his Sight and hearing Him with His Hearing. (139)
>
> *Wheresoe'er ye turn, there is the Face of God.* Things lie hidden in their opposites, and but for the existence of opposites, the Opposer would have no manifestation. (140)

Merton was concerned with many of the passages which remind a person to accept both the blessings and the trials of life with an equal heart and to love God's will for us whether it brings ease or contraction into our lives:

> The Outwardly Manifest is veiled by naught but the strength of the manifestations, so be present with Him, nor be veiled from Him by that which hath no being apart from Him. Stop short at the illusion of forms, nor have regard unto the outward appearance of receptacles. Do not know Him only in His beauty, denying that cometh unto thee from His Majesty, but be deeply grounded in all the states, and consider Him well in opposites. Do not know Him in expansion only when He vouchsafeth, denying Him when He witholdeth, for such knowledge is but a veneer. It is not knowledge born of realization. (142–143)
>
> Be turned unto God, welcoming all that cometh unto thee from Him. Busy thyself with naught but let everything busy itself with thee, and do thou busy thyself with proclaiming the Infinite and saying there is no god but God, utterly independent therein of all things, until thou comest to be the same in either stare.... (144–145)

In "The Symbolism of the Letters of the Alphabet," Merton was particularly interested in the writings of Shaikh al-'Alawi with regard to the metaphysics of the manifested world and the nature of the Godhead, whose Essence is to be found in Qualities.

In "The Great Peace," Dr. Lings explains:

> The rhythm to which the breathing is subjected is the rhythm of creation and dissolution, of Beauty and Majesty. Breathing in represents creation, that is, the Outward Manifestation of the Divine Qualities...breathing out represents the "return" of the Qualities to the Essence, the next intake of breath is a new creation, and so on. The final expiring symbolizes the realization of the Immutability which underlies the illusory vicissitudes of creation and dissolution, the realization of the truth that "God was and there was naught else beside Him, He is now even as He was...." (159)
>
> The fullest attainment of inward Peace means the shifting of the consciousness from a secondary or illusory centre to the One True Centre, where the subject is...no longer created being but the Creator. This is in fact what is meant

by "concentration"; it follows therefore that for one who is truly concentrated, the symbolism of breathing is necessarily inverted: breathing in becomes absorption of all in the Oneness of the Essence, and breathing out is the Manifestation of the Divine Names and Qualities. (159)

To say that beyond his created plenitude Universal Man has an aspect of total extinction means that beyond this extinction he has an aspect of Absolute Plenitude, for his extinction is simply the measure of his capacity to receive. (160)

According to Shaikh al-'Alawi:

[A] Gnostic may be dead unto himself and unto the whole world, and resurrected in his Lord, so that if thou shouldest ask him of his existence he would not answer thee inasmuch as he hath lost sight of his own individuality. Abû Yazîd al-Bistâmî was asked about himself and he said, "Abû Yazîd is dead—May God not have mercy on him!" This is the real death; but if on the Day of Resurrection thou shouldest ask one who hath died only the general death "Who art thou?" he would answer "I am so-and-so," for his life hath never ceased and he hath never sensed the perfume of death, but hath simply passed on from world to world, and none graspeth the meaning of the real death save him who hath died it. Thus have the Sufis a reckoning before the Day of Reckoning, even as the Prophet said: "Call yourselves to account before ye be called to account." They laboured in calling themselves to account until they were free to contemplate their Lord, and theirs is a resurrection before the Resurrection. (161)

Extinction and submersion and annihilation come suddenly upon the Gnostic, so that he goeth out from the sphere of sense and loseth all consciousness of himself, leaving behind all his perceptions, nay, his very existence. Now this annihilation is in the Essence of Truth, for there floweth down over him from the Holiness of the Divinity a flood which compelleth him to see himself as the Truth's Very Self in virtue of his effacement and annihilation therein. (163)

Regarding extinction from oneself and subsistence in God, the great Andalusian saint, whose tomb has become the spiritual center of Alexandria in Egypt,

Abû'l 'Abbas al-Mursî used to pray, "O Lord, open our inward eyes and illumine our secret parts, and extinguish us from ourselves, and give us subsistence in Thee, not in ourselves." (167)

The point is made that even though someone be blessed with Union with God, this in no way absolves him from following the revealed law. To be fully mature in the spiritual life

one should combine outward stability with inward o'erwhelmedness, so that one is outwardly spiritual effort and inwardly contemplation, outwardly obedient to

God's command and inwardly submissive (*mustaslim*) to His Utter Compulsion and that the Supreme State belongs to those "who combine sobriety (*sahw*) with uprootedness (*istilam*)"...so that outwardly they are among creatures and inwardly with the Truth, integrating two opposite states and combining the wisdom of each. (168)

In the same vein, Merton marked passages which discussed the true cause of the great sadness Jacob felt at the loss of Joseph. A disciple of Shaikh al-'Alawî had inquired of his master how the "beauty of Joseph could have diverted [Jacob's] attention from the beauty of the Truth," and the Shaikh explained:

Jacob's exceeding sorrow was not for the person of Joseph but because Joseph was for him a place of the Manifestation of the Truth, so that when Joseph was by, Jacob's own presence with God was increased in intensity. (164)

Therefore the Truth trieth those whom He loveth by the sudden disappearance of the form, so that their vision may be deflected from the part unto the whole, as He did with Jacob. (165)

Merton also highlighted a magnificent line from al-Ghazali (d. 1111 CE), which refers to this meeting of the finite with the Infinite:

Each thing hath two faces, a face of its own and a face of its Lord; in respect of its own face it is nothingness, and in respect of the Face of God it is Being. (169)

Among the many ideas that attracted Merton in "Gnosis" is one regarding sight:

But the Shaikh affirms that it is none the less possible for the outward eye, while still "in this world," to see the Truth, provided that it can first achieve a perfect co-ordination with the inward eye. [Footnote by Dr. Lings: During this life, the Saint's "resurrection in God" is a resurrection of the soul, not yet of the body. But through the coordination just referred to, he may also have foretaste of the resurrection of the body.] (172)

The outward eye is the ray of the inward eye and the *faqîr* should not open his outward eye (in the hope of seeing Reality) until the connection hath been established between it and his inward eye. When, in virtue of this connection, his outward eye hath become pure inward vision, then he will see the Lord of the verse *Naught is like unto Him* with all his faculties, just as he will also hear Him with all his faculties.... (172)

The sight cannot attach itself unto nothing, and that therefore no object of sight can be void of the outward manifestation of the Truth, for things in themselves are naught. (174)

Merton was interested in the meaning and inner purposes of the ritual ablution before prayer in Islam, and the symbolism of water. In respect that everything returns to the Archetype, the world is compared to an iceberg and man, to the water flowing from its sides, melting back to Essence. Among the paragraphs which Merton singled out is:

The purpose of the ablution in Islam is the removal of inward impurity symbolized by various modes of outward impurity.... The meaning of defilement (*hadath*), continues the Shaikh, is ephemeral existence (*hudúth*), that is, the existence of other than God. This is not ousted from the heart of the Gnostic, and its film is not removed from his inward eye to be replaced in his sight by Eternity, save through his finding the Water and his Purification therewith. Except he be purified by It, he is far from the Presence of his Lord, unfit to enter It, let alone to sit therein. Likewise the slave will not cease to suppose the existence of defilement in all creatures until he have poured this Absolute Water over their outward appearance. Without It he will not cease to condemn them, and how should his verdict be revoked when he seeth their defilement with his eyes, and when his Heart believeth in the independent existence of creation? (182–183)

In "The Ritual Prayer," Merton is seen to have taken a special interest in the deepest significance of the positions in Muslim prayer. Shaikh al-'Alawi explains that after the worshipper begins his prayer by raising his hands and proclaiming "God is Most Great," or *Allahu Akbar,* he begins gradually to draw himself in more and more as he approaches the Divine. The extremity of Nearness is attained by the state of prostration.

The Prophet said: "The slave is nearest his Lord when in prostration." At his prostration he descendeth from the stature of existence into the fold of nothingness, and the more his body is folded up, the more his existence is folded up.... (187–188)
   Before his prostration the Gnostic had the upright stature of existence, but after his prostration he hath become extinct, a thing lost, effaced in himself and Eternal in his Lord.... (188)
   When the worshipper hath obtained the degree of prostration and hath been extinguished from existence, he prostrateth himself a second time that he may be extinguished from that extinction. Thus is his (second) prostration identical with his rising up from (the first) prostration, which rising signifieth subsistence. (188)
   He is prostrate with regard unto the truth, upright with regard unto creation, extinct (even as a Divine Quality is extinct) in the Transcendent Oneness, subsistent in the Immanent Oneness. Thus is the prostration of the Gnostics uninterrupted, and their union knoweth no separation. The Truth hath slain them with a death that knoweth no resurrection. Then He hath given them Life, Endless Life, that knoweth no death. (189)
   After the final prostration before the end of the prayer, the worshipper resumes the sitting position from which, after expressions of devotion to God and invocations of Peace on the Prophet, himself and all the faithful, he seals

the prayer by turning his head to the right with the words *As-Salâmu 'alaikum*—Peace be on you! (190)

Of this final sitting position the Shaikh says: He must take a middle course when he returneth unto creation, that is, he must be seated, which is midway between prostration and standing, that he may make good his intercourse with creation. For if he went out unto creatures in a state of being prostrate, that is, in a state of extinction and obliteration, he could take no notice of them. Nor must he go out unto creation standing, that is, far from the Truth as he used to be before his extinction, for thus would he go out unto creation as one created and there would be no good in him and none would profit from his return. Even so he must take a middle course, and "midmost is best in all things." It is said: "Long live the man who knoweth his own worth and taketh his seat beneath it!" Now a man gaineth knowledge of his worth only at his obliteration. Thus is a sitting position required of him after his obliteration. (190)

On the subject of meditation, the Algerian master wrote:

Meditation may be on things that are made, but not on the Essence, even as the Prophet said: "Meditate upon all things, but meditate not on the Essence lest ye perish." Thought is only used with regard unto what is made, but when the Gnostic hath attained unto the Maker, then is his thought changed to wonderment. Thus is wonderment the fruit of thought, and once it hath been achieved the Gnostic must not swerve from it nor change it for that which is its inferior. Nor can he ever have enough of wonderment at God, and indeed the Prophet would say: "O Lord, increase me in marveling at Thee." Meditation is demanded of the *faqir* whilst he be on his journey. One meditateth on the absent: but when He that was sought is Present in Person, then is meditation changed into wonderment. (190–191)

Merton also underlined these words regarding the wasting of one's time:

Trifling, for the Gnostic, is being busied with that which concerneth him not, once he hath realized the degree of Perfection; and everything except being busied with God is such frivolity and trifling as justifieth neither a turn of the head thereunto nor the waste of a moment of time thereon. (191)

In the section on the funeral prayer, parallels between the spiritual and the physical death struck Merton. As one will be passive in the hands of whoever washes one's body at death, so should the disciple be in the hands of his master "lest he be left with all his impurities upon him by reason of his stubbornness and willfulness and want of passivity." Merton must have wrestled with the fame which came in conjunction with his writings. Perhaps this was one of the reasons why he highlighted the following:

"Bury thine existence in the earth of obscurity, for if a seed be not buried it bringeth not forth in fullness." (Ibn Ata Allah d. 1309 CE)

[The Shaykh says:] "Indeed, there is nothing better for the disciple than obscurity after attainment, and no harm is greater for him than fame at that moment, that is, at the moment of his entry unto God, not afterwards, for after his burial in the earth of obscurity there is no harm in the spreading of his fame inasmuch as the growth hath come after the roots were firm, not before, so that there is no doubt that he will bring forth in fullness." (193–194)

Analogously, by a symbolism parallel to this last, the realization of Supreme Sainthood is mirrored in the funeral prayer. Just as the body yields up the soul at death, so the soul, at spiritual death, yields up the Spirit. The Shaikh says: "Bodily death taketh not place without the Angel of Death, and even so spiritual death taketh not place save through the intermediary of a Master who knoweth how to grasp the Spirits of his disciples."

"The soul is precious, yet for Thee will I exchange it,
And being slain is bitter, yet in Thy Good Pleasure is it sweet." (194)

In the funeral prayer itself, the four affirmations of the greatness of God are recited so that the one who has died may be reminded of the four Aspects of Being, the Firstness and Lastness, and Outward Manifestation and Inward Hiddenness. Then this soul can find no outlet: "His spirit departeth and his body goeth to nothing, inasmuch as the directions of space exist no longer for him through his finding not even so much as the breadth of a fingertip left vacant by these four Aspects, whithersoever he turneth. Even if he turn unto himself, he findeth that he himself is one of the Aspects, and so it is wherever else he turn, according to His Words *Wheresoe'er ye turn, there is the Face of God*. Thus when the rapt one turneth his face unto himself [he] seeds in the mirror of his existence the Face of God."

Thus, in the service itself, the seeker has a final reminder of his essential nothingness before God—which indeed would seem to be the goal of Realization.

The final phrase of this work which Merton noted was a Prophetic saying revealed by God in His Words. One cannot help but imagine that Merton's writings and efforts were intended to please his Lord and draw men to His Remembrance and His worship.

The dearest of men unto Me is he who maketh Me dear unto men, and maketh men dear unto me. (195)

NOTES

Reprinted from a work published by Fons Vitae with the permission of the publisher.

1. The most recent edition is titled *A Sufi Saint of the Twentieth Century, Shaikh Ahmad Al-'Alawî, His Spiritual Heritage and Legacy* (Cambridge, U.K.: The Islamic Texts Society, 1993). It contains two new chapters which Dr. Lings now feels would have been of great interest to Merton.

2. *Faqir*, pl. *fuqara*—this term refers to someone who becomes a disciple of a master with the intention of emptying himself for God. The root "f-q-r" means "poverty" or "emptiness." A spiritual martyr is someone who has achieved this emptiness and can be said to have achieved what Saint John of the Cross meant by "Die before you die." Humility is a form of this effort.

15

THE SUFI WAY OF LOVE AND PEACE

Nasrollah Pourjavady

To speak of love as one of the pillars of world peace may at first sound like a meaningless truism. Everyone would agree that animosity, war, and strife come to an end once love and friendship come in between. A more careful examination of the relation between love and peace, however, shows that what seems to be a truism is not really so. We know that having love and compassion for all of humanity, and in fact for all of God's creatures, are fundamental teachings in most religions, yet the history of religions has witnessed many wars and even holocausts. In our own time, acts of terrorism are committed for the sake of religious goals. In the face of all of this we need to answer the question: How can atrocious and violent acts of killing innocent people be justified by any religion that claims to have peace, love, and compassion for all humanity as its primary goals and objectives?

Wars have been waged not only by the followers of different religions, but also by different groups and sects within the same religion. We do not need to mention how the Protestant and Catholic sects in Christianity have treated each other in the past or how Sunni and Shiite Muslims fight each other even today in some Muslim countries. How can the followers of two religions, who claim to worship a merciful and compassionate God and follow almost the same ethical teachings, fight with one another and kill each other? Even more, how can the followers of two sects of the same religion kill each other in the name of one and the same God?

The answer to these questions, I believe, lies in the way that the adherents of different religions and sects, *madhahib* (sing. *madhhab*),[1] have interpreted the original vision or revelation of their religion, and the kind of relationship they have established between the human being and God. The basic teachings of a religion, which are found in its scriptures, can be read and understood differently by different people in each religion. Moreover, people can enter into different kinds of relationships with their Lord. To use the language of the Muslim theologians (*mutakallimun*) and some mystics, particularly the followers of the school of the Andalusian Sufi Ibn ʿArabi

(d. 1240 CE), God has many Names and Attributes. People in different circumstances and at different times may approach God through one or another of these Divine Names and Attributes, thereby entering a particular relationship with Him.

Let me illustrate this point by giving some examples of different names of God in Islam. One of these is *al-Ghani,* literally meaning "the Rich," which implies the Divine Attribute of Self-Sufficiency. God is said to be *al-Ghani,* while human beings, and in fact all creatures, are said to be poor (*faqir*) and in need of Him (see, for example, Qur'an 35:15).[2] All creatures are in the same relationship with God, the Self-Sufficient Being, because they need Him for their existence. God is also named Lord (*al-Rabb*), which denotes another relationship that human beings may have with the Divine Being (see, for example, the first verse of the Qur'an, "Praise be to God, Lord of the Worlds"). If a person recognizes God as his or her Lord, then he or she is the Lord's vassal (*marbub*), or His slave or servant (*'abd*). When a person worships God, he or she enters into another relationship with Him. In this relationship, God is the Worshipped One (*ma'bud*), whereas the human being is the worshipper (*'abid*).

One of the most significant relationships between the human being and God is *'ubudiyya,* which is most often translated as "servitude." However, to be more exact, the term means "slavery." God is the Master—the Lord—and the human being is His slave or servant. Another relationship that has played a prominent role in Muslim religious thinking, particularly among the mystics, is love. According to this relationship, God is the Beloved (*mahbub* or *ma'shuq*), while human beings are the lovers (sing. *muhibb*). As a lover of God, the Sufis say that the human being "makes love" with the Divine Beloved and finally reaches a state of union (*wisal*) with Him.[3]

These two relationships—that of master–slave and beloved–lover—between God and man have had a great impact on the lives of Muslims throughout the centuries. Though both relationships exist together in Muslim religious experience, each has its own characteristics and has shaped the religious mentality and the social and cultural life of Muslims in different ways. The main characteristic of the master–slave relationship is power and domination versus submission. The Qur'an states that the religion of God is submission (*al-Islam,* Qur'an 3:19). The Lord dominates and imposes His will on the slave, and the slave must offer total submission to the Lord. In the words of an Arabic saying, "Whatever the slave has is in the hands of his Master." The slave (*'abd*) owns nothing, not even himself or herself. This is why the word *'abd,* as a description of the relationship between the human being and God, is best translated as "slave." The human being's submission to the Lord takes different forms in the acts of worship that one performs. This is expressed symbolically in the different postures that one makes during prayer, where the slave bows down before the Lord.

The love relationship between the human being and God also has its own characteristics, some of which are similar to the master–slave relationship. For example, the lover must submit (*aslama,* from the same root as *islam*) to the will of the Beloved. However, this is not done out of servitude, but rather out of love and the desire to unite with the Beloved. In other words, the lover, by virtue of love itself, has a propensity to identify with the Beloved. There is another important difference between a love relationship and a master–slave relationship: whereas the latter is characterized by power and domination, the former is characterized by love and beauty. Muslim theologians, philosophers, and mystics have divided the Divine Attributes into two distinct types: those belonging to the category of *jalal* ("glory" or "majesty") and those belonging to the category of *jamal* ("beauty"). The two kinds of relationships between the human being and God can be subsumed under these two categories of attributes. The master–slave relationship is characterized by the attribute of *jalal,* while the lover–beloved relationship is characterized by the attribute of *jamal.* To use expressions made famous by the historian of religion Rudolf Otto, we might say that the master–slave relationship represents the *mysterium tremendum,* whereas the lover–beloved relationship represents the *mysterium fascinans.*[4]

The feeling of power in the *mysterium tremendum* and the feeling of desire in the *mysterium fascinans* cause two different psychological states to arise in the personalities of the slaves of God and the lovers of God, respectively. The religious mentality of a person who sees himself or herself as a slave of God is different from the religious mentality of a person who tries to be a lover of Divine Beauty. These different mentalities will also have an effect on the relationships that both types of believers establish with other people. Just as those who see themselves as slaves of the Lord have a different mentality from those who try to love and adore Absolute Beauty, a society that is dominated by the idea of the power of God, the *mysterium tremendum,* is not the same as a society that is dominated by the idea of love, the *mysterium fascinans.* I shall try to show this difference by relating a historical incident that took place over 12 centuries ago.

In the year 877 CE charges were brought against a group of Sufis in Baghdad by a Hanbalite traditionalist named Ghulam al-Khalil. These Sufis were the famous spiritual master Abu'l Husayn Nuri and his friends Raqqam and Abu Hamza. The story of their trial and what Nuri did when the executioner was going to carry out his execution is reported in several sources, including the *Kashf al-Mahjub* (The Unveiling of the Veiled) of 'Ali ibn 'Uthman al-Jullabi al-Hujwiri (d. 1071 CE):

> When Ghulam al-Khalil persecuted the Sufis, Nuri and Raqqam and Abu Hamza were arrested and conveyed to the Caliph's palace. Ghulam al-Khalil urged the Caliph to put them to death, saying that they were heretics (*zanadiqa*), and the Caliph immediately gave orders for their execution. When the executioner

approached Raqqam, Nuri rose and offered himself in Raqqam's place with utmost cheerfulness and submission. All the spectators were astounded. The executioner said: "O young man, the sword is not a thing that people desire to meet so eagerly as you have welcomed it; and your turn has not yet arrived." Nuri answered: "Yes, my doctrine is founded on preference (*ithar*). Life is the most precious thing in the world. I wish to sacrifice for my brethren's sake the few moments that remain. In my opinion, one moment of this world is better than a thousand years of the next world, because this is the place of service (*khidmat*) and that is the place of proximity (*qorbat*), and proximity is gained by service." The tenderness of Nuri and the fineness of his saying astonished the Caliph (who was informed by a courier of what had passed) to such a degree, that he suspended the execution of the three Sufis.[5]

The above story is usually cited as an example of the practice of preference (*ithar*) by the Sufis. In fact, it comes at the beginning of Hujwiri's chapter on preference in *Kashf al-Mahjub*. *Ithar,* as an altruistic act, is one of the manifestations of love and compassion. Thus, the doctrine that Nuri referred to in his response to the executioner was both the doctrine of preference and the doctrine of love. Nuri and his Sufi friends felt that the best way to approach God and to relate to him is through love. In fact, one of the charges brought against Nuri was that he said, "I love God, and God loves me." Nuri's act of preference on behalf of his friends was the outcome of his love for God. His action represents the selflessness of submission in the lover–beloved relationship, whereas the action of the Caliph and his executioner represents the element of power in the master–slave relationship.

Nuri's doctrine obviously seems praiseworthy and in accordance with orthodox beliefs. Then why was he condemned by al-Khalil for having said, "I love God, and He loves me?" The problem lies in the word that Nuri used to express his idea. The word that is commonly used by Muslims to express the love relation between human beings and God is *hubb*. This is, in fact, the word that is used in the Qur'an when it says, "[God] loves them and they love Him" (Qur'an 5:54). Nuri himself referred to the same verse when he was defending himself against his enemy's allegation. However, his argument was not accepted because he used the Arabic word *'ishq* instead of *hubb*. The difference between these two words is that while *hubb* is a generic word that is used to express love and friendship in general, *'ishq,* which means "desire," usually refers to the love that exists between lovers, that is, between a man and a woman. At that time, there was a grave controversy about the use of the word *'ishq* for expressing a person's relationship to God, and Nuri was one of the first Sufis who dared to do so. This controversy seems quite similar to the one that existed earlier for the Christian mystic Pseudo-Dionysius (ca. fifth or sixth century CE), when he used the Greek word *eros* instead of *agape* when he referred to the love of God.[6]

Although Nuri failed to convince his opponents that one can use the word *'ishq* to express the human relationship with God, the Sufis increasingly began to use this word for the very same purpose. The use of this word and its derivatives (such as *'ashiq,* "yearner" or "desirer," and *ma'shuq,* "the one desired or yearned for") became even more popular when the Sufis began to express their ideas and mystical experiences through poetry, particularly in Persian. By the early twelfth century CE, an entire metaphysics was constructed on the idea of *'ishq.*

One of the best expositions of the doctrine of mystical love in Islam can be found in a rather small book titled *al-Sawanih* (literally, "Auspicious Omens"), which may be translated roughly as "Meditations on Love."[7] Written by Ahmad al-Ghazali (d. 1126 CE), the younger brother of the famous theologian Abu Hamid al-Ghazali (d. 1111 CE), the *Sawanih* is composed of some 70 short chapters, all of which deal with the metaphysics and psychology of love. As a spiritual heir of the famous Sufi martyr Hallaj (d. 922 CE), Ahmad al-Ghazali believed in Essential Love, an idea that was adopted by many mystics and Persian poets. According to this doctrine, Love is not simply a Divine Attribute, but the very Essence of God. Love is the basic principle, the *arche* of the entirety of existence, as well as the driving force of everything that exists.

Ahmad al-Ghazali expresses his ideas mainly through metaphors and romantic anecdotes. For example, Love is said to be a bird that has left its nest in Eternity and has flown into this world of temporal existence for a brief sojourn before returning to its nest. In its essence, Love is absolute unity (*tawhid*), but in its journey to this world, it appears both as the lover and as the beloved. The lover par excellence is the Spirit (*ruh*), the Neo-Platonic *nous,* which has been separated from its origin and now yearns for union. Just as the origin of the lover is Love itself, the origin of the beloved is Love too. The Beloved is absolute Beauty (*jamal*), which manifests itself to the lover and brings him or her back to his or her origin. This metaphysical event has a corresponding analogy in the phenomenal world. In fact, the journey of the Spirit back to the Beloved must be accomplished through human beings. It is the spirit in man that seeks union with the divine Beauty, the Beloved. This mystical union is achieved through the self-annihilation of the lover. Once the lover loses his or her identity in the Beloved, all that remains is the Beloved, who is itself identical with Love. This is how unity (*tawhid*), the basic principle of faith in Islam, is realized.

The doctrine of Essential Love, as expounded by Ahmad al-Ghazali and other Persian Sufis and poets, presents a view of the human being and the world that is different from the view based on the master–slave relation. In the master–slave relation, the human being is always the slave and God is always the Master. The position of each side is fixed. God wills and commands, while the human being is obliged to obey. In the lover–beloved relation, however, the positions of the lover and the beloved are not fixed. In other words, the love relation between the human being and God is reciprocal. At times, the human being is the lover whereas God is the

Beloved, but at other times God is the Lover whereas man is the beloved. This is why Nuri said, "I love God and God loves me." Another famous Sufi, Abu al-Hasan al-Kharaqani (d. 1034 CE), used to say, "At times, I am [God's] Abu al-Hasan and at times [God] is my Abu al-Hasan." Ecstatic utterances such as these are said to express the same idea as the Qur'anic statement, "[God] loves them, and they love Him" (Qur'an 5:54).[8] The Sufis have even claimed that God's love for the human being precedes the human being's love for God, and if it were not for the fact that God had favored the human being with His Essential Love, Mercy, and Compassion, the human being could never love God or His creatures.

The human being's love for God's creatures brings us to another characteristic of the love relationship in Islam. In the master–slave relationship, God the Master orders the human being to be kind to His creatures. In the love relationship, however, the human being loves all other human beings, and indeed all creatures, because the human being loves God. One's love for God and His creation are ultimately affected by the same cause. Ahmad al-Ghazali and the other mystics that followed the doctrine of Essential Love believed that Love has a single nature. Whether it is God's love for the human being, the human being's love for God, the human being's love for other human beings, the love between a man and a woman, or the love between a mother and her child, it is all of the same nature, the difference being only in the context and the intensity, not in the essence.

This idea of the oneness of Love is similar to what some mystical philosophers, such as Mulla Sadra (d. 1640 CE), and Illuminationist (*ishraqi*) philosophers, such as Suhrawardi (d. 1191 CE), said about existence and light. According to these philosophers, existence (*wujud*) is a single reality, wherever it may be and in whatever object it is found. The same is true of light. The light of the sun and the light of a candle, for example, are a single reality, although they exist in different degrees. Existence too, whether it is predicated of God, of the human being, or of any other existing thing, is one and the same reality, even though in each one of these subjects this reality has a different degree. The differences that we perceive are simply differences of "analogical gradation" (*tashkik*): both existence and light are unitary realities, but in different things they have different degrees of intensity or weakness.

What we have said about the essential oneness and the analogical gradations of love, light, and existence applies to beauty (*jamal*) too. Beauty is one single reality whether it is absolute or relative, whether it is in the spiritual realm or the phenomenal world, whether it is in the human body, in the sunset, or in a flower. The only difference is in its intensity or context. Since beauty is one single reality, love for a beautiful object is a manifestation of love for the absolute or divine Beauty. To see and appreciate sunlight, whether it is in a garden or on a mountain, or simply a ray shining through a window into a room, is ultimately to appreciate the essence of light.

Likewise, to love other human beings is to love God. There is no such thing as truly profane beauty, just as there is no such thing as truly profane love. The only problem is that sometimes one loves a relative form of beauty and mistakenly thinks that it is absolute Beauty. The love of a relative form of beauty, such as in the form of a human being, should act as a transition—a bridge—that takes the lover toward absolute Beauty, the Supreme Being.

The lover's union with the Beloved is the ultimate goal of the spiritual quest. In the early history of Sufism, some mystics felt that this goal could not be attained in this life, but only in the next life, when the lover went to Paradise. Muslims also believed that the believer could only experience the beatific vision of God in Paradise. The experience of reaching the presence of the Lord in Paradise and seeing Him face-to-face is implied in the Qur'an, where it says that in Paradise the believers are greeted with a greeting of *salam* from their Lord (Qur'an 36:58). Besides being the Muslim greeting, *salam* also means "peace" or "well-being." Thus, it is important that the Divine Beloved greets the Lover in this way. The above verse of the Qur'an demonstrates that Perfect Peace is found in Heaven and that it proceeds from God Himself. In fact, *al-Salam* ("The Peace-Maker") is one of the Divine Names that is mentioned in the Qur'an (Qur'an 59:23). Since Perfect Peace and well-being is experienced in its most essential form in Heaven, the Qur'an also calls Paradise *Dar al-Salam* ("The Abode of Peace," Qur'an 10:25).

Although the state of *salam* is most truly experienced by the believer in the Hereafter, human beings can also enjoy it to some degree in this life too. God sends *salam,* to his Prophets, such as Noah, Abraham, and Moses. *Salam* in the sense of peace in this world is but a reflection of the absolute *salam* experienced by believers in Paradise. Not only does God bestow *salam* upon the hearts of His Prophets and the believers here in this world, but the believers themselves also wish well-being and peace on each other when they meet.

But is it also possible for a believer, as a lover of the Divine Beloved, to experience the Heavenly *salam* in this life too, or do we have to wait until we die and go to Paradise? In the first two or three centuries of Islamic history, Muslims generally believed that the Heavenly Peace and the vision of God that it entails could be experienced only after death. However, in later centuries, particularly after the mystics developed the doctrine of Love, Muslims began to believe that one could have such an experience in this life too, though in a different way. While one could see the face of the Lord and hear His voice through one's eyes and ears in Paradise, here in this world the lovers of God could have that experience only in their hearts. The only exception was the Prophet Muhammad, who actually had a vision of God and experienced Perfect Peace and well-being in his night journey to Heaven (*mi'raj*). According to the Qur'an, the Prophet experienced the Heavenly state of *salam* throughout that night, until the rising of the dawn (Qur'an 97:5).

The journey of the Prophet toward the Divine Beloved has been shared and relived by many saints, or "Friends of God" (*awliya' Allah*), throughout Islamic history. Thanks to the presence of these saints in Muslim societies, believers have been able to enjoy the grace (*baraka*) of the Peace that accompanies the vision of God and union with the Beloved. It is precisely this inner spiritual Peace, this *salam,* which is needed more than ever in our turbulent world today. In order to attain any degree of it, we Muslims need to follow the path of Love shown to us by the Prophets and saints. It is only by virtue of this path that we can enter the lover–beloved relationship with God, a relationship that requires us to forget hatred and wish mercy, forgiveness, and compassion upon all of humanity. *Wa al-Salam* ("And Peace").

NOTES

This chapter originally appeared as the paper, "The Islamic View of Love as a Pillar of Peace," which was delivered at the colloquium, "Truth, Justice, Love, Freedom: Pillars of Peace," Vatican City, December 1, 2003. It is reproduced here by permission of the author. (Ed.) following a note signifies that the note was added by the general editor of this set.

1. The Arabic word *madhhab* literally means "way" or "path," "the way in which one proceeds." In Arabic usage, it most commonly takes the connotation of "method" or "procedure," in the sense of the method or procedure of a particular school of Islamic jurisprudence. Hence, *madhhab* is most often understood as a synonym for "school of practice" especially a school of Islamic law. In Persian, these meanings are extended to include belief in formal doctrines. Hence, Dr. Pourjavady's use of *madhhab* as meaning "sect" or "religion." (Ed.)

2. In this verse, the Divine Name *al-Ghani* also carries the connotation of absoluteness: "Oh people! You are poor and in need of God (*al-fuqara' ila Allah*), but God is the Self-Sufficient, the Praiseworthy (*wa Allahu huwa al-Ghani' al-Hamid*)." (Ed.)

3. The terms "make love" and "union" should not be taken literally, but are metaphorical or mythological in nature. Sufis often use terms with sexual connotations, such as *'ishq* ("desire") and *wisal* ("union"), as vehicles of comparison, to convey the idea that the spiritual and mystic union of the human being with God is a oneness that can only be compared to the most intense feelings of unification that a person experiences in day-to-day life. Since the ideal goal of love is the merging of two souls into one, this metaphor may also be used to describe the goal of the Gnostic (*'arif*), the "knower" of God. (Ed.)

4. These terms come from Otto's book, *Das Heilige,* usually translated in English as *The Idea of the Holy.* According to Otto, the human experience of religiosity comes from the dialectical relationship between two mysteries. *Mysterium tremendum* ("The Great Mystery") refers to the fear of unknown powers, the awe and dread that people have of forces beyond their control; *mysterium fascinans* ("The Fascinating Mystery") refers to the attractive power of the Holy, which draws people toward it

even against their will, like a moth to a candle flame. The moth to a candle flame analogy was often used by Sufis to express the attractive power of the love of God, which draws them ever closer until their human selves are annihilated in the "flame" of the Divine Essence. See Rudolf Otto, *The Idea of the Holy,* trans. John W. Harvey (1923; repr., London, Oxford, and New York: Oxford University Press, 1958), 12–40. (Ed.)

5.   'Ali ibn 'Uthman al-Jullabi al-Hujwiri, *The Kashf al-Mahjub: The Oldest Persian Treatise on Sufiism,* trans. Reynold A. Nicholson (1911; repr., London, U.K.: Luzac & Company, Ltd., 1976), 190–191.

6.   The Greek word *eros* means "desire" or "yearning," as does the Arabic word *'ishq.* The Greek word *agape* is equivalent to the Arabic words *hubb* ("love") and *rahma* ("mercy"), depending on the context. In his discourse on the Divine Names, Pseudo-Dionysius uses *eros,* in the sense of divine longing, yearning, or passion, to describe the motivating force of creation. Most Christian theologians, however, would use the term *agape,* which connotes a more compassionate form of love, in such a context: "The divine longing (*eros*) is Good seeking good for the sake of the Good. That yearning (*eros*) which creates all the goodness of the world pre-existed superabundantly within the Good and did not allow it to remain without issue. It stirred [God] to use the abundance of his powers in the production of the world." *Pseudo-Dionysius: the Complete Works,* trans. Colm Luibheid and Paul Rorem (New York: The Paulist Press, 1987), 79–80. Pseudo-Dionysius, who may have been Syrian in origin, was one of the most influential mystical thinkers of early Christianity. His works would have been widely known in Greek and Syriac among the Nestorian Christians of Baghdad during the time of Nuri and would have been widely known in Latin translation in late twelfth-century Spain, during the time of Ibn 'Arabi. (Ed.)

7.   See Ahmad al-Ghazali [*sic.*], *Sawanih. Aphorismen über die Liebe* (*Sawanih. Aphorisms on Love*), ed., Helmut Ritter (Istanbul, 1942). (Ed.)

8.   The full Qur'anic verse in which this statement appears is as follows: "Oh you who believe! If any of you turns away from his religion, God will bring forth a people that He will love as they love Him, who are humble toward the believers, stern toward the unbelievers, who strive in the way of God and do not fear the blame of the blamers. This is the Grace of God, which He gives as He wills, for God is the All-Comprehensive, the All-Knowing" (Qur'an 5:54). (Ed.)

16

SUFI WOMEN'S SPIRITUALITY: A THEOLOGY OF SERVITUDE

Rkia Elaroui Cornell

The earliest book about Sufi women in Islam is *Dhikr al-niswa al-muta'abbidat al-sufiyyat* (Memorial of Female Sufi Devotees), by the great systematizer of Sufi doctrine, Abu 'Abd al-Rahman al-Sulami (d. 1021 CE). Sulami, a resident of the city of Nishapur in eastern Iran, describes Sufi women as practicing a Theology of Servitude. He depicts this theology as a practice-oriented complement to the more theoretical doctrines followed by Sufi men.[1] The Theology of Servitude that was practiced by Sulami's Sufi women is based on the idea that spiritual engagement operates on two levels: an outer (*zahir*) level and an inner (*batin*) level. Each of these levels also has an outer and an inner dimension. On the inner level of spiritual engagement, the outer dimension consists of an engagement with God; this is because God is conceived as being outside of one's self (*nafs*). The inner dimension of the inner level of spiritual engagement consists of an engagement with one's own soul (*ruh*); this is because the soul represents a transcendence of the self (*nafs*), but it is also found within the self. The outer level of spiritual engagement in Sufi women's Theology of Servitude consists of religious practices that are part of the Sufi woman's engagement with her self. The outer dimension of these practices concerns the types of practices employed to discipline and transform the self. The inner dimension of the outer level of spiritual engagement concerns the transformation of the spiritual understanding that the religious practices and spiritual disciplines are meant to bring about.

According to Sulami, Sufi women are different from ordinary Muslim women because they practice *ta'abbud*: literally, "making oneself a slave" (*'abd*). *Ta'abbud* is the Arabic term that Sulami uses to designate the Theology of Servitude. For Sulami, *ta'abbud*, the Theology of Servitude, is the essence of Sufi women's spirituality. It is their means to divine inspiration, and it is the spiritual method that distinguishes them from their male Sufi counterparts.

Although Sulami makes the Theology of Servitude a characteristic of Sufi women, the concept for which it stands has long been part of Islamic piety. The Arabic term for worship (*'ibada*) means "servitude." The famous statement about worship in the Qur'an (Qur'an 51:56), "I have not created Jinn and humankind except to worship me (*illa li-ya'buduni*)," shows that the concept of servitude is all-inclusive: it envelops not only humans, but other forms of creation as well. The Theology of Servitude is also expressed in the Hadith, the Prophetic traditions of Islam. For example, in the *Musnad* of Ibn Hanbal (d. 855 CE), the Prophet Muhammad states that one of the names most favored by God is *'Abd Allah* (Slave of God). The other name most favored by God is *'Abd al-Rahman* (Slave of the Bestower of Grace). Both names include the term *'abd*, "slave."[2]

In the Qur'an, the concept of *Islam*—the submission of the self to God—is frequently expressed in terms of servitude. "Selling oneself to God" is the quintessential attribute of the true believer and is one of the spiritual traits that Islam shares with both Judaism and Christianity. This is stated explicitly in the following verse:

> Verily God has purchased from the believers their persons and possessions in return for Paradise. They fight in the cause of God and they slay and are slain. This is a binding promise on God, stated in truth in the Torah, the Gospel, and the Qur'an. Who is more faithful to his promise than [God]? So, rejoice in the sale of yourself that you have concluded, for it is the supreme achievement.

(Qur'an 9:111)

In his exegesis of the Qur'an titled *Haqa'iq al-tafsir* (The Realities of Qur'an Interpretation), Sulami often discusses the Theology of Servitude through the words of Ahmad ibn 'Ata' (d. 921 CE), a famous Sufi of Baghdad. In these passages, another term for servitude is used: *'ubudiyya,* which is commonly understood as "worshipfulness," but literally means "slavery." In his commentary on the Chapter on Women in the Qur'an (Qur'an 4, *Surat al-Nisa'*), Sulami quotes Ibn 'Ata' as saying: "Servitude is a combination of four traits: (1) to be true to one's covenants; (2) to preserve moral rectitude; (3) to be satisfied with whatever one finds; (4) to patiently bear what has been lost."[3]

Being true to one's covenants corresponds to the outer dimension of the outer level of spiritual engagement described above. Engagement with God is expressed in the Qur'an by the covenant struck between God and humanity before the creation of Adam (Qur'an 7:172). Engagement with other human beings depends on other types of covenants such as oaths and contracts, which figure prominently in the Qur'an as well (see, for example, Qur'an 16:94; 5:1, 5:89). Both types of engagements require renewal and reaffirmation, and both types rely on moral rectitude (Ibn 'Ata's second trait of servitude) for their fulfillment. Moral rectitude is the key to the outward process of spiritual engagement. In Islam, moral rectitude entails the emulation of the Prophet Muhammad's actions and the embodiment of his moral fiber, which is fundamental to the concept of *Sunna*. The Qur'an states: "And you [Muhammad] are of great moral character" (Qur'an 68:4). Ibn 'Ata's third and fourth traits of servitude, which are to be satisfied with whatever one finds and to patiently bear what has been lost, correspond to the inner dimension of the outer level of spiritual engagement. These disciplines correspond to the Qur'anic teaching to regard the life of the world as nothing but a "sport and a pastime" (Qur'an 6:32), and help the seeker on the spiritual path turn her attention from the outer life of the world toward the Abode of the Hereafter and the inner life of the soul.

Elsewhere in *Haqa'iq al-tafsir* Sulami states: "Servitude (*'ubudiyya*) is built on six principles: (1) exaltation of God without reservation; (2) shame, which consists of the restlessness of the heart; (3) trial, which consists of desire; (4) fear, which consists of the abandonment of sin; (5) hope, which consists in following the example of the Prophet Muhammad and realizing his moral character; (6) awe, which consists of the abandonment of choice."[4] Most of these principles could be applied to any religion other than Islam with little or no modification. Exaltation of God is symbolic of a resolute faith. Falling for sin or debauchery causes shame and remorse for the ethical and moral person. Trials and tribulations shake one's faith to its core whenever they occur. Fear of punishment for evil deeds haunts everyone with a conscience. Hope for salvation or happiness, when channeled through divine exemplars such as prophets or spiritual masters, is a universal human aspiration. Awe of the Transcendent causes egos to melt away. In such a state, the believer abandons the idea that she is the architect of her own destiny. What is left is: "There is no god but God" (*la ilaha illa Allah*), the fundamental statement of divine unity (*tawhid*) in Islam and the basis of the Islamic creed. This is the Qur'anic meaning of servitude. It is the complete surrender or "sale" of oneself to God.

According to Ibn 'Ata', the sale of oneself to God meant above all else the suppression of the human ego, which, like the self in general, is designated by the Arabic term *nafs*. In the words of Ibn 'Ata', "The worst of your enemies is the *nafs* that is between your two sides."[5] This inner battle within the self is a prerequisite for the inward spiritual engagement that comprises the second, deeper dimension of the Theology of Servitude. The salvation of the soul, says Ibn 'Ata', can only be purchased with servitude.[6] Ja'far al-Sadiq (d. 765 CE), the sixth Shiite Imam stated: "The faithful slave of God must rely on three sets of foundational practices (*sunan*): the *Sunna* of God Most High, the *Sunna* of the Prophet Muhammad (Peace be upon him), and the *Sunna* of the Friends of God (*sunnat awliya' Allah*). The *Sunna* of God is the concealment of divine secrets. Allah Most High said: '[God alone] knows the unseen, and he does not allow anyone to be acquainted with

His mysteries' (72:26). The *Sunna* of the Messenger of God (Peace be upon him) is the experiential knowledge of creation. The *Sunna* of the Friends of God is the fulfillment of covenants and endurance in hardship and calamity."[7]

A similar understanding of servitude can be found in *Slavery as Salvation,* Dale B. Martin's study of the rhetoric of slavery in early Christianity. Realizing that the metaphor of slavery in the Gospels and the letters of the Apostle Paul stood for more than just humility, Martin examined late antique slavery in its full sociohistorical context and found that it was a complex institution. In the late Roman Empire, where social, economic, and political ties were often based on patronage, slavery might paradoxically be used as a metaphor for authority.[8] In a wealthy household, the slave-manager (Gr. *oikonomos*) would often have a considerable amount of authority. As a loyal and devoted servant of his master, a trusted slave might even have more authority than a free person of low status. A similar state of affairs existed in the Muslim world of Sulami's day, where relationships of loyalty and intimacy with a powerful patron were also expressed through the rhetoric of servitude. By making a vocation out of service to their divine Master, the Sufi women who practiced the Theology of Servitude could free themselves from the constraints that would normally have limited their role in society. In both cases, the early Christian and the medieval Muslim, slavery to God meant liberation, both from slavery to the self and from slavery to other human beings. Servitude to the Lord trumps servitude to all lesser lords, including one's own self. This is such an important concept in Islam that the word "lord" (*rabb*) as a status category is used only for God. For human beings, the word "lord" is only used in a metaphorical sense, as in the phrases, "head of the family" (*rabb al-ʿaʾila*) and "the intellectuals" (literally, "the lords of the intellects," *arbab al-ʿuqul*).

It is in this wider context of the Theology of Servitude that we must understand the statements made by Sufi women such as ʿAʾisha bint Ahmad of Merv (d. late tenth century CE): "When the slave seeks glory in his servitude, his foolishness is revealed."[9] Just as the religious metaphor of slavery stands for more than humility, this statement is more than just a warning against the egoism of virtue. Islam, like Christianity, inherited much from late antiquity, including the relationship of slavery as an institution to wider, patronage-based social structures. In the Gospel of John, the Apostles of Jesus, as Slaves of Christ, are rhetorically transformed into the Friends of Christ and thus become figures of religious authority.[10] Likewise, for Sulami, being a Slave of God (*ʿabd Allah*) was necessary for becoming a Friend of God (*wali Allah*). Thus, the glory that ʿAʾisha bint Ahmad warns her associates to avoid is not only that of pride in one's virtue but also the vainglory of seeking sainthood for the worldly patronage that it bestows.

Further comparisons can be made between the Christian and the Islamic uses of servitude as a religious metaphor and a spiritual practice.

Besides sharing a common understanding of slavery as a path to salvation, medieval Muslims and early Christians saw servitude as a way of overcoming the limitations of human nature.[11] Certain traditions that are critical of women in Islam attribute woman's inadequacy to the deficiencies of the female nature. For example, a well-known hadith in *Sahih al-Bukhari* (ca. 860 CE) reports that the Prophet Muhammad informed a group of women that they were deficient in both intellect and religion.[12] Because of traditions such as these, it is not surprising to find that overcoming human nature—and especially the female nature—was a prominent concern for Sufi women. Commenting on the famous hadith: "He who knows himself (or his inner self) knows his Lord" (*man 'arafa nafsahu 'arafa rabbahu*), Futayma the wife of the Sufi Hamdun al-Qassar (d. late ninth century CE) remarks: "When a person truly knows herself, her only characteristic is servitude and she takes pride in nothing but her master."[13] This statement is perhaps intentionally ambiguous. Does Futayma mean to say that the Master who must be served before all else is God? Or does she mean to say that a woman serves God by serving her husband as her master? Maybe she means both, because Futayma's husband was a famous Sufi spiritual master. Either way, it is clear that the spiritual path for Sufi women was opened by servitude. The Sufi woman 'Unayza of Baghdad (d. first half of the tenth century CE) stated: "Human forms [literally, 'the molds of human nature'] are mines of servitude" (*qawalib al-bashariyya ma'adin al-'ubudiyya*).[14]

A major advantage of the Theology of Servitude was that it freed early Sufi women from the constraints imposed on them by their societies. As Slaves of God, they could separate themselves from the ordinary masses of women who did not share the same spiritual vocation. Choosing an independent life as "career women" of the spirit, they could travel without a chaperone, mix socially with men, teach men in public assemblies, and develop intellectually in ways that were not accessible to their non-Sufi sisters. This focus on spirituality as a personal vocation explains the surprising comment made by the Sufi woman Nusiyya bint Salman (d. early ninth century CE) upon the birth of her son: "Oh, Lord! You do not see me as someone worthy of your worship. So because of this you have preoccupied me with a child!"[15]

As stated above, the spiritual method of the Theology of Servitude works on the outer and inner natures of the human being at the same time. Outwardly, it cultivates the Sufi attributes of scrupulous abstinence (*war'*), patience, poverty, and humility. Without these attributes, the human being is a slave to the ego-self. In the words of the female ascetic Umm Talq (d. mid-eighth century CE), "The ego-self (*nafs*) is a king if you indulge it, but it is a slave if you torment it."[16] Inwardly, the Theology of Servitude cultivates the attributes of fear, worshipfulness, gratitude, and reliance on God (*tawakkul*). These are the attributes that lead to perfection in religion, according to the words of the famous tradition: "Worship God as if you see Him; for if you do not see Him, surely He sees you."[17]

Sulami's book of early Sufi women implies that once women start practicing the Theology of Servitude, it is no longer acceptable for male authority figures to claim that women are deficient in religion, for servitude is the truest form of submission to God. Even more, because such women are successful in overcoming the lower aspects of their human natures, the highest levels of religious knowledge are now accessible to them. The limitlessness of this potential is reflected in the statement of Umm 'Ali, a Sufi woman from Nishapur, whose brother Abu Mansur ibn Hamshadh (d. 998 CE) was a famous preacher and acquaintance of Sulami: "One who is confirmed in the knowledge of servitude will soon attain the knowledge of lordship."[18] Umm 'Ali's point is made even more strongly in the words of Surayra al-Sharqiyya, a disciple in Nishapur of the Sufi master Abu Bakr al-Tamastani al-Farisi (d. 951 CE): "Eventually, servitude vanishes and only lordship remains."[19]

The above discussion has demonstrated that the Theology of Servitude practiced by early Sufi women is a key to many different types of spiritual engagements. The essence of this practice is to transcend the ego-self by "selling one's soul" to God. When stripped of its egoistic attachments, the human soul cannot be labeled as either male or female. The statements and teachings of early Sufi women, which were inspired not by the ego-self (*nafs*) but by the providentially motivated and divinely guided spirit-soul (*ruh*), are universal in their application. Thus, they are able to provide guidance for all human beings, regardless of gender. This, in fact, was why Sulami chose to devote an entire book to them. Today, a conservative reaction across the Muslim world has made of women—both body and soul—a major battlefield in the struggle between an idealized Islam and the West. The result of this struggle, in places as diverse as Afghanistan, Saudi Arabia, Pakistan, Somalia, Iraq, and Darfur, has been to deprive the Muslim woman of her personality and to make her an object for the exploitation of men. It is noteworthy and perhaps highly significant that many of the movements of religious reform in Islam that are most critical of women's role in society also condemn the religious perspective of Sufism. Sulami's book of Sufi women was lost to the Muslim world for more than 500 years, only to be discovered by accident in Saudi Arabia (and ironically in the library of Muhammad ibn Saud University, a major center of Wahhabi teaching) in the early 1990s. One cannot help but feel that the rediscovery of this work was meant to be, and that in current times, when freedoms of personal and religious expression are under severe attack in much of the Islamic world, the voices of the early Sufi women again need to be heard.

NOTES

1. Biographical information on Sulami can be found in the Introduction to Abu 'Abd al-Rahman al-Sulami, *Early Sufi Women, Dhikr an-niswa al-muta'abbidat*

as-sufiyyat, Translation and Introduction by Rkia E. Cornell (Louisville, Kentucky: Fons Vitae, 1999), 54–60.

2. See Ahmad ibn Hanbal, *Musnad,* 14/245.

3. Paul Nwyia, ed., *Trois Oeuvres inédites de Mystiques musulmans: Shaqiq al-Balkhi, Ibn 'Ata', Niffari* (Beirut, 1973), 45. This work contains only selected portions of Sulami's *Haqa'iq al-tafsir.*

4. Abu 'Abd al-Rahman al-Sulami, *al-Haqa'iq: Tafsir al-Qur'an al-Karim bi lisan ahl al-haqa'iq* (The Realities: the Interpretation of the Noble Qur'an in the Language of the People of Transcendent Reality). Sulami's exegesis of the Qur'an has not yet been edited definitively in Arabic. The manuscript from which the above quotation is taken was originally copied in 1854 and was registered in the manuscript collection at Bulaq, part of the city of Cairo, Egypt, in 1895 (Cairo: Dar al-Kutub al-Misriyya, ms. 481), 78.

5. Nwyia, *Trois Oeuvres inédites,* 60.

6. Ibid., 63.

7. Sulami, *al-Haqa'iq* manuscript, 81.

8. Dale B. Martin, *Slavery as Salvation: The Metaphor of Slavery in Pauline Christianity* (New Haven and London: Yale University Press, 1990), 56–57.

9. Sulami, *Dhikr an-niswa,* 258.

10. Martin, *Slavery as Salvation,* 54.

11. See, for example, the following statement made in the early Christian hagiographical tradition about the fourth-century ascetics of the Egyptian desert. These are "true servants [literally, "slaves"] of God...[through whom] the world is kept in being, and that through them too human life is preserved and honoured by God." Benedicta Ward, *The Lives of the Desert Fathers: The Historia Monachorum in Aegypto,* trans. Norman Russell (London and Oxford: Mowbray and Collins, 1980), "Prologue," 49–50.

12. See, for example, Muhammad ibn Isma'il al-Bukhari, *Sahih al-Bukhari,* Kitab al-zakat: al-Zakat 'ala al-aqrab (Book of the Alms Tax: the Alms Tax for Near Relatives), hadith nos. 257 and 258.

13. Sulami, *Dhikr an-niswa,* 206.

14. Ibid., 248.

15. Ibid., 92.

16. Ibid., 118.

17. Muslim ibn al-Hajjaj an-Nisaburi (d. 875 CE), *Sahih Muslim bi-sharh al-Nawawi* (Beirut, n.d.), vol. 1, 152–160.

18. Sulami, *Dhikr an-niswa,* 244.

19. Ibid., 246.

17

FATIMA AL-YASHRUTIYYA: THE LIFE AND PRACTICE OF A SUFI WOMAN AND TEACHER

•

Leslie Cadavid

INTRODUCTION

The following autobiography is taken from the writings of a twentieth-century woman saint and scholar from Palestine. Fatima al-Yashrutiyya (1891–1978) was the daughter of the Shadhili Sufi Shaykh 'Ali Nur al-Din al-Yashruti (d. 1899 CE), whose spiritual center (*zawiya*) was in Acre, Palestine (now part of the State of Israel). As one of Shaykh al-Yashruti's few surviving children, Fatima was the object of much affection and attention. When she was two years old, her father began to take her with him to attend meetings of theologians and Sufis. She was evidently gifted, for when the Shaykh died in 1899 at the venerable age of 108, and Fatima was but eight years old, she resolved to undertake the search for the knowledge that she had begun to taste, and took it upon herself to read as many books as she could on all aspects of Sufism and Islam. She continued these studies for the greater part of her life and used to meet regularly with scholars and Sufis throughout the Middle East. It was exceptional for a Muslim woman living in the early part of the twentieth century to meet in this way with men and to converse freely on scholarly topics. However, Fatima's behavior can be explained by her exceptional gifts in the fields of learning and also by the fact that she had already been well acquainted with the scholars of the day as a child. A popular legend says that the early Muslim theologian Hasan al-Basri (d. 728 CE) related of the woman saint Rabi'a al-'Adawiyya (d. 801 CE), "I passed one whole night and day with Rabi'a speaking of the Way and the Truth, but it never occurred to me that I was a man nor did it occur to her that she was a woman."[1]

Fatima al-Yashrutiyya never married, nor does she mention any possibility of marriage. This, too, was unusual and can perhaps be explained by her wholehearted devotion to the pursuit of knowledge and spiritual realization, which took precedence over all else in her life. She died in 1978 in Beirut at the age of 87. She wrote four books: *Rihla ila al-Haqq* (A Journey Toward the Truth), *Masirati fi Tariq al-Haqq* (My Journey on the Path of the Truth), *Mawahib al-Haqq* (Gifts of the Truth), and *Nafahat al-Haqq* (Breaths of the Truth). It is rare to find among the Sufis a woman who wrote of her path to God for later generations to read. Indeed, few women Sufis wrote at all; for the most part we must content ourselves with later writings about them by their male followers or admirers. This rarity makes Yashrutiyya's writings all the more valuable.

In *A Journey Toward the Truth* we find the life story of Fatima's father, recounting his travels from his home in Tunisia, where he was born in 1791, to his final residence in Acre, Palestine. His life spanned more than a century and saw great changes in the Muslim world as so-called "progress" and Westernization crept in. Fatima al-Yashrutiyya would perhaps never have written her first work were it not for the fact that several disciples and friends had requested it of her, and she was then divinely inspired to write. This first book and the rest of her works were written primarily for the disciples of the Yashrutiyya Sufi order and not so much for outsiders unfamiliar with the world of the *tariqa* (Sufi spiritual path). In her works, *Sayyida* Fatima ("Lady Fatima," a term of respect) is full of praise for the Sufi way; she explains what the Sufi way is and how one must follow it, depending on the predisposition of one's soul. The last work she wrote was *My Journey on the Path of the Truth,* which contains her autobiography as well as descriptions of many members of her family. *Gifts of the Truth* and *Breaths of the Truth* tell about life in the Yashrutiyya Sufi order and record numerous miracles that graced her father and his disciples. The most important of Sayyida Fatima's works are *A Journey Toward the Truth* and *My Journey on the Path of the Truth,* and it is almost exclusively from these that the selections reproduced below have been taken. In translating these selections, I excluded the customary formulas following the mention of the Prophet Muhammad ("may peace and blessings be upon him") or following the name of a deceased saint or relative ("may God be pleased with him"), to ease the experience of the reader in English. I also use parenthetical notes to define or explain a word, such as *tariqa* (spiritual brotherhood), to minimize the need for endnotes.

The Yashrutiyya Sufi order (*tariqa*) is a branch of the Shadhiliyya *tariqa* founded by Abu al-Hasan al-Shadhili (d. 1258 CE), a spiritual master of Moroccan-Tunisian origin who spent the latter half of his career in Alexandria and is buried on the Red Sea coast of Egypt. Shaykh al-Yashruti's master was Shaykh [Muhammad ibn Hasan Zafir] al-Madani (d. 1847 CE), and Shaykh al-Madani's master was Mulay al-'Arabi al-Darqawi (d. 1823 CE), the founder of the Darqawiyya Sufi order, one of the most prominent branches of the Shadhiliyya in North Africa.[2] The Yashrutiyya Sufi order has many adherents throughout Palestine, Lebanon, and Syria, as well as in East Africa and even as far as South America.

Although more than one shaykh was elected to succeed Shaykh al-Yashruti during Sayyida Fatima's lifetime, it is safe to say that it was she who carried the *baraka* (blessing) of the order. Although she did not have a formal leadership role in the order, she was authorized to initiate others into it. Visiting disciples were interested in meeting her above everyone else. An acquaintance that knew her related to me that on one occasion some visiting African disciples lifted her onto their shoulders out of joy and reverence for her. She was, according to all accounts, very beautiful. Even when she was in her eighties, her inner radiance shone forth, making her seem like a young woman. Jean-Louis Michon, a Swiss architect and Muslim scholar, met Sayyida Fatima in the late 1970s in Beirut. He recounted that the meeting was "marvelous, she was nearly eighty, without a wrinkle. She had a radiant face like a young girl, full of life yet very serene." This account makes one think of the famous Andalusian Sufi Muhyiddin Ibn 'Arabi (d. 1240 CE), who was taught by an elderly woman saint named Fatima in Cordoba. He related that despite her great age, she possessed the beauty of a young girl. Ibn 'Arabi accorded women a very high spiritual position and saw them as a manifestation of the mercy (*rahma*) of God. He was not the only man in Islam to venerate women in this way. Throughout its history, the Muslim world has known many saintly women, whose *baraka* has survived down to the present. Fatima (d. 632 CE), the daughter of the Prophet Muhammad, is one to whom some Muslims turn for intercession. Despite the fact that she was the mother of the Prophet's grandsons, Hasan and Husayn, she was given the honorific title of "virgin" (*batul*) because of her great purity of soul. Fatima al-Yashrutiyya was named after none other than this great woman of early Islam.

Rabi'a al-'Adawiyya, who was mentioned earlier, is famous throughout the Islamic world as the master of the Sufi path of Love. For Rabi'a, love for God was the motive behind every act, as her most famous and oft-quoted words reveal: "I have not served God from fear of Hell, for I should be like a wretched hireling if I did it from fear. Nor have I served God from love of Paradise, for I should be a bad servant if I served for the sake of what was given. Instead, I have served God only for the love of Him and desire for Him."[3] The love spoken of by Rabi'a is the highest station of Islamic mysticism and is equivalent, in its essence, with the station of gnosis, the intimate knowledge of God. In like manner, Ibn 'Arabi said in a famous poem: "My heart has opened to every form. It is a pasture for gazelles, a cloister for Christian monks, a temple for idols, the Ka'ba for the pilgrim, the tables of the Torah and the book of the Qur'an. I practice the religion of Love. In whatsoever direction its caravans advance, the religion of Love shall be my religion and my faith."[4] One could interpret the meaning of love as Rabi'a used it in a similar manner. Thus, it becomes the supreme state of union with the Spirit, where all individuality has melted away and there remains only the consciousness of God in His Essence.

The fact that so many scholars from both East and West came to visit Fatima al-Yashrutiyya during her lifetime demonstrates the importance of her position in the world of Islam and Sufism. Indeed, her education in the disciplines of jurisprudence, theology, and Sufism was unrivalled for a woman of her background. In 1973, she wrote a paper as a contribution to a conference in Houston, Texas, that reflects her status as both a learned scholar and a profound thinker. In it she wrote:

> The salvation of the soul and the attainment of knowledge of God is the legacy of purification. We maintain, therefore, that Sufism is the most noble and excellent of all the sciences because its subject is the knowledge of God, His names, His qualities, and His deeds. While the virtue of acquiring knowledge in all fields is the duty of every Muslim, every branch of knowledge derives its honor from the level of that which it seeks to know and the fruits thereof. The study of the physical world as the handiwork of God Almighty is a natural and noble activity of man. It is obvious that man's finite intellect, if he is on the right path, is drawn by and moves toward the Infinite. Thus, the knowledge of God is more noble and complete than the knowledge of anything else knowable, and the fruits of it lead to felicity in this world and the next. Moreover, the seeker of knowledge is usually affected by that which he seeks, such that gradually his life and soul are molded by the qualities and attributes of the "known." Thus, the knowledge of every attribute of God leads to a spiritual state.[5]

When asked about the vitality of the Yashrutiyya Sufi order at the end of the 1970s, Sayyida Fatima said: "Ours is a materialistic age, but there *are* those who follow the Way. Good men are always in the minority. But that does not matter. Numbers are not what count. One person can be worth more than thousands. Many thousands are not worth one good man."

THE AUTOBIOGRAPHY OF FATIMA AL-YASHRUTIYYA

I was born in 1891 and raised in my father's *zawiya*—that of the Shadhiliyya Yashrutiyya in Acre, Palestine. When I was born, my father was 100 years old. This occasion caused much celebration in our house and in the *zawiya*, for my honored father did not have many surviving children. He passed on to the next world when I was just eight years old. There was a woman in our *zawiya* who was thought by all to be a very pious person, so when my mother gave birth to me, my father went to her and said, "I would like you to give me a blessed name for my child, which I have at last been given." She replied, "Is there any name more noble than that of your grandmother and ancestor, *Sayyidatuna* (Our Lady) Fatima al-Zahra', the daughter of the Prophet?" Thus, I was honored with that noble name.

It was always a source of pride and happiness to me that I bore a great physical resemblance to my father. I was given the same shape of face and

cheekbones, similar facial features and nose, and a white complexion.
My hands, with their long fingers and fair complexion, are also inherited
from him. Anyone who saw me as a child knew that I was the Shaykh's
daughter on account of our great likeness. The *zawiya* in Acre was a meeting
place for men of learning and law, of Sufism and gnosis. Ever since my eyes
first saw the light of day, I found myself living among these learned men
and attending study circles, spiritual counsels, and meetings of scholars and
jurists. My father favored me and by his kindness to me directed me toward
those fields of religious education that emphasized religious sciences and
Sufism and that encompassed outward and inward knowledge. For this
reason, he allowed me to sit in the circles of Sufi learning where he spoke
and which the most learned theologians attended. I began to do this
regularly when I was four years old. I was the only child and the only female
who devoted herself to lessons of this sort. My father was well aware that he
would eventually leave my sister and me alone in the world, so he wanted
me to begin my pursuit of knowledge of religion and Sufism, to which my life
was to be devoted in the future. This explains the extraordinary attention
with which he guided me toward these subjects.

Our life at home in the time of my honored father was one of happiness,
lightheartedness, and well-being—a life of simplicity and ease, with few com-
plications. Illuminated by the light of faith and good works, it was a life of
learning and mystical striving, of worship and nobility of character. My father
was a most holy irradiation of the Divine Essence, endowed with the nature
of the Messenger of God, walking in his footsteps through all the stations
of outward and inward perfections, not lingering at any one of them, but
understanding the truth in all of them. He was heir to the Muhammadan
nature in all its perfection, immersed in the overflowing bounty of the
divine ocean, and a perfected, divinely inspired guide. He was an example of
devotion toward his parents and family, a generous and noble husband,
a gentle and kind father, and a man whose humanity encompassed both
men and animals with gentleness and mercy. During the course of his
life he married four times, but he never had more than one wife at a time.
He had a great respect for women and recognized their rights and duties;
moreover, he made efforts to raise their level of knowledge and learning.
When he married my honored mother, after his former wife had passed
away, she was illiterate so he appointed a private tutor for her to teach her to
read and write. After her lessons he used to teach her something of Islamic
law, Hadith, Sufism, and the like, encouraging her to work and serve God,
striving in His path toward perfection. Thus, my mother attained, by her
human and spiritual striving, the highest station in relation to the divine.

My father's concern with raising the level of women's spiritual knowledge
was not confined to his wives, daughters, and granddaughters alone. In our
house, religious lessons were held daily, which were attended only by
women. My father used to choose a book and a subject, and ask a woman

teacher named Sayyida Umm Isma'il al-Dimashqi to give the lesson. Often, he would attend the session himself and offer explanations. It was obligatory for all members of our house, as well as those in isolation, visitors, and those living nearby to attend the religious lessons, and it was also obligatory for all the women of our house, even children, to pray five times daily. Every child over the age of seven years had to pray, fast, and recite the litany (*wird*) of the Yashrutiyya Sufi order. We had a special room in our house for chanting verses of the Qur'an, where we went every morning, each with her own copy. One of us would read a portion of the Holy Book aloud; then each would read whatever amount she could accomplish by herself in a voice so low it was almost a whisper, and after this we would all leave to carry out our household duties. A number of women from the important families of neighboring towns used to visit us. One of the first women to receive an initiation from my father was from this group.

The circles of invocation that took place in the *zawiya* were for men only, for my father said, "Circles of invocation are for men, not women." However, this did not mean that women in the *tariqa* were cut off from the practice of invocation. Every year in Ramadan we prayed the extra prayers in our house, with my father assigning for us a leader in prayer. After the night prayer and the voluntary prayers, we women would recite the litanies of the Shadhiliyya Sufi order together and then listen as a part of the Qur'an was recited. The house in which we lived during the life of my father and afterward was not only a place of residence, like other homes, but was also like a mosque, in which the five daily prayers were performed and the Qur'an was read in the intervals. My father lived just as the other disciples did in his home: praying, reciting litanies, and giving himself up to worship and obedience, but in addition he was a guide to lead people toward God. He only ceased reciting the litanies with others after he had passed his hundredth year. My sister Maryam once asked him, "Honored father, do you still recite the litanies at your great age, and in your spiritual station?" He replied, "The Messenger of God used to keep vigil at night until his feet were swollen, even after God had forgiven him his former sins and those that were to come. When he was asked about this, he said, 'Am I not, then, a grateful servant?'" In the same way, my father never ceased to get up at night for prayer and vigil up until the night before he passed on to the Eternal Abode. He spent his time in worship of God night and day, eating and sleeping but little, and living for God and in God. He used to partake of sweetened coffee and tea, and usually stayed in the *takiya,* only returning to the house to eat and sleep.[6] At times he ate with his disciples, for he spent most of his time with them, and he prayed the dawn prayer with them in the mosque behind the *imam* (leader of the communal prayer). When he passed his 100th year, he began to pray in his room, and then go down to the *takiya* (Prayer Hall), as was his custom. He used to enjoy walking in the fresh air and would pay visits to the tomb of the Prophet Salih or to the tomb of a saintly man of the area.[7]

We used to sleep with my father in one room. He was very kind to us and treated us with the gentlest of fatherly care and the greatest tenderness. He was concerned with the circumstances of all the women in the house along with the servants and tried to make them happy if possible. It is certain that the women among his disciples who attained realization and knowledge of God and His Messenger—those to whom God gave victory and aid from His Messenger—were so many that there is not space here to write all of their names. Suffice it to say that my honored father declared that in the city of Safad (Safed in present-day Israel) alone, there were 40 women who had realized God.

My sister Maryam was born two years after me, at the beginning of 1893. We lived under the care of my father and mother when we were children, then under the care of my mother after my father departed to Paradise, and then together after my mother died, until Maryam left this world to meet her Lord in 1975. When Maryam was a small child, no more than one year old, she used to hear the voice of the *muezzin* making the call to prayer, "God is most great! God is most great!" Whenever she heard him, she would raise her hands over her head and say "*Allahu Akbar!*" meaning, "God is most great!"

My sister was this way in all aspects of her life. When she reached the age of six, she began to show signs of traveling on the Path. My mother told me that after getting into bed and going to sleep, my sister used to wake up every night, sit up in her bed, look around her, and ask, "What is the explanation of such and such a verse from such and such a Sura of the Qur'an?" The women in the room would awaken, awestruck, and say nothing. Then my sister would begin explaining the verse and her explanation would be correct, according to those who heard her. Next she would ask those present, "What is the meaning of such and such a hadith?" Again, the women were silent in amazement. My sister would then give the explanation of the hadith, what happened in it, and its chain of transmission. She would remain doing this for some time, until sleep once more overcame her. The next morning, those who had heard her would ask her about what had happened the previous night, but she knew nothing of what she had done and it was as though she had experienced nothing unusual. She continued this way for four months, and eventually my mother became very upset and often wept for her. Finally, she decided to ask my sister what she saw when she was in that state. One night after my sister had gone to sleep, she awoke, sat up, and began explaining verses of the Qur'an. Those who were present asked her what she saw, and she said, "She sees before her wide, green fields in which there are many people listening to her, and at her side is a man carrying a wreath radiant with light, which he wishes to place on her head." My mother said to her, "Tell them, 'My mother is sad, she does not want this for me, but wants me to be as I am in the daytime. She pleads with you and asks God for help so that you help her.'" My sister began to repeat this. The wish was repeated for 10 nights until God accepted my mother's desire and my sister ceased to have these experiences. God the glorious had brought her back from the station of inebriation (*sukr*) to that of perfect sobriety (*sahw*). My sister combined both the beautiful and the majestic in her character, and was the embodiment of mercy. She ascended the ladder of the Path with humility through all of the stations, witnessing and unveiling the Truth, for she resembled our father both outwardly and inwardly.

My father used to sit and devote himself to the prolonged invocation of the name of God while facing the direction of Mecca. At these times, I often sat next to him, for I wished to see him in this state. The special circumstances in my life seldom permitted me to play with other children of my age. This did not upset me, however, for I felt happy and proud to sit with the learned men before my honored father, attending his lessons. Of course, I was not completely prevented from having close friends who were dear to me during my childhood. My father was kind to them too; he treated them with gentleness and told me to behave with kindness toward them.

Once, when I was six years old, I asked my mother, "Who created me?" "God," she answered. "And who created you?" I asked. "God," she said. "And who created my father?" "God." "And who created our Prophet Muhammad?" "God," she said. "And who created God?" "No one created Him," she said. "He has always existed, even before creating us." "How was He before He created us?" I asked, and she said, "Ask your father." At that moment he was sitting in the same room as us, and was reciting the litany, rosary in hand. I stood before him, kissed his hand, and repeated to him what I had said to my mother. Whenever I asked him about anything, he gave me a complete answer, as though one of his senior disciples were asking the question. When I asked him my question as I had done to my mother, he looked at me, smiling, and repeated the tradition of the Prophet as follows: "[God] was in darkness. Beneath Him was air and above Him was air, and He created His Throne upon the water." Then he closed his eyes, completely absorbed, and continued narrating the tradition, his hands resting on his knees.

I was very intimately linked with my father. I accompanied him physically and spiritually wherever he was, whether at home, in the *takıya,* in the prayer room, or in towns and villages. I remember how he used to go to the Friday prayer and to the two feast day (*'Id*) prayers accompanied by large groups of disciples. I remember how I used to go with him, never parting from him, saying the prayer behind the *imam* along with the others. At times, I went up with Hajj Salim, who was one of my father's disciples, to the roof of the mosque to pray with the men who gave the call to prayer. One of the dearest memories I have of my childhood is of a dream I had one night while asleep in my bed. I saw the Prophet Muhammad (peace and blessings be upon him) lying very still, asleep in my father's bed. Upon seeing him, I was seized with a great fear and began to cry and shout out: "O my father! O my lord, O my master, O my grandfather, O my beloved, O Messenger of God!"

At this he opened his eyes, and looked at me, smiling. Then he sat up in the bed, drew me to him, and held me to his noble chest, blessing me, and I could feel his breaths entering with mine into my breast. The next morning, when I told my father of the vision I had, his eyes filled with tears and he wept from joy, saying to me, "God will give you victory, my daughter, by the grace of those pure, noble breaths."

On another night, I once again had a vision while asleep, and when I awoke in the morning, I set off to look for my father to tell him of it. I found him that day standing with a group of visiting disciples outside the door to the great hall of the *zawiya*. I approached him and said, "O my lord! I saw in my sleep that I was standing before the gate of Paradise. The guardian angel opened the gate, and called to me, saying, 'Enter.' 'I will not enter,' I said. 'Why?' he asked. 'I will not enter until my father's disciple Hajj Salim Baliq enters.' 'Then let him enter,' the Summoning Angel said. Still I remained where I was and did not enter. I heard the Summoning Angel say a second time, 'Enter.' I replied, 'I will not enter.' 'Why?' he asked. 'I will only enter when all of our brethren have entered,' I said, and he replied, 'Then let them enter.' It was then that I awoke." When my father heard this, his eyes were filled with tears, and I heard him say to our brethren, "My daughter Fatima is a true disciple, for she loves all of the brethren on the Path. May my Lord grant her victory!"

On the 16th night of Ramadan, in the year 1316 of the Hijra (January 28, 1899), my father said his obligatory prayers, then stayed awake and kept vigil for half the night in spite of being 108 years old at the time. He then retired to his bed, which was in the same room in which he worshiped. There, in perfect repose and silence, he left this world to meet his Lord just before dawn. He was one who pleased God and whose soul was in peace, for he possessed confidence in God to the greatest possible degree and had spent his entire life in the service of the primordial (*hanif*) religion by guiding aspirants and spreading the teachings of Sufism far and wide. My relationship with my father was founded upon veneration, respect, and great spiritual love. Because of this love, which filled all my thoughts and my heart, I am helpless to describe here the extent of the grief and pain I felt upon his passing to the everlasting Paradise. From the moment the news of his death reached my ears, I felt as though I had fallen from heaven down to earth. I left our house and went to the *zawiya*, wandering without knowing where I was going. It is true, of course, that I was only eight years old when my father passed away, but whoever had lived as I had lived, in his shadow and among the most eminent leaders in thought and learning, and whoever had enjoyed guidance such as his would no doubt have experienced the events and changes that came to pass not as a small child, but as an adult possessed of a fully mature mind. I can remember that on the third day after my father passed away, I was afflicted with an illness that confined me to my bed as a result of my extreme grief and pain. While, in bed I picked up the Qur'an and began reading *Surat al-Kahf* (Qur'an 18, The Cave). I came to the verse that says, "And their father had been righteous, and thy Lord intended that they should come to their full strength and should bring forth their treasure as a mercy from their Lord" (Qur'an 18:82). Upon reading this verse, I felt a great peace entering my soul, bringing rest to my mind and calm to my wounded heart. I realized at that moment that God, Glorious and Most High, would not forsake me, and that my father's care for me ever since I came into this world was clear proof that God had taken my hand and would guide my footsteps and illuminate my heart so that I would be shown what was best for me in my religious and worldly life.

I was afraid that after my father's death I would lose the opportunity to attend meetings of scholars and doctors of the law and that I could no longer go to the study circles that were attended by scholars and Sufis who came from various parts of the city and from distant towns to hear my father's discourses, explanations, and interpretations. Fortunately, however, my link with these learned men was not broken at all after his death; in fact, they became even kinder to my sister and me. The bonds between us were strengthened and the roots of our relationship deepened and remained strong throughout my life. Such friendship had a great impact upon me and was to influence the formation of my character. As the Shadhili master Taj al-Din Ibn 'Ata'illah al-Iskandari (d. 1309 CE) said in his *Kitab al-Hikam* (Book of Aphorisms): "Do not befriend one whose state does not inspire you, or whose words do not lead you to God." This was the direction toward which my father had led me and which he wished me to follow. Without doubt, it was my mother who helped the most to nurture the growth of the Sufi spirit in my sister and me after my father's departure from this earthly life. She always urged us to practice what our father had desired of us. Among the things that helped us realize this goal were a library at the *zawiya* that contained precious and valuable books and my father's private library in our house. Although I was still very young, I decided to try to read many of the books in these libraries, so that through their instruction I might obtain of my father's teaching what I otherwise would have missed.

I asked my mother for permission to veil myself in front of the great scholars and the male disciples of my father. She consulted with my brother Ibrahim and with the scholars and brethren that we knew, but they all agreed that I should not be permitted to use the veil when I was with them. She did permit me, however, to dress as I had done in the days of my father, and meet these men in our house wearing a wide, white prayer scarf on my head. In the street, I went veiled like the rest of the young ladies of the day, for in that time this practice was observed most strictly.

I cannot be certain at what point in my life I learned to write. Moreover, I do not remember sitting before a teacher and learning writing from him, and I cannot recall the first time I ever picked up a pen. All I can remember is that I wanted to learn to write ever since I began to understand the nature of things. After my father's death I used to see Hajj Salim writing letters to his family. I would take one of these letters, put a thin piece of paper over it, and trace onto it what he had written in his letter. He would watch me doing this, and after some weeks he asked me, "What are you doing, mistress?" "I am drawing the word on the thin paper," I replied. "I am just playing with it." He said, "Are you able to understand the meaning of the words you are writing?" "Yes," I said. "Have you forgotten that I have completed the Qur'an and know some of its verses by heart?" He said, "Then read what you have written." So I read it, and he said, "Now I will write a line for you and you copy it out for me." So I tried and succeeded in copying the line of words without using the thin paper. Hajj Salim went on teaching me to write in this way, and that is why my handwriting resembles Hajj Salim's. I remember that after I wrote the first line, Hajj Salim went to tell the good news to my mother, saying, "My lady, little Fatima has learned to write by herself through the blessing of her father!" My mother was very happy at this, as was everyone else in the house at that time.

The home in which a child is raised has a great and lasting influence on her and determines to a large degree the formation of her personality. I remember my sister 'A'isha, the firstborn of my father, when she was about 90 years old. I never saw her without a book in her hand. In her free time, she used to see to her religious duties, reciting the litanies and invoking the name of God. After this, she spent most of her time reading books. She not only read religious works on theology and Sufism, but also books on history, literature, and ancient and modern poetry. She was very happy to see me at the age of nine or ten, with so much determination, working hard to read as much as possible to increase myself in wisdom and learning. My mother feared that I read too much, especially during my severe bouts of asthma, but my sister 'A'isha used to say to her, "Let her read. She will attain greatness in society and in the Sufi Way, if God Most High wills. This strong motivation to acquire knowledge, even when she is just a young child, has to manifest itself somehow in the world. My sister will obtain what she desires, with God's permission." In my father's *zawiya* there were a number of Qur'an reciters who knew the Holy Book by heart and who were well known for their beautiful voices. I grew up loving to listen to the recitation of verses of the Wise Book and to hear the songs and rhymed poems that were composed by the Sufis of our Yashrutiyya Tariqa. In this way, I memorized many verses of the Qur'an as well as Sufi songs and poems, and I began to acquire a taste for the arts, poetry, and music in an age in which there were no radios, televisions, or tape recorders.

As I entered my adolescence, God granted me recovery from my asthma, from which I had suffered constantly for 10 years. However, because of my prolonged illness, I never regained a strong constitution and was in need of care and supervision for the rest of my life with respect to food, rest, and social activities. The doctors had advised for my benefit that we spend time in coastal and inland areas, and in lowlands and mountains so as to have a periodic change of climate. Therefore, we would journey each year in the spring and summer to the mountains of Palestine, Lebanon, and Damascus. We continued in this way until war broke out in western Libya, waged by the Italians who had first brought their troops into Beirut but were defeated by the Ottoman Turkish army. During this time, it was dangerous to remain near the coast. Everyone living in such areas was anxious, especially in the city of Acre, which was still a fortified town of military importance. Many of the inhabitants of the city left to live in nearby villages and mountain areas, fearing an attack by the Italians. After passing a few weeks with our family in fear and apprehension, we decided that there was no alternative but to follow the course of the other citizens of Acre. We asked leave of my brother Ibrahim, and then went with my mother, my sister Maryam, and my cousins Anisa and 'Abda to the *zawiya* in the mountain village of Tarshiha, 24 kilometers northeast of Acre. It was cold up in the mountains and the village sometimes even had snow in the winter. When we went there it was the beginning of March, and we traveled over a rough, unpaved road. We stayed in Tarshiha for three months and during this period my health became worse and I suffered a relapse because of the cold weather. Added to this was the fact that I did not like living in this village, for I had too many fond memories of spending the summer months there with my father, and receiving huge groups of visitors from various parts of Syria who came to seek his counsel. Were it not for the Italian war (that is, World War I), which forced me to stay there for three months, I would have preferred to go to the mountains of Lebanon.

Whenever we went on our seasonal trips, my father's disciples would welcome us with joy and celebration and show great affection toward us. This was a reminder to us that they remained devoted and full of love for my father, adhering to his teachings and directions in spite of his passing away to the next world. Throughout our lives our mother never forbade us anything that gave us pleasure, provided it was in conformity with the Noble Path of the Sufi order and the accomplishment of God's commands. We were, may God be praised, objects of trust, esteem, and respect for whomever we met, whether they were disciples of my father or acquaintances from outside the Yashrutiyya order.

Life in Acre was unsettled after the establishment of the "Nation of Unity and Progress" in Turkey.[8] I used to spend a few weeks at a time in Acre and then go to Haifa, alternating between the two. In the spring we often went to Sidon in Lebanon or Damascus, or took an excursion in Palestine. People in our country had joined forces four months before the declaration of war by the Ottoman government on the Allies in 1914. At that time, I was suffering from gastric fever, so my mother decided that we should stay in Damascus for the duration of the war. My mother and sisters waited for me to recover, and when I had partially overcome my sickness but was still feeling weak, we prepared to leave Acre. However, we could not find any carriage or animals to take us to the train station, which lay outside of Acre, because the Ottoman army had taken possession of all means of transportation in the region. I was still too weak to go by foot from our house in the old city to the train station, so my cousin Sidi Hasan carried me there in his arms. We were very sad to leave the city that housed the remains of my father. However, at that time we did not think that we would be kept away for long, and hoped that we would surely be able to return to our beloved city one day. My mother, my sister Maryam, and my cousin Anisa traveled with me, while my brother Ibrahim remained in Acre with his family, along with my cousin Sidi Hasan.

The war caused poverty, hunger, destruction, disease, and the death of multitudes of people. Even though in World War I our country did not become very involved with the armies engaged in battle, our people suffered deeply from the hardships that resulted from it. The Arab regions of Syria were swept by a wave of typhoid fever at that time, and I remember during my stay in Damascus that there was severe hunger that grew worse every day, especially during the last two years of the war. It became a common sight to see men starve and die in the streets, and whenever we went out of the house we saw men, women, and children in distress crying, "We are hungry! We are hungry!"

While I was in Damascus in my youth, I would receive scholars, doctors of the law, and learned men of that city, and during the war, others who had fled from Acre to Damascus. When I met with them I wore the complete veil according to the Shari'a. My presence in Damascus during that period, and my freedom in the realm of the law and the arts, afforded me a precious opportunity. Because I had become acquainted with many of the learned men of that time, I was able to broaden my understanding and deepen my knowledge of diverse subjects. I developed a strong and independent personality that has endured throughout my life. It was my great good fortune to be able to take advantage of the opportunity to live in Damascus, for it was in those days an important center of Islamic scholarship.

Following the end of World War I, with its grief and misery, people throughout the country once more felt safe and returned to their normal way of life, going back to the homes that they had fled. We too returned to our home in Acre and took up our permanent residence there as before the war. From time to time, we would take trips to Damascus or Lebanon to visit friends or for a vacation, and then return to our home. In addition, we often spent the winter months in Cairo, which was a major center of religion, law, literature, and the arts. The first time we went there was in 1920, just after the war. We traveled by train from Palestine and were some of the first women to go to Egypt following the war. During our stay in Cairo, we rented a house in the new part of the city, which was at that time no more than a small village. The house that we found for ourselves there became like

a miniature *zawiya,* for we met there with other disciples of my father as well
as with scholars and literary men. The situation was similar for my female
companions. We occupied ourselves with reading both classic and contemporary works, books translated from other languages, as well as literary and
scholastic journals, and when we met we would discuss our readings.
The majority of my companions were gifted women with literary and writing
abilities. Some of them were poets and members of the highest ranks of the
women's revival movement in Egypt.

In the years following the war, the eyes of the people were opened to the
true nature of what had happened to them. Revolution came to Egypt in
the time of Sa'd Zaghlul (d. 1927), followed by revolution in Damascus
and other regions of Syria, and hints of revolution in Palestine as well.[9] Thus,
we did not feel settled no matter where we were. There was then a manifest
need for women to be more visible in order for them to participate in the
organization and planning of Arab society. In spite of this ambience, I always
tended toward a Sufi perspective. This was not surprising, for I saw myself
first as a worshipper of God, the Majestic and Powerful, through my journey-
ing on the Straight Path and through my love for knowledge, realization, and
learning. My father was my master and guide, and I made great efforts to
guard the filial and spiritual link with him. I had certain physical weaknesses
in those early days, which gave rise to the illnesses that afflicted me my health,
and which called for special attention. I have lived a fragile life, one in which
my schedule of eating, sleeping, and meeting with visitors have always been
regulated. Thus, I was never able to live in a town cut off from contact with
the outside world, or in one where there were no doctors and medicines
available, in spite of my attraction to and love for the beauty of nature.

I kept company only with people of learning, mystical knowledge, and the
arts. This was not out of any egoism or pride on my part, but because I had
sat among such people since I was a child, and the valuable lessons I learned
in those meetings on all aspects of knowledge had given rise to this tendency
in my soul. I was drawn to these worthy scholars and felt a desire deep within
my heart to be where they were. This compelled me to return time and again
to the cities of Damascus and Cairo, for it was in these important centers of
learning that such scholars were to be found. I was strict with myself, keeping
watch over my soul to the extreme limit of conservatism; I never for one day
interrupted my prayers or reciting the litanies, even when I was traveling to
Cairo, Damascus, or Lebanon, and I set aside times when I went into seclu-
sion to invoke God's name. In these moments, I felt a peace that I cannot
describe adequately in words, except to say my soul was engulfed by a most
profound feeling of contentment. This was indeed the station of worship
(*'ibada*) of God the Creator, the One. He said, "Worship thy Lord until
certitude cometh to thee" (Qur'an 15:99).

In another part of my life at this time I had women friends, the daughters
of elite families who had an appreciation for the arts. We used to meet

together for singing, socializing, and to discuss various subjects. We would listen to the songs of women who were blessed with beautiful voices, or had skill in rendering a piece of music according to its proper rhythm and melody. In this way, I passed the period after World War I.

I did not forget to worship and persevere in Sufi practices, but at the same time I did not cut myself off from the social world that surrounded me and of which I was a part. My relations with many of the great scholars and saintly people were strengthened, and by the grace of God I was confident and secure in all that I did at that time. It is well known to those familiar with history that the Palestinian revolution raged fiercest in the year 1936, and during that year there was great violence, fighting, and rioting. It was a year that was different from the rest of the years of the revolution and was therefore called the "Revolution of '36." The general history of this affair I leave to historians, and will only include what happened to my family and me during this period, which went on for nearly three years, and which lasted until just before the breakout of World War II in 1939.

When the revolution of 1936 broke out, I was recovering from a bout of dysentery, which had previously afflicted me two years earlier. At the time I came down with it, it took a great toll on me, for I already had a weak constitution due to the asthma that I had suffered from in my youth. This illness caused me a great deal of discomfort and pain, and my overall health was very slow to improve. At that time, I was still living with my mother and sister in Acre, and when my mother saw that my health was not improving at all, she decided that we should go to Beirut and seek the advice of well-known doctors there. She was also motivated by the events taking place in Palestine at that time. We left for Beirut in the beginning of 1935 and rented a house there. Thus, when the worst of the Palestinian revolution came in 1936, I was in Beirut recovering from my illness. It was necessary for me to watch over my health carefully for a few years before I regained my strength, and even then I was delicate and susceptible to further bouts of sickness for a long time. Both my stay in Beirut, a city of learning and intellectualism, and my confinement to my house encouraged me to read a great deal about various subjects. I benefited from learning more about various ideas and views in different fields. This stay also enabled me to meet with several philosophers and scholars, either through their visits to our house or by attending their lectures, if my health permitted. Thus, in this period I was able to increase my store of knowledge, particularly in the domain of philosophy and in the realm of Sufism.

After we had spent nearly three years in Beirut during the period of the Palestinian revolution, World War II was declared in 1939. A few weeks later, we left Beirut and moved to Damascus, but after two months returned to Lebanon. It had become clear to us that we could not stay in Damascus during winter, as it was extremely cold, and my mother was no longer young and needed to see the doctors in Beirut with whom she was accustomed and

who were familiar with the details of her health. Thus, we stayed for the
summer in the city of Aliya in the mountains of Lebanon and stayed for the
winter months in Beirut on the coast. In spring we would travel either to
Acre or to Damascus, depending upon the conditions of transportation at
the time. Days, months, and years passed in this way, traveling from one city
to another and hoping to be able to return to our country and live in Acre
after the war.

At the end of the third year of the war, I sat down one day to write some
letters. However, without intending to do so, I wrote a discourse on Sufism
of over seven pages in length. I was amazed at what I had done, and felt that
a spirit, or rather a hidden voice, had urged me to write about the Path and
about my father and his Sufi message. The moment I finished writing these
pages I hastened to show them to my mother, who encouraged me, saying,
"Do as you are ordered. This is a fruit of the blessing your father bestowed
upon you." I remembered then that my friends who were doctors of
the law and scholars had asked me to write a book that would relate the
story of my father's life, his deeds, and his message. I knew then that the
duty of writing this book had fallen to me, and that I would confirm what
had come to pass in my father's life and tell of the grace God had bestowed
upon him.

Thus, I began to write my first book, which is titled *A Journey Toward the
Truth*. This work begins with an introduction to Sufi doctrine, followed by a
description of my father's doctrine, his life and influence on Sufism, and
something about the Shadhiliyya Sufi order. I remember that when writing
some of the chapters of this book, it was necessary for me to refer to some
of the books of the Sufi masters. In spite of my complete faith in the sanctity
of Shaykh Ibn 'Arabi (may God be pleased with him), I neglected to make
use of his valuable works, for I thought, "Shaykh Muhyiddin has some enemies, and I do not want to open the door of dispute by referring to him."
From the moment this thought passed through my mind, I was no longer
able to continue writing; my hand was paralyzed for three years, unable to
complete the work without knowing why. Then one day a woman disciple
from Damascus came to visit us in Beirut, and during her stay she saw my
father in her sleep. She kissed his hand in her vision and asked him why
I had stopped writing. He answered, saying, "Because Fatima has shut the
door upon Shaykh Muhyiddin, may God be pleased with him." The next
morning, this disciple related her vision to me. I asked forgiveness of God
and repented of my erroneous thoughts. Then I hastened to the books of
Shaykh Muhyiddin and began to read them and absorb their wisdom. During
my study of his works, I came across a poem that he wrote called "Journey to
the Truth" (*Rihla ila al-Haqq*). This title pleased me, so I gave it to my book
as well, guided by Shaykh Muhyiddin's example. The writing of my first book
took just under 14 years to complete. I wrote down what came to me in
humility and devotion, telling of the graces that our Sufi order enjoyed.

I only wrote when I felt composed in the depths of my soul. Then I would seclude myself in my room to record my memories and write about what I had learned of Sufism.

After the end of the Second World War, we decided to remain living in Beirut, as we had grown accustomed to life there and it had become an absolute necessity to have a doctor nearby, especially for my mother. However, we still used to visit our home in Acre once or twice a year for a few weeks during spring or autumn. We remained in Beirut until the great Palestinian disaster of 1948, when we were compelled along with most other Palestinians to flee from our homes, an emigration from which we have not been able to return to this day.[10]

My new permanent residence in Beirut afforded me the opportunity to continue pursuing intellectual activities in spite of my delicate health, for this city was and still is one of the most important centers of learning and thought in the Arab world. The existence of several universities, along with the freedom of thought, speech, and publishing that existed there, encouraged diverse views and beliefs to manifest themselves and interact with each other, through the media of newspapers, magazines, and books, or in lectures and debates. Life in Beirut differed from that of other Arab countries, for groups of people from different nations and regions had immigrated there, and each of these groups had its own customs, traditions, and ways of thinking. Thus, if one experiences life in Beirut he will not be able to decide whether he is in an Oriental or a Western country, so distinct and peculiar is its character. However, the absolute and unrestricted freedom of thought, speech, and action can reach a point of near chaos. There were those in this beautiful city who advocated the adoption of Western urbanization wholesale, while another, more moderate group called for people to learn from the West, but to keep their Arab heritage—in other words, to blend Oriental and Western modes of thought. There were others who were conservative and did not believe in importing anything from the West. They wished to retain the philosophy and customs of the traditional world and to revive that which had been forgotten or had fallen into disuse. This era of the Palestinian emigration has been the longest period of my life, extending over more than 30 years. It began in 1948, and continues to this day at the end of 1978, as I write this chapter of my memoir. Only God knows how long this situation of exile will continue. From the start of this period, we have been living in Beirut, so from the point of view of daily life these years can be seen simply as a continuation of our life there.

Nothing changed for me during this time, and I continued to work on my book until it was completed in 1954. In April of that year, my mother left this world—may God have mercy on her—after having suffered a great deal from illnesses and having spent her whole life caring for us and serving the disciples of the *Tariqa*.

THE ZAWIYA OF THE YASHRUTIYYA IN MY FATHER'S TIME

The *zawiya* is a place where religious rites are performed. It is a place for prayer, fasting, night vigil, reflection, invocation, meditation, and total concentration on God. It is there that the litanies are recited, circles of *dhikr* (invocation) are held, and the disciple (*faqir,* literally "poor one") cuts himself off from anything other than God, the Glorious. It is in the *zawiya* that knowledge of God and realization are sought, where union with God, the Mighty and Majestic, is witnessed and realized, and where the disciple is extinguished in love of God and His Messenger. The *takıya* is the great sanctuary of the *zawiya,* with a high dome, in which the five daily prayers and sessions of *dhikr* are held. There are in addition many rooms in the *zawiya* to house visitors during their stay and for those disciples who are in retreat from the world. Then there are the small houses in which the families of those in retreat live. There are special sections for the old and sick, for the poor followers of the Path, and one house set apart for women. The Shaykh's house was in the vicinity of the *zawiya,* where he lived with his wife and children. The greatness of the *zawiya* was due not to the beauty and grandeur of its outward appearance, but to the great saintliness of its Shaykh and his divine station, for he was filled by God with mystical secrets and lights, and with knowledge and understanding.

This was how our *zawiya* was in my honored father's time: The spiritual life there was sweet with worship, remembrance, mysteries, and divine illuminations. Winds of grace and holiness swept through the realms of religious learning, both outwardly and inwardly, during the meetings of *dhikr,* in lessons of literature and the arts, during meditation, and in singing spiritual songs. This holy breeze wafted throughout the atmosphere of the Sufi, for although Islamic learning has many aspects, it is in essence a spiritual education that can be reduced to the acts of worship and remembrance of God. Every evening, study circles were held in our *zawiya* where lessons of Islamic Law, Hadith, Qur'an commentary, and Sufism were taught as well as other aspects of the sciences of the outer law and inner truth. In those days, the *zawiya* resembled an institute of learning that was attended by various groups of people, not only for the purpose of following a spiritual path and seeking enlightenment, but also to benefit from the sacred spring of wisdom, each to the extent of his desire and need for religious education and spiritual direction.

Adherents of both exoteric and esoteric knowledge attended the sessions of *dhikr.* They included men of authority, the rich, and the poor. Sometimes it happened that a person could not find a place to sit in that great sanctuary on account of the multitude of people who used to come to listen to our Shaykh. My honored father performed the five daily prayers in the *takıya* along with his representatives (sing. *muqaddam*), elder disciples, visitors, disciples in retreat, and those living nearby, who also came to pray with him. The great number of visitors to the *zawiya* filled one with awe and reverence. The rows of men at prayer were often so numerous that they even overflowed into the outer hallways of the mosque. The practice of invocation is mentioned clearly in several places in the Qur'an, such as in the following verses: "Remember God with much remembrance, and glorify Him morning and evening" (Qur'an 33:41–42); "...Those who remember God standing, sitting, and lying on their sides" (Qur'an 3:191); and "Is it not in the remembrance of God that hearts find peace?" (Qur'an 13:28). There are also many *ahadith* that speak of the right to invoke and to hold sessions of *dhikr*. Of these, the following was transmitted by Tirmidhi: "The Messenger of God said: 'Whenever you pass by the meadows of Paradise, graze therein.' They asked, 'O Messenger of God, what are the meadows of Paradise?' He replied, 'The circles of *dhikr*.'" The Prophet (peace and blessings be upon him) also said: "Verily God has angels who travel about seeking out the circles of *dhikr*, and whenever they come upon one, they surround it and God says to them, 'Enfold them in My mercy, for they are of those who sit together (to invoke) and whose sitting thusly will not cause them sorrow.'"

The Sufi disciple who is attached to God's path may be in isolation from the world, or he may work and earn his living as others do. The one in isolation must cut himself off from that which is apart from God, and devote himself completely to Him. The other, for his part, enters the Path while continuing in his outward life, working to earn his living and performing his worldly duties. In this respect, disciples are divided into two groups, yet they are all united in a common path under the direction of a realized Shaykh who has been given the authority to guide. For the aspirant who follows a spiritual path under a perfected Shaykh, all of his experiences and states exist only as a reflection of those of his master, and come about by means of him. This is what is meant when it is said that the Sufi state of extinction (*fana'*) is divided into three stages: The first extinction is in the Shaykh, the second extinction is in the Muhammadan Essence, and the third extinction is in God, the Mighty and Exalted. The attainment of the second level of extinction should not sever the fundamental link between the disciple and his Shaykh, for the successful and joyful disciple is he who never forgets his master, regardless of his spiritual state or station. Those who work in the world are divided into three subcategories: first, those who earn their livelihood in their own countries and who come to visit their Shaykh and return home again; second, those who work and live in the town near the *zawiya;* and third, those who emigrate from their country in order to be near their Shaykh or to find work for themselves in the nearby town.

Those who have been placed by their Lord, the Glorified and Most High, in the station of isolation from the world (*khalwa*) live in the *zawiya* near the master. Having devoted themselves to God in this way, they no longer turn toward the world. There were a great number of these disciples in our *zawiya,* men who came from all social classes and ethnic origins. Among them were Arabs, Turks, Moroccans, Indians, Persians, and Sudanese. These disciples were outwardly and inwardly brethren in God: men who conformed to the Muhammadan Sunna in order to purify their souls and polish their characters, to efface their lower selves, and become immersed in the consciousness of the essence of God Most High.

Advancement on the path of the Sufi masters is not obtained by holding circles of *dhikr* openly, for this is something that everyone owes to God. Rather, it is obtained by practicing the remembrance of God in secret through repeating the Supreme Name, *Allah*. This is the second pillar of the Path of the Masters of the Shadhiliyya, the first being the existence of a realized and perfected Shaykh, for without him the one who practices remembrance (*dhikr*) would not be able to attain the peace and fulfillment contained in the invocation. The disciple who wishes to practice the invocation should choose a peaceful, quiet place, during the night or the day, but more often at night, where he can sit to remember God, with knees either drawn up, as a sign of humility, or cross-legged and in both cases wrapped in a cloak. It was related that the Prophet Muhammad used to sit with his knees drawn up, holding a garment wrapped around him. The most important invocation is the invocation of the Supreme Name, *Allah.* Without this Name, no victory will come to the aspirant, nor will he attain to the station of sainthood save by invoking it. Moreover, he cannot truly invoke unless he cuts himself off from everything other than the One Invoked.

The Shadhiliyya Sufi method is founded on the Holy Book and the Sunna of the Prophet Muhammad, the search for knowledge, and the frequent practice of invocation in an attitude of worshipfulness and consciousness of the divine. This means of calling upon God is the easiest and most direct of spiritual paths, for it does not entail great hardship or much strenuous effort. The primordial light lying dormant within the soul gains strength through the light of knowledge and through the light of invocation, so that the soul is rid of its defects and impurities. It can then draw nearer to the Divine Presence until it is completely absorbed and the invocation burns away all thoughts of anything other than the One Invoked.

People are often heard to say that the occupants of Sufi dwellings live a life of indolence and ease, but in our *zawiya* it was not thus. Each disciple had duties that he performed to the best of his ability, depending on his preparation and education. These duties were not a burden for him, but were part of life in the *zawiya* and were done in an attitude of friendship and affection toward others. All of the disciples were equal before God; the wise and learned taught the illiterate and the common man, striving to teach the doctrinal knowledge that makes the Muhammadan initiation accessible to him. The strong dealt gently with the weak, and the elevated man gave guidance to his humbler brother.

The Shaykh appoints a representative (*muqaddam*) in the *zawiya*, who is authorized to initiate others into the Yashrutiyya order, to educate disciples, to lead the sessions of *dhikr*, and to teach religious studies. This representative must be someone who is well educated and eloquent, possessed of an excellent character, and endowed with wisdom and understanding. He must combine in his person knowledge of both legal and spiritual matters. He could be chosen either from those who live in isolation from the world or from those working in the world, for neither is more worthy than the other for this position. Concern for health and cleanliness was of the greatest importance in our *zawiya*, indeed to a degree that surpasses description. If my honored father fell ill, the doctor was summoned immediately, and thus it was with his wife and family or any of his disciples. If someone needed to be under a doctor's supervision, he was sent to the hospital in Acre. If he had to undergo surgery in one of the bigger hospitals in Beirut, he was sent there. If he needed a change of climate he went to the mountains, and whenever someone was afflicted with an infectious disease he was isolated from the rest of the disciples. Thus, in spite of the great numbers of visitors, whether nomads or settled folk, the concern for health and cleanliness was paramount. In reality, life in our *zawiya* was not like the life of dervishes, but instead was a life of spiritual progress combining invocation, learning, worship, and realization. Through carrying out our human duties and diligently striving to attain the levels of perfection—and by this last I mean the spiritual stations—one could arrive at the station of proximity to God Most High.

Our *zawiya* offered food to visiting disciples, and we often had no less than 400 or 500 visitors every day, apart from those living there in retreat with their wives and children. These visitors stayed in the *zawiya* and at mealtimes the tablecloths were laid and the disciples sat in groups to eat, while some helped to serve, carrying jugs of water and singing spiritual songs. During the feast days the number of visitors could reach between 1,000 and 2,000 each day. Whatever money accrued from religious charities was spent on the *zawiya*, as well as any other money and gifts the disciples offered to it. The Shaykh's money, when he had any, was also spent on the *zawiya* and thus everyone participated in its upkeep. If the *zawiya* happened to own some farmland or olive groves, farmers who were in retreat would cultivate it, till it, gather the harvest, pick the fruit, and put the olives in a press to extract the oil. They also worked at transporting provisions and raising livestock. Some worked at weaving clothing, combing cotton from the beds, buying necessities from the market, sweeping, cleaning, polishing, and whatever else was necessary for the maintenance of the *zawiya*.

The majority of those in retreat in our *zawiya* in my father's time were from elite and very old families. My father used to exhort them to give wholehearted devotion to their spiritual practices and to extinguish themselves in the love of God and His Messenger. He treated them as a father would his children, never differentiating between them and my brother Sidi Muhyiddin. In fact, he often said, "If Muhyiddin were not a disciple, I would not be disposed to love him." My brother Sidi Ibrahim came from Tunis, bringing his wife and children after the death of our brother Muhyiddin. Although at that time our master had no male children other than Sidi Ibrahim, he ordered him to follow the Path as if he were in isolation from the world for some years along with the other disciples before coming to live in his father's house. Sidi Ibrahim slept with the disciples and assisted them by helping to construct buildings, carrying clay with his hands, and wearing dyed linen garments. My sister's son Sidi Hasan led the same life. Our brother in God Sidi Mahmud al-Lahham related the following account from his brother Sidi 'Abdallah—both of them were sons of the great Shaykh Muhyiddin al-Lahham: "We were in the *zawiya* and heard news of the arrival of Sidi Ibrahim, the son of our great master, in Haifa. I was with a group of our disciples from Damascus, and we all decided to go to Haifa and take the rest of the disciples to the *zawiya* to welcome him. Now our Shaykh was nearby and when he saw our group he said, 'Do not behave with Sidi Ibrahim as the disciples of Shaykh So-and-So behave with his sons; they pamper and entertain them and dress them in silk. As a result, the children start to walk about and look at themselves and become cut off from closeness to God.' So we remained in the *zawiya*, and not one of us went to welcome the Shaykh's son. He came with his family and entered the *zawiya* unaccompanied." My father also said to some disciples after my brother's arrival in Acre, "Leave him to be taught by the members of our order." Our Shaykh was ascetic in the true sense of the word. He avoided the things of this world in spite of the fact that he was always being offered them. If he were given something he would spend it in God's name.

The disciples were extinguished in their love for their master, and preferred a life of isolation to that of work in the world so they could be near him at all times. However, the Shaykh did not order any of his disciples to leave their professions, businesses, or posts; the perfected one is he who moves among ordinary people while performing his duties. There is no work that God has made lawful that does not help the servant draw nearer to His presence. It only deters those who lack pure intentions in their work, whether it is in the field of learning, labor, or a professional career. A disciple once came to our master and asked permission to leave his work and give himself up completely to worship. The Shaykh said, "Remain in your shop and work and pray to your Lord. That is better for you than begging for food from people." The disciples were proud of their affiliation and used to boast of having visions of our noble Shaykh. They would compete with each other and believed that if his gaze merely fell upon a disciple he was transported to a higher state, and would attain realization. But the Shaykh himself knew that the divine light was not limited in this way and could come to the disciple anywhere, even if he were at the end of the earth.

Many visited the Shaykh for the purpose of acquiring his qualities and attributes, which were an embodiment of the Muhammadan nature. When our brother 'Uthman Pasha, a Turkish minister in the Ottoman state, once visited him, he said to our Shaykh, "I have been honored with a vision of our master. Am I not then better than 'Ali Rida Pasha?" The Shaykh answered him by saying, "Being united to the essences is better than being united to the qualities." When Shaykh Hafiz 'Uthman, the famous Turkish reciter of the Qur'an, came to visit my father, he composed a poem during his journey at sea. When he entered the *zawiya* my father asked about the poem he had composed, although no one had known anything about it. The Hafiz was astonished and asked, "Do you know what is hidden, or has a spirit inspired you?" Our Shaykh replied, "Do you not recite the Noble Qur'an?" "Certainly," he said. "God has said in His Mighty Book: 'The Knower of the Unseen, which He reveals unto none save every Messenger whom He has chosen (62:26–27).' I am of those whom the Messenger of God has chosen, for I am descended from him and linked to him." At this, Hafiz 'Uthman was filled with joy and entered into the Way of the Shadhiliyya. He was one of those who attained to knowledge of God. The Shaykh also said to him while giving a talk one day, "You are of those who have preserved the Qur'an in your memory. Our Lord, the Glorious and Most High, has favored us with you." Shaykh Hafiz 'Uthman answered, "With those who put the prescriptions into practice." Our Shaykh said, "Is there anyone aside from our Prophet who practices everything in the Qur'an? Rather, do you not practice only a part of it, even if only a single letter?" "Certainly," he said. The Shaykh replied, "This suffices." He also said, referring to the Sufi masters, "When you are told that there lives in Syria a great and wise man, learned in the sciences of the outward and the inward and in gnosis and realization, one possessing pleasing qualities and Muhammadan characteristics, that which comes to you is the Lore of Certainty (*'ilm al-yaqin*). When you have abided with him and realized his outward and inward qualities, and found him to be above that which they have described to you, your knowledge of him becomes the Truth of Certainty (*haqq al-yaqin*). So what is it that has disappeared between yourself and him, when neither he nor you have changed, and there has been no increase or decrease in his being or in yours? The answer is that what has disappeared is your ignorance of him."

NOTES

Reprinted from a work published by Fons Vitae with the permission of the publisher. (Ed.) following a note signifies that the note was added by the General Editor of this set.

1. Farid al-Din 'Attar (d. 1230 CE), Section on Rabi'a al-'Adawiyya in *Tadhkirat al-Awliya* (Memorial of the Saints) translated in Michael A. Sells, *Early Islamic*

Mysticism: Sufi, Qur'an, Mi'raj, Poetic, and Theological Writings (New York and Mahwah, New Jersey: The Paulist Press, 1996), 161.

2. Shaykh Muhammad ibn Hasan al-Madani was originally from the city of Mecca. In 1807, he left Arabia on a spiritual journey to Morocco, where he met Mulay al-'Arabi al-Darqawi in 1809. He also met a number of other famous Sufi shaykhs, including the West African revivalist Sidi Mukhtar al-Kunti (d. 1811) and Ahmad ibn Idris al-Fasi (d. 1837 CE), a Moroccan shaykh and Sufi reformer then residing in Arabia. Eventually settling in the region of Tripoli in Libya, Shaykh al-Madani founded the Tariqa al-Shadhiliyya al-Madaniyya, which, along with the Sanusiyya Tariqa, was one of the two great Sufi orders of Libya during the nineteenth century. Shaykh al-Yashruti, who was then living in Tunis, became acquainted with the Madaniyya order because of the close relations between Tunisia and Libya. See Martin Lings, *A Sufi Saint of the Twentieth Century: Shaikh Ahmad al-'Alawi, His Spiritual Heritage and Legacy* (Berkeley and Los Angeles: University of California Press, 1973), 70–71; See also R.S. O'Fahey, *Enigmatic Saint: Ahmad ibn Idris and the Idrisi Tradition* (Evanston, Illinois: Northwestern University Press, 1990), 71. (Ed.)

3. Margaret Smith, *Rabi'a the Mystic A.D. 717–801 and Her Fellow Saints in Islam* (1928 Cambridge University Press first edition; repr., San Francisco: The Rainbow Bridge, 1977), 102.

4. These famous lines by Ibn 'Arabi come from the collection of poems titled *Tarjuman al-ashwaq* (Interpreter of Desires). They have been reproduced and translated in many different ways. For an edition and translation based on Ibn 'Arabi's own commentary to this collection of poems, see *The Tarjuman al-Ashwaq: A Collection of Mystical Odes by Muhyi'ddin Ibn al-'Arabi,* trans. Reynold A. Nicholson (1911; repr., London: Theosophical Publishing House, Ltd., 1978), 66–70. (Ed.)

5. Chris Waddy, *The Muslim Mind* (Lanham, Maryland: New Amsterdam Books, 1990), 164–165.

6. *Takiya* is an Arabic term that means "place of repose." Among the Yashrutiyya Sufis, the term is used for a domed prayer hall. *Takiya* is the origin of the Turkish word *tekke,* which is a synonym for *zawiya* (literally, "corner"), a Sufi meeting place. (Ed.)

7. The Prophet Salih is mentioned in several Suras of the Qur'an. Salih was the prophet of a people called Thamud, who are described in the Qur'an as building castles in the plain and hewing houses out of hills (Qur'an 7:78). When they reject the One God, Salih warns his people that their gardens, springs, tilled fields, and date-palm groves will not last forever (Qur'an 25:146–149). The Qur'an also states that at the time of its revelation, one could see the dwellings of Thamud empty and in ruins (Qur'an 27:52). Clearly, Thamud were an Arab trading people because their ultimate transgression was to unlawfully hamstring a camel that was consecrated to God (Qur'an 11:64). For this sin, God destroyed them with an earthquake. The Qur'anic descriptions of Thamud fit the Pre-Islamic Nabataean civilization, centered at the capital city of Petra in modern Jordan, quite closely. The inhabitants of Petra built temples and castles in the plain and hewed tombs and other buildings out of solid rock, as described in the Qur'an. Archaeologists have also determined that Petra's prosperity was brought to an end by massive earthquakes in the years 363 and 561 CE. The association of the Prophet Salih with the Nabataeans is further strengthened by name of *Mada'in Salih* (Cities of Salih), which was given by local Arabs to a

famous Nabataean site in northwestern Saudi Arabia. Although the tomb of Salih that Shaykh al-Yashruti visited in Palestine is quite far from Petra, the greatest kings of Petra were occasionally known to have controlled Palestine and Syria as far north as Damascus. In a famous episode in 2 Corinthians 11:32–33, the Apostle Paul escapes from Damascus and the clutches of the Nabataean King Aretas by being lowered in a basket from the city walls. For a good description and overview of the history of Petra and the Nabataeans, see Jane Taylor, *Petra* (Amman, Jordan: Al-'Uzza Books, 2005). (Ed.)

8. In 1913 the Committee of Union and Progress, also known as the Young Turks, took over direct control of the Ottoman government. The general Mustafa Kemal, who took the title of *Ataturk* (Father of the Turks) in 1934, assumed control of the secular government of Turkey in 1919 and ruled the nation until his death in 1938. After the end of World War I and the signing of the Treaty of Sèvres in 1920, the Republic of Turkey was established in 1923, followed by the formal abolition of the Ottoman Empire in March 1924. (Ed.)

9. Sa'd Zaghlul (ca. 1860–1927) and other leaders of the *Wafd* (Delegation) Party of Egypt started a series of nationalist demonstrations against the British protectorate and ruling dynasty of Egypt in 1919. Their movement espoused a social revolution that advocated, among other things, the control of the Egyptian economy by Egyptians, the abandonment of the veil by women, women's participation in social life and nationalist politics, the destruction of the quasi-aristocratic pasha class, the assumption of power by people of peasant background, and the removal of the Turkish element from Egyptian politics. See Afaf Lutfi al-Sayyid-Marsot, *Egypt's Liberal Experiment: 1922–1936* (Berkeley and Los Angeles: University of California Press, 1977), 43–72. (Ed.)

10. The "Great Palestinian Disaster of 1948" of which Fatima al-Yashrutiyya refers are the events surrounding the creation of the State of Israel and the first Arab-Israeli war. These events led to the flight and in some cases the forcible evacuation of much of the population of northern Palestine. (Ed.)

18

GOD'S MADMAN

Daniel Abdal-Hayy Moore

1

I saw a *majdhub*[1] at the Ka'ba
   and O, was he crazy!
He took old men's canes and
   threw them on the ground in the
path of people doing *tawaf*[2]
then paraded back and forth jubilantly,
    crazy eyes gleaming.

He walked off in people's sandals,
   gesturing, crying out in
    hoarse, weird Arabic
phrases repeated
   over and over. He was

about thirty, black hair, unruly
   beard, wiry, intense, O
    very intensely laughing and
insistently repeating things to a
   crowd both
    visible and invisible that
seemed to ignore him—*God's clown!*

He shuffled past in lady's shoes.
He was courteously escorted away by one of the
   guards. Later he
sauntered by in a different robe, white
   cap and

shoes altogether, momentarily
pinched from someone, still
muttering to himself. *In front of*
    God's House! Ecstatically
        rambunctious. Handsome,
more radiant than most. Fashioned directly from
        God's hands. Let loose
    among us. Out of control. But

not altogether: I saw him
walk past with an open
    Qur'an in one hand as if
making a point,
waving his free arm, insisting on
    something unknown to me in his
crazy discourse to
        no one listening. I feared he might
throw the Qur'an down as he did the
    canes and sandals, but
majdhubs are directly under God's command—
        he was bodily
guarding the Word of God. He may have been
exhorting us to do so.
    Starry eyes zigzagging back and forth
        pouring light. Then

turning his head and
        laughing!

2

What is attraction to God? The *majdhub* is
    attracted to Allah with all
restraints removed, drawn magnetically,
tossing all scruples away, actually tossing his
        resistance more than his
    scruples, he's beyond
scruples, though some may be
even more scrupulous than the scholars about
    every little thing,
fearful in the Majestic Presence of Allah that one
detail of the Prophet's *Sunna* be neglected, one

thought be
out of line—
that's their "craziness." Others

to God's Beauty go, like flocks of doves in
    twilight, they laugh and sing
        enthusiastically, weep and
lament, laugh and cry, in
        crazy spirals of God's love.

Who knows what's
going on in their hearts.

He knows! That's
all they care about!

The moon reflected in a
pan of piss: God's Light in
    this world!

The delicate petals of a hidden
blue flower unfurling.

Beetles black as Ethiopian princes
passing on a black rock
        in the black of night.

Love expressed in an instant like a
tight-rope flung across the
    Grand Canyon and
        stepped out on,
high above silver clouds, first time
    without teetering...

Rumi said: *If you want God's Love
don't turn your back to the sun.*

These mad flotsams ride waves
        eternally beating our
    shores. They let themselves be
pushed and lifted
        by God alone.

They love the Light.

NOTES

This poem first appeared in Daniel Abdal-Hayy Moore, *Mecca/Medina Time-Warp*. Reprinted from a Zilzal Press chapbook, by permission from the author.

1. *Majdhub,* God-enraptured one.
2. *Tawaf,* the ritual of circumambulation around the Ka'ba in Mecca.

19

JIHAD IN ISLAM

Shaykh Muhammad Hisham Kabbani

In this chapter we would like to shed light on the meaning of Jihad, a term that has become universally known today. One can find countless interpretations of this term which differ from its true spirit and the meaning that God intended it in the Holy Qur'an and in the narrations of the Prophet (May God bless and preserve him). On the contrary people are using the term Jihad in this time in a way that suits their own whims without realizing the damage that they are causing Islam and Muslims.

What is meant by Jihad? The concept of "holy war" does not occur in the term Jihad, which in Arabic would be *al-harb al-muqaddasa*. Throughout the entire Qur'an, one cannot find a term that expresses the meaning "holy war." Rather the meaning of combative Jihad expressed in Qur'an or Hadith is simply war.

That said, I will show in this chapter, that Jihad in the classical sense does not simply mean war. In fact Jihad is a comprehensive term which traditionally has been defined as composed of 14 different aspects, only one of which involves warfare.

In this chapter we will explain unambiguously the different aspects of Jihad defined by the Prophet together with what renowned mainstream Muslim scholars have written about this subject citing them at length in order to arrive at an accurate understanding of this term.

Islamic thought includes all educational endeavors and scholarly opinions made in distinguishing Islam's core principles, its simplicity and its tenderness and compassion in its approach to all aspects of human relations.

Today there are many individuals who study Islam from a superficial point of view and emerge with their own ideas and imaginary interpretations which often diverge greatly from the established legislation in the area of study. Because of such studies lacking a true basis in Islamic jurisprudence, many non-Muslims are given an improper understanding about Islam.

So in this chapter we will return to the original source texts bringing up the issue of Jihad in order to explain its various different facets and clarify its understanding once and for all.

THE MEANING OF JIHAD

Jihad in its basic meaning is "to struggle" as a general description. Jihad derives from the word *juhd,* which means *al-ta'b,* fatigue. The meaning of *Jihad fi sabil Allah,* struggle in the Way of God, is striving to excess in fatiguing the self, to exhaust the self in seeking the Divine Presence, and to bring up God's Word, all of which He made the Way to Paradise.

For that reason God said:

> And strive hard (*jahidu*) in (the way of) God, (such) a striving as is due to Him.

> (Qur'an 22:78)

It is essential to understand that under the term *jahidu* come many different categories of Jihad, each with its specific context. The common understanding of Jihad to mean only war is refuted by this tradition of the Prophet's:

> A man asked the Prophet "Which Jihad is best?" The Prophet said, "The most excellent Jihad is to say the word of truth in front of a tyrant."[1]

The fact that the Prophet mentioned this Jihad as "most excellent" means that there are many different forms of Jihad.

IBN QAYYIM'S FOUR CATEGORIES OF JIHAD

Islamic scholars, from the time of the Prophet until today, have categorized Jihad into more than 14 distinct categories. Jihad is not simply the waging of war, as most people today understand. War in fact, or combative Jihad, according to many scholars, is only one of 14 different categories of Jihad.

In his book *Zad al-Ma'ad,* Ibn Qayyim al-Jawziyya divided Jihad into four distinct categories:

1. Jihad Against the Hypocrites

   a. By heart

   b. By tongue

   c. By wealth

   d. By person

   2. Jihad Against the Unbelievers

     a. By heart

     b. By tongue

     c. By wealth

     d. By person

   3. Jihad Against the Devil

     a. Fighting Satan defensively against false desires and slanderous doubts about faith that he throws toward the servant.

     b. Fighting Satan defensively from everything he throws toward the servant of corrupt passion and desire.

   4. Jihad of the Self

     a. That one strives to learn guidance and the religion of truth of which there is no felicity or happiness in life or in the hereafter except by it. And when one neglects it, one's knowledge is wretched in both words.

     b. That one strives to act upon religion after he has learned it. For the abstract quality of knowledge without action, even if one commits no wrong, is without benefit.

     c. That one strives to call to God and to teach Islam to someone who does not know it. Otherwise he will be among those who conceal what God had revealed of guidance and clarity. His knowledge does not benefit him or save him from God's penalty.

     d. That one strives with patience in seeking to call to God. When the creation harms him he bears it all for the sake of God.[2]

IBN RUSHD'S CATEGORIZATION OF JIHAD

Ibn Rushd, in his *Muqaddima*, divides Jihad into four kinds:

1. Jihad of the heart
2. Jihad of the tongue
3. Jihad of the hand
4. Jihad of the sword.[3]

Jihad of the Heart—The Struggle against the Self

The Jihad of the heart is the struggle of the individual with his or her own desires, whims, erroneous ideas, and false understandings. This includes the struggle to purify the heart, to rectify one's actions, and to observe the rights and responsibilities of all other human beings.

Jihad of the Tongue—Education and Counsel

Ibn Rushd defines Jihad of the tongue as:

> To commend good conduct and forbid the wrong, like the type of Jihad God ordered us to fulfill against the hypocrites in His Words, "O Prophet! Strive hard against the unbelievers and the hypocrites" (Qur'an 9:73).

This is the Jihad the Prophet waged in struggling to teach his people. It means to speak about one's cause and one's religion. This is known as the Jihad of Education and Counsel.

God first revealed:

> Read in the name of Thy Lord!

> (Qur'an 96:1)

The first aspect of the Jihad of Education is through reading. Reading originates with the tongue.

> O Prophet! strive hard *[jahid]* against the unbelievers and the Hypocrites, and be firm against them.

> (Qur'an 9:73)

Jihad of the Hand—Development of Civil Society and Material Progress

Jihad of the hand includes the struggle to build the nation through material development and progress, including building up civil society, acquiring and improving every aspect of technology, and societal progress in general. This form of Jihad includes scientific discovery, development of medicine, clinics and hospitals, communication, transportation, and all necessary underlying infrastructure for societal progress and advancement, including educational institutions. Building also means to open opportunities to the poor through economic programs and self-empowerment.

Another aspect of Jihad by Hand is through writing, for God said:

> He taught by means of the pen, taught mankind what he did not know.

> (Qur'an 96:4–5)

The meaning of writing includes the use of computers and all other forms of publication.

Jihad of the Sword—Combative War

Finally, Jihad of the hand includes struggle by the sword (*jihad bi-l-sayf*), as when one fights the aggressor who attacks him in combative war.

JIHAD IN HISTORY AND LAW

Following this brief summary, let us now consider the nature of Jihad more fully as it appears in the history and law of Islam. Sa'id Ramadan al-Buti, a contemporary Sunni scholar from Syria, states in his seminal work on the subject *Jihad in Islam*[4]:

> The Prophet invited the unbelievers peacefully, lodged protests against their beliefs and strove to remove their misgivings about Islam. When they refused any other solution, but rather declared a war against him and his message and initiated the fight, there was no alternative except to fight back.[5]

The most fundamental form of Jihad, usually overlooked in today's pursuit of newsworthy headlines, is the Jihad of presenting the message of Islam—*da'wa*. Thirteen years of the Prophet's 23-year mission consisted purely of this type of Jihad. Contrary to popular belief, the word Jihad and related forms of its root word *jahada* are mentioned in many Meccan verses in a purely noncombative context.

Combative Jihad in the technical usage of Islamic law means "the declaration of war against belligerent aggressors." It is not a haphazard decision taken by anybody but only by the leader of the nation. The principles of Islamic jurisprudence state that the actions of the leader must be guided by the interests of the people.

The Jihad of Education

Thus, we see that the building blocks of today's concept of rights were present in the Prophet's message from its very outset when the Jihad of Education took on the aspects of struggle in the Messenger's first years of preaching, as the chiefs of the Meccan tribes sought to suppress the freedom of expression, speech, and debate that were sought by the Prophet in teaching the new faith. God states in the Qur'an:

Invite (all) to the Way of thy Lord with wisdom and beautiful preaching; and argue with them in ways that are best and most gracious: for thy Lord knoweth best, who have strayed from His Path, and who receive guidance.

(Qur'an 16:125)

Calling people to Islam and making them acquainted with it in all its aspects through dialogue and kind persuasion is the first type of Jihad in Islam, in contrast to the imagined belief that Jihad is only of the combative form. This is referred to in the Qur'an where God says:

So obey not the disbelievers, but strive against them (by preaching) with the utmost endeavor with it (the Qur'an).

(Qur'an 25:52)

Here the word "strive," *jahidu,* is used to mean struggle by means of the tongue—preaching and exhortation—and to persevere despite the obstinate resistance of some unbelievers to the beliefs and ideals of Islam.

Ibn 'Abbas

Ibn 'Abbas and others said that God's words "strive with the utmost endeavor" denote the duty of preaching and exhortation as the greatest of all kinds of Jihad. Ibn 'Abbas said that "with it" refers to the Holy Qur'an.[6] Thus, the form of Jihad here considered as most essential by Ibn 'Abbas, cousin and associate of the Prophet and foremost exegete of the Qur'an, is the call to the Word of God, the Jihad of Education.

Imam Malik bin Anas

Imam Malik bin Anas stated in *al-Mudawwana al-kubra:*[7]

The first of what God has sent His Messenger is to call people to Islam without fighting. He did not give him permission to fight nor to take money from people. The Prophet stayed like that for thirteen years in Mecca, bearing all kinds of persecutions, until he left for Medina.

Ibn Qayyim al-Jawziyya

Ibn Qayyim al-Jawziyya says in *Zad al-Ma'ad:*

God commanded the Jihad of Education when He revealed: "Therefore listen not to the Unbelievers, but strive against them with the utmost strenuousness, with the (Qur'an)" (Qur'an 25:51, 52). This is a Meccan chapter, therefore

[God] commands therein the Jihad of the non-Muslims by argumentation, elocution and conveying the Qur'an.[8]

Imam Nawawi

Imam Nawawi in his book *al-Minhaj*, when defining Jihad and its different categories, said:

>...one of the collective duties of the community as a whole (*fard kifaya*) is to lodge a valid protest, to solve problems of religion, to have knowledge of Divine Law, to command what is right and forbid wrong conduct.[9]

Imam al-Dardir

The explanation of Jihad in Imam al-Dardir's book *Aqrab al-Masalik* is that it is propagating the knowledge of the Divine Law by commanding right and forbidding wrong. He emphasized that it is not permitted to skip this category of Jihad and implement the combative form, saying, "the first [Islamic] duty is to call people to enter Islam, even if they had been preached to by the Prophet beforehand."[10]

Imam Bahuti

Similarly, Imam Bahuti commences the chapter on Jihad in his book *Kashf al-Qina'* by showing the injunctions of collective religious duties (*kifayat*) that the Muslim nation must achieve before embarking on combative Jihad, including preaching and education about the religion of Islam, dismissing all the uncertainties about this religion and making available all the skills and qualifications which people might need in their religious, secular, physical, and financial interests because these constitute the regulations of both this life and the life to come. Hence, *da'wa*—performing the activities of propagating Islam and its related fields of knowledge—is the cornerstone of the "building" of Jihad and its rules; and any attempt to build without this "cornerstone" would damage the meaning and reality of Jihad.[11]

Dr. Sa'id Ramadan al-Buti

Sa'id Ramadan al-Buti says in his book *Al-Jihad fil-Islam*:

>The most significant category of Jihad was the one established simultaneously with the dawn of the Islamic *da'wa* (calling for Islam) at Mecca. This was the basis for the other resulting kinds accorded with the situations and circumstances.[12]

Removing all misconceptions and stereotypes in clarifying the image of Islam held by non-Muslims, building a trusting relationship, and working with them in ways that accord with their way of thinking are all primary forms of Educational Jihad. Similarly, establishing a strong community and nation which can fulfill all physical needs of its people, thereby creating for them conditions in which the message will be heard, rather than being lost in the strife and struggle of everyday life, are requirements and form a basic building block of the Jihadic concept. These foundations fulfill the Qur'anic injunction:

> Let there arise out of you a band of people inviting to all that is good, enjoining what is right, and forbidding what is wrong: and these it is that shall be successful.
>
> (Qur'an 3:104)

Until this is accomplished the conditions of combative Jihad remain unfulfilled.[13]

Sayyid Sabiq

Sayyid Sabiq, in his renowned work *Fiqh al-Sunna,* says:

> God sent His Messenger to all of mankind and ordered him to call to guidance and the religion of truth. While he dwelled in Mecca, he called to God by using wisdom and the best exhortation. It was inevitable for him to face opposition from his people who saw the new message as a danger to their way of life. It was through the guidance of God that he faced the opposition with patience, tolerance and forbearance. God says: "So wait patiently (O Muhammad) for thy Lord's decree, for surely thou art in Our sight" (Qur'an 52:48). "Then bear with them (O Muhammad) and say: Peace. But they will come to know" (Qur'an 43:89). "So forgive, O Muhammad, with a gracious forgiveness" (Qur'an 15:85).
>
> Here we see that God does not permit the fighting of evil with evil, nor to wage war on those who oppose the message of Islam, nor to kill those who cause discord among the Muslims. And He said: "Nor can goodness and Evil be equal. Repel (Evil) with what is better: Then will he between whom and thee was hatred become as it were thy friend and intimate!" (Qur'an 41:34).
>
> As the persecution continued, it became harder and harder to bear, reaching its peak when the Quraysh conspired against the life of the Noble Messenger. At this time, it became imperative that he migrate from Mecca to Medina, both for his personal safety, for the very survival of the new faith, and in an effort to avoid war. Thus thirteen years after the commencement of Qur'an's revelation, the Prophet ordered his companions to emigrate to Medina.

Here, we see that the Prophet did not engage in repulsing the aggressive attacks against the Muslims by his tribesmen but sought to avoid conflict and avoid their persecution by means of migration.

Establishment of the Islamic Nation-State

Sayyid Sabiq continues:

"And when those who disbelieve plot against thee (O Muhammad) to wound thee fatally, or to kill thee or to drive thee forth; they plot, but God (also) plotteth; and God is the best of plotters" (Qur'an 8:30).

Medina thus became the new capital of Islam. As a nation-state for the Muslims, and their new home, an entirely new political situation had evolved. Whereas before the Muslims had been a persecuted minority with no land or political base, upon establishing Medina as a nation ruled by the legislation of Islam, and a sanctuary to which new Muslims under persecution could flee, it was imperative to protect this homeland from the aggressive designs of the enemy, who sought nothing less than the complete extirpation of the Muslim faith and killing of its adherents. Thus when the enemies opened war against them the situation of the Muslims became gravely dangerous, taking them to the brink of destruction at the hands of the enemy, in which case the very message was in danger of being lost.[14]

So Jihad in its combative sense did not come about until after the Prophet and his companions were forced to leave their country and hometown of Mecca, fleeing for safety to Medina after 13 years of propagating the call to the faith and calling for freedom of belief. God said:

But verily thy Lord,- to those who leave their homes after trials and persecutions, - and who thereafter strive and struggle [for the faith] and patiently persevere, - Thy Lord, after all this is oft-forgiving, Most Merciful.

(Qur'an 16:110)

So we see that after the migration to Medina, God described Jihad as a struggle which was suffered patiently through persecution and trial.

First Legislation of Combative Jihad

Even then the legislation to fight was not made until the Meccans set out to eliminate the newly established Islamic nation, by building an army and setting forth with the intention of assaulting and destroying the community in Medina.

Sayyid Sabiq continues:

The first verse revealed regarding fighting was:
    Sanction is given unto those who fight because they have been wronged; and God is indeed Able to give them victory; Those who have been driven from their homes unjustly only because they said: Our Lord is God. For had it not been for God's repelling some men by means of others, cloisters and churches

and oratories and mosques, wherein the name of God is oft mentioned, would assuredly have been pulled down. Verily God helpeth one who helpeth Him. Lo! God is Strong, Almighty. Those who, if We give them power in the land, establish worship and pay the poor due and enjoin kindness and forbid iniquity. And God's is the sequel of events.

(Qur'an 78:39–40)

This verse shows that permission for fighting is granted for three reasons:

1. The Muslims were oppressed by their enemies and expelled by them from their homes unjustly for no reason except that they practiced the religion of God and said, "Our Lord is God." They then came under the obligation to take back the country from which they had been expelled.
2. Were it not for God's permission for this type of defense, all places of worship (including churches, synagogues, and mosques), in which the name of God were remembered, would have been destroyed (see Denial of Religious Freedom for a more detailed explanation of this aspect) because of the oppression of those who aggressively oppose belief.
3. The goal of victory in Islam is to establish freedom of religion, to establish prayer, to give charity and to command the good and forbid evil.

This last justification also means that as long as the preaching and practice of Islam are not circumscribed, the Muslims cannot fight a Jihad against a country in which Muslims freely practice their religion and teach Islam.

In the second year after the Migration, God ordered the Muslims to fight by saying:

Warfare is ordained for you, though it is hateful unto you; but it may happen that ye hate a thing which is good for you, and it may happen that ye love a thing which is bad for you. God knoweth, ye know not.

(Qur'an 2:216)

This verse shows that warfare was disliked in general, and was not something sought after; despite this, it was called for at times when the security of the nation was threatened by external belligerency.

Thus, with a simple and studious examination of the relevant verses, we discover that there were two different kinds of Jihad: that of Mecca and that of Medina. The Jihad in Mecca was primarily by education. In Medina Jihad was by two methods:

1. education
2. fighting, but only after the enemies attacked the Prophet within his own city-state. Additionally, the Muslims who had been expelled invoked the right to return to their homeland, and if opposed, to use force.

As explained earlier, there are 14 different categories of Jihad, only one of which entails fighting. Since it is this, the combative Jihad, which is now the focus of this chapter, I will now speak on the principles of such combat.

Combative Jihad was authorized only after the Prophet migrated along with his followers from Mecca to Medina, having been persecuted and expelled from their country fleeing from persecution and torture. This is not unlike what we see today: people fleeing from persecution in their home countries, becoming refugees in foreign nations. And the supporters, *al-Ansar*, of Medina, welcomed the refugees (*al-Muhajirun*) and shared with them all they possessed of their wealth and their homes.

The struggle in the way of God, *al-jihad fi sabil Allah*, which the Prophet began by teaching the Qur'an in Mecca, was primarily one of enlightenment and education, whereas in Medina his message became the basis of civic society and social life. This is borne out by the emphasis the Prophet made on caring for the poor, the emancipation of slaves, giving rights to women and building a civic society by levying taxes on the rich to benefit the poor, and by establishing community centers and community homes in which people could meet. These teachings were brought to a society in Mecca in which injustice ruled, and for this reason the Prophet was persecuted and fled to Medina. There he was able to establish a nation-state based on freedom of speech and freedom of religion where all religions flourished together without conflict.

In establishing this society in Medina, the Prophet sought to keep his new nation safe, just as today every country has security as a dominant concern. Therefore, he built up an army of his followers to keep his borders safe from enemy attack. In particular the Muslims were under threat due to the Prophet's teaching opposing the hegemony of tyrants.

Thus, Medina became the first city for the believers in which the new message, Islam, was established and the Prophet and his followers sought to keep it safe. Just as all nations do today, they built up an army and weaponry. And, just as is done in the modern world, if anyone attacks a nation, its citizens are obliged to respond and repel those who attack them.

So the majority of Muslim scholars including Imam Abu Hanifa, Imam Malik, and Imam Ahmad ibn Hanbal say that combative Jihad is to defend oneself and to repel the aggressors.

RELIGIOUS FREEDOM OF NON-MUSLIMS

It is a right for the People of the Book to practice the laws of their religion, and to maintain judges and courts, enforcing the rules of their own religion among themselves. Their churches or temples are not to be demolished nor are their crosses (religious symbols) to be broken.

The Messenger of God said, "Leave them to what they worship."

Additionally, the right of a Christian or a Jewish spouse of a Muslim is that she may go to her church or to her temple. It is not the right of her husband to prevent her from going.

Islam permits non-Muslims to eat the foods that their religion allows. Swine are not killed nor is wine destroyed as long as it is permitted to them. Therefore, non-Muslims have more latitude than the Muslims, who are prohibited from drinking wine and eating pork.

They have the freedom to follow their own laws of marriage, divorce, and charity and to conduct these affairs as they wish without any conditions or limits.

Their honor and rights are under the protection of Islam, and they are given freedom to the right of deliberation and discussion within the limits of reason and decorum, while adhering to respect, good conduct and avoiding rudeness and harshness. God says:

> And dispute ye not with the People of the Book, except with means better (than mere disputation), unless it be with those of them who inflict wrong (and injury): but say, "We believe in the revelation which has come down to us and in that which came down to you; Our God and your God is one; and it is to Him we bow (in Islam)."
>
> (Qur'an 29:46)

> If one amongst the Pagans ask thee for asylum, grant it to him, so that he may hear the word of God; and then escort him to where he can be secure. That is because they are men without knowledge.
>
> (Qur'an 9:6)

This also shows that even if polytheists come to the Muslims, seeking to live and work in their nation for any reason, it is ordered to grant them safety and security to demonstrate the great care and compassion Islam takes in the care of others. Such are free to move where they like. This clarifies the understanding that combative Jihad is only against those who actively disturb the peace.

In the view of some schools of jurisprudence, Islam mandates equal punishment for Muslims and non-Muslims except for those things permitted in their faith such as drinking wine or eating pork.

Islam makes lawful eating what the People of the Book slaughter and Muslim men are permitted to marry their women. God says:

> This day are (all) things good and pure made lawful unto you. The food of the People of the Book is lawful unto you and yours is lawful unto them. (Lawful unto you in marriage) are (not only) chaste women who are believers, but chaste women among the People of the Book, revealed before your time,-

when ye give them their due dowers, and desire chastity, not lewdness, nor
secret intrigues....

(Qur'an 5:5)

Islam sanctions visiting and counseling their sick, offering them guidance,
and dealing with them in business. It is established that when the Messenger
of God passed to his Lord, his armor was given as credit for a debt from a
Jewish person.

In another case, when some of the Companions sacrificed a sheep the
Prophet said to his servant, "Give this to our Jewish neighbor."

It is obligatory for the leader of the Muslims (caliph) to protect non-
Muslims who are in Muslim lands just as he would protect Muslims and to
seek the release of non-Muslims who are captured by the enemy.

The Messenger of God forbade killing non-Muslims when he said:

> The one who kills a convenanter (*dhimmi*) will not smell the fragrance of
> paradise.[15]

It can truly be said that in Arab and Muslim nations, the Christians,
the Jews, and all other non-Muslims are in fact covenanters, for they pay
their taxes supporting the nation's standing army. Thus, it is the duty of the
ruler to protect the safety of the covenanter. The concept of a covenant of
protection, while not explicitly spelled out today, is fulfilled through
government taxation.

The popular, yet controversial, Islamic scholar Shaykh Yusuf al-Qaradawi
said:

> Jihad is an obligation on everyone but not killing and fighting.

Citing Ibn Qayyim's division of Jihad into 14 different levels including
struggle against the ego, struggle against Satan, and the establishment of
education, only one of them being combat against an aggressor, Shaykh al-
Qaradawi
states:

> Whoever looks into the sources as to the understanding of Jihad, will see
> that one can be a *mujahid* [of the 14 categories] but it is not necessary to be a
> combatant; that is only when combat is forced on you by the invasion of your
> country.

FORCED CONVERSION

We have seen above that the foundation of Jihad is Islamic propagation
(*da'wa*). The question often asked is whether Islam condones or teaches

the forced conversion of non-Muslims. This is the image sometimes projected by Western scholars and as any Muslim scholar will tell you, it is seriously flawed. The Qur'an clearly states:

> There is no compulsion in religion, the path of guidance stands out clear from error.

> (Qur'an 2:256; 60:8)

In this verse, the phrase "path of guidance" (Ar. *rushd*) refers to the entire domain of human life, not just to the rites and theology of Islam.

There is no debate about the fact that pre-Islamic Arabia was a misguided society dominated by tribalism and a blind obedience to custom. In contrast, the clarity of Islam and its emphasis on reason and rational proofs excluded any need to impose Islam by force. This verse is a clear indication that the Qur'an is strictly opposed to the use of compulsion in religious faith. Similarly, God addressed the Prophet saying:

> Remind them, for you are only one who reminds.

> (Qur'an 88:21)

God addresses the believers, urging them to obey the injunctions of Islam:

> Obey God, and obey the Messenger, and beware (of evil): if you do turn back, then know that it is Our Messenger's duty to proclaim (the message) in the clearest manner.

> (Qur'an 5:92)

This verse makes it clear that the Messenger's duty is only to proclaim and preach the message; it remains to each individual to accept and to follow.

As for forced conversion, no reliable evidence exists that Muslims ever intended or attempted to impose the specific rites and beliefs of Islam. The histories of Central Asia, Spain, India, the Balkans, and all of Southeast Asia are concrete proof of this.

Islam's History of Good Treatment of Non-Muslims

It is thus well established in history that when persecution took place in non-Muslim lands against the People of the Book, they would seek refuge with the leader of the Muslims (caliph), and this refuge was not refused. A well-known example of this is the plight of the Jews in Andalusia after it was conquered by the Spanish and taken from the hands of the Muslim Moors. With the imposition of the infamously cruel Inquisition in 1492,

Jews and Muslims had no choice but to flee their homes, convert to Catholicism, or die. The Jews sought the protection of Sultan Suleyman of the Ottoman Empire, and asylum was granted. For this reason, one finds a sizable population of Jews in Istanbul, which was the seat of the Ottoman Empire at that time.

CONDITIONS FOR COMBATIVE JIHAD

The ruler, the Imam, is completely answerable to the people and their legal apparatus, the most important representatives of whom are the scholars. The position of the law is that Jihad is permissible only when it can be proven that

- there are aggressive designs against Islam;
- there are concerted efforts to eject Muslims from their legally acquired property; and,
- military campaigns are being launched to eradicate them.

At such a time the ruler can declare and execute the provisions of combative Jihad.

Precondition: Leadership

Dr. Buti in *Jihad in Islam* says:

It is known that Islamic Shari'a rules can be divided into two groups: first, the Communicative Rules (*ahkam al-tabligh*) that inform you how to behave in your life, including all matters of worship and daily life, and second, the Rules of Leadership (*ahkam al-imama*) which are related to the judicial system, the Imam or leader.

The Rules of Leadership are those rules that have been directed from the leader to the citizens. In the time of the Prophet he was leader, so this applied to anything directed from the Prophet to the Muslims. After the Prophet, such directives became the responsibility of the caliph, his successor. This means that the Imam of the Muslims is the leader of every Muslim nation. He is the person responsible for the application of the rules as he sees fit. These rules are flexible within the geographical, societal, and cultural norms of the nation, which the leader can exercise by God's grace, to apply them for the benefit of all the people.

Declaring combative Jihad is the foremost responsibility of the Imam (leader, president, or king of a nation). He is the only responsible person that can declare the time and place of Jihad, lead it or terminate its mission. It is in no way the responsibility of individual Muslims to declare Jihad without the order of the leader. Note in this regard the ulama are not in the position to issue a call for combative Jihad.

There are two kinds of combative Jihad. One is the combative Jihad to fight a nation which attacks a Muslim nation. The second category of combative Jihad, which is called *al-sa'il,* means the fight against an assailant, attacker, or violator. We will not go into this aspect as it falls under the Communicative Rules, not the Rules of Leadership. This is based on the hadith related by 'Abdullah ibn 'Umar, in which the Prophet said, "He who is killed in defense of his belongings, in self-defense, or in defense of his religion is a martyr."[16]

The category *al-sa'il* refers to someone defending his private possessions as when someone attacks him at home or his business in order to steal, to harm, or out of hatred due to differences of religion. This does not come under the aspect of Leadership, where nations are involved.[17]

Ibn Qudama

It is an essential precondition that there be a leader of the Muslims, an Imam, to declare combative Jihad. In *al-Mughni,* Ibn Qudama, a respected scholar of the Hanbali school, states:

Declaring Jihad is the responsibility of the Ruler and consists of his independent legal judgment. It is the duty of the citizens to obey whatever the Ruler regards appropriate.[18]

Dardir

Dardir says: "Proclaiming Jihad comes through the Ruler's assignment of a commander."[19]

Jaza'iri

Abu Bakr al-Jaza'iri states that the pillars of combative Jihad are:

A pure intention that it is performed behind a Muslim Ruler and beneath his flag and with his permission.... And it is not allowed for Muslims to fight without a Ruler because Allah says: "O ye who believe! Obey God, and obey the Messenger, and those charged with authority among you" (Qur'an 4:59).[20]

Tahanui

According to *Kashf al-Qina'a* by Tahanui:

Ordering combative Jihad is the responsibility of the Imam and his legal judgment (*ijtihad*) because he is the most knowledgeable about the enemy's status and their nearness or farness, their intention and conspiracy.[21]

Qirafi

Qirafi said:

The Leader is the one who has been chosen for the foreign policy of his county, and he has been entrusted by the people to conduct the common affairs of the state, sign treaties, forbid wrong deeds, suppress criminals, fight aggressors, and settle people down in their homes and the like.[22]

Mawardi

Mawardi, a Shafi'i authority, while enumerating the obligations of a Muslim ruler says:

His sixth obligation is to conduct [combative] Jihad against those who show hostility against Islam....[23]

Sarakhsi

Sarakhsi in *al-Mabsut* said:

The Ruler of the Muslims must always exert all efforts to lead an army himself or dispatch a military detachment of Muslims; and trust in God to aid him in achieving victory.[24]

Sharbini

Sharbini said:

Collective-duty Jihad becomes applicable when the Imam fortifies the frontiers (to gain equal military parity with the enemy), reinforces the fortresses and ditches, and arms his military leaders. It also becomes relevant by the Imam or his deputy's leading the army....[25]

The Pakistani monthly *Renaissance* in discussing the authorization for declaring combative Jihad says:

Both the Qur'an and the established practice of the Prophets of God explicitly say that Jihad can only be waged by a state. No group of people have been given the authority to take up arms, because individual groups if given this license will create great disorder and destruction by fighting among themselves once they overcome the enemy. A study of the Qur'an reveals that the Makkan Surahs do not contain any directive of combative Jihad for the fundamental reason that in Makkah the Muslims did not have their own state.

Islam does not advocate "the law of the jungle." It is a religion in which both human life and the way it is taken hold utter sanctity. Thus Islam does not give Muslims any right to take life unless certain conditions are fulfilled. So, it was

not until an Islamic state was established in Madinah that the Qur'an gave
the Muslims permission to take up arms against the onslaught mounted by the
Quraysh: "To those against whom war is made, permission is given [to fight]
because they have been oppressed and verily God is Most Powerful to help them.
[They] are those who have been expelled from their homes without any basis,
only because they said: 'Our Lord is God'" (Qur'an 22:39–40).

Consequently, the Prophet never retaliated in Makkah to the inhuman treat-
ment which was given to him as well as to some of his Companions. He preferred
to suffer and be persecuted than to counterattack his enemies, since Muslims at
that stage had not fulfilled this all-important prerequisite of combative Jihad:
establishment of a state.

Similarly, the earlier prophets were not allowed by the Almighty to wage war
unless they had established their political authority in an independent piece of
land. For instance, the Prophet Moses, as is evident from the Qur'an, was
directed to wage war only after he had fulfilled this condition. Since the Prophet
Jesus and his Companions were not able to gain political authority in a piece of
land, they never launched an armed struggle to defend themselves, despite
intense persecution.

Consequently, there is a consensus among all authorities of Islam that only an
Islamic state has the authority to wage Jihad. [And where is the Islamic state today, with its fundamental principles? Therefore one easily concludes that today
there is no valid state under which to wage combative Jihad.] Groups parties
and organization have no authority to raise the call to arms. Whoever undertakes
war without the authorization of the ruler in fact disobey the religion.[26]

Referring to the prerequisite of state authority, the Prophet said: "A Muslim ruler is the shield (of his people). A war can only be waged under him and
people should seek his shelter (in war)."[27]

Sayyid Sabiq

This last condition is so explicit and categorical that all the scholars of the
Muslim Umma unanimously uphold it. Sayyid Sabiq, while referring to this
consensus, writes:

Among *kifaya* obligations, there is a category for which the existence of a ruler is
necessary e.g., [combative] Jihad and administration of punishments.[28]

Zafar Ahmad 'Uthmani

Zafar Ahmad 'Uthmani, a Hanafite jurist, writes:

It is obvious from the Hadith narrated by Makhul[29] that Jihad becomes
obligatory with the ruler who is a Muslim and whose political authority has been
established either through nomination by the previous ruler similar to how Abu
Bakr transferred the reins [of his Khilafah to 'Umar] or through pledging of
allegiance by the *'ulama* or a group of the elite…in my opinion, if the oath of

allegiance is pledged by the *'ulama* or by a group of the elite to a person who is not able to guard the frontiers and defend the honour [of the people], organize armies, or implement his directives by political force, and neither is he able to provide justice to the oppressed by exercising force and power, then such a person cannot be called "Amir" (leader) or "Imam" (ruler). He, at best, is an arbitrator and the oath of allegiance is at best of the nature of arbitration and it is not at all proper to call him "Amir" (leader) or an "Imam" (ruler) in any [official] documents nor should the people address him by these designations.... It is not imperative for the citizens to pledge allegiance to him or obey his directives and no [combative] Jihad can be waged alongside him.[30]

Imam Farahi

In the words of Imam Farahi:

In one's own country, without migrating to an independent piece of land, [combative] Jihad is not allowed. The tale of Abraham and other verses pertaining to migration testify to this. The Prophet's life also supports this view. The reason for this is that if [combative] Jihad is not waged by a person who holds political authority, it amounts to anarchy and disorder.[31]

Albani

The Salafi scholar Albani, stressing the necessity of Jihad being established by the ruler of the Muslims, said:

In the present time there is no Jihad in the Islamic land. While undoubtedly there is combat taking place in numerous places, there is no Jihad, established under a solely Islamic banner that abides by Islamic legislation.

From this we can understand that it is not permitted for a soldier to act according to his own wishes, but that he is obliged to follow the rules of the commander and his commands and that the commander must be delegated with proper authority by the caliph of the Muslims. So we can ask ourselves today, "Where is the Caliphate of Muslims in the present time?" Since there is no Caliphate, the fundamental principle of leadership is no longer present. Thus, while there still remains combat between one nation and another, it is no longer considered as fulfilling the religious obligation that Jihad entails.

The preceding quotations represent only a sampling of many quotes from scholars regarding combative Jihad and demonstrate the responsibility of the Imamate in ordering it. The Imam (Ruler) in fact is the only one responsible for repelling aggressors and for seeing what actions are fitting for the country. The actual title, whether he be called Imam, caliph, king, or president, is not important—his position as ruler is what counts. The leader is the one who has been elected to administer the foreign policy of his nation, and he has been entrusted by the people to conduct the common affairs of the state, sign treaties, forbid wrong deeds, suppress criminals, fight aggressors, and settle people down in their homes and the like.

This specific duty can never devolve on a group of people living in a country who act against a government by terrorizing innocent citizens. It is not acceptable in Islam by any means for someone to declare combative war if he is not in the position of leadership.

The many aforementioned rulings of scholars and the many verses of Qur'an and Hadith refute the methods of the so-called "Islamic parties" who establish states within the state and act as if they are the rightful rulers of the Muslims.

Their methodology is to initiate war by attacking non-Muslims in their countries, and they do this without the permission of the Muslim rulers or the Muslim nation and without the consensus of its scholars. What happens then? The result is that everyone suffers from the disastrous consequences of their actions. This subject is discussed in detail in Rebellion Against Rulers.

Self-Defense

Naturally every community has the right to self-defense, and in the case of Islam, where religion is the primary dimension of human existence, war in defense of the nation becomes a religious act. A lack of understanding of this quality of Islam, its nonsecularism, has also contributed considerably to the fear that when Islam talks about war it means going to war to convert. This might be true in other cultures, but Islam must be allowed to speak for itself.

Dardir says of this:

Jihad becomes a duty when the enemy takes [Muslims] by surprise.[32]

Dr. Buti shows that fighting in this case is an obligation of the community as a whole.

This is based on the Prophet's saying, "He who is killed in defense of his belongings, or in self-defense, or for his religion, is a martyr."[33]

God said:

God does not forbid you from those who do not remove you from your homes (by force) and who do not fight you because of your religion, that you act kindly and justly towards them....

(Qur'an 60:8)

This verse mentions a fundamental principle of Islam regarding Muslim/non-Muslim relationships. Muslims are enjoined to act kindly and justly toward members of other faiths except in two circumstances: first, if they dispossess Muslims of their legitimate land rights, and second, if they engage in hostilities toward Muslims by killing or attacking them, or show clear intent to do so (*al-hiraba*) because of their religion. In the second eventuality, it is the duty of the Muslim ruler to declare combative Jihad as a defensive action to repel such attacks.

It is evident from the Qur'an and other sources that the armed struggle against the polytheists was legislated in the context of specific circumstances after the Prophet had migrated from Mecca to Medina. There he secured a pact with the Jewish and Arab tribes of the city, who accepted him as the leader of their community. In the milieu of this newly founded base of operations, under the governance of Divine legislation and the leadership of the Prophet, Islam attained the status of a nation with its corequisite territory and the accompanying need to protect its self-interests. At that time the divine command was revealed permitting Jihad, but this occurred only after:

- Persistent refusal of the Meccan leadership (the Prophet being in Medina at the time) to allow the practice of Islam's religious obligations, specifically to perform the Hajj at Mecca. Note that despite this belligerency, the Prophet agreed to a truce.

- Continuous unabated persecution of Muslims remaining at Mecca after the Prophet's emigration to Medina triggered an armed insurrection against Qurayshite interests in the Hijaz.

- Meccans themselves started military campaigns against the Muslims at Medina with the sole objective of eradicating Islam.

- Key security pledges were abrogated unilaterally by a number of tribes allied to the Prophet, forcing him into a dangerously vulnerable position.

These conditions for defensive Jihad involving armed struggle were then clearly specified in the Qur'an:

And fight in the way of God those who fight against you, and do not transgress [limits] for God likes not the transgressors.

(Qur'an 2:190)

Explaining this verse, Sayyid Sabiq states:

This verse also consists of prohibiting aggression due the fact that God does not love aggression. This prohibition is not abrogated by any verse and is a warning that aggression is devoid of God's love. Verses that consist of such warnings are not abrogated because aggression is tyranny and God never loves tyranny. Therefore a legal war is justified only when it is to prevent discord and harm to the Muslims and for them to have the freedom to practice and live according to their religion.[34]

God says:

> Will you not fight a people who have violated their oaths and intended to expel the Messenger while they did attack you first?

(Qur'an 9:13)

The clear picture that emerges here is that the command to fight was given in relation to specific conditions. Thus, the declaration of war is not an arbitrary act at all.

> To those against whom war is made, permission is given (to fight), because they are wronged;- and verily, God is most powerful for their aid.

(Qur'an 22:39)

Expulsion

The Qur'an then goes on to describe the conditions of those who are permitted to fight:

> They said: "How could we refuse to fight in the cause of God, seeing that we were turned out of our homes and our families?"

(Qur'an 2:246)

> (They are) those who have been expelled from their homes in defiance of right,- (for no cause) except that they say, "our Lord is God." Had not God checked one set of people by means of another, there would surely have been pulled down monasteries, churches, synagogues, and mosques, in which the name of God is commemorated in abundant measure. God will certainly aid those who aid his (cause);- for verily God is full of Strength, Exalted in Might, (able to enforce His Will).

(Qur'an 22:40)

Explaining this verse, Imam Abu Ja'far ibn Jarir at-Tabari explained that were God not to check one set of people by means of another, then "monasteries belonging to Christians, synagogues belonging to Jews and mosques belonging to Muslims, where God's Name is often mentioned, will all be destroyed." Thus, Islam advocates the upholding of religious freedom, not for Muslims alone, but as is stressed by the order of the religions mentioned in the verse in which the rights of non-Muslims are upheld first, and lastly those of Muslims.

The Qur'an then goes on to describe the attributes of those whom He ordains for defense of the faith, and who protect the right of religious freedom, saying:

> (They are) those who, if We establish them in the land, establish regular prayer and give regular charity, enjoin the right and forbid wrong: with God rests the end (and decision) of (all) affairs.

> (Qur'an 22:41)

Here God describes the defenders of the faith as those who are sincere and pious, for they establish prayer and give charity, prevent wrongdoing, and enjoin good conduct.

Denial of Religious Freedom

In later times, the Muslims engaged in warfare to establish the "Pax Islamica" or Islamic Order. The legal and political order must flow from the divine imperative (the Qur'an and the Sunna). It alone guarantees the rights of every individual by keeping in check all the dark psychic tendencies of man and so prevents him from indulging in antisocial behaviors and from political aggression, right down to the commonest criminal act. It is for this reason that the Qur'an calls on the believers to go forth in defense of those whose rights and liberty have been trampled by the unbridled tyranny of oppressors and conquering armies, or who are prevented from freely hearing the word of God espoused to them by preachers and educators. God says:

> How should ye not fight for the cause of God and of the feeble among men and of the women and the children who are crying, "Our Lord! Bring us forth from out this town of which the people are oppressors! Oh, give us from Thy presence some protecting friend! Oh, give us from Thy presence some defender."

> (Qur'an 4:75)

This verse gives two explanations, among other reasons for fighting:

1. First is fighting in the cause of God, which is the intent the religion calls for until discord has vanished and the religion is practiced freely for God alone. This means one cannot fight a Jihad against a country in which Muslims can freely practice their religion and teach Islam to others.
2. Second is fighting for the sake of the weak, such as those who converted to Islam in Mecca, but were unable to undertake the migration to Medina. The Quraysh tortured them until they prayed to God for liberation. They had no means of protection from the persecution of the oppressors.

God permitted armed Jihad against an aggressor, when He said:

> Lo! God hath bought from the believers their lives and their wealth because the Garden will be theirs: they shall fight in the way of God and shall slay and be slain. It is a promise which is binding on Him in the Torah and the Gospel and the Qur'an.

> (Qur'an 9:111)

So the rule of repelling aggression is not specifically for Muslims but is also the role of anyone following the Torah and the Gospel—the right to fight those who attack them. Giving oneself in God's Way means repelling the aggressor. "A promise binding on Him in truth" means that God took this promise on Himself as a right, not only in the Qur'an but also in the Torah and the Gospel, giving the believers the Garden of Paradise in exchange for their selves and their lives.

He said, "God bought from the believers their lives and their wealth." This means to give one's wealth for building up society, for the welfare of others, and for establishing hospitals, schools, and civic society.

Can Muslims Fight if Religious Practice is Not Proscribed?

God said:

> God forbids you not, with regard to those who fight you not for (your) Faith nor drive you out of your homes, from dealing kindly and justly with them: for God loveth those who are just.
>
> God only forbids you, with regard to those who fight you for (your) Faith, and drive you out of your homes, and support (others) in driving you out, from turning to them (for friendship and protection). It is such as turn to them (in these circumstances), that do wrong.

> (Qur'an 60:8–9)

One sees here that God does not hinder the Muslims from dealing justly and kindly with those who do not fight them for their religion. Thus, we see that Muslims today live in many non-Muslim nations, and they are living in peace, observing all their religious obligations and are free to practice their faith.

Today one cannot find any nation in which mosques are forced to close, or the authorities are removing the Qur'an or other religious books, or where Muslims are prevented from praying, paying their poor-due, fasting, or attending the pilgrimage. Instead we find that all Muslims today are free to practice their faith in every nation around the globe.

We find that in non-Muslim universities Islamic texts, including large troves of ancient manuscripts, are preserved.

> Surely God loves those who are just.
>
> (Qur'an 5:42)

This shows that Islam urges the believers to practice goodness with those who do good to them, and thus they are not permitted to attack them.

> If one amongst the Pagans ask thee for asylum, grant it to him, so that he may hear the word of God; and then escort him to where he can be secure. That is because they are men without knowledge.
>
> (Qur'an 9:6)

This also shows that even if polytheists come to the Muslims, seeking to live and work in their nation for any reason, it is ordered to grant them safety and security to demonstrate the great care and compassion Islam takes in the care of others. Such are free to move where they like. This clarifies the understanding that combative Jihad is only against transgressors.

Possibility of Success

Jihad against countries that are guilty of oppression and persecution only becomes compulsory after all political negotiations have failed, if the enemy is set on aggression. Additionally, the Muslims may fight when there is a likelihood of success. The state must make preparation of whatever is necessary from weapons, materials, and men with the utmost possible scope as God says:

> Make ready for them all thou canst of (armed) force.
>
> (Qur'an 9:6)

This means that the leader must prepare and establish what is necessary of weapons, materials, and men with the utmost possible scope, as well as spending to the utmost from the nation's capability and expending every effort, for it is God's rule that without strength one cannot fight, for to do so would result in killing oneself and killing one's people and the creation of mayhem (*fitna*), which in fact is worse than killing, for God says:

> Tumult and oppression (*fitna*) are worse than slaughter.
>
> (Qur'an 2:191)

Creating mayhem (*fitna*) might grow to become a war or become a hate crime against innocent people. That is why God said it is worse than killing. *Fitna* is the work of *munafiqin*, hypocrites. This is in fact conspiracy, the result of which may be a great war instigated between one or more nations, which may end up in the death of thousands or millions of innocents.

> Now God has lightened your [task] for He knows that there is weakness among you. So if there are of you a hundred steadfast persons, they shall overcome two hundred, if there are a thousand of you, they shall overcome two thousand with the leave of God and God is with the patient.

> (Qur'an 8:66)

Thus, God declares that if the ratio of Muslim warriors to their opponents is half (1:2) they may fight and they will be given Divine Support in an open fight facing the enemy directly, warrior-to-warrior. This was a reduction from the original ratio, in which the believers were obliged to fight even if the ratio of Muslims to their opponents was one to ten.

Without Adequate Fighting Capacity Should War Be Instigated?

The rule "Without adequate fighting capacity war should not be instigated" also means that if the enemy is more than twice the Muslim force, then there is no possibility of success and therefore at that time one must not set forth. To do so will create nothing but *fitna*—a state of destruction and confusion.

Here the following questions arise: How can a group declare combative Jihad against an entire nation, when the group possesses no more than a few dozen or a few hundred dedicated warriors? If it is not permitted for 19 people to fight a group in excess of 38, what then about instigating war against a massively fortified and armed nation of over 250 million, such as Al Qaeda has done? This is in reality nothing more than mayhem, and the result is endangerment of the entire Muslim Umma. This is nothing but *fitna*—confusion, sedition, disorder, and mayhem—and the Prophet declared those who create turmoil to be under God's curse:

> Confusion/sedition/mayhem (*fitna*) is dormant. God curses the one who rouses it.

Today's radicals justify combative Jihad without state authority by citing the skirmishes carried out by one of the Muslim converts against the Meccans. *Renaissance*'s Shehzad Saleem explains:

> We know from history that after the treaty of Hudaybiyya, Abu Basir defected to Madinah. According to the terms of the treaty he was duly returned back to the Quraysh by the Prophet. He was sent back in the custody of two people of the

Quraysh. He killed one of his two custodians and again defected to Madinah. When he arrived in Madinah, the Prophet was angry with what he had done. Sensing that the Prophet would once again return him to the Quraysh, he left Madinah and settled at a place near Dhu'l-Marwah, where later on other people joined him. From this place, they would attack the caravans of the Quraysh.

If these guerrilla attacks are analyzed in the light of the Qur'an, the basic thing which comes to light is that whatever Abu Basir and his companions were doing was not sanctioned at all by Islam. The Qur'an says that the actions and deeds of a person who has not migrated to Madinah are not the responsibility of the Islamic state: "And as to those who believed but did not migrate [to Madinah], you owe no duty of protection until they migrate" (Qur'an 8:72).

Not only did the Qur'an acquit the newly founded Islamic state of Madinah from the actions of these people, we even find the following harsh remarks of the Prophet about Abu Basir when he returned to Madinah after killing one of his two custodians:

"His mother is unfortunate! Though he is in the right, he is going to ignite the flames of war."[35]

IS ISLAM BY NATURE HOSTILE TO NON-MUSLIMS?

The idea, often postulated in the media, that Islam is hostile to non-Muslims simply because they are non-Muslims is a major misconception. According to the majority of scholars, beyond the conditions described above, there exists no valid reason to hold any hostility toward non-Muslims. Sayyid Sabiq says:

> The relationship of Muslims with non-Muslims is one of acquaintance, cooperation, righteousness and justice for God says: "O mankind! We created you from a single (pair) of a male and a female, and made you into nations and tribes, that ye may know each other (not that ye may despise each other). Verily the most honoured of you in the sight of God is (he who is) the most righteous of you. And God has full knowledge and is well acquainted (with all things)" (Qur'an 49:13).
>
> And in advising righteousness and justice He says: "God does not forbid you from those who do not remove you from your homes (by force) and who do not fight you because of your religion, that you act kindly and justly towards them..." (Qur'an 60:8).
>
> Among the bases of this relationship are the mutual, general well being (or welfare) of a society and the strengthening of human relations.[36]

The reference in these verses is to the non-Muslims in general.

Loyalty and Enmity (al-wala' wa al-bara'a)

Many of today's self-appointed Islamic leaders and scholars state:

Enmity for the sake of God (*al-bara'a*) means to declare opposition in deed, to take up arms against His enemies....[37]

Sayyid Sabiq says:

This meaning does not prevent friendship with non-Muslims. The prohibition exists only when friendship with non-Muslims is meant in aggression against the Muslims. Serious dangers to the existence of Islam come from assisting non-Muslims who are [actively] working against the Muslims, weakening the power [and security] of the believing society.

As far as the relationship between the Muslims and non-Muslim subjects (*dhimmis*) living in Muslim nations, Islam calls for harmony, peace, good manners and courtesy, friendly social intercourse, mutual welfare and cooperation for the sake of righteousness and good conscience.

Even with regard to those who fight against the Muslims, despite their enmity, God says:

It may be that God will grant love (and friendship) between you and those whom ye (now) hold as enemies. For God has power (over all things); And God is Oft-Forgiving, Most Merciful.

(Qur'an 60:7)

DOES ISLAM CALL FOR ONGOING WAR AGAINST NON-MUSLIMS?

Some Orientalists as well as some radical interpreters of Islam assert that Islam condones an ongoing combative Jihad, and that it means a continual war upon the non-Muslims until they repent and accept Islam or else pay the poll tax. However, the majority of Muslim scholars reject this view, citing as evidence:

...and if any of the polytheists seeks your protection then grant him protection, so that he may hear the Word of God, and then escort him to where he can be secure, that is because they are men who know not.[38]

(Qur'an 9:6)

The Imams argued from this that as long as the unbelievers are willing to live peacefully among the believers our divine obligation is to treat them peacefully, despite their denial of Islam. The succeeding verse affirms this:

So long as they are true to you, stand you true to them. Verily! God loves those who fear God.

(Qur'an 9:7)

This verse instructs the Muslims to observe treaty obligations with meticulous care, and not to break them unless the other side breaks them first.

On the basis of the clear arguments of the scholars of Qur'an and Hadith, the majority concluded that physical fighting is not a permanent condition against unbelievers, but is resorted to only when treaties are broken or aggression has been made against Muslim territory (*dar al-Islam*) by unbelievers.

On the other hand, educating non-Muslims about Islam *is* a continuous Jihad, per the agreed-upon, multiply transmitted hadith:

> The Messenger of God said, "I have been ordered to *fight* the people until they declare that there is no god but God and that Muhammad is His Messenger, establish prayers, and pay *Zakat*...."[39]

In his book *al-Jihad fil-Islam*, Dr. Sa'id Ramadan al-Buti explains this hadith in detail based on the understanding of the majority of jurists, showing that linguistically the word "fight" here and in many other places does not refer to combat, rather to struggle, including in its scope *da'wa*, preaching, exhortation, and establishment of the state apparatus whereby Islamic preaching is protected. It does not mean forcing anyone to become Muslim at the point of a sword, and numerous examples can be cited from the life history of the Prophet showing that he never forced conversion, nor did his successors.

Dr. Buti explains that the linguistic scholars of Hadith showed that the word *uqatil* used by the Prophet in fact means "fight" and not *aqtul*, "kill." In Arabic, this word is used in terms of defending against an attacker or an oppressor; it is not used to mean attack or assail.

In light of this, Dr. Buti shows that this hadith connotes:

> I have been ordered by God to fulfill the task of calling people [peacefully] to believe that God is One and to defend any aggression against this divine task, even though this defense requires fighting aggressors or enemies.[40]

Dr. Buti explains that this hadith is reminiscent of a saying by the Prophet on the occasion of the Treaty of Hudaybiyya:

> where he told his mediator, Badil ibn Waraqa, "But if they do not accept this truce, by God in whose Hands my life is, I will fight with them, defending my Cause till I get killed."[41]

By these words, Badil ibn Waraqa was tasked with inviting the Quraysh to peace, and simultaneously, warning of the ongoing war which had already exhausted them. Dr. Buti remarks:

> The Prophet's words "I will fight with them defending my Cause," in this context certainly means that he, while inclining to peace with the enemy, would react to their combative aggression in the same way, if they had insisted on their aggression.[42]

Note also that in the years after the Treaty was signed, it was the Quraysh who violated the treaty. Near the end of the seventh year after the migration to Medina, the Quraysh along with the allied Banu Bakr tribe attacked the Banu Khuza'a tribe, who were allies of the Muslims. The Banu Khuza'a appealed to the Prophet for help and protection.

The Banu Khuza'a sent a delegation to the Prophet requesting his support. Despite the Meccan provocation and clear violation of the treaty, the Prophet avoided acting in haste to renew hostilities. Instead he sent a letter to the Quraysh demanding payment of blood money for those killed and the disbanding of their alliance with the Banu Bakr. Otherwise, the Prophet said, the treaty would be declared null and void.

Quraysh then sent an envoy to Medina to announce that they considered the Treaty of Hudaybiyya null and void. However, they immediately regret-ted this step—and therefore, the leader of Quraysh Abu Sufyan himself traveled to Medina to renew the contract. Despite having been the greatest enemy of the Muslims, and despite the Quraysh already being in violation of the pact they had solemnly entered into, no hand was laid on this Qurayshi chief—someone who is infamous for his persecution and harm to Muslims in Mecca. He was even permitted to enter the Prophet's mosque and announce his desire to reinstate the treaty.

From this, one can argue that if a state of unbelief were sufficient pretext for war, then the Prophet would have been warranted in seizing Abu Sufyan and initiating hostilities against the Quraysh then and there. However, on the contrary, Abu Sufyan came and went from Medina freely and only after some time were the hostilities renewed based on the Meccans' aggressive violation of the pact.

God says:

> ...and fight the *mushrikun*, [polytheists Pagans] all together as they fight you all together. But know that God is with those who restrain themselves.

> (Qur'an 9:36)

Here, we understand "fight the unbelievers collectively as they fight you collectively" means "treat them in the same way as they treat you." Commenting on this, Dr. Buti says, "You should deal with the unbe-lievers kindly and equitably, unless they are rampant and out to destroy us and our faith. Hence the motive for [combative] Jihad becomes self-defense."[43]

Finally God says:

> So, if they hold aloof from you and wage not war against you and offer you peace, God alloweth you no way against them.

> (Qur'an 4:90)

This verse refers to the people who were not among those involved in fighting the Muslims and who stayed away from the battle between the two groups, and this is what Islam calls for. The above is an explicit statement from God, that it is not permitted to fight with those who are not engaged in belligerency, despite their being nonbelievers in Islam.

WHO IS INVOLVED IN COMBAT?

Communal Obligation

Let us begin with the most prevailing common understanding held by both Muslims and non-Muslims, who are not Islamic scholars, that Jihad means war against unbelievers.

Combative Jihad is not an obligation on every Muslim, rather it is a communal obligation (*fard kifaya*) fulfilled when someone takes on the duty to repel the enemy. God says:

> And the believers should not all go out to fight. Of every troop of them, a party only should go forth, that they (who are left behind) may gain sound knowledge in religion, and that they may warn their folk when they return to them, so that they may beware.
>
> (Qur'an 9:122)

Here, God shows that combative Jihad is not for everyone. If a group of people have been assigned to go for combative Jihad by their leader, the rest must not go. Rather their duty is to stay behind and study, in order to educate themselves and to educate others.

So from this verse, God splits the people who participate in Jihad into two categories: one group goes to battle and the other stays behind to develop the understanding of religion in order to teach others. So even when combative Jihad has been called for, both those who go forth to combat and those who stay behind to develop the understanding of religion are participants in Jihad. This verse makes those who stay behind and study the religion equal to those who go forth to battle, by saying: "their duty is to stay behind and study, in order to educate themselves and to educate others."

In this verse God emphasizes that not all believers should go out to fight. This indicates that there is a decision to be made: who will go to fight and who will not? This implies the existence of a leadership that must first decide if it is necessary to fight or not. It is not the case that people from here and there may issue a call to go for fighting, which will result in nothing but anarchy.

Mu'adh ibn Jabal related:

> Acquire knowledge because doing so is goodness, seeking it is worship, reviewing it is glorifying God and researching it is Jihad....[44]

From this we can see that to learn the religion becomes more important than participation in battle, for it will elaborate for you all the beliefs and the rulings that Muslims must follow in their lives. Understanding the rulings of the religion, including those related to Jihad, is essential and can only be accomplished by study and education. If someone has not studied comprehensively the rulings of Jihad, he will easily come to the conclusion that every issue that is raised entails combative Jihad, whereas this is indeed not the case.

Conscription

Participation in combative Jihad becomes assigned to an individual when he is ordered by the leader to be present in the line of fire:

> The Messenger of God said: "There is no migration (after the conquest of Mecca), but Jihad and good intention. So when you are called to go forth in stopping aggression, then do so."[45]

This means that when you are called forth by your leader (I have explained before who has the right to issue a declaration of war), the Imam, you must obey, as that is part of obedience to God, the Prophet, and those in authority. And the condition for such a declaration of war is when the enemy suddenly attacks a land. In that case combative Jihad is incumbent on its inhabitants and they must go forth to defend their nation from aggression.

Along with this it is incumbent on any group, who seek to fight as soldiers in the way of God against aggression by unbelievers, to first pledge themselves to their leader—someone who fits the profile of an Imam from knowledge, piety, and effectiveness—who organizes the army. Thereafter they organize their ranks and prepare to fight.

Setting forth when called is *mandatory* on the Muslim when he is: male, possesses sound reason, has attained the age of maturity, is healthy, and whose family possesses sufficient funds for what they need until he completes the duty assigned to him by the leader.

God said, setting the rules for Jihad, "the believers should not all go out to fight" (Qur'an 9:122).

The verse begins with this statement to emphasize that not every person goes forth to battle, and it goes on to explain "from every troop of them, a party only should go forth, that those who are left behind may gain some knowledge in religion and that they may warn their folk when they return to them that they may beware."

God is showing that from every group, only a part of them goes forth. That means the army is to be formed from different citizens from various parts of the country, "from every group of them," which today means that volunteers or recruits who have been assigned to fight and who have been trained go forth to fight, while the rest of the citizens remain behind to train and educate themselves.

> Not unto the weak nor unto the sick nor unto those who can find naught to spend is any fault (to be imputed though they stay at home) if they are true to God and His messenger.

(Qur'an 9:91)

This verse means that there is no obligation on those who have a weak personality, or a radical mentality, nor on those who have no talent, to go forth, for war will not be good for them. This indicates that only those persons selected by the Ruler or his appointed leaders should go forth; not those who might commit rash actions because of excessive emotional zeal nor those who are mentally ill and might commit crimes like throwing bombs, suicide attacks, and so forth.

As Ibn Qayyim al-Jawziyya said in *Zad al-Maʿad*:

> The Prophet said:
>   The fighter is the one who fights himself in obedience to God and the one who emigrates is the one who emigrates from iniquities.[46]
>   The Jihad of the self is a prerequisite over the Jihad against the enemy in the open and initial basis for it.
>   Without a doubt, the one who does not fight his self (or someone who does not do what he is commanded and does not leave what has been forbidden and goes to battle in the way of God) it should not make combative Jihad against the external enemy. How is it possible for him to fight his [external] enemy, when his own enemy which is right beside him, dominates him and commands him? Since he did not wage war on the [internal] enemy of God, it is even more impossible for him to set out against the enemy until he fights himself.[47]
>   "There is no blame for the blind, nor is there blame for the lame, nor is there blame for the sick (that they go not forth to war)" (Qur'an 29:17).

Surprise Attack

When the enemy suddenly arrives at a place where the Muslims reside, the inhabitants are obliged to go out and fight them and it is not allowed for anyone to be exempt from this obligation.

Age Requirement

Ibn ʿUmar said, "I was presented to the Messenger of God at the time of the battle of Uhud when I was fourteen years of age, and he did not give me permission to fight."

This is because Jihad is not obligatory except on the one who has reached the appropriate age.

Jihad of Women

'A'isha asked, "O Messenger of God, is Jihad necessary for women?" He said, "Jihad without fighting. Hajj and 'Umra [are their Jihad]."[48]
God says:

> And covet not the thing in which God hath made some of you excel others. Unto men a fortune from that which they have earned, and unto women a fortune from that which they have earned. (Envy not one another) but ask God of His bounty. Lo! God is ever Knower of all things.

> (Qur'an 4:32)

It is reported by 'Ikrima that some women inquired about Jihad and other women said, "We wish that God would grant us a portion of what the military expeditions receive from the reward of what the men share."
This does not prevent women from going out to treat the wounded.
It is reported that the Prophet was out on a military expedition and Umm Salim was with him and other women from the Helpers. They were giving water to the fighters and treating the wounded.[49]

Parents' Permission

In the case of a major, obligatory combative Jihad, parents' permission is not required, but as far as the voluntary combative Jihad is concerned, their permission is required.
Ibn Mas'ud related:

> I asked the Messenger of God which action is most loved by God and he said, "Prayer in its time." Then I said, "Then what?" and he said, "Being good to your parents." Then I said, "What after that?" He said, "Jihad in the way of God."[50]

Ibn 'Umar said:

> A man came to the Prophet and asked permission for combative Jihad and he said, "Are not your parents alive?" He said, "Yes." Then he said, "Then ask them first, then fight."[51]

One does not go out in Jihad except if he has completed providing for the needs of his family and the service of his parents. For this is the prerequisite of Jihad; even more it is the best Jihad.

JIHAD BETWEEN MUSLIMS

Properly speaking Jihad, in the case of internal dissension, occurs only when two conditions are met: (1) the presence of a just leader (*Imam*); (2) an unjustifiable insurrection. In Islam, allegiance and obedience to a *just* authority is obligatory.

It must be noted also that rebellions against authority and especially political authority have no place in the concept of Jihad. In this age of relativism, the spirit of rebellion seems to have penetrated every layer of society. However, Islam and its principles cannot be made subservient to these cultural trends.

In some of the contemporary "Islamic" groups, Jihad has been adapted to a virtually Marxist or Socialist concept of class revolt aimed at overthrowing the authority of the state. In the often fervently materialistic milieu of contemporary political and revolutionary ideologies, Islam is inevitably reduced to nothing more than a social philosophy. This reductionism amounts to an abysmal misunderstanding of the essential function of Islam, which is to turn the face of the human being away from the world of disharmony and illusion toward the tranquility and silence of Divine awareness and vision. Inward Jihad, as we alluded to at the beginning of this chapter, has a key role to play in this respect.

SEEKING PEACE

The Ruler, the political leader of the country, has the power to ratify peace treaties consistent with the interests of the Muslims.

God said:

Enter into peace completely and do not follow the steps of Satan.

(Qur'an 2:208)

And:

And if they incline to peace, incline thou also to it, and trust in God.

(Qur'an 8:60)

Sayyid Sabiq states:

This verse is the command to accept peace when the enemy accepts it, even if their acceptance is known beforehand to be deception and deceit.[52]

God says:

And fight them until there is no more tumult or oppression, and there prevails justice and faith in God; but if they cease, let there be no hostility except against those who practice oppression.

(Qur'an 2:193)

From this verse we see that fighting is exhorted until oppression is ended. Thus, with the words "but if they cease" God legislates that once justice prevails and no one is prevented from observing his or her belief in God, then fighting should end. God grants that arms be set aside, "except against those who practice oppression."

And fight them until there is no more tumult or oppression, and there prevail justice and faith in God altogether and everywhere; but if they cease, verily God doth see all that they do.

(Qur'an 8:39)

Thus, peace is not only permitted but called for, after the adversary, even if still antagonistic, ceases his aggression. However, precaution and watchfulness is not to be abandoned in this situation, for here God reminds the Muslims of His Own Attribute, "verily God doth see all that they do."

The Prophet said, after establishing the Islamic state in Medina, that the way of the Muslims is one. No single group can autonomously declare war or fight, nor can any one group make peace by itself, but the entire country must make peace. A peace treaty can be made by the country's leader, and all subjects of the country are bound by that decision, regardless of whether the leader was appointed or elected. The final decision is up to the ruler after his consultation with others.

If a state has no leader then it must select one, or all the neighboring states and nations may come together and agree on a treaty with any foreign country. This applies today in the case of the Middle East Crisis. This applies as much to peace as it does to war. No individual or group may come forth and declare a Jihad, for such will be a false Jihad. All Muslim nations and their leaders must come together for a decision of war or peace and that is the only accepted process.

It is imperative to keep in mind that all verses about Jihad were revealed at specific times and pertaining to specific historical events. Our concern to-day is that radical extremists employ these verses outside their proper historical and revelatory context, merely cutting and pasting together what suits their evil inclinations, without accurate or sufficient knowledge of the applicability of such verses.

TAXATION

Ibn Qudama said that a treaty of peace involves agreeing with combatant non-Muslims for an end to hostility for a period of time, whether it involves paying a tax or not. He asserted that Muslims are allowed to make peace treaties that do not require non-Muslims to pay a tax, because the Prophet of God did so on the occasion of the Hudaybiyya Treaty. Ibn Qudama says that Imam Ahmad ibn Hanbal gave this opinion as did Imam Abu Hanifa.[53]

CONDUCT OF COMBAT

Prohibition of Killing Noncombatants

Islam prohibits utterly the killing of those who are not actual military personnel.

The Prophet sent the following message to his military leaders who were setting forth in the way of Jihad to stop hostile advances and defend Muslim territories:

> Advance in the name of God, with God, on the pattern of the Messenger of God. That means do not kill the elderly, infants or children and women. Do not exceed the proper bounds. Gather your spoils and make peace "and do good. Lo! God loveth those who do good" (Qur'an 2:195).[54]
>
> The Prophet passed by a woman who was killed and said, "She was not engaged in fighting." The Prophet then sent to the Muslim leader Khalid ibn al-Walid the following message, "The Prophet orders you not to kill women or servants."[55]

This was to show that the reason for the prohibition of killing the woman was due to the fact that she was not with the fighters. The inference here is, "the reason we fight them is because they fight us, not on the simple principle that they are disbelievers." This is clear evidence that the woman was not a fighter and the Prophet prohibited her killing. From the strong expression the Prophet made, going so far as to send a letter to his topmost military commander, we see how concerned he was to prevent any such incidents and to insure that every single Muslim warrior was aware of the rules of combat.

Some questions arise here: When someone explodes a bomb or commits a suicide attack in a public place, how many innocent women, children, and elderly people are killed? If for one woman's death, the Prophet scolded his top general, Khalid ibn al-Walid, what then about killing twenty, thirty, or even hundreds of noncombatants, some of whom may even be Muslims?

Just as the Messenger of God forbade the killing of women and the young, he forbade killing priests.

The first caliph Abu Bakr as-Siddiq's commandment to the leader of the first Islamic military expedition after the Prophet was:

...No hermit should be molested...Only those should be killed who take up arms against you.[56]

So we see from these various narrations of the Prophet—and there are many more like them—that the Prophet prohibited the Muslims from fighting anyone, Muslims or non-Muslims, even if they are unbelievers, if they are not transgressors against the security of the nation.

This shows that terrorist acts, in particular suicide attacks which kill indiscriminately, are utterly unacceptable forms of combat, even during valid combat authorized for the defense of the nation.

Prohibition of Burning the Enemy

It is prohibited to burn the enemy with fire because the Messenger said, "Kill [the enemy] but do not burn him. For no one punishes with fire except the Lord of the Fire."[57]

This hadith illustrates the Prophet's emphasis on mercy and avoidance of harm when he established laws of conduct on the battlefield. In modern times only were such rules of warfare established, as in the Geneva Conventions, in which it is impermissible to kill or torture prisoners of war. Similarly, we see that 1,400 years ago, the Prophet established details of the rules of warfare in which even using fire in combat was prohibited, something which modern legislators of warfare have been loathe to adopt.

According to this hadith, weapons of fire are not approved by God. God prohibited burning, yet the majority of attacks by Islamic groups today involve bombs and explosions, such as the attacks on the World Trade Center on 9/11, where 3,000 people were incinerated.

Prohibition of Mutilating the Dead

'Imran ibn Husayn said the Messenger of God encouraged us to give charity and forbade us from mutilation.[58]

Prohibition of Despoiling

Abu Bakr al-Siddiq commanded the leader of the first Islamic military expedition after the Prophet saying:

"No fruit-bearing trees are to be cut down and no crops should be set on fire. No animal should be killed except those slaughtered for eating...Only those should be killed who take up arms against you."[59]

Suicide Attacks

One of Islam's fundamental principles is the sanctity of life. Islam prohibits the killing of noncombatants, except those involved in a direct battle face-to-face between warriors. There is simply no room for maneuver in Islam to justify the killing of innocents, even as a form of mass retribution, which many radicals today use as justification for their large-scale attacks on civilians, for Islam prohibits blood feuds and specifies retribution only toward the one who commits a crime.

God says:

Slay not the life which God has made sacrosanct unless it be in a just cause.

(Qur'an 6:151)

And whoever kills a believer intentionally, his recompense is Hell to abide therein, and the Wrath and the Curse of God are upon him, and a great punishment is prepared for him.

(Qur'an 4:93)

Since no one can say for sure that a specific person is not a believer, it becomes forbidden to kill any human being without just cause.

Suicide itself is specifically prohibited:

Kill yourselves not, for God is truly merciful to you.

(Qur'an 4:29)

and:

Throw not yourselves into the mouth of danger.

(Qur'an 2:195)

Thus, we see the general principle enunciated here that killing oneself is forbidden. The Qur'an did not leave anything without an explanation. This is a general principle that no one is permitted to kill another or to kill himself.

Killing Noncombatants

The one who attacks the enemy in repelling his aggression, fighting under the authorized leader of the Muslims, and fights and is killed becomes a martyr (*shahid*). But to attack a public location where the ones killed are killed randomly without knowing if they are combatants or not is forbidden.

Today's militant radical Islamists cite a ruling by the Shafi'i scholar Mawardi in which he stated that when involved in combative Jihad, if the enemy has mixed noncombatants among warriors either by chance or intentionally as "human shields" then Muslim archers are allowed to fire on the enemy, despite the fact that due to the randomness of shooting, noncombatants might die. Expanding on this point, they argue that this ruling justifies bomb attacks against civilian areas.

This is nothing but a distortion of the law to suit their purposes. The ruling is very specific in that it allows such attacks on the assumption that it is only the combatants that are targeted by the archers, not the civilians, who only happen to be present or, in the worst case, have been placed as "human shields." The assumption of the jurist is also that the Muslims and the enemy are engaged in face-to-face fighting, between combatants. However, the attacks carried out by such militants in fact do not target combatants: rather they are typically placed in public locations more frequented by civilians, including innocent women, children, and nonmilitary persons.

In Islamic law, one cannot build a case on doubtful assumptions, such as "those people are likely all engaged in fighting Muslims." Such an argument is false, and the result is the killing of innocents without justification.

Prohibition of Suicide

Islam utterly forbids suicide. On this the Prophet said:

Whoever kills himself in the world with anything, then God will punish him by that same thing on the Day of Judgment.[60]

The Prophet said:

Among those who were before you, there was a man who was inflicted with wounds. He felt despair, so he took a knife and with it he cut his hand; blood kept flowing until the man died. God the Exalted said, "My slave has caused death on himself hurriedly; I forbid Paradise to him."[61]

Abu Hurayra narrated:

We were in the company of God's Messenger on an expedition, and he remarked about a man who claimed to be a Muslim, saying, "This (man) is from the people of the (Hell) Fire." When the battle started, the man fought valiantly until he was wounded. Somebody said, "O God's Apostle! The man whom you described as being from the people of the (Hell) Fire fought valiantly today and died." The Prophet said, "He will go to the (Hell) Fire." Some people were on the point of doubting (the truth of what the Prophet had said). Suddenly someone said that the man was still alive but severely wounded. When night fell, he lost patience and committed suicide. The Prophet was informed of this, and he said, "God is Greater! I testify that I am God's Slave and His Apostle." Then he ordered Bilal to announce amongst the people:"None will enter Paradise but a Muslim, and God may support this religion (i.e. Islam) even with a disobedient man."

The Prophet said:

Whoever throws himself down from a high mountain and kills himself will be throwing himself down from a mountain in the Fire of Hell for all eternity. Whoever takes poison and kills himself will be taking poison in the Fire of Hell for all eternity. Whoever kills himself with a weapon (literally, iron) will be holding it in his hand and stabbing himself in the stomach in the Fire of Hell for all eternity.[62]

The Prophet said:

Indeed, whoever (intentionally) kills himself, then certainly he will be punished in the Fire of Hell, wherein he shall dwell forever.[63]

A person [engaged in battle] killed himself with a broad-headed arrow. The Messenger of God said, "As for me, I will not pray over him."

Even a Mufti of the most fundamentalist school of law in Islam, the "Wahhabi/Salafi" school of thought, declared that suicide bombings have never been an accepted method of fighting in Islam. The Mufti of Saudi Arabia Shaykh 'Abd al-'Aziz Al Shaykh declared, "To my knowledge so-called 'suicide missions' do not have any legal basis in Islam and do not constitute a form of Jihad. I fear that they are nothing but a form of suicide, and suicide is prohibited in Islam." This echoes an earlier *fatwa* by his predecessor, the late Saudi Mufti Shaykh 'Abd al-'Aziz ibn Baz.

Like the suicide attackers of September 11, those who commit such atrocities in the name of religion are offenders. They can find no support for their actions in our creed. Nor can those who blow up themselves and others indiscriminately in shopping centers, theaters, or houses of worship find any justification in the faith's pristine teachings.

One justification that the terrorists make is the following account from the life of the Prophet in which the Prophet's paternal cousin Zubayr ibn al-'Awwam was participating in a battle against the Byzantine Army. Zubayr said to a group of Muslim soldiers, "Who will promise to go with me and fight our way through the enemy lines until we reach the end of their lines, then go around their camp back to our current position?" A group of fighters said, "We promise." Zubayr led a group of fighters and fought their way through many enemy lines until they reached the end of the Roman camp. They then went around the Roman camp and returned to the Muslim army.

The logic the terrorists use is that Zubayr and his companions were certain to die and thus committed suicide while fighting the enemy. In fact Zubayr did not tell his companions "Let us kill ourselves," before going on this challenging task. He only exposed himself and them to what is commonly expected in any form of warfare—the possibility of being killed by the enemy. He did not intend to die, but to fight, and with God's support to win, or else to die by the enemy's hand. This is not suicide, rather it is bravery and heroism. Thus, the terrorists' "logic" is shown for what it is, illogical.

Islam has always required perfect chivalry and discipline. For that reason, soldiers are ordered to endure and fight even in the face of tremendous odds. The Islamic rules of military conduct never permit using civilians as targets or as hostages. In Islam, even so-called "collateral damage" is unacceptable. Therefore, if a Muslim kills himself, along with innocents, it is a doubly forbidden act.

Shaykh Yusuf al-Qaradawi issued a *fatwa* condemning the tragic suicide attacks of 9/11, stating: "Even in times of war, Muslims are not allowed to kill anybody save the one who engages in face-to-face confrontation with them." He added that Muslims are not allowed to kill women, old persons, or children, and that haphazard killing is totally forbidden in Islam. Shaykh Qaradawi on another occasion defined terrorism as "the killing of innocent people...with no differentiation between the innocent and the foe."

Another widely followed religious scholar, Sayyid Tantawi, Grand Shaykh of Islam's highest institution of learning, the University of Al-Azhar, has said that attacks against women and children are "not accepted by Islamic law." Al-Azhar's Research Academy, shortly after the 9/11 attacks, declared that a "Muslim should only fight those who fight him; children, women and the elderly must be spared." Therefore, terrorism and its crime against civilians is impermissible under any interpretation of Islamic law. This ruling does not change based on geographical locality.

The Prophet said:

> Whoever fights under the banner of a people whose cause is not clear, who gets flared up with family pride, calls people to fight in the cause of their family honor or fights to support his kith and kin, and is killed, dies in a state of spiritual and moral ignorance (*jahiliyya*).
>
> Whoever indiscriminately attacks my Umma, killing the righteous and wicked among them, sparing not even those firm in faith, and fulfilling not a pledge made with whoever was given a promise of security, has nothing to do with me and I have nothing to do with him.[64]

This shows us very clearly that those who indiscriminately attack both Muslims and non-Muslims by suicide bombings, killing innocent people, and without focusing on anyone in particular, are rejected completely by the Prophet. Such is the case in many Muslim countries today, including the land of Hijaz, Pakistan, Darfur, Egypt, Algeria, Iraq, and so forth. What is taking place in these nations today is clearly described in this hadith, "Whoever indiscriminately attacks my Umma, killing the righteous and wicked among them, sparing not even those firm in faith."

Emphasis in this hadith on "fulfilling not the pledge made with whoever was given a promise of security" is reference to those citizens who keep their civic obligations by paying taxes and pledging their allegiance to the government. Thus, both Muslim and non-Muslim citizens are encompassed in the scope of meaning of this hadith, and as for those who aggress against them, "he has nothing to do with" the Prophet and the Prophet has "nothing to do with him."

If someone asks, "What about suicide bombings against non-Muslims?" We say: "This is utterly wrong."

False Rulings Supporting Suicide Attacks

Often those who justify suicide attacks cite as evidence the story of the Companion Bara' ibn Malik at the Battle of Yamama, in which the Muslims fought the false prophet Musaylima the Liar, who had begun the war by attacking the Muslims.

> The Muslims gained ground against the idolaters the day of Yamama until they cornered them in a garden in which Musaylima was staying. Bara' ibn Malik said: "O Muslims, throw me to them!" He was carried aloft until when he was above the wall, he penetrated [the enclosure]. Then he fought them inside the garden until he opened it for the Muslims and the Muslims entered. Then God killed Musaylima.
>
> Bara' threw himself onto them and fought them until he opened the gate after having received more than eighty cuts. Then he was carried away and tended. Khalid [ibn al-Walid] visited him for a month.[65]

The Companion threw himself into the ranks of the enemy, in order to throw open the fortress door, knowing full well that he would likely be killed in the process.

Studying this analogy, one finds that it is not relevant, for in the incident cited the two combatant armies were fighting face-to-face. In the process Bara' did not kill innocent people. He threw himself at the enemy with the intention of either opening the door or dying in the attempt. In fact his death was expected at the hands of the enemy, not by his own action. And this, like the earlier example of Zubayr ibn al-'Awwam, is exemplary of chivalry and bravery, not of the intent to commit suicide. In addition, Bara' did not die, but survived his wounds.

Suicide bombings are actions in which innocent people are killed; some might even be supporters of one's cause, while others are innocent. Thus, the above example does not apply. Such an act on the contrary is not suicidal; it is an act of bravery which is accepted in every nation and culture.

This means that whoever goes on his own and declares his own rulings, independent of the ruler of the Muslim Nation, falls under the label of

Jahiliyya—pre-Islamic ignorance and unbelief. Such a person establishes his own group and his own false rulings on fighting, causing all people to fall into tribulation due to his aggression.

The Hadith demonstrate the Prophet Muhammad's emphatic opposition to those who would declare a false combative Jihad. They also demonstrate that the Prophet predicted that people would arise who would create havoc and confusion, who would be arrogant and proud of themselves, and who despite appearances were in fact fighting for the sake of their families and tribes. This is not Jihad by any means but in fact falsifies the concept of Jihad as a whole.

We have seen that the Prophet extended shelter to a combatant pagan who was promised shelter by a Muslim woman. How then can we allow today's beheadings of those people who are working to help bring stability and support human rights in Iraq? The terrorists take innocent people, who have been given shelter by the existing government and are noncombatants, and behead them as combatants.

"Whoever indiscriminately attacks my Nation killing the righteous and the wicked among them, and fulfilling not a pledge made with whoever was given a promise of security, has nothing to do with me and I have nothing to do with him."

This portion of the hadith makes it abundantly clear that if someone attacks a person whose safety has been pledged by the nation's government to uphold, the Prophet abandons the attacker and disassociates himself from him. For the believer, nothing could be more distressing than for the Prophet to abandon him.

PRISONERS OF WAR

In regard to prisoners of war, God says:

At length, when ye have thoroughly subdued them, bind a bond firmly (on them): thereafter (is the time for) either generosity or ransom: Until the war lays down its burdens.

(Qur'an 47:4)

It was related from Umm Hani bint Abi Talib, who said to the Prophet, "My brother 'Ali said he will kill a person to whom I gave shelter, so-and-so son of Hubayra," who was a combatant pagan at that time. The Prophet said, "We shelter the person whom you have sheltered."[66]

In a similar vein is the hadith where the Prophet said: "He who gives a promise of safety to a man in regards to his life, then kills him, I am innocent of the actions of the killer, even if the one killed was a disbeliever."

It is established that the Prophet captured prisoners yet never did he compel or force anyone to embrace Islam. The same holds true for his Companions.

The Companions of the Messenger of God used to ransom captives and rejected killing them saying, "What would we gain from killing them?"

REBELLION AGAINST RULERS

The scholar Ibn Nujaym said, "It is not permitted for there to be more than one state leader (*Imam*) in a time period. There may be many judges, even in one state, but the leader is one."[67] Bahjuri said, "It is an obligation to obey the leader, even if he is not fair or trustworthy or even if he committed sins or mistakes."[68] Abu Hanifa's school says that the head of state, the Imam, cannot be expelled for being a corrupt person (*fasiq*).[69]

Bahjuri

Bahjuri said, "...You have to obey the Ruler even if he is oppressive."

This means that a group or an individual is not permitted to declare war against the ruler of a nation, especially by means of terrorizing the people through planting bombs and suicide attacks which kill innocents and incite mayhem.

And in his commentary on *Sahih Muslim* Bahjuri said, "It is forbidden to rise against the ruler."[70]

Amin Ahsan Islahi

While commenting on the underlying reasons that form the basis of state authority for combative Jihad, Amin Ahsan Islahi writes:

> The first reason [for this condition] is that God Almighty does not like the dissolution and disintegration of even an evil system until a strong probability exists that those who are out to destroy the system will provide people with an alternative and a righteous system. Anarchy and disorder are unnatural conditions. In fact, they are so contrary to human nature that even an unjust system is preferable to them...this confidence [that a group will be able to harmonize a disintegrated system and integrate it into a united whole] can be placed in such a group only if it has actually formed a political government and has such control and discipline within the confines of its authority that the group can be termed as *al-Jama'a* [the State]. Until a group attains this position, it may strive [by religiously allowable means] to become *al-Jama'a* – and that endeavor would be its Jihad for that time – but it does not have the right to wage an "armed" Jihad.

The second reason is that the power which a group engaged in war acquires over the life and property of human beings is so great that the sanction to wield this power cannot be given to a group the control of whose leader over his followers is based merely on his spiritual and religious influence on them [rather than being based on legal authority]. When the control of a leader is based merely on his spiritual and religious influence, there is not sufficient guarantee that the leader will be able to stop his followers from *fasad fi'l-ard* (creating disorder in the society). Therefore, a religious leader does not have the right to allow his followers to take out their swords (that is to wage an armed struggle) merely on the basis of his spiritual influence over them, for once the sword is unsheathed there is great danger that it will not care for right and wrong and that those who drew it will end up doing all [the wrong which] they had sought to end. Such radical groups as desire revolution and the object of whom is nothing more than disruption of the existing system and deposition of the ruling party to seize power for themselves play such games – and they can, for in their eyes disruption of a system is no calamity, nor is it cruelty or any kind an evil. Everything is right to them [as long as it serves their purpose].[71]

Hudhayfa ibn al-Yaman narrated a hadith in which he said:

The Prophet said, "there will be after me leaders who do not follow my guidance and do not follow my *Sunna,* and there will be among them men whose hearts are like those of Satan in the body of a human being." And I asked the Prophet, "What should I do at that time if I reach it?" He said, "listen and obey the ruler, even if he lashes your back and takes your money, listen and obey."[72]

In another narration, Awf bin Malik said, "O Prophet of God, do you recommend that we fight them?" He said, "No, don't fight them as long as they do not prevent you from your prayers. And if you see from them something that you dislike, dislike their acts, but do not dislike them. And do not take your hand out from obedience to them."[73]

It is narrated from 'Abdullah ibn 'Abbas that the Prophet said:

If someone dislikes his ruler, he must be patient, because if he comes against the ruler in a rebellious or destructive manner by only a handspan and dies, he dies in a state of pre-Islamic ignorance (*jahiliyya*) and sin.[74]

Other hadiths with similar purport are:

The Prophet said, "There will be over you leaders whom you will recognize and disapprove of; whoever rejects them is free, whoever hates them is safe as opposed to those who are pleased and obey them." They said, "Should we not fight them?" He said, "No, as long as they pray."

The Prophet said, "The best of your leaders are those you love and they love you, you pray for them and they pray for you. The worst of your leaders are those who anger you and you anger them and you curse them and they curse you." We replied, "O Messenger of Allah should we not remove them at that?" He said, "No, as long as they establish the prayer amongst you...."[75]

These source texts are clear evidence that whoever lives under a particular government must obey the ruler and live peacefully. They are prohibited from taking up arms against him. Uprising or violence by any group against the ruler is completely rejected in Islam and was prohibited by the Prophet and will be a cause of death on the way of ignorance (*jahiliyya*). Thus, Islam considers rebellion against the ruler a great iniquity. These hadiths affirm that one must be patient with one's ruler, even if he commits oppression. These hadiths refer to the leader of a nation, not the leader of a small group. Therefore, groups that take up violent struggle against their regimes are prohibited in Islam and are by default illegal and blameworthy.

In fact the true path to correction of the mistakes of a ruler is according to the hadith "a most excellent Jihad is when one speaks a word of truth in the presence of a tyrannical ruler."[76] Note here the hadith does not mention fighting the ruler, but rather praises the one who corrects the ruler by speech. Armed and violent opposition to a state regime can never be recognized as Jihad in the way of God, despite the claims of many groups. Unfortunately we see today countless individuals and groups who label their rulers and their governments apostates or unbelievers, thereby giving themselves the excuse to declare "Jihad" against them, asserting that this is because they do not rule by what was revealed to the Prophet. Even worse, they go further by terrorizing and killing government officers, members of the armed forces, and public servants, simply because they are easy targets. These groups use a "militant Islamic" ideology to justify such felonious action, declaring the ruler, the government, and its officers to be criminals standing in the way of "true Islam," who must be eliminated. Thus, those who are innocent of any crime, but who are earning a living and raising their families, such as officers and officials of ministries and departments, county and city officials, and police, become targets of these extremist ideologues. Such groups do not hesitate to kill them in surprise attacks, terrorizing the entire nation by blasting here and there, and harming the innocent.

If the ruler commits a mistake, it is not permitted to label him an apostate, nor to indoctrinate people to use militancy to oppose him. In the time of the Prophet after the conquest of Mecca, a Companion named Hatib ibn Abi Balta assisted some of the enemies by supporting them extensively and passing them secret information. It may be that no one today supports a tyrannical ruler as Hatib supported the unbelievers at that time.

When questioned as to his motives, Hatib replied:
O Prophet of God! Don't hasten to give your judgment about me. I was a man closely connected with the Quraysh, but I did not belong to this tribe, while the other emigrants with you had their relatives in Mecca who would protect

their dependents and property. So, I wanted to compensate for my lacking blood relation to them by doing them a favor so that they might protect my dependents. I did this neither because of disbelief nor apostasy nor out of preferring disbelief (*kufr*) to Islam.

The Prophet of God said, "Hatib has told you the truth."[77]

We see here that the Prophet, though fully aware of Hatib's actions, never considered him to be outside the fold of Islam, nor did he inflict any punishment on him. Regarding Hatib and his support of the unbelievers God revealed the following verse:

O you who believe! Do not take My enemy and your enemy for friends: would you offer them love while they deny what has come to you of the truth, driving out the Messenger and yourselves because you believe in God, your Lord?

(Qur'an 60:1)

Though the verse reprimands Hatib showing him to be in the wrong, nonetheless God did not take him out of the state of faith, but yet continued to address him with the honorable title "O you who believe," despite his assisting the enemies of Islam.

This constitutes proof that even if someone assists a regime that does not support Islam, one cannot harm that person as the Prophet did not inflict any punishment on Hatib. One wonders then how today so many groups freely label those working for the government as renegades and apostates and issue fierce edicts to kill them? Their work with the government might be for their livelihood or for building a bridge of trust for the Islamic community to ensure a better future relationship or a better understanding of Islam. Such actions are baseless in Islam and are founded on an extremist ideology, far removed from the middle path which always constitutes this blessed religion of God.

THE INNER JIHAD

Islam is not a rhetorical religion, but it is based on unity, love, and rational action. Soon after the Prophet's death, Islam radiated outwardly from its earthly center, the Ka'ba, the physical symbol of Divine Unity (*tawhid*). Jihad was the dynamic of this expansion. Outwardly it embodied the power of Islam against error and falsehood, while inwardly it represented the means of spiritual awakening and transcending the self. Referring to this, the Prophet said while returning from battle:

We are now returning from the lesser Jihad to the greater Jihad, the Jihad against the self.[78]

The Prophet is reported to have said during the Farewell Pilgrimage:

> ...The Fighter in the Way of God is he who makes Jihad against himself (*jahada nafsahu*) for the sake of obeying God.[79]

God says in the Holy Qur'an,

> Those who have striven for Our sake, We guide them to Our ways.

(Qur'an 29:69)

In this verse, God uses a derivative of the linguistic root of the word "Jihad" to describe those who are deserving of guidance, and has made guidance dependent on Jihad against the false desires of the soul. Therefore, the most perfect of people are those who struggle the most against the selfish promptings of the ego for God's sake. The most obligatory Jihad is that against the base side of the ego, desires, Satan, and the lower world.

The great Sufi Abu al-Qasim al-Junayd said:

> Those who have striven against their desires and repented for God's sake, shall be guided to the ways of sincerity. One cannot struggle against his enemy outwardly (i.e. with the sword) except he who struggles against these enemies inwardly. Then whoever is given victory over them will be victorious over his enemy, and whoever is defeated by them, his enemy defeats him.

CONCLUSION AND POLICY RECOMMENDATIONS

It is apparent that the understanding of Jihad as a concept is dismally blurred by the ongoing rhetoric employed by financially empowered Islamist activists and extremist scholars. Disregarding centuries of classical scholarship, using a simplistic, literal approach to the Qur'an and holy traditions of the Prophet, they have built a convincing picture of Jihad as militant, continuing warfare between the Muslims and the non-Muslims—a situation they contend will persist until the end of time.

The only way to dispel the false notions of Jihad put forth by the extremists, who are massively funded by external sources, is an equally strong effort put forth by Muslim governments in the reeducation of their populations, in particular the youth, with a correct understanding of this concept. Such efforts must be sustained and ongoing and must have the support of modern, moderate Muslim scholars in each nation.

We propose the following recommendations for each nation engaging in these reeducation efforts:

1. follow-on discussions to create a response to the current abuse of the term Jihad;

2. development and staging public presentations to educate the public based on the information and discussions in (1);

3. publish literature detailing the accurate definition of Jihad and distributing this literature in large quantities;

4. encourage modern, moderate scholars to stand up and speak up in opposition to the extremists;

5. create a national podium for modern, moderate scholars;

6. publish in public media the proceedings of the above-mentioned debates and discussions by modern, moderate scholars.

NOTES

1. *Musnad* of Ahmad ibn Hanbal. Similar *ahadith* are narrated in Abu Dawud and Tirmidhi.

2. Ibn Qayyim al-Jawziyya, *Zad al-Ma'ad.*

3. *Muqaddima,* Ibn Rushd (known in the Western world as Averroës), 259.

4. Muhammad Sa'id R. al-Buti, *al-Jihad fil-islam* (Beirut: Dar al-Fikr, 1995).

5. Ibid., 44.

6. Ibid., 16.

7. Imam Malik bin Anas, *al-Mudawwana al-kubra,* 180.

8. Ibn Qayyim al-Jawziyya, *Zad al-Ma'ad.*

9. Nawawi, *al-Minhaj,* 210.

10. Imam al-Dardir, *Al-Sharh al-Saghir.*

11. Mansur bin Yunus al-Bahuti, *Kashf al-qina'a,* 33.

12. Buti, *Al-Jihad fil-islam,* 16.

13. *Musnad* Ahmad. Similar ahadith are narrated in Abu Dawud and Tirmidhi.

14. Sayyid Sabiq, *Fiqh al-Sunna,* 2nd ed., vol. 3 (Beirut: Daru'l-Fikr, 1980).

15. Ibn Majah reported it in his *Sunan,* from 'Abd-Allah bin 'Amr.

16. Narrated by Abu Dawud, ibn Majah, Tirmidhi, and Ahmad.

17. Buti, *al-Jihad fil-islam,* 108–109.

18. Ibn Qudama, *al-Mughni,* vol. 9, 184.

19. Dardir, *al-Sharh al-Saghir,* vol. 2, 274.

20. Abu Bakr al-Jaza'iri, *Minhaj al-Muslim,* chapter on Jihad.

21. Tahanui, *Kashf al-qina'a,* vol. 3, 41.

22. Qirafi, *al-Ahkam fi tamyiz al-fatawa,* 24.

23. Abu'l-Hasan 'Ali al-Mawardi, *al-Ahkam al-sultaniyya,* 1st ed. (Beirut: Daral-Kitab al-'Arabi, 1990), 52.

24. al-Sarakhsi, *al-Mabsut,* vol. 10, 3.

25. Sharbini, *Mughni al-muhtaj,* vol. 4, 210.

26. Shehzad Saleem in "No Jihad without a State," *Renaissance Monthly,* December 1999.

27. Bukhari.

28. *Fiqh al-Sunna*, 30. Cited by Shehzad Saleem in "No Jihad without a State," *Renaissance Monthly*, December 1999.

29. The complete text of the *Hadith* is:

Makhul narrates from Abu Hurayra who narrates from the Prophet: "*Jihad* is obligatory upon you with a Muslim ruler whether he is pious or impious, and the prayer is obligatory upon you behind every Muslim whether he is pious or impious even if he is guilty of the major sins." (*Sunan Abu Dawud*, No. 2171)

30. Zafar Ahmad 'Uthmani, *Lila al-Sunan*, 3rd ed., vol. 12 (Karachi: Idarat al-Qur'an wa al-'Ulum al-Islamiyya, 1415 AH), 15–16. Cited by Shehzad Saleem in "No Jihad without a State," *Renaissance Monthly*, December 1999.

31. Imam Farahi, *Majmu'a tafasir-i-farahi*, 1st ed. (Lahore: Faran Foundation, 1991), 56. Cited by Shehzad Saleem in "No Jihad without a State," *Renaissance Monthly*, December 1999.

32. Dardir, *al-Sharh al-Saghir*, vol. 2, 274.

33. Abu Dawud and Tirmidhi.

34. Sayyid Sabiq, *Fiqh al-Sunna*.

35. Bukhari.

36. Sayyid Sabiq, *Fiqh al-Sunna*.

37. Muhammad Sa'id al-Qahtani, *al-Wala' wa al-Bara'a*, trans. Omar Johnstone.

38. The singular exception to this consensus being the opinion of Imam Shafi'i.

39. A mass-transmitted hadith narrated by Bukhari, Muslim, Abu Dawud, Tirmidhi, an-Nasa'i, Ibn Majah from Abu Hurayra.

40. Buti, *al-Jihad fil-islam*, 58.

41. Bukhari.

42. Buti, *al-Jihad fil-islam*.

43. Ibid., 92.

44. Imam Ibn Rajab al-Hanbali, *Warathat al-Anbiya'*, chap. 8, 37–38.

45. Bukhari reported it from Ibn 'Abbas.

46. Ahmad recorded it in his *Musnad*, from Fadala ibn 'Ubayd.

47. Ibn Qayyim al-Jawziyya, *Zad al-Ma'ad*.

48. Related by Muslim and Bukhari.

49. Muslim, Abu Dawud, and Tirmidhi.

50. Muslim and Bukhari recorded it.

51. Bukhari, Abu Dawud, and an-Nisa'i. Tirmidhi graded it sound.

52. Sayyid Sabiq, *Fiqh al-Sunna*.

53. Ibn Qudama, *al-Mughni*, vol. 12, 691–693.

54. Abu Dawud narrated it in his *Sunan* from Anas bin Malik.

55. Narrated in the *Sunan* of Abu Dawud from Rabih ibn Rabi', and Tabari narrated a similar tradition in his *al-Awsat* from Ibn 'Umar. Similar narrations are related in Ibn Majah, and Ahmad from Hanzala.

56. Cited in *Ta'rikh al-Tabari*, vol. 3, 226–227.

57. Abu Dawud narrated it in his *Sunan,* from Muhammad ibn Hamza al-Aslami from his father.

58. Narrated in Bukhari.

59. Cited in *Ta'rikh al-Tabari,* 226–227.

60. Reported by Abu Awana in his *Mustakhraj* from the hadith of Thabit ibn al-Dahhak. A similar hadith is reported by Abu 'Imran by al-Bazzar but its chain contains Ishaq ibn Idris who is rejected as a Hadith source.

61. Bukhari.

62. Reported by Bukhari, 5778.

63. Bukhari (5778) and Muslim (109 and 110).

64. Muslim.

65. The first narration is by Baqi ibn Makhlad in his *Musnad* narrated from Ibn Ishaq. The second is from Thumama, from Anas. Both are cited by Hafiz Ibn Hajar in *al-Isaba fi Tamyiz al-Sahaba,* vol. 1, 279–280.

66. Bukhari and Muslim.

67. Ibn al-Nujum, *Al-Ashbah wal-nadha'ir,* 205.

68. Al-Bahjuri, *Sharh Sahih Muslim,* vol. 2, 259.

69. Imam Abu Hanifa, *Sharh al-'aqa'id al-nasafiyya,* 180–181.

70. Al-Bahjuri, *Hashiyyat al-Bahjuri 'ala sharh al-Ghizzi,* vol. 259.

71. Islahi, Amin Ahsan, *Da'wat-i-Din awr us ka Tariqah-i-kar* (Urdu), chap. 14, 241–242.

72. Al-Bahjuri, *Sharh Sahih Muslim.*

73. Ibid.

74. Bukhari and Muslim.

75. Narrated in Darimi's *Sunan,* and a similar hadith is related in *Musnad* Ahmad.

76. Narrated by Abu Sa'id al-Khudri in Abu Dawud and Tirmidhi.

77. Bukhari.

78. Ghazali in the *Ihya'.* 'Iraqi said that Bayhaqi related it on the authority of Jabir and said: There is weakness in its chain of transmission. According to Nisa'i it is a saying by Ibrahim ibn Ablah.

79. Tirmidhi, Ahmad, Tabarani, Ibn Majah, and al-Hakim.

80. Related on the authority of Abu al-Darda by Ahmad, Tirmidhi, Ibn Majah, Ibn Abi al-Dunya, al-Hakim, Bayhaqi, and Ahmad also related it from Mu'adh ibn Jabal.

20

LETTER TO MANKIND

Daniel Abdal-Hayy Moore

I have been to the center of the earth.
Jules Verne didn't get it right.
It's not down in cavernous bowels of igneous
   rock swathed in
     sulfurous fumes.
The serpents of the self and its idolized distractions
     are the only monsters to
    come at you out of the rocks.

I have been to the Ka'ba at Mecca
as pure as a heartbeat, as stunning in time and
space as a precious diamond decreed by God to be
    cut by the hand of man to
   mirror His Glory.

All is clarity there, and concentration.

The ears are filled with a joyous noise.

The eyes behold God's plan in the
masses of humanity that pass there that
reduce in every case to one: One heart before
One God in one moment in time,
the most public place on earth for the
most private encounter with our
Lord.

I've sat among its people, I've
stood in the first rows of prayer facing
   the House, black cloth covering

stone,
I've bowed and prostrated as
swallows wheel in a
    sky so saturated with
light as to scintillate with a jagged
        indelible brightness.

This is still man's major crossroad.

Around the Ka'ba even the worst of men
    for a while
        regain their innocence
    and are renewed.
If they are lost in awe and tears flow and they
    call on Allah with each heartbeat
they are in Paradise.
If they walk around the House of Allah
    chatting and distracted they are
still in God's Garden, so powerful is the
    presence there.

The Ka'ba is of a
blackness that is not black, of a
    dimension that has no
        size, of a
cubeness that has no
    shape in space,
neither size, shape nor color define it,
yet it is
    such-and-such a dimension in
        roughly cube shape with a
golden door set in its side and a
golden rainspout over one edge at the top
made of square blocks of gray stone caulked with
    white and
covered over with fine black brocade to the ground
    embroidered at the top with the
golden calligraphy of God's Word.

Inside it is empty.
(I was there one morning when they
    rolled a wooden stairway to the
    door and opened it and the
        crowd came to a halt and

gasped, and many of us
    burst into tears—I nearly
was able to enter, but
dignitaries and pilgrims with special
   green cards were the
     only ones allowed—
but I saw men in the darkness inside
face the inner wall and do the prayer,
prostrating to Allah from inside facing out in the
    holy space we pray towards
     every day *outside* facing *in!*)

White and pearly gray marble slabs make a
floor from the Ka'ba to the edge of the
mosque courtyard for the millions of
feet to pace, even the feet of
   cats, lean felines of Mecca, one seen
doing the seven prescribed circuits, a
   perfect pilgrim of a cat,
before wandering off among the human
    multitudes.

Faces float forward from the faces we
    bear until I think all the
faces on earth are present there,
even unbelievers, even non-Muslims
    represented by the
intensity in the faces of those
who go around God's House—
no one on earth ignored by God, no one
    not brushed by
     angels' wings, no one
in this creation of His
left in utter desolation, but is
    sustained and
conveyed into His
    Presence.

This is the heart of the world.

The self of man.

The spirit of our consciousness in
   life and death.

Distinctions blurred and distinctions
   sharpened at the same time.

Heavens rolled up, seas
dried, earth-prints erased.

No one's gone anywhere.
No one's done anything. No one's

taken a step or even the minutest
breathtaking space of separation
   away from the

House of Allah at the

center of the earth of mankind in

space in Mecca in what is now Saudi Arabia

January 6, 1996,

Philadelphia, Pennsylvania, the United

States of America,

3:25 A.M. one cold winter morning

in my bed on earth

at the feast of our Lord.

NOTE

This poem first appeared in Daniel Abdal-Hayy Moore, *Mecca/Medina Time-Warp*. Reprinted from a Zilzal Press chapbook, by permission from the author.

INDEX

———————————————•———————————————

About the Editor and Contributors

————————————— • —————————————

VINCENT J. CORNELL is Asa Griggs Candler Professor of Middle East and Islamic Studies at Emory University. From 2000 to 2006, he was Professor of History and Director of the King Fahd Center for Middle East and Islamic Studies at the University of Arkansas. From 1991 to 2000, he taught at Duke University. Dr. Cornell has published two major books, *The Way of Abu Madyan* (Cambridge, U.K.: The Islamic Texts Society, 1996) and *Realm of the Saint: Power and Authority in Moroccan Sufism* (Austin, Texas: University of Texas Press, 1998), and over 30 articles. His interests cover the entire spectrum of Islamic thought from Sufism to theology and Islamic law. He has lived and worked in Morocco for nearly six years and has spent considerable time both teaching and doing research in Egypt, Tunisia, Malaysia, and Indonesia. He is currently working on projects on Islamic ethics and moral theology in conjunction with the Shalom Hartmann Institute and the Elijah Interfaith Institute in Jerusalem. For the past five years (2002–2006), he has been a key participant in the Building Bridges Seminars hosted by the Archbishop of Canterbury.

KAMRAN SCOT AGHAIE received his PhD in History from the University of California, Los Angeles, in 1999. He is Associate Professor of Islamic and Iranian History at the University of Texas at Austin and currently serves as Director of the Center for Middle Eastern Studies at the University of Texas. His main publications include *The Martyrs of Karbala: Shi'i Symbols and Rituals in Modern Iran* (2004) and *The Women of Karbala: The Gender Dynamics of Ritual Performances and Symbolic Discourses of Modern Shi'i Islam* (2005). His research interests include modern Iranian history, Islamic studies, Shi'ism, gender studies, historiography, religious studies, nationalism, and economic history.

KARIMA DIANE ALAVI is Director of Education at the Dar al-Islam educational center in Abiquiu, New Mexico. She presents workshops on Islam both at Dar al-Islam and at national conferences. She has been interviewed on Spirituality TV and on National Public Radio. In the 1970s, she taught at the University of Isfahan, Iran. Upon her return to the United States, she taught Islamic Studies at the Sidwell Friends School in Washington, D.C. With Susan Douglass, she authored the curriculum unit *Emergence of Renaissance: Cultural Interactions Between Europeans and Muslims*. Alavi has also published articles for social studies publications and for Muslim and Christian magazines.

LESLIE CADAVID began her studies of the Arabic language at the age of 16, when she moved with her family to Cairo, Egypt. She attended the School of Oriental and African Studies at the University of London, and Indiana University in Bloomington, Indiana. Besides the autobiography of Fatima al-Yashrutiyya on which she is presently working, she has also published *Two Who Attained* (2005), a translation of selected works by the twentieth-century Muslim saints, Ahmad al-'Alawi and Fatima al-Yashrutiyya. She is also working on translations from Spanish into English for a publisher in Spain.

DAOUD STEPHEN CASEWIT currently resides in Rabat, Morocco, where he has been serving as Executive Secretary of MACECE (the Moroccan-American Commission for Educational and Cultural Exchange) since 1996. He holds an MA in Applied Linguistics (1984) and a BA (1983, *summa cum laude*) in Arabic Studies from the American University in Cairo. He also served as Director of ALIF (Arabic Language Institute in Fez) from 1991 to 1996. From 1984 to 1988, he resided in Medina with his family of four and taught at the university there. He has published articles on various subjects in scholarly journals dealing with the unique traits of Medina, the concept of Hijra, and teaching English as a second language to Muslim learners. He is currently working on a book-length historical guide to Medina.

RKIA ELAROUI CORNELL is Senior Lecturer in Arabic at Emory University. For the previous six years (2000–2006), she was Research Associate Professor of Arabic Studies at the University of Arkansas. A native of Morocco, she obtained a degree in secondary education from the Women's Regional Normal School in Meknès, Morocco, and finished an eight-year contract with the Moroccan Ministry of Education. From 1991 to 2000, she was Assistant Professor of the Practice of Arabic at Duke University. In 1999, she published *Early Sufi Women,* a translation of an early work about Sufi women by the Persian mystic Abu 'Abd al-Rahman al-Sulami (d. 1021 CE). Cornell has given numerous lectures and conference presentations on the subjects of Qur'anic exegesis, women in Islam, and language pedagogy. She is currently preparing a book on the woman saint Rabi'a al-'Adawiyya and an advanced reader in premodern Arabic literature.

VIRGINIA GRAY HENRY-BLAKEMORE is the director of the interfaith publishing houses Fons Vitae and Quinta Essentia. She is a writer and video producer under contract with the Book Foundation, U.S. director of photography and children's book publisher Dar Nun, and cofounder and trustee of the Islamic Texts Society of Cambridge, England. She is an accomplished lecturer in art history, world religions, and filmmaking. She has taught at Fordham University, Cairo American College, and Cambridge University. She is also a founding member of the Thomas Merton Center Foundation. Virginia Gray Henry-Blakemore received her BA from Sarah Lawrence College, studied at the American University in Cairo and Al-Azhar University, earned her MA in Education from the University of Michigan, served as Research Fellow at Cambridge University from 1983 to 1990, and is scheduled to receive her PhD from Canterbury, Kent, in 2008.

SHAYKH 'ALI JUM'A is the Grand Mufti (Chief Jurisconsult) of Egypt. He is considered to be one of the most respected and qualified traditional Islamic scholars alive. He has mastery of numerous Islamic sciences but specializes in the science of the Foundations of Islamic Law (*usul al-fiqh*). He follows the Shafi'i school of Islamic jurisprudence. Shaykh 'Ali Jum'a did not enter the religious establishment in his boyhood. He first studied at the Faculty of Commerce, obtaining his BA from Ain Shams University in 1973. He then enrolled at the University of Al-Azhar, obtaining a BA in 1979, an MA in 1985, and a PhD in Shari'a and law in 1988. Shaykh 'Ali Jum'a is also the preacher (*khatib*) of the Sultan Hassan Mosque in Cairo. He has authored around two dozen books on various aspects of Islamic thought and jurisprudence. He is Editor of the *Encyclopaedia of Hadith,* a subproject of the greater Sunna Project of the Thesaurus Islamicus Foundation, which aims at documenting and publishing all works related to Prophetic narrations or Hadith. He is also a member of the editorial advisory board of Fons Vitae, an interfaith publishing house based in the United States.

SHAYKH MUHAMMAD HISHAM KABBANI is a world-renowned author and religious scholar. He has devoted his life to the promotion of the traditional Islamic principles of peace, tolerance, love, compassion, and brotherhood, while opposing extremism in all its forms. The Shaykh is a member of a respected family of traditional Islamic scholars. Shaykh Kabbani received a bachelor's degree in chemistry and studied medicine. In addition, he holds a degree in Islamic Law and a license to teach, guide, and counsel religious students in Islamic spirituality from Shaykh Muhammad Nazim Adil al-Haqqani of the Naqshbanidiyya Sufi brotherhood. Shaykh Kabbani has published a large number of books in English on classical Islam and spirituality. He has hosted three international conferences, which drew leaders and scholars from around the world. As an important voice for traditional Islam, Shaykh Kabbani is sought for counsel by journalists, academics, and government leaders. He serves on the boards of a number of religious and educational organizations.

BARRY C. McDONALD edited *Seeing God Everywhere: Essays on Nature and the Sacred* (2003). He also coedited, with Patrick Laude, *Music of the Sky: An Anthology of Spiritual Poetry* (2004). His poetry has appeared in numerous journals, including *Sacred Web, Crosscurrents, Sophia, The American Muslim,* and *Sufi.*

DANIEL ABDAL-HAYY MOORE is a widely regarded American Muslim poet. His first book of poems, *Dawn Visions,* was published by Lawrence Ferlinghetti of City Lights Books in San Francisco (1964). He became a Sufi Muslim in 1970, performed the Hajj in 1972, and lived and traveled in Morocco, Spain, Algeria, and Nigeria. Upon his return to California, he published *The Desert is the Only Way Out* in 1985 and *Chronicles of Akhira* in 1986. A resident of Philadelphia since 1990, he has published *The Ramadan Sonnets* (1996) and *The Blind Beekeeper* (2002). He has also been the major editor for a number of works, including *The Burda of Shaykh Busiri* (2003), translated by Hamza Yusuf, and *State of Siege* (2004), the poetry of the Palestinian poet, Mahmoud Darwish, translated by Munir Akash.

SEYYED HOSSEIN NASR is University Professor of Islamic Studies at George Washington University in Washington, D.C. He is one of the most prolific and influential Islamic scholars alive. Professor Nasr is the author of over 50 books and 500 articles on Islamic science, religion, and the environment, in four languages. His best known works include *Three Muslim Sages, An Introduction to Islamic Cosmological Doctrines, Science and Civilization in Islam, Ideals and Realities of Islam,* and *The Heart of Islam: Enduring Values for Humanity.* He attended MIT as an undergraduate. Upon his graduation from MIT, Nasr obtained a master's degree in geology and geophysics and went on to pursue his PhD in the history of science and learning at Harvard University. After Harvard, he returned to Iran as a professor at Tehran University, and then at Arya Mehr University, where he was appointed President in 1972. He was Dean of the Faculty and Academic Vice Chancellor of Tehran University from 1968 to 1972. He was also a student of 'Allama Tabataba'i, a traditional Iranian scholar whose commentary on the Qur'an, *Tafsir al-Mizan,* is very popular. In the 1970s, Empress Farah Pahlavi of Iran appointed Professor Nasr head of the Imperial Iranian Academy of Philosophy, the first academic institution to be created in accordance with the intellectual principles of the Traditionalist School. He was forced to leave Iran after the Islamic Revolution of 1979. Nasr took up positions at the University of Edinburgh and then at Temple University, followed by George Washington University, where he has been since 1984 to the present day.

NASROLLAH POURJAVADY was born in Tehran. He went to the United States in 1963 to study Western philosophy and having obtained his BA in 1967 returned to Iran and earned his MA and PhD from the University of Tehran. Subsequently, he taught philosophy and mysticism at Sharif University of Technology in Tehran, and then at the University of Tehran, where he is now a full professor. He has also taught as a visiting professor at Colgate University (2002) and at Gregorian University in Rome (2005). Over the last 30 years, Professor Pourjavady has written some 20 books as well as over 100 essays and articles in the fields of Islamic mysticism, philosophy, and Persian literature. He was the general editor of a monumental three-volume work on Iranian art and culture, *The Splendour of Iran* (2001). As the founding director of Iran University Press, the largest academic publishing house in Iran, he supervised the publication of some 1,200 academic books and 11 periodicals in Persian, English, French, and German for 24 years, until the spring of 2004. He is a member of the Academy of Persian Language and Literature, which awarded him the Academy's Persian Literature Award in 2004. He received the Alexander von Humboldt Research Award in 2005.